JEAN-CLAUDE COLIN, MARIST

Donal Kerr

Jean-Claude Colin, Marist

A FOUNDER IN AN ERA OF REVOLUTION AND RESTORATION: THE EARLY YEARS 1790-1836

the columba press

First published in 2000 by

the columba press

55A Spruce Avenue, Stillorgan Industrial Park, Blackrock, Co Dublin

Cover by Bill Bolger
Origination by The Columba Press
Printed in Ireland by Colour Books Ltd, Dublin.

ISBN 1 85607 314 9

Contents

Foreword

After the upheaval of the Enlightenment and the French Revolution, the early nineteenth century saw a remarkable revival in Christian Churches. Already in 1799 when Pope Pius VI died a prisoner in France, Catholics were quietly laying the foundation for a renewal of the Church. With the return in 1814 of 'the most Christian King', Louis XVIII, a thoroughgoing effort of restoration developed. New needs were perceived and new organisations developed to meet them. Bishops undertook vigorous efforts to renew and reform their dioceses, new religious orders of priests, brothers and sisters sprang up, older ones revived and the laity took a major role in the work of re-evangelisation. A sign of the revival of Christianity was the renewed effort to spread the Christian message. Protestants began missions in India and Oceania, Orthodox in Siberia and Alaska, Catholics in India, China and the Americas. For the Catholic Church, the main missionary thrust came from Rome where Cardinal Mauro Cappellari, head of Propaganda Fide, who became Pope Gregory XVI in 1830, was devoted to the missions. At the same time, many local initiatives took place and, in particular, the Association for the Propagation of the Faith, established in Lyon in 1822, gave the laity the opportunity of participating in missionary work through prayer, through financial support and by encouraging mission vocations.

In the story of the renewal of Catholicism in Europe and of its expansion across the world, Jean-Claude Colin (1790-1875) played a modest but not insignificant part. His family and parish had suffered much during the Revolution and he lost both of his parents before he was five years old. A quiet shy boy with a deep devotion to the Virgin Mary, his only wish was to be alone with God, yet he made his priestly studies for the diocese of Lyon almost unwillingly. The year before ordination, a student in the seminary in Lyon told him and some others of a revelation he had in which the Blessed Virgin asked for a society dedicated to her. Colin saw in this project the possibility of combining the priesthood with the unassuming, almost hidden, way of doing good which he believed was how Mary helped the early Church. From the time the group of seminarians pledged itself to found the Society in 1816, he devoted himself to writing its rule. Colin, a founder despite himself, became involved in negotiating with bishops, nuncios and the Roman Curia for approval. Approval took twenty years. Even then it was the determination of Pope Gregory xvi to expand Catholic missions to all the Pacific that brought the break-through. Colin had long pledged his fellow-Marists' willingness to go wherever they were needed and he and his group of twenty received Rome's request to take on the mission to Western Oceania with joy. The acceptance of the mission brought the approbation of the priests' branch of the Society of Mary and propelled it and Colin on to the wider world stage.

The title, *A Founder in an Era of Revolution and Restoration* indicates that this volume intends to give prominence to the background of his life and to those people who influenced him and his project. The sufferings of the French Revolution help to explain why he grew up a shy, retiring youth; the Restoration of the monarchy in 1814 placed him in the context of a resurgent Church engaged in a determined effort at renewal. It is at this time in his adult years that Colin, in dialogue with his age, shaped both his own distinct identity and a new Society. For him restoration was not all reaction. He intuitively grasped that in the post-Revolutionary world, those who would win people for God, must be as unobtrusive as Mary in their work, 'hidden and unknown', as his favourite expression ran.

The first part of this biography presents a writer with a difficulty for, in 1841, over a period of four days, Colin systematically burnt his papers. His justification was that posterity would have more to do than to occupy themselves with him and that if the story of the Society were ever to be written, it should be written like biblical history in which God's action alone counts. Although the loss is a grievous one, for only his personal papers let us know what he was thinking at key moments in his life, other sources are ample. In all, over 400 contemporary documents survive. There exists, too, a wealth of later documents that treat of the period. In his eleven volumes of hand-written Mémoires, the chronicler of the Society, Gabriel-Claude Mayet, a Marist priest, went to great pains to conserve accurately Colin's conversations and continually interrogated others about the early years of the Society. Although memoirs are selective, yet Mayet was honest, careful and well placed to sift the truth. Some of Colin's sermons also survive and the archives of the Roman Congregations, of the Marist Brothers and Sisters and those of the dioceses of Lyon, Belley and Pinerolo provide further documents. Fathers Jean Coste and Gaston Lessard (with the collaboration of Seán Fagan for volume 2) collected and edited close on a thousand of the relevant documents dealing with this period in the four volumes of their monumental *Origines Maristes*. Those volumes, with copious notes and commentaries, were essential for this work.

From the renewal of Marist studies which the work of Coste and Lessard generated, many other scholars have contributed significantly to Marist studies, as a glance at publications like *Forum Novum* and *Maristica* shows. To their work and to valuable articles in *Marist Notebooks,* the Marist Brothers' journal, the present writer is indebted. Of the biographical studies of Colin over that period, Stanley Hosie's lively biography, *Anonymous Apostle,* has proved useful. Franco Gioannetti's work *A Spirituality for our time; Jean-Claude Colin,* is concerned with the relevance of his spirituality today, while placing him, too, in his historical context. I have been fortunate to be able to use Sister Hyacinth's translations in *Recollections: Mother Saint Joseph* and *Correspondence of Mother Saint Joseph;* those of Edwin Keel in his *Book of Texts,* and those of William Stuart and Anthony Ward in *A Founder Speaks* and *A Founder Acts.* The other translations are my own.

It is a pleasure to acknowledge my indebtedness to many individuals. In the first place I wish to thank the Marist Fathers' general administration. My thanks, too, to Madame Marie-Madeleine Plancher, Jean Coste's sister, for her interest and for furnishing a photocopy of the memoirs of their ancestor, Benoît Coste: 'Mes souvenirs de soixante ans'. Larry Duffy and Phil Graystone read many sections of the typescript; the late Patrick Bearsley, Charles Girard, Sister Joan McBride, Professor Kevin B. Nowlan and George Skelton read it in full. To all of them I owe a debt of thanks for many useful suggestions. I am grateful to Carlo Maria Schianchi, the archivist of the Marist Fathers Archive (APM) in Rome for his ready help on all occasions; to Renato Frappi for patient work on the maps and photographs; to the Marist Sisters in Rome and in Belley, in particular to Sisters Jane O'Carroll and Winifred Rose. Among many others who were helpful were Marist Fathers Pierre Allard, Mauro Filippucci, Justin Taylor, Mervyn Duffy, Alexandre Rodet and Craig Larkin. I am obliged also to the community at Monteverde for their support. I want to thank, too, Marists of the Irish Province and all the Marist family for their interest and support. I am grateful to Ursula and Marcella Ní Dhálaigh for their very thorough proof-reading. In a special way I want to thank Alois Greiler whose valuable assistance has been generously forthcoming at all times. I owe most to Gaston Lessard for his advice, encouragement and assistance over the years.

My hope is that this volume may help people understand better the man whose ideas and leadership made the Society of Mary a reality.

Abbreviations

APM	Archives Marist Fathers, General house, Rome.
b.	born
CGC	Lessard, G. ed., 'Projet d'édition des lettres écrites par Jean-Claude Colin pendant son généralat (1836-1854)', 9 fascicles (Hull-Rome, 1986-1990).
CMJ	Historical Committees of the Marist Fathers and Marist Sisters eds, *Correspondence of Mother Saint Joseph, Foundress of the Marist Sisters* (1786-1858) (Rome-Anzio, 1966).
Doc. Docs	Document(s)
ed. eds	Editor, editors
FA	J. Coste ed., *A Founder Acts. Reminiscences of Jean-Claude Colin by Gabriel-Claude Mayet,* English translation by William Joseph Stuart and Anthony Ward (Rome, 1983).
FHSM	*Fontes historici Societatis Mariae,* Rome.
FS	J. Coste ed., *A Founder Speaks. Spiritual Talks of Jean-Claude Colin,* English translation by Anthony Ward (Rome, 1975).
Ibid.	ibidem [same place, reference]
IMJ	Historical Committees of the Marist Fathers and Marist Sisters eds, *Index Mother Saint Joseph. Foundress of the Marist Sisters (1786-1858)* (FHSM, 6), (Rome, 1977).
M.	Monsieur; normal title for laymen, but used also for priests.
OM	J. Coste and G. Lessard eds, (with the collaboration of Seán Fagan for volume 2) *Origines Maristes (1786-1836)* (FHSM, 3), 4 vols (Rome, 1960-1967).
ord.	ordained
p. pp	Page, pages
prof.	professed
RMJ	Historical Committees of the Marist Fathers and Marist Sisters eds, *Recollections: Mother Saint Joseph, Foundress of the Marist Sisters (1786-1858)* (FHSM, 5) (Rome, 1971).
VM	APM, section Villa Maria, Sydney
vol. vols	Volume, Volumes

List of Illustrations and Maps

CHAPTER 1

The French Revolution, the Oath and Saint-Bonnet-le-Troncy

The year Jean-Claude Colin was born - 1790 – was a dramatic year in France and the decade that followed it proved among the most troubled periods in the history of his native land. His life and his life's work were decisively marked by the civil strife that began at that time. The conflict that convulsed France and led to the disruption of the Colin family life, with brutal confiscations, police raids, and threats to the life of the father of the family, had its source in the Revolution of 1789 and, in particular, in the oath to the Civil Constitution of the Clergy which the Revolutionaries imposed on priests in 1790. Jean-Claude's father, Jacques Colin, was a farmer at Barbery, a hamlet two kilometres from the village of Saint-Bonnet-le-Troncy, in the Haut Beaujolais, in central France. The year Jean-Claude was born the parish of Saint-Bonnet had two hundred and twenty-six 'hearths' (that is properties which entitled the owner to vote) or a population of one thousand one hundred and twenty five. Saint-Bonnet, a village far from the great centres of eighteenth-century France, was situated in the canton of Thizy, in the district of Villefranche and in the newly-constituted department of the Rhone. The district's capital was the growing and prosperous textile town of Villefranche on the Saone, some forty kilometres to the east, with a population of almost five thousand. Almost equidistant from Saint-Bonnet was Roanne, a large town to the west, which, however, was on the Loire and capital of the department of the Loire. The city of Lyon, the capital of the department of the Rhone, was thirty miles to the south at the meeting of the Rhone and Saone. Running through the valley in which Saint-Bonnet is situated, and in many ways the most important physical feature of the area, is the river Azergues. The Azergues is a tributary of the Saone and, during the winter, it often swelled into dangerous torrents. The Colin family had lived in that valley since the seventeenth century or earlier. They were farmers who, like their neighbours, supplemented the family income in the winter months by weaving, and the earnings from the two occupations enabled them to live in modest comfort. The family was devout. Jean Colin, Jean-Claude's grandfather, recited the Little Office of the Blessed Virgin daily and used to tell the children stories from the Bible. In 1771, Jean's son, Jacques, at the age of twenty-four, married the fourteen-year-old Marie Gonnet. Unlike the Colins, the Gonnets could be described as professional people. Marie's father, Jean-Baptiste, following in the

13

footsteps of his father and grandfather, was a master surgeon and Marie's second brother, Paul, later became a surgeon in the navy. Given the social distinctions of the time, it was not usual for a peasant to marry the doctor's daughter though it is probable that a surgeon – earlier on the surgeon was also the barber – did not carry the same prestige as today. Still, the alliance may indicate the good standing of Jacques Colin, his attractiveness to Marie, or his determination to climb the social scale. If one can judge by the profound grief Jacques is reported to have experienced when Marie died, they were very attached to each other and in the later accounts by their sons, Pierre and Jean-Claude Colin, there was never a hint of discord in the family. Jean-Claude Colin was born on 7 August 1790. He was the eighth member of this family but his sister, Marie-Anne, born on 10 September 1788, had died soon after birth. An ordinary family, in a quiet backwater of France, there was nothing to distinguish the Colins from any other family in that close-knit community that constituted the parish of Saint-Bonnet-le-Troncy in the late eighteenth century. The times, however, were far from ordinary, for an extraordinary sequence of events was upsetting the very pattern of life throughout France. The people of Saint-Bonnet, too, would be caught up in its maelstrom.

Eighteenth-century France, with a population of twenty-six million people, was the most populous country in western Europe and probably the wealthiest and most powerful. Like most of Europe, France was a monarchy where the king, in theory at least, was an absolute monarch whose authority was believed to derive from God. In practice, the king's power was limited by the ancient rights and privileges of classes and corporations such as the Church, the nobility, and the high court.[1] Ninety-five percent of France's twenty-six million inhabitants was Catholic and the Catholic Church was recognised as the Church of the nation. The maxim ran that there was but 'one law, one faith, one king'. The state of the Church varied from one province to another and, within the provinces, dioceses and parishes also differed. In general, however, the Church was solidly based and the practice of the faith almost universal. The clergy was held in general esteem. The Counter-Reformation had succeeded in one of the key objectives of the Council of Trent; it was producing a far better type of priest to carry out the Church's mission. The Sulpicians, the Eudists, and the Vincentians, with government support, had established excellent seminaries where candidates for the priesthood were trained in theology and the administration of the sacraments and their conduct subjected to careful vetting before they were accepted for ordination. More than any other single factor these seminaries had brought about a general rise in the level of priestly formation.

---

1. The high courts of Paris and of each province, called parlements, had acquired important political powers before the Revolution.

The results were noticeable: throughout France, the priests were generally seen as well-trained, devoted pastors and, indeed, as the cream of society.

The eighteenth century, however, had not been without difficulties for the Church in France, and in certain areas historians can now detect some early stages of what would be later seen as dechristianisation. Vocations had fallen, with the number of clergy dropping by over twenty-five per cent in the half-century before 1790. The middle classes may not have been so devout as earlier, or their devotion showed in a different way.[2] A certain resentment existed within the ranks of the clergy for, while the bishops and abbots, almost all aristocratic, possessed enormous revenues, the priests were badly remunerated and had no say in the running of the Church at a higher level. Within the clergy, too, the supporters of Jansenism, a type of Catholic puritanism, had been locked in battle with Rome and the majority of bishops. The controversy had ended with the crushing of Jansenism but enough Jansenists remained to embitter the struggle that was to come. A more pervasive influence was Gallicanism. Gallicanism, a complex phenomenon, was the collective name for doctrines and practices that claimed to be based on the so-called 'freedoms of the Gallican Church'. Its main thrust was to claim for the Gallican or French Church a degree of independence from Rome. It held, too, that ecumenical councils were above the pope, whose *ex cathedra* statements were not infallible unless they received the consent of the Church. Gallicanism also had a strong political dimension insofar as the French kings, claiming ancient and historically-doubtful prerogatives, used these Gallican 'freedoms', not only to deny any interference from Rome in the affairs of France, but also to take to themselves virtual control over the Church in France. Every seminary professor and holder of high office was bound to take the oath to Gallicanism before taking office. From the middle of the century, too, the Church faced a new threat, this time from the Enlightenment. Writers like Voltaire, Rousseau and Diderot, some deists, others atheists, attacked revealed religion, in particular the Catholic Church. Their new theories were brilliantly argued in the salons of the rich and popularised in the *Encyclopédie*. During this period, too, the Catholic Church was weak at its centre, for little positive leadership came from Rome, where the popes since the death of Benedict XIV in 1758, although respectable men, were of mediocre calibre. The papacy proved feeble in the face of the Catholic princes influenced by the Enlightenment, as became abundantly clear when they forced Pope Clement XIV, in 1773, to suppress the Jesuits.

Despite those tensions and the erosion caused by the Enlightenment, the position of the Church in France appeared quite healthy. Its presence was evident everywhere. Hospitals, orphanages, schools, and universities were in its

2. O. Hufton, 'The French Church', W. J. Callahan and D. Higgs, eds, *Church and Society in Catholic Europe of the Eighteenth Century* (Cambridge, 1979), pp 14-15.

hands. In every village throughout France, the parish church was the centre of life, and the peal of its bells regulated the day, the week, and the year of the people. Apart from his all-important spiritual role, the priest was the official registrar of births, marriages, and deaths and on Sunday at Mass he read out not merely parish notices but the king's ordinances. King Louis XVI, who ascended the throne in 1774, was a sincere Catholic who took seriously his coronation oath to uphold the Church. The central position of the Church was not questioned. The 'cahiers de doléances' or grievance books of 1788 are a telling witness to its accepted position. The reason why these books were drawn up has a direct bearing on this story.

In 1788, Louis XVI decided to call a meeting of representatives of the three 'Estates' or classes in the land, the clergy, the nobility, and the commoners. As was customary on the rare occasions when the three Estates met, he invited each parish to draw up a 'cahier de doléances' or copy-book in which it listed its grievances and requests. These grievance books of the parishes throughout France are extant and provide a remarkably rich account of France as many of its people saw it on the eve of one of the greatest changes in its history. As the object and title of the cahiers or grievance books indicate, it was a one-sided exercise: the people were called on to specify their complaints, for this was to be the unique opportunity to have them remedied. In the cahiers that survive, the calls are for more services and less tax. The clergy and nobility paid no taxes and the commoners, on whom all the burden fell, demanded that they begin to pay their fair share. The grievance books, however, did not question the role of the Church. Indeed, some of them called for a strengthening of its position in society. Calls for Church reforms figured quite low.[3]

The grievance book of the third estate of Saint-Bonnet-le-Troncy reveals how some of the inhabitants saw their parish and its problems and paints an interesting picture of the parish into which Jean-Claude was born.[4] In their three-thousand-word statement they complained that they faced harsh physical difficulties. They live, they tell the king, in the heart of the mountains. In winter torrents plunge down from the heights sweeping unwelcome clay into their carefully cultivated fields, causing great damage to the harvests. Since it is so exposed to the elements, their parish is at the mercy of the ravages of storms, hail, and frost. Even apart from such seasonal hazards, their land, they explain, is arid, providing grain for but one third of the year. To compensate for these disadvantages to their agriculture, they had established a weaving and cotton-spinning industry. This industry, so essential to complement their farming

3. G. Shapiro, 'Les demandes les plus répandues dans les cahiers de doléances,' M. Vovelle, ed., L'image de la révolution française, vol. 1 (Oxford, 1990), p. 9.
4. C. Faure, Cahiers de doléances du Beaujolais pour les États généraux de 1789 ... (Lyon, 1939), pp 112-116.

income, was being destroyed, however, by unfair foreign competition, the result of a disastrous commercial treaty which the foreign minister, Count Charles de Vergennes, had signed with England in 1786. The ruin of both weavers and merchants was the inevitable result. A further matter for complaint was the distance they had to travel to buy and sell at the fairs and markets and they asked for a new road between the two major towns of Roanne and Villefranche. The grievance book went on to criticise the nobility and the clergy who, it complained, possessed almost half the land and the best portion of it. It demanded a fairer tax system where clergy and nobility would also pay their share. It went further and criticised Church property in terms far stronger than in the great majority of other grievance books throughout the country. If the king wanted to raise money, it maintained, one of the best ways to do so would be to 'take over the land and property given over as prebends in times of ignorance and in centuries when the clergy held sway over the third estate and skilfully deprived it of these possessions as a way of opening to it the gates of paradise.' The words are pure Enlightenment language and could have come straight from the writings of Voltaire or Diderot. Only one quarter of the grievance books throughout the country called for any confiscation of the Church's land, and a minuscule part – just two per cent – wanted them nationalised.

Invaluable though this document is in furnishing us with a first-hand account of Saint-Bonnet-le-Troncy a year before Jean-Claude Colin's birth, it has to be interpreted with care. Many of the grievance books were based on master-copies drawn up in Paris or other cities to make a strong case for the third estate. Many again were drafted not by the ordinary people of the parish as such, but by politically involved people, lawyers and others. In Arras, for example, Maximilien Robespierre, later the leader of the Jacobins who instigated the Reign of Terror during the Revolution, drew up the statement of grievances. As regards Saint-Bonnet, there is a further difficulty in ascertaining how representative the document is of the feelings of the parishioners. The parish had two hundred and twenty-six 'hearths'. All of those were expected to assemble in order to draw up their book and to elect their deputies. To judge from the document, only twenty-five, or less than a tenth, came. The book itself was signed by sixteen parishioners, including the mayor. This number is low compared with most other villages in the Beaujolais. How representative were these twenty-five, and in particular the sixteen who signed the book, it is impossible to say. The grievance book, however, provides some insight into the physical and economic difficulties under which Jacques Colin and his fellow parishioners laboured. It records, too, what at least some of the parishioners of Saint-Bonnet-le-Troncy thought about the affairs of their parish and the envious eyes they were casting on the privileges and property of nobility and clergy.[5]

5. This cahier is that of the third estate only; the clergy drew up their own cahiers.

These grievance books were drawn up in 1788-9 to prepare for the meeting of the Estates that Louis XVI had called to deal with a major financial crisis. Prosperous and stable though France was, a series of costly wars, particularly the recent successful war in support of the American rebels against England, and a chaotic revenue system, had bankrupted the state. The representatives of the three Estates – the clergy, the nobility and the commoners – assembled at the château of Versailles in May 1789 to solve the crisis. In the past, when they had met, each Estate had brought its grievance book before the king, voted the extra revenue he needed, and went home. This did not happen in 1789. The Estates met in early summer and, within a short period, this old-fashioned gathering, which had in the past been no more than three separate consultative bodies, had transformed itself into an all-powerful 'National Assembly'. This National Assembly saw itself as having the mission of constituting a new France on a democratic basis. In a delirium of reforming enthusiasm it proclaimed the Rights of Man, abolished privilege, and reduced the influence of the king. The Church was not opposed to this revolution. The transformation of the cumbersome Estates General into a dynamic, omnipotent National Assembly owed much to the clergy, most of whom shared this glorious new vision. It was they who brought the three Estates together to form one National Assembly; they bailed out the bankrupt exchequer by placing the great wealth of the Church at the disposition of the nation; they were among the ablest legislators in the formulation of the historic Declaration of the Rights of Man. Nor could it be said that the revolution was opposed to the Church. Yet in those heady early months it was the Church more than any other body that lost out. Tithes were abolished without compensation and the nation took over the Church's wealth although it undertook to provide for the clergy. Then, in February 1790, the National Assembly 'opened' the monasteries and the monks and nuns were allowed and later encouraged to leave. Disquieting though these last changes were to some, they caused no serious alarm. That only came when, on 12 July 1790, the Assembly brought in a 'Civil Constitution for the Clergy'. In introducing this measure, the Assembly maintained that it did not intend to interfere with the doctrine of the Church nor with its inner spiritual life and that the Civil Constitution, as the word 'Civil' implied, was concerned only with regulating the external relation of the Church to the nation. In fact, however, the new law interfered with the structures of the Church in a way that dismayed some of the best-disposed clerical members at the Assembly. In order to make dioceses coterminous with the newly-constituted departments, it reduced the number of dioceses from a hundred and thirty-five to eighty-three. Of greater significance was the manner it decided on for appointing bishops and curés or parish priests. This was to be done by election. Bishops were to be elected by the same electorate as members of the National Assembly and curés by the electors for the district administrative assembly. In practice, this meant that in a number of areas Protestants could vote for the election of bishop or curé. The constitution, too, reduced the role of the pope to a minimum. It specified that 'the new bishop may not apply to the pope for confirmation, but shall write to him as the visible head of the universal Church.'

Such changes were more than mere organisational ones. Alarmed, the bishop-members of the Assembly did their best to persuade the Assembly that the Civil Constitution was too radical. The majority of deputies, however, insisted and it became law. Even then a compromise might have been arranged. What changed all was the oath. When it became apparent that there would be resistance to the Civil Constitution, the Assembly took this one grave step further and demanded that the clergy swear an oath accepting it. The Assembly was preparing the way for the first and major split in the country, for the oath marks a turning point in the Revolution and indeed in French history, creating a division in France that has never been completely bridged. The bishops in the Assembly remained steadfastly opposed and demanded that the Church be given the opportunity through a Council to deliberate on the matter. They were refused. Yet, despite threats from the mob, who paraded the streets of Paris shouting 'hang the rebels,' only two of the forty-four bishops at the Assembly took the oath: the cynical bishop of Autun, Charles-Maurice de Talleyrand, and the vacillating coadjutor bishop of Bâle, Jean-Baptiste Gobel. Gobel became archbishop of Paris and would later exchange his mitre for the red bonnet of the revolution. The reaction of the bishops outside the Assembly was awaited with anxiety by both sides. It could not have been more decisive. Of the hundred and thirty-three bishops in France, only four agreed to take the oath.[6] The bishops had given a clear lead in massively rejecting the oath: would the rest of the Church follow their lead?

The priests were now given two months during the winter of 1791 to swear allegiance to the Civil Constitution. The issues involved were of the most serious consequence for the whole Church, laity and clergy. Would the new constitution with its sweeping re-organisation of the Church be accepted or not? It would touch profoundly the lives of the priests. 'The [...] oath staked out a real and deadly serious obligation, wherein a failure to conform entailed a clergyman's ejection from his functions and his ostracism from the community of the Revolutionary nation.'[7] The reaction among the small group of clergy engaged

6. If one includes bishops who were not ordinaries (that is, in charge of a diocese), the total is seven out of a hundred and sixty. These included Étienne Loménie de Brienne, cardinal archbishop of Sens, and his nephew and coadjutor. Before the Revolution, Louis xvi had rejected Brienne for Paris, protesting that the archbishop of Paris should at least believe in God. Of the others, the most notable were Talleyrand and Gobel.

7. T. Tackett, *Religion, Revolution, and Regional Culture in Eighteenth-Century France. The Ecclesiastical Oath of 1791* (Princeton, 1986), p. 3.

in education was in line with that of the bishops. Of the seminary professors, only twenty-four out of a total of three hundred and twenty-seven took the oath. Of far more importance for the country, however, would be the reaction of the fifty-one thousand parish clergy who represented the Church for the ordinary people in every corner of the land. Surprising though it may appear later, the majority of priests did not imitate the bishops. Over twenty-seven thousand, or from fifty-two to fifty-five per cent of the parish clergy, accepted the oath. Some twenty-four thousand rejected it and this number increased when it became known that Pius VI, who was pope from 1775 to 1799, opposed it. By autumn 1792, the percentage who took the oath had dipped slightly below fifty per cent.[8] The reasons for taking or rejecting the oath varied from parish to parish. Sometimes a powerful local personage, usually the priest, led the people for or against it, sometimes it was the people who pressurised the priest. When King Louis, whom the priests trusted, finally, if reluctantly, accepted the Civil Constitution, many were reassured and took the oath. Where there was more than one priest on his own, as in the towns, the oath was more often than not rejected. In areas where Jansenism had been strong, more priests took the oath than elsewhere.

For us, today, the surprise is that so many priests accepted the oath; for the Assembly in Paris, the surprise was that so many rejected it. The revolutionaries were not against the Church; on the contrary, they believed so strongly that the Church was part of the Nation that they could not accept that it would not enter fully into the national reorganisation they had planned for it. Despite the warnings of the bishops in the Assembly, they were sure that, under pressure, the Church would accept. So it was that they insisted on the oath. It was not suprising that the priests did not follow the example of the bishops. For long, the bishops, recruited almost exclusively from the aristocracy, had been out of contact with their clergy. There was little scandalous about the lives of the bishops and many were good pastors of their people. Nevertheless, many others were worldly. The great wealth of the bishops contrasted with the poverty of the priests, and the run-up to the elections to the Estates General had seen frequent conflict between them. Some bishops were accused of being more interested in preserving their wealth and privileges than in defending the rights of the Church. Furthermore, at the very time when their lead might have had most effect, many bishops did not give any lead at all. Many simply abandoned their dioceses, others did not speak out and others still, perhaps as many as a third, waited until after late January before condemning the oath. By then it was too late, for most of the priests had had to decide one way or another.[9] Nor did

8. Tackett, *Religion,* pp 41-3.
9. Tackett calculates that of the eighty-three episcopal condemnations that can be dated, twenty nine came after late January. Tackett, *Religion,* p. 112, footnote 56.

Rome prove of much help. The reaction of Pius VI was slow and it was only in early summer, four or five months after most of the priests had gone through the ceremony of oath-taking, that his disapproval became known. Pius was totally opposed to the oath. He was afraid to offend the French clergy who were Gallican and touchy about papal interference and, in any case, the popes did not then have the same influence in France that they were to have a century later. Furthermore, Pius feared that the National Assembly would confiscate his dominions in Avignon and the Venaissin. By summer 1791 scores of bishops had packed their bags and fled the country. The Church had lost its leaders and was now headless as well as divided. Worse was to follow. Even as the oath was being taken, violent clashes broke out between rival groups, particularly where the people or the clergy rejected the oath. As in so many other parishes throughout France, the oath was to have profound effects on Saint-Bonnet and on the Colin family.

The Civil Constitution had changed Saint-Bonnet's location in the ecclesiastical world. Prior to 1790, it had formed part of the diocese of Mâcon but it had now become part of the diocese of Rhone-et-Loire, which was co-extensive with the departments of the same name. The archbishop of Lyon, Yves-Alexandre de Marbeuf, whose proud title was 'Primate of Gaul,' refused to take the oath and, as early as December, publicly condemned the Civil Constitution. He fled to Brabant in the Austrian Netherlands, but his vicars general kept in touch with him and one of them, Father Jacques Linsolas, an unrelenting opponent of the Revolution, maintained the organisation of the 'Roman' or 'refractory' Church, that refused the oath.

Marbeuf was soon replaced. An election was held and the electorate chose Antoine-Adrien Lamourette, an ex-Vincentian and a protégé of Count Mirabeau, the foremost leader of the Revolution in its early stages. On 27 March 1791, Gobel, now archbishop of Paris, consecrated Lamourette as the new constitutional archbishop of Lyon. Before that date the priests throughout the diocese had had to take a decision, for the oath-taking ceremony began during the winter of 1790-91. In the parishes, the ceremony was a community experience and took place on Sunday morning, after Mass, when the priests publicly read the formula in the presence of the parishioners who came in great numbers for such occasions. In some parishes the ceremony was followed by a little celebration. When the final count was taken in the diocese of Rhone-et-Loire, it was clear that the vast majority of the priests had accepted the new arrangement. Of the four hundred and ninety-eight priests, four hundred and thirteen took the oath, bringing the percentage of jurors, or oath-taking priests, to eighty-three! This was well above the national average. The exception to the overwhelming trend was Lyon, the capital city of the department, where only five of the fourteen curés took the oath. The opposition to the oath was in keeping with a general trend in the larger cities, where seventy-five per cent of the clergy refused the oath.

What would happen in Saint-Bonnet? Would the curé, Benoît-Marie Cabuchet, or his curate, Jean Favret, swim against the tide? On 6 January 1791 both parish priest and curate took the oath. Since four fifths of the clergy in the area had done the same, the action of the Saint-Bonnet clergy was normal enough. What was unexpected was that five or six months later Father Cabuchet changed his mind and refused to read the pastoral instruction of the constitutional bishop, Lamourette. What had happened in the meantime? The pope's condemnation probably played some role. The reason tradition gives was the resolute action of the parishioners. Pastors did not want to lose the support of their people and in Saint-Bonnet, if one can credit the reports given later, the people were strongly opposed. Their reaction is enshrined in the story of the wolf in the sheepfold, a story told with slight variations by both Jean-Claude and Pierre Colin.[10]

According to the Colins' account, Father Cabuchet went to see Bishop Lamourette, who had taken up residence in Lyon on 12 April 1791. On his return, after the gospel on Sunday he began to read the bishop's pastoral instruction to the congregation. Suddenly, an elderly parishioner jumped to his feet, grabbed his hat and cried out: 'Let's get out of here; the wolf is in the sheepfold; quick, quick, let's go.' The whole congregation spilled out of their seats and rushed out the door. Cut short so abruptly, the startled celebrant went no further with the reading but after mass hurried over to consult a neighbour, Father Dimery, curé of Saint-Vincent-de-Rheins. What passed between them is not known but Dimery returned with him to the parish in time for vespers and reassured the agitated parishioners that he would sing vespers himself. After the Magnificat had been sung, however, Cabuchet rose and asked pardon of the people for the scandal he had given them. He refused to read the bishop's pastoral and either renounced the oath or added such reservations to it as to nullify it. A legend would have it that the elderly parishioner who raised the cry of 'wolf' was Jean-Claude's father, but Jacques Colin was no old man in 1791. It could possibly have been Jean-Claude's pious grandfather but there is no corroboration whatever for this supposition. Besides over-simplification in the Colins' account of the whole incident, particularly as regards Cabuchet's attitude to the oath, there are elements in this story that present difficulties.[11] Why did the congregation make no move in January when Cabuchet took the oath? The oath-taking was a public affair performed openly on a Sunday after Mass in the presence of the congregation. Did anything happen in the meantime or is there any reason why the parishioners waited half a year before

10. OM, docs 527, 6-7; 704, 1-10.
11. OM 2, pp 546-7.

registering their displeasure? The strength of popular protest that summer as registered in the account given by both the Colins is corroborated a few months after the 'sheepfold' incident by Father Peloux, his successor, who spoke of 'the resistance of almost all the inhabitants' to himself, presumably because he had taken the oath. Why was this resistance so strong and yet took so long to manifest itself?

Distrust of the bishop of Lyon, Adrien Lamourette, was a central element. The Saint-Bonnet people, according to one account, were worried and angered that Cabuchet went to this new bishop at Lyon; their diocese was Mâcon, they complained, and they did not belong to Lyon.[12] Perhaps it was the content of Lamourette's pastoral instruction which Cabuchet had begun to read that provoked the crisis. Since Lamourette issued more than one in the few months after his arrival, it is not clear which pastoral instruction caused the uproar. His first was dated 12 May and was a reply to the criticisms of the exiled Archbishop Marbeuf, who, through his vicars general, continued to exercise authority in the diocese. Although this first instruction blamed the non-juring clergy for raising up a spirit of fanatical fury, it was a comparatively mild document. In a second instruction on 16 July, however, Lamourette has this to say of the pope's condemnation of the Civil Constitution:

> The Roman court's doctrinal judgment on the ecclesiastical constitution of France [...] is heretical in that it divides the bishops, [...]. This judgment is inconsiderate, rash, in that it disturbs the peace of a great kingdom and sows in it the sparks of civil war. [...] This judgment is scandalous and immoral in that it advocates an odious and simoniacal concordat [...].[13]

If this was the pastoral that Cabuchet read out after the gospel on that Sunday morning, the unmeasured condemnation of papal action as 'heretical, rash, and scandalous', the shock and fury of those loyal to Rome becomes understandable. The pope's brief of 10 March 1791 condemning the Civil Constitution had reached Paris by 20 March and his opposition to it had become widely known by early summer. It is possible, then, that it was the Roman aspect of the question that provoked the change of heart among parishioners and pastor alike. Local issues may have been involved but, essentially, the reasons for rejecting the oath were religious. This was the case throughout France generally.[14] Some historians believe that the attitude of the people to the

12. OM, doc. 704, 2.

13. Charles Monternot, *Yves-Alexandre Marbeuf, ministre de la feuille des bénéfices, archevêque de Lyon, 1734-1799* (Lyon, 1911), pp 127-32.

14. After decades of examining other reasons, based on sociology, politics, economics, or on the opposition of town versus country, it is now generally accepted that the primary reason for the rejection of the Civil Constitution was religious. F. Furet, 'Constitution civile du clergé', F. Furet and M. Ozouf, eds, *Dictionnaire critique de la Révolution française: institutions et créations* (Paris, 1992), pp 217-19.

oath constituted the first referendum on the Revolution. For Cabuchet, Father Dimery's timely intervention provided much-needed advice and support, at a time when close on nine tenths of his fellow priests in the area had taken the oath.[15] As for the parishioners, already their 'cahier de doléances' of 1789, with its many criticisms, provided indications that there were strong-minded people in the parish ready to take a stand on what they considered their rights.

Cabuchet's refusal to read the bishop's pastoral and the restrictions he added to the oath angered the authorities at Villefranche, and so they sacked him from his position as curé and held new elections. On 8 August, the electors chose as curé a Father Peloux, who had been a Capuchin until the government suppressed the religious orders in February 1790. Peloux accepted but immediately ran into trouble. Pierre Colin gave a colourful account of Peloux's arrival in the parish. When the people living on the hillside saw the priest on the slope opposite climbing up towards the village, they cried out at the top of their voices, 'Au loup, au loup,' 'Wolf, Wolf,' as they were accustomed to do to warn against the presence of a wolf. When the villagers heard the commotion, they rushed out of doors. Then, as the unfortunate priest trudged towards his presbytery, from every corner of the parish arose the mournful howl of 'loup, loup'. It was an unfortunate and cheerless beginning to his ministry. His name, 'Peloux,' sounded like 'loup', which made it all the easier for people to hoot and jeer him. Pierre Colin recounted that this dismal reception made a profound impression on the children present.

If Pierre, who was then only five, could recall Peloux's unpleasant reception, he would have witnessed another scene closer to home. Before Peloux moved into the presbytery, Cabuchet moved out. He brought his belongings to Jacques Colin's house at Barbery and came to live there. It was there he exercised his priestly functions, baptising and, probably, celebrating the Mass. There, too, other refractory priests came, no doubt to sustain one another in their opposition to the new order of things in the Church. What impression this bizarre series of events had on the family, one can only guess. Jean-Claude, an infant of no more than a year, was too young to remember any of it but it would have been part of the family lore as he grew from infancy to boyhood. Jacques Colin's action in welcoming the priest and taking in his furniture was brought to the notice of the directory in Villefranche, and they summoned him to appear before them for questioning. He went the twenty miles, probably on foot, to the town to be subjected to interrogation, persuasions, and threats.[16] The authorities warned him to attend the Mass of the constitutional priest but

15. For the context of support that the presence of fellow priests provided for non-juring priests, see Tackett, *Religion*, pp 122-3, 289.
16. M. Cattin, *Mémoires pour servir à l'histoire ecclésiastique des diocèses de Lyon et de Belley, depuis la Constitution civile du clergé jusqu'au Concordat ...* (Lyon, 1867), p. 84; OM, doc. 890, 5.

he promised nothing. The family tradition, as picked up by Jean-Claude, relates that when he came home his anxious family, instead of welcoming him with joy, began to weep. 'You promised to go to the juror's Mass,' they cried. 'No, no, children,' he replied, 'I promised no such thing; I would rather die.'[17]

Meanwhile the trials of the juring priest, Father Peloux, continued. Almost all the parishioners rejected him from the very first day he came to Saint-Bonnet and only four or five families came to his services. The resistance turned violent. The women, Jean-Claude told Peter Julian Eymard, filled their aprons with stones to throw at him.[18] This statement, however, came forty years after the events and Jean-Claude could not have had any personal recollection of such harassment but it accords with what was happening in many places in France, where the women, particularly, harassed the 'intruders,' as they called them, often assaulting them physically. They were boycotted, the door to the parish church locked against them and offensive jokes played on them. In one parish, when the 'intruding' priest opened the tabernacle, a mouse jumped out. One new bishop, Monsignor Pouderous, was known as 'the bayonet bishop' for he needed an army escort with fixed bayonets to enter his diocese of Béziers![19] In Caen, some hundreds of women stoned the intruder, chased him into his church and tried to hang him from the choir loft. The role of the women of France in resisting the oath and in rebuilding the Church shattered by the Terror was remarkable. Was Marie Gonnet involved? No evidence of that exists.

On All Saints Day, after a little over two months in the parish, Peloux abandoned it for good. He retired not merely because of the opposition but for reasons even more compelling. He had taken the oath and had accepted Lamourette as archbishop, he told the authorities, because he believed that the pope would accept him. When, however, he became aware that the pope would not recognise Lamourette he was dismayed. '[A]ccording to my religious principles,' he stated bluntly, 'I regard the approval of the Holy Father as absolutely necessary.' For these religious reasons, he abandoned all claim to the parish. 'My religion is my first duty,' he explained, 'my second is obedience to the laws of the fatherland.' As regards the oath, he now added the significant reservation

17. OM, doc. 527, 9-10.
18. OM, doc. 527, 8. Although in the text this incident appears to refer to Peloux, it may well relate to Peloux's successor, Laussel. The trouble between intruding priest and resisting parishioners had taken a more violent turn during Laussel's time. Saint Peter Julian Eymard (1811-68), Marist priest, 1839; provincial, 1845; left Marists to found Blessed Sacrament Fathers and the Servants of the Blessed Sacrament, 1856.
19. The rector of La Chapelle-Janson (Ille-et-Vilaine) was jeered and pelted with stones. Priests in Lozère who took the oath were chased from their parishes by knife-wielding women. Tackett, *Religion*, pp 166-80. Supporters of the oath used similar violence against clergy who refused to take it.

that it be 'without prejudice to the submission I owe to the legitimate pastors of our religion.'[20] He returned to the parish where he had been curate for a while. Later, apparently, he fled abroad.[21] Nothing further is heard of this priest, whose perplexity mirrors that of so many priests caught up unwittingly in the tangle created by the Revolution. Most of the 'constitutional' clergy had taken the oath with the intention of serving both faith and fatherland and many of them were to die on the scaffold for the Catholic faith.

On 11 November, shortly after Peloux left the parish, Saint-Bonnet elected a new municipality which included Jacques Colin. It sent to Lyon to persuade Cabuchet to return as curé and on 26 November he returned in triumph, welcomed by the municipality. The bells of Saint-Bonnet pealed joyfully and delighted parishioners fired shots in the air to express their satisfaction. From then until February 1792 he exercised his functions openly in the parish church. The authorities, however, decided to send in another constitutional priest as pastor. An election was held on 25 March 1792 and this time a Father Laussel was elected. Laussel, a priest from Languedoc, was a 'patriot priest' committed to the new régime, and founded the *Journal du département de Rhone-et-Loire* to promote revolutionary ideas. In Saint-Bonnet he was met with fierce opposition. Posters disparaging him were displayed and, according to Laussel, the municipality was unwilling to remove them. Shots were fired through his window at night. Matters reached a climax at vesper time on 29 June 1792. Laussel rang the bell for vespers. When the congregation assembled, however, he left in a hurry with his housekeeper and three or four friends for the fair at Saint-Nizier. This annoyed the parishioners. According to Laussel's friends, however, he departed to avoid being left at the mercy of a mob of rebels. When he returned, a crowd of twenty parishioners gathered and began to abuse him. So threatening did they appear that one of Laussel's escort drew his pistol in defence. Twelve of Saint-Bonnet's citizens now denounced their municipality to the Revolutionary directory at Villefranche. Their opponents organised a boycott of Laussel, who was then refused the very necessaries of life. He was forced to appeal for help to the directory of Villefranche, who drafted in a hundred soldiers to protect him. Laussel had had enough. A short while later he abandoned his troublesome parish and headed up to Paris, where he was soon in the confidence of the powerful minister of the Interior, Jean-Marie Roland de la Platière, who gave him a roving commission as 'an apostle of liberty.' He confided the parish of Saint-Bonnet to a curate, another juring priest, Claude Blanc, while he went on to play an important role in Lyon as procurator of the commune. During the Reign of Terror in Lyon he denounced

20. Peloux to the administrators of the district of Villefranche, 12 January 1792 (Archives départementales du Rhône 4 L 72; copy APM 917 Rhône).
21. In all, between thirty and forty thousand priests fled the country during the Revolution.

'the priestly caste, the furious enemy of liberty.'[22] Of the ministry of Blanc in Saint-Bonnet, nothing is known.

The Revolutionaries in the National Assembly toughened their line in 1792 and in May they decreed that those priests who did not take the oath were to be deported. In September of that year, came the massacres in Paris when between two hundred and twenty and two hundred and sixty priests were killed by a mob, many of them in the grounds of what is now the Institut Catholique. The question put to them before they were hacked to death was simply: 'Did you take the oath?' They could have saved their lives by agreeing to accept it but they did not. This horrific incident, which sealed in blood the hostility between the Church and the Revolution, shows how the oath became a symbol.

Meanwhile, at Villefranche, the authorities replaced both the mayor and procurator of Saint-Bonnet and sent a commissary named Perrin to oversee new elections. Angry with Laussel for not remaining at his post, they ordered him to return to Saint-Bonnet and summoned him, in vain, before the tribunal to explain his non-residence. They had a new municipality elected and, blaming Cabuchet and his adherents as the troublemakers, they decided to deal with them. Among those singled out for investigation was Jacques Colin and, on 25 June 1793, the justice of the peace of Thizy issued an order for his arrest. For whatever reason, no arrest was made. The next intervention by the authorities proved more dangerous, for the extreme left wing of the revolution – the Jacobins – had taken control in Paris and the Reign of Terror had begun. Lyon, the second city of France, together with other parts of France rebelled against their dictatorship. Reacting energetically against the threat, the Jacobin Committee of Public Safety, the effective ruler of the country, sent armies to invest Lyon. At the same time, it sent roving commissioners throughout the country with full powers to bring the rebels in the provinces to heel. Three of these 'representatives of the people,' Jacques Reverchon, Sébastien Delaporte and Claude Javogues, whom the historian, Hippolyte Taine, described as 'the Nero of [the department of] Ain', came to the department of Rhone-et-Loire, where they played an important role in combating the rebellion in Lyon. At a meeting at their headquarter at Mâcon in August 1793, they took time to examine the incidents at Saint-Bonnet and issued strict orders to the district authorities at Villefranche to settle the matter forthwith. Jacques Colin, Étienne Plasse, and Jacques Rollin were to be arrested for opposing conscription, for encouraging 'fanaticism' – the term they now used for the Catholic religion – and for applauding the rebels of Lyon. The representatives gave the Villefranche authorities just three days to carry out their orders. Jolted into activity, the members of the Villefranche directory issued a new order for the

22. L. Trénard, *Révolution française dans la région Rhône-Alpes* (Paris, 1992) pp 270-1, 274, 335, 354-6, 371-3.

arrest of the three. They instructed Badet, administrator of the district, to take as many gendarmes and national guards as were necessary to track down the three and lodge them in the jail at Villefranche.[23] Despite the new urgency in the pursuit, Badet failed totally. Jacques Colin had fled to the woods of Crest above his farm. How many swoops the police made on the Colin house at Barbery over the next year is not recorded but they never found their prey. The dread that the head of the household would be caught, imprisoned or guillotined made it an extremely difficult time for the Colin family. The atmosphere in this tiny community had become totally poisoned and, in the province, a civil war had begun. The republicans were proving ruthless. In October 1793, after a bitter struggle, they had captured Lyon and exacted a fierce revenge on their opponents, shooting or guillotining up to two thousand of them. Among them were a hundred and thirty-five priests.[24] The Constitutional Archbishop, Adrien Lamourette was among the guillotined. Before his death he solemnly retracted the oath.[25]

All over France suspected enemies of the Revolution feared the same fate. An anti-religious fury gripped the revolutionaries. Up to then they had supported the constitutional or patriotic Church – which the revolution had established – against the refractory Church loyal to Rome, but now they began a campaign for the total dechristianisation of France. Intense pressure was brought to bear on priests to abandon their priesthood and burn their ordination letters. Some twenty thousand priests, almost exclusively of the Constitutional Church, abdicated their priestly functions. A register of Lyon priests lists a hundred and sixty-three who 'de-priested'. Extraordinary pressure was brought on the priests to marry, for the revolutionaries perceived the marriage of the priests as the symbol of a final break with the Church. 'Marriage or the guillotine', was the choice. Imprisonment, exile or execution became the order of the day for all suspected of not conforming to the new regime.

Sunday was abolished because it was the Lord's day, and those who kept it were threatened with prison for being the accomplices of the liberty-killing tactics of the priests.[26] The saints were erased from the names of towns, and

23. Livre du comité de surveillance révolutionnaire. Registre de la commune de Bonnet le Tronsit, 27 March 1794 (Archives départementales du Rhône 33 L 51; copy APM 917 Rhône).

24. Of the fourteen thousand persons executed by the revolutionary tribunals, nine hundred and twenty were clergy and one hundred and twenty-six nuns. Many others were shot or drowned, or died in prison awaiting deportation. The proportion of clergy executed was six or seven times more than the average. If later persecutions are included, between two and three thousand clergy were put to death. B. Cousin, M. Cubells, R. Moulinas, *La pique et la croix:Histoire religieuse de la Révolution française* (Paris, 1989), p. 168.

25. J. Linsolas, *L'Église clandestine de Lyon pendant la Révolution,* vol. 1, 1789-1794 (Lyon, 1985), pp 183-4. Archbishop Gobel of Paris, who had ordained Lamourette bishop, also died on the scaffold reconciled to the Roman Church.

26. Trénard, *Révolution,* p. 504.

'Saint-Bonnet' became 'Bonnet-la-Liberté.' Children were named after Roman heroes, or flowers and vegetables; some children were 'baptised' in a republican ceremony with incongruous names like 'Celery.' Terror was the order of the day and it touched all France. Not unlike the cultural revolution in China, vandalism became commonplace. On the high altar of Notre-Dame, in Paris, one of the greatest churches of the Christian world, the revolutionaries enthroned an actress of doubtful morals, vested as the goddess of Reason. In Lyon, on 6 December 1793, the revolutionaries held a patriotic festival: a donkey was dressed in pontifical vestments, and before him went a dragon in alb and chasuble, holding in his hand a ciborium from which the donkey ate hay. The chapels and oratories in the city were transformed into warehouses. In Belley the goddess of Reason was enthroned and relics were profaned. In Le Puy the venerated black madonna was burned; in the Bugey the belfries were torn down. The Villefranche authorities, lamenting that Catholicism still persisted, forbade pilgrimages as a waste of good time, favouring debauchery, and serving the cupidity of the clergy.

Those who hid the Roman priests were in real danger. Marguerite Coste, of Montpellier, was guillotined on 5 May 1794 for harbouring a priest named Étienne Berhaudon. Jacques Colin and his friends had reason to fear for their lives. Two meetings of the revolutionary committee of Saint-Bonnet, in March and in May 1794, detailed a formidable list of charges brought against him by his fellow parishioners. After their failure to arrest him, they employed other means of harassment. In December 1793, they had seized his vineyard.[27] In June 1794, they confiscated the last harvest of wine from his cellar and sold it off. Jacques remained constantly on the run, sleeping in the woods and in barns, never, according to Jean-Claude, sleeping more than two nights in his own house for over a year.[28] The plight of Marie Gonnet with her eight children – the oldest, Claudine, a girl of seventeen, and the youngest, Joseph, a babe-in-arms – was equally painful. While her husband was in constant danger of his life, their home remained under surveillance and subject to frequent police raids. Nothing was safe any longer in the house. Their home was pillaged, whether by the gendarmes, the soldiers, or the hostile republican minority in the parish, is not clear. Their furniture, too, was sequestered and officially sealed. Financially, physically, and psychologically it was a fearful time for the mother of a young family.

The end came unexpectedly. On 27 July 1794, Robespierre, the chief support of the Terror, fell a victim to it himself. His enemies, fearful for their own safety, united to denounce him and, with some hundred of his partisans, he died on the guillotine. The Terror was over and persecution, in its intense form,

27. 16 December 1793 (Archives départementales du Rhône 1 Q 746).
28. OM, doc. 889, 5.

ceased for the moment. In August 1794, a month after the fall of Robespierre, Jacques Colin was pardoned. His sequestered furniture and even the price his wine fetched were returned to him. He had been over a year on the run. Now, finally, he could return to his wife and family and they could restart a normal life. A few months later, under a new law of 21 February 1795 guaranteeing freedom of religion, Cabuchet was able to return to the parish. Much needed renewing, for the religious divisions and the absence of a priest had upset the religious life of the parish. Yet it seemed possible that the parish of Saint-Bonnet, its curé, and the Colins could now return to normality.

The oath to the Civil Constitution had shattered the unity of Church and Nation, family and parish and was to leave a permanent scar on French society. In the midst of the strife it had unleashed, it evoked much heroism, and the events in Saint-Bonnet from 1790 to 1794 constitute a minor epic in this story. The Colins always regarded their parents and Cabuchet as heroes, indeed martyrs, of that fierce persecution. Forty years later, when the local historian of the revolution, M. Ruivet, vicar general of Belley, set himself the task of recording the heroism of those priests and Christian families who had suffered for the faith during these persecutions, he singled out the Colin family. After recounting the heroism of Jacques and Marie Colin and noting that they were the parents of the Marists Pierre and Jean-Claude, he added, 'This father and this mother merited well to have such children.'[29]

29. OM, doc. 890, 6.

CHAPTER 2

Colin's Boyhood:
From the Terror to the Concordat

Few contemporary documents are extant concerning the Colin family in the months following the father's return home for good in 1794. Later, however, some glimpses are recorded in the reminiscences of the two Marist sons – Pierre and Jean-Claude. In 1848, Pierre gave a touching account of his mother to Father Gabriel-Claude Mayet, the chronicler of the Society:[1]

> I'll never forget the goodness of that tender mother. During the last years of her life, although I was quite young, I never tired of gazing at her; just to fix my eyes on her face made me happy. On returning from a walk, when I was five or six, seeing her from afar, I would run towards her, jump up on her lap, take her face in my little hands and cover it with kisses. She did not stop me. Then I got down and was content.[2]

Yet she was not over-indulgent. One day when he used some inappropriate words, she gently reproved him. When he repeated them, she reproved him again but more strongly. When he insisted on repeating them, she rose without a word and slapped him.[3] A precious vignette of her occurs in two stories treasured by the family – poignant because of the circumstances which gave rise to them. Seriously ill and sensing she would not recover, Marie impressed on her children that the only mother they had now was their heavenly mother, Mary, the mother of God. Anxious for their earthly welfare also, she begged her brother-in-law to take care of them. Marie died on 20 May 1795. She was only thirty-seven. Although her husband, Jacques, personally reported her death to the authorities, he may have been ill, which would explain her unusual request to her brother-in-law. Certainly, Jacques was heart-broken at her death and local tradition records that day after day he came grieving to her grave. Within less than three weeks, on 9 June, he, too, died. He was forty-eight. What caused their deaths is not known but, many years later, Jean-Claude told Fathers Jean Jeantin and Georges David, his close collaborators in later years, that they contracted the illness that brought both to an early grave, while they were on the

---

1. Gabriel-Claude Mayet (1809-94), b. Lyon, ord. 1836, Marist novitiate 1837. His invaluable 'Mémoires originaux' on Jean-Claude Colin and the history of the Society run to 6,000 closely-written pages.
2. OM, doc. 681, 1.
3. Ibid.

run from the law.[4] Marie had never been on the run, however, and for the previous nine months Jacques had been at home. Yet, the long period of hardship and strain had, no doubt, taken a toll on them both and Jean-Claude and Pierre were right in seeing them as 'martyrs' of the Revolution. Before the year was out, another bereavement followed. Two days after Christmas, Jean Colin, senior, the grandfather, died at the age of eighty-two. The year 1795 had been a sad one for the Colins.

The roots of people's later traits, especially their difficulties, are often traced to 'traumas' of early childhood. One can only guess at the devastation caused by the absence of one parent on the run from the law and then the simultaneous loss of both on a family that had already suffered much. The eight surviving children were still quite young, ranging from Claudine, who was nineteen, to Joseph, who was just two. Arrangements had to be made for their future. Two weeks after the father's death, the two families, Colins and Gonnets, met to make provision for the orphans. Seven of the Colin family and two of the Gonnet family appeared before Benoît Sautallier, justice of the peace at Thizy, and an official act was drawn up, appointing Sébastien Colin, paternal uncle of the children, as guardian. This document is the only account extant of the extended family – uncles, uncles through marriage, cousins and cousins through marriage – who interested themselves in the orphans. It reveals that all the Colins except two lived in the commune of Saint-Bonnet. One lived at Saint-Vincent-de-Rheins, another at Saint-Nizier-d'Azergues, while the two Gonnets lived at Ranchal, all villages within a few miles of Saint-Bonnet. Sébastien Colin, Jacques Colin's brother, was named first in the document for, if one excepts the eighty-two-year old grandfather, he, as the sole surviving child of Jean and Claudine Colin, was head of the family. Since he was a bachelor it is not surprising that he was chosen to be the legal guardian of the orphans.[5]

Sébastien, or Bastien as he was known, was a weaver like his brother, Jacques. He was a kindly uncle who took his new responsibility seriously. Thenceforth he was for the young Colins 'le parrain' – their sponsor. Their guardian, protector, and uncle, he had become in many ways the central person in their life. Was he a 'dreamer'? A conscientious, perhaps timid, and even scrupulous man he clearly was, as his fear of failing in his obligations towards his wards suggested.[6] There are indications that he had difficulty in coming to terms with life. Although his brother and his father could write, he could not. He never married and, late in life, his business collapsed. A story survives that

---

4. Jean Jeantin (1824-95), b. Savoy, professed 1847; author of a six-volume biography of Colin. Georges David (1827-1907), b. Lyon, prof. 1848; esteemed as novice-master.
5. OM, doc. 13.
6. OM, doc. 527, 14.

gives a brief glimpse into the family life and is revealing of his character. The children were warming themselves around the fire but were misbehaving. Uncle Sébastien became so annoyed with them that he threatened: 'Alright, children, you are bold; I am leaving you and I'll get married and I shall divide you out left and right.' The poor children burst out sobbing and Bastien retreated to his room. There he had, or believed he had, an extraordinary experience. Marie Gonnet, his dead sister-in-law, either appeared or spoke to him. 'Bastien,' she implored him, 'don't abandon my children!' Poor Bastien cried out, 'Marie, Marie, I'll not marry, I shall not abandon them.'[7] Immediately, he returned to the children and said: 'Children, weep no more; I'll never abandon you.' This story was told by Father Eugène Colin, Bastien's grand-nephew, whose father, Joseph, was one of the children. Eugène Colin commented that, while it was possible that he did hear a voice, Bastien was much given to seeing and hearing extraordinary things and never went out at night without seeing some apparition. While omitting the rebuke at the fireside, Pierre and Jean-Claude also recounted the same story of Sébastien and Marie Gonnet. It was an incident which they retained long afterwards for Sébastien's threat had touched a sensitive nerve – the panic the children felt of being abandoned once more.[8] It shows the soft-hearted goodness of Sébastien but may indicate, too, a certain unreal, dreamlike quality in his make-up. Bastien proved a devoted guardian and cared well for the upbringing and education of his orphaned nephews and nieces as Jean-Claude later testified when at the point of death.

Possibly before the parents' death, Jeanne-Marie, or Jeannette as she was called, the youngest surviving girl in the Colin family, had been sent to be brought up in the nearby village of Poule. The curé of Poule, Gabriel Captier, who had been curate in Saint-Bonnet and had remained in contact with the family, may have made the arrangements.[9] Perhaps he had also arranged another matter for the family for from his parish, too, there came another person whose role during Jean-Claude's boyhood was quite significant. This was the house-keeper, Marie Échallier. When Marie came to Barbery is not certain but, while she may have come before the death of the parents, it is more likely that Sébastien hired her because he felt unable to cope on his own with the young children.[10] Marie Échallier has been accused of having a negative impact on the children and especially on Jean-Claude right into his adult years. Little is

7. OM, docs 819, 130; 850, 1.

8. OM, docs 493, 2 and additions d, e; 527, 13; 819, 130; OM 3, pp 721-2.

9. G. Lessard, 'Claudine of Lyon: the French Connection,' Hyattsville, 28 November 1981, p. 6, unpublished paper in author's possession. Claudine Colin later cooperated with Captier in estab-lishing a Catholic educational institute.

10. Jean-Claude states on one occasion that she was seventeen years with them. For this state-ment to be accurate she would have had to enter the Colin household in 1789, before the death of the parents, for when Jean Colin married in 1806 she returned to Poule where she died. This

known about her and the impression is given that she was a wrinkled old dragon who tied Jean-Claude in a psychological knot, particularly in sexual matters, permanently affecting his attitude to women. She was neither wrinkled nor old for when she was asked to take charge of the Colin household she was no more than twenty-four![11] She was born in the little village of Poule in 1771 and died there in 1834. When she came to Barbery she was unmarried which, at her age, was already late for a French peasant girl. Jean-Claude gave her high praise, thanked providence that the housekeeper Sébastien found was not of a different sort, but added the cryptic remark that, 'quite young as we were, we, and he, too, would have been at risk, if the servant he had found had been a worldly servant.'[12] A not unreasonable interpretation of this remark is that he thanked God that the young woman who came to take over the household on the death of his mother was not a smart, presentable, worldly young woman anxious to make her way in life, who might have wasted their inheritance or even induced the weak-minded Sébastien to marry her, and the children's recurring fear of being abandoned once more would have been realised. Instead there came into the house the pious, plain, parsimonious, but unambitious and down-to-earth Marie who served them faithfully for eleven years or more.[13] This young woman was both demanding and, by present-day permissive standards, prudish. Jean-Claude admitted to Fathers Maîtrepierre and Mayet that she was strict and insisted on obedience in matters concerning religion and in the modesty she demanded from the children.[14] Many years later, in 1867, Father François Yardin, a friend of the family, accompanied Jean-Claude on a historic visit to his eldest brother and godfather, Jean, now blind and very anxious to meet him. Present during this last meeting of the two elderly brothers, Yardin had been primed by Mayet to take note of what he could learn about the Colins' childhood. Yardin reported back to Mayet that Marie Échallier was a pious person but dominating. The children held her in high regard but also feared her. In particular, on days she was preparing to go to confession, it was not pleasant to be in her presence.[15]

does not fit in with Jean-Claude's other statement that Sébastien was the person who found Marie, which is more likely. It accords well with the difficulty Sébastien faced in bringing up the family on his own. OM 3, p. 994-5.

11. Confusion arose from an expression *'toute badinée'* which occurs in a note Maîtrepierre added to Jean-Claude's account of his family. 'Badinée' means crumpled like paper that has been folded and creased. Gaston Lessard, however, discovered that in Lyon 'toute badinée' meant 'not in a mood for jesting'. OM 2, doc, 527 q; OM 3, p. 994-5, note 4; OM 4, p. 505; Ad. Vachet, *Glossaire des gones de Lyon* (Lyon 1907, Laffitte Reprints, Marseille 1983), p. 24.

12. OM, doc. 527, 14. The French word 'mondain' has been translated 'worldly' but it can also indicate a high style of living.

13. OM 3, p. 994-995, note 4; OM 4, p. 505.

14. OM, doc. 527, addition q. Denis-Joseph Maîtrepierre (1800-72), assistant and provincial-visitor to Colin, 1839; novice-master, 1841; assistant general 1854-66.

15. OM, doc. 889, 2.

Yet, if demanding and dominating, Marie had many good qualities. Jean-Claude, in his account to Peter Julian Eymard, in 1842, thanked God for Marie Échallier and the way she cared for them. She was, he said, a good, very pious, very thrifty young woman.[16] Jean-Claude's words are kindly but even allowing for some indulgence on his part the high praise he gave Marie Échallier – 'she took the place of a mother' – cannot be ignored. Her lengthy service is itself impressive. Elsewhere Jean-Claude, while blushingly admitting that he knew nothing of the facts of life until adulthood, saw it as God's good grace that he grew up under the supervision of such a good and devout person who took no nonsense.[17] Such was the reserve that she implanted in him that even the slightest immodesty shocked him; when he went to the seminary, he dressed and undressed under the bedclothes. Yet to see this training as unusual would be unhistorical. From at least the seventeenth century, French society had become protective of the morals of children. Jansenists and Jesuits, the two great opposing schools of religious thought in eighteenth-century France, were in total agreement on this point. That gentle saint, Francis de Sales, and that great educator of youth, John Baptist de la Salle, insisted that 'mothers and fathers must teach their children to cover their own bodies when going to bed.'[18] It is not surprising, then, that Marie Échallier, who took on the care of this large young family and who by temperament was strict on herself, if not scrupulous, felt obliged to make sure that her young charges were preserved from the depravity of the world, a depravity which the Revolution had aggravated. In matters of moral behaviour, she insisted on being obeyed.

Despite their shortcomings, Sébastien's and Marie Échallier's part in the Colins' upbringing was vital. The Revolution had created a crisis for the handing on of the faith. Throughout pre-revolutionary France, especially in the villages and countryside where there were no primary schools, it had been the custom for the curé to instruct the children in their faith after the Sunday Mass. By 1792, as a result of the persecution, there was neither regular Sunday Mass nor children's instruction. Where the parents could read and had a manual, they took on the instruction of their children, as happened in John Vianney's family, growing up at the same time at Dardilly, some twenty-five miles from Saint-Bonnet. For the orphaned Colins, however, the burden of some basic religious training fell largely on the shoulders of the bachelor uncle and this young peasant woman of twenty-four. Neither of them was particularly well equipped for such a task but at least they instilled in the children some of the rudiments of religion.

Yet neither the conscientious upbringing of the dreaming uncle nor the

16. OM, doc. 527, 14.
17. OM, doc. 539, 2-3.
18. Cited in Philippe Ariès, *L'enfant et la vie familiale sous l'ancien régime* (Paris, 1973), p. 121.

moral surveillance of the strict young housekeeper could take the place of the love of a father and mother. The children had suffered a sense of loss, an absence of parental affection and they so dreaded the departure, even temporary, of another member of the family that they hid rather than face the normal goodbyes. Jean-Claude was a lonely child with a nervous stutter. His path to enchantment from the unfriendliness of his world was to take a book and wander off to the woods above his home – the woods of Crest – where his father and Father Cabuchet would have often taken refuge from the revolutionary police. Although, as he admitted, he was timid by nature and quivered with fear at the slightest noise, he loved the dark, deep solitude of the wood, and to the tall fir trees he would preach little sermons. Later on, he gathered other children around him and preached to them the sermons he heard from the curé or the lessons he learned at school from Sister Martha.

This mention of lessons is a reminder that besides Sébastien and Marie Échallier there was a third and more formal influence on Jean-Claude's education – Sister Martha – the 'ex-nun'. Who Sister Martha was and where she came from is not known nor is it clear when the Colin children began to go to her for instruction.[19] One of the first acts of the Revolution, even before its disagreement with the Church on the oath, was to 'open the gates of the convents.' Religious life had declined in France during the latter half of the eighteenth century, particularly among male religious.[20] The National Assembly first forbade the taking of solemn religious vows and suppressed those orders which did not have a teaching or nursing role. As this decree affected only contemplative and mendicant orders, and those orders involved in active work were not suppressed, there was little public outcry though some of the bishops, de Bonal of Clermont and La Fare of Nancy, became alarmed at the interference of the state in matters outside its realm. The revolutionaries, however, described its action as 'opening' the convents and a 'liberation' of the religious unjustly confined there. It was also an opportunity, though the revolutionaries did not as readily acknowledge it, to enrich the state and individuals with monastic property. The suppression of public vows was only a beginning. In the face of mounting pressure the religious, monks and nuns, were forced to abandon monasteries and convents. Many returned to the lay life and some married. For most it was a bewildering and painful period as, deprived of their old way of

19. Thomas Gilbert, curé of Saint-Bonnet from 1803, mentions 'a good woman' who looked after the schooling of the children 'to the best of her ability'. She is probably Sister Martha. Gilbert to Joseph Courbon, Vicaire Général, à Lion, 19 Feb. 1804; Archives de Lyon. Etat des paroisses 1804. Saint-Nizier-d'Azergues (Canton) Saint-Bonnet-le-Troncy. Copy in APM. Jean Coste mentions a Marthe-Marie Plasse (1778-1828) born in Saint-Bonnet who may well be the same person. OM 4, p. 518.
20. J. Le Goff and R. Rémond, *Histoire de la France religieuse,* vol. 3 (Paris, 1991), pp 184-190.

life, they attempted to cope with a new, and often hostile, environment. Few
of the expelled nuns wanted to marry, many were unwanted by their relatives,
who regarded them as a burden or an embarrassment. Quite a number of them
were anxious to teach religion and played an important role in handing on the
faith in the dark days of religious persecution. One of those, the well-loved
Sister Martha, ran a school in Saint-Bonnet which the young Colins attended.
Only one incident of their school days survives which Jean-Claude later retailed.
One day there was a dance in the village square and, fascinated, he half-opened
the door to watch it. Sister Martha, for whom dances were probably scandalous, spied him and meted out exemplary punishment. No further information
about Sister Martha and her school has survived. Who paid her and to whom
was she responsible? When did she begin to teach? Possibly after the fall of
Robespierre, though more probably around 1798, when the second Terror had
eased somewhat.

Probably Sister Martha taught elementary education though religion would
have been the important part of her teaching. She may have used the pre-
revolutionary catechisms of the diocese of Mâcon or she may have used the
new catechisms drawn up by the bishops opposed to the Revolution. The horrors of the Revolution were seen as the result of sin for which expiation had to
be made. The catechism, which the missionaries sent by Father Jacques
Linsolas, vicar general of Archbishop Marbeuf of Lyon, brought with them to
instruct the people, was militantly anti-revolutionary, rigorous, and austere.[21]
What many of those new catechisms had in common was their detestation of
the constitutional Church, which they denounced, often harshly, as schismatic.
It may well have been one of the new catechisms that Sister Martha used to give
Jean-Claude and his brothers their first lessons in Catholic doctrine. Loyalty to
Rome remained an essential part of Jean-Claude's creed.

The fact that there would have been no Christian education of the children
were it not for the generous efforts of Sister Martha is a reminder of the continuing abnormal situation of the Church. In the period between August 1795
and June 1799, France was ruled by a Directory, consisting of three Directors,
generally hostile to the Church. At first, however, active persecution ceased.
Profiting from the decree of the liberty of cults in 1795, both Churches – for
the constitutional Church and the Roman Church still existed side by side –
began to re-organise. Across the borders, from Germany, Spain and Italy, and
over the sea from England flocked thousands of the exiled, Roman or 'refractory' priests as their enemies called them.[22] The bishops, who were regarded by

21. Jacques Linsolas (1754-1828), vicar-general of Archbishop de Marbeuf of Lyon; principal
organiser of the Roman Church in Lyon during the Revolution. C. Ledré, *Le culte caché sous la
révolution: les missions de l'abbé Linsolas* (Paris, 1949).
22. The clergy who took the oath to the constitution are referred to as 'constitutional' or 'juring.'

the revolutionaries as enemies of the Revolution, prudently remained abroad so it fell to the laity and priests, such as Linsolas in Lyon, to organise the Roman Church again.[23] The constitutional bishops, on the other hand, were on the spot and, headed by Henri-Baptiste Grégoire, bishop of Blois, gave the lead to the re-organisation of their church.[24] The two sets of clergies, Roman and constitutional, that emerged from the campaign of dechristianisation were much weakened. Some of the finest of the Roman clergy had died on the scaffold or of maltreatment on prison ships. The constitutional Church fared worse. Thousands of its clergy had abandoned their ministry, married, or even torn up their letters of ordination and become active persecutors of the Church, while others had gone over to the Roman Church. In all, it had lost seventy percent of its priests and over fifty percent of its bishops. To make good the losses was an impossible task, for the seminaries had been closed and recruits were few. Both sets of clergy were that much older and ill-treatment or suffering while on the run had broken many of them in health and spirit. Some priests were too afraid to come out of hiding or, when they did, reluctant to resume their priestly duties: in one town in eastern France – Levier, in the Doubs – the priest refused to say Mass, but the women of the parish took up sticks, beat him into the church, and forced him to celebrate.[25] The priests' fear was not unreasonable, as the recurrence of persecution a year later proved.

To add to the confusion, Catholics remained bitterly divided. Although both Roman and constitutional churches had suffered dreadfully under the Terror, they still remained hostile to one another. In the autumn of 1795 a new problem arose. Since the spring of that year a majority in the National Assembly wanted religious peace and, in an effort to win over more of the clergy, the government replaced the constitutional oath by a new one which demanded only obedience to the laws of the Republic. After the unfortunate experience of earlier oaths, it might have been better if no oath had been demanded. Would this new oath, with little religious content, finally bring peace to the troubled country? All depended on how the church would respond.

Opinions were divided. There was little guidance to be had from either bishops, most of whom were still in exile, or from the pope, Pius VI, who hesitated to interfere. In Paris, Father Jacques-André Émery, superior of the Sulpicians and vicar general to the archbishop of Paris, advised accepting the

---

23. J. Linsolas, *L'Église clandestine de Lyon pendant la Révolution,* 2 vols (Lyon, 1985, 1987).
24. Henri-Baptiste Grégoire (1750-1831); studied at Metz under Adrien Lamourette; constitutional bishop of Rhone-et-Loire, and later Blois. Grégoire, who espoused a 'Catholic Enlightenment', remained committed to the Catholic faith despite separating himself almost completely from Rome.
25. Hufton, 'Reconstruction', p. 45.

oath.[26] From his post in the seminary at Saint-Sulpice in Paris and later during a long imprisonment at the time of the Terror, Émery, who, after the flight of the bishops, had shown remarkable courage in helping and counselling the clergy, was essentially a moderate for whom religious peace was the priority. In Lyon, however, the influential Linsolas took a hard line and rejected the new oath out of hand. Most exiled bishops, removed from the scene, raised the cry of a new 'sell-out', and Pius VI inclined that way too. To an extent, this divergence of views was a foreshadowing of the conflict during the nineteenth century between the liberals and the intransigents in the French Church, between those who attempted to reconcile the Church with the Revolution and those who would have no truck with what they saw as a bloodstained monster.

While this dispute was dividing the Roman clergy, government actions complicated matters further. In September 1797, the three Directors, worried at the waves of returned emigrants, whom they perceived as enemies of the Republic, staged a coup d'état, renewed the penal laws and began to enforce them vigorously. Priests who wanted to celebrate Mass had to take a new oath – this time an 'Oath of Hatred of the Monarchy.' Even the eirenic Émery could not go that far, though he endeavoured to exonerate those who did. This oath was part of the 'Fructidorean' Terror, so called because introduced on 18th of Fructidor, or 4 September, 1797. This new and ferocious Terror was better organised and more systematic than the first Terror.[27] A law authorising police raids on houses suspected of harbouring refractory priests was strictly applied. Another law made priests who disturbed the peace liable to be deported without trial or right of defence – a measure so broad in application that it could be applied to almost any priest in the country. The astute Directory preferred to avoid executions lest they alienate people but the alternative they chose was as grim – exile to the dreaded Devil's Island in Guyana. Exile to Guyana had been used during the first Terror but was now systematically adopted to crush the recalcitrant clergy. Arrested without trial, denied all right of appeal, the priests were loaded on to carts, often chained like animals, and transported, in the dead of winter, from village to village, serving thus as a stern warning to others. From all over France these carts with their human cargo converged on

26. Jacques-André Émery (1732-1811) superior-general of the Sulpicians, 1782; worked for religious reconciliation and peace; played an important part in the negotiations that resulted in the concordat; refounded the Sulpicians and re-opened the seminaries at Saint-Sulpice and Lyon; friend and adviser to Fesch, whom he reconciled to the Church and the priesthood. Despite his firm support of papal authority, he was highly respected by Napoleon. The Sulpicians, or Company of Priests of Saint-Sulpice, founded in 1641 by Jean Jacques Olier, dedicated themselves to the training of priests and ran seminaries in many parts of the world.
27. B. Plongeron, P. Lerou et R. Darteville, *Pratiques religieuses, mentalités et spiritualités dans l'Europe révolutionnaire 1770-1820: Actes du colloque Chantilly 27-29 novembre 1986* (Paris, 1988), p. 510-511.

the west coast. There, in the harbours of Bordeaux and La Rochelle, a number of prison hulks were riding at anchor and on to those as many as possible of the priests were packed. They were bound for Guyana. The remaining priests were interned on the islands of Ré and Oléron near La Rochelle to await their turn for transportation. Sufficient ships were not found, however, and, in any case, few could leave port, for the English fleet patrolled the high seas off the French coast. As a result, over two thousand unfortunate priests lived for months crowded together in wretched conditions in the island prisons or on the prison hulks. Those crowded on the boats were the worst off, for they were piled together, without room to move in stifling and infectious conditions. Rarely were they allowed on deck to breathe clean air. Many of them died. A few ships slipped past the English blockade and reached Guyana. Of the two hundred and fifty-six who were landed there, a hundred and eighteen died within the following two years in this 'exile without consolation, without hope, without relations, without friends, without help.'[28]

The ongoing struggle between the Catholic Church and the Revolution was not merely at local and national level but had by 1798 reached an international intensity. Eight hundred of the priests awaiting transportation to Guyana were Belgian! From being a purely French affair, the Revolution had become European. Its armies had overrun modern-day Belgium, the Netherlands, Spain, parts of Germany and Italy, and wherever they came they brought their anti-Church laws. In February 1798, they entered Rome. A year later they arrested Pius VI, 'Citizen Pope,' as they called him. Then, in March 1799, they transported him up the length of Italy and finally over the Alps into France in an agonising journey that lasted five months. The intention was to bring him to Dijon but Pius, now eighty-two, was too ill and when they reached Valence, sixty miles to the south of Lyon, he could go no further. There, on 29 August 1799, he died, and the revolutionaries, who would not allow him to be brought back to Rome, had him buried without pomp or ceremony. The officials who reported to the government the death of 'Giovanni Angelo Braschi, exercising the profession of pontiff,' maintained that they were burying Pope Pius the Last! To many it appeared to be the end of the papacy and the Roman Church.[29]

Yet if the fortunes of the papacy looked black in 1799, the French Church was staging a remarkable revival. Even before the Terror, the Roman church

---

28. Brumault de Beauregard, *Mémoires*, vol. 2, p. 209, cited in A. Latreille, *L'Église catholique et la révolution française*, vol. 1 (Paris, 1946), p. 254. Brumault de Beauregard was the only one of the six priests of the diocese of Poitiers to return from Guyana.

29. P. Baldassari, *Histoire de l'enlèvement et de la captivité de Pie VI ... traduite de l'italien ... par M. l'abbé de Lacouture* (Paris, 1839), is a moving account of the last days of Pius VI by a priest who accompanied him from Italy.

continued to ordain priests, mostly in the anonymity of Paris, where it was easier to evade the eyes of the police.[30] From 1794, when the first Terror came to
an end, Catholics made a determined and sustained effort to rebuild their
Church. The new Terror launched by the Directory had certainly exiled,
imprisoned, and put to death many priests, but it had not halted this rebuilding. A strong feeling of the need to make reparation for the sins and crimes of
the day was evident. On the corpse of Father Jean Rochelé, executed on 24 July
1798 at Colmar, in Alsace, was found the prayer: 'O my divine Saviour, cast
your regard of mercy on our unfortunate church! Have mercy on this unfortunate portion of your church,' a prayer repeated in substance by other devout
Christians at the period, including Sophie Barat, foundress of the Sisters of the
Sacred Heart.[31] Anxious particularly for the future, both the constitutional
church and the Roman church began opening seminaries to train young men
for the priesthood. The Roman church was particularly successful. Since the
bishops were in exile, the priests and lay people took the initiative. In their pres-
byteries, curés began to teach promising young candidates Latin, and before
long little seminaries were springing up all over France.

If religion had begun to flourish again, at least in some parts of France, there
was still the question of which of the two Catholic churches would prevail.[32]
The efforts of the constitutional clergy, many of them devout and courageous
priests, were coordinated by their bishops and, after the first Terror, they were
more acceptable to the authorities than the Roman church for they took the
new oaths without difficulty. They held a synod in Paris in 1797 where, surprisingly, they renounced the Civil Constitution which had established their
Church, drew up a plan for reconciliation with Rome and a programme of
rechristianisation. They only succeeded in annoying the Directory without
reconciling the Roman clergy. Their efforts at recruitment were largely unsuccessful. The parish schools, which the Roman clergy was establishing so successfully,
did not materialise. Few recruits entered the seminaries they had re-opened.[33]
More ominous still, the people, particularly the women, rejected their ministry.
The bands of priests which the energetic Grégoire, the leading constitutional

---

30. C. Dumoulin, 'Le réveil du recrutement sous le Directoire et le Consulat, indice de l'échec
de la déchristianisation,' *Christianisation et déchristianisation: Actes de la neuvième rencontre
d'histoire tenue à Fontevraud les 3, 4 et 5 octobre 1985* (Angers, 1986), p. 195.
31. J. de Viguerie, 'Pour une histoire spirituelle de la France pendant la révolution,' *Les résistances
spirituelles: Actes de la dixième rencontre d'histoire tenue à Fontevraud les 2, 3 et 4 octobre 1986*
(Angers, 1987), pp 115-120.
32. The revival of Christianity was not as marked in all areas. See J. de Viguerie, 'Examen de
quelques hypothèses au sujet de la révolution française et de la déchristianisation', *
Christianisation et déchristianisation; actes de la neuvième rencontre d'histoire religieuse tenue à
Fontevraud les 3, 4, et 5 octobre 1985* (Angers, 1986), pp 177-185.
33. Dumoulin, 'Le réveil du recrutement,' p. 195.

bishop, organised, encountered rejection everywhere. The people, they reported back, would not come to them for confession nor, when they opened their churches, did they ask them to officiate. Although they (the constitutional clergy) offered their services free while the refractory clergy demanded payment, the people opted for the latter. The women certainly wanted no truck with priests who they felt had compromised themselves by accepting the oath in 1791 and again in 1795. A furious Grégoire complained that his church was strangled by 'the vicious and seditious women.'[34] Devastated by its losses, which it proved unable to repair with new recruits, rejected by most of the faithful, who derided it, and deserted by the state that founded it, it was losing out to the Roman church.

The end of 1799 brought an improvement in the fortunes of the Church for, in November, the Directory was overthrown and the 'Consulate,' dominated by Napoleon Bonaparte, took over. On 28 December, the Consulate proclaimed freedom of worship but the freedom it promised did not come immediately, since Bonaparte, whose future policy was foreshadowed in this decree, was not in total control. Within a few months, however, on 5 June 1800, Napoleon told an astonished Catholic clergy in Milan that he wanted 'to secure and guarantee the Catholic, apostolic, and Roman religion'. When, a fortnight later, he won the decisive victory at Marengo which gave him control of Italy and established his preeminence in France, he celebrated it with a *Te Deum* in Milan cathedral. In addition to northern Italy, France now controlled Belgium and the Rhineland, in all of which the Catholic religion was firmly rooted. This influenced Napoleon, when secure of his power after Marengo, he sent out feelers for peace with the Church. How would the papacy and the church react to this initiative?

A pope – for, to the chagrin of revolutionaries, Pius VI proved not to be the last – had been elected three months before Marengo, at a prolonged conclave held not in Rome, but in the safety of a monastery on the island of Saint George, in Venice. Although he defiantly took the name of his predecessor, the new pope, Pius VII, a saintly monk, was indifferent as to the forms of civil government and was ready to speak to Napoleon. Fierce opposition faced the pope and the future emperor, but both were determined to find an agreement and long and painful negotiations ensued. Napoleon bullying, cajoling, lying by turns, drove a hard bargain and the concessions which the pope had to make were considerable. Finally, on 17 July 1801, a concordat between the French government and the Holy See was signed. Pius agreed not to protest against the wholesale confiscation of the church's property. Bishops were to take a simple oath of allegiance to the constitution. The key question was what was to happen to the bishops who had courageously resisted the Civil Constitution and

34. Grégoire, 8 March 1795, cited in Hufton, 'Reconstruction', p. 23.

gone into exile rather than accept it. Most of them were still alive and lived in hopes of returning to their sees. Napoleon insisted that they be dismissed. The pope and the curia were startled. Finally, under extreme pressure, Pius asked the bishops, in the interests of peace, to abandon their sees. He declared, however, that if they did not, he would go ahead and install new bishops in their place. In fact, although he avoided saying so explicitly, Pius VII deposed the entire hierarchy! Rarely, if ever, has a pope taken such a dramatic measure. There was uproar in the curia. The cardinals divided sharply on the question – fourteen for and fourteen either totally opposing the concordat or accepting it with reservations. Forty-seven of the bishops resigned immediately but thirty-six refused to resign and a number sent the pope a dignified *Very Respectful Protest*.[35] Pius VII went ahead, however, and a new episcopate, nominated by Napoleon and appointed by the pope, was established. Pius had made sacrifices which caused him much pain and brought him much odium. There were gains, however, which made the concessions worthwhile. Foremost, was the restoration of public worship in France. Once more the churches were open, and the faithful could hear the word of God and receive the sacraments. Another gain was the ending of the schism. Although Pius had to accept twelve of the constitutional bishops as part of the new hierarchy, the state withdrew its support from the constitutional Church. A further advantage gained by the Holy See was unsought but no less real – Gallicanism had been dealt a serious, though not a mortal, blow. Napoleon's religious policies were as Gallican as those of any of the kings, and many bishops remained Gallican but the pope's dismissal of the whole French hierarchy was a serious setback for fullblown Gallicans. Despite the hard bargaining, Rome and France, and indeed most of Europe, rejoiced that finally a settlement had been agreed. The next Easter Sunday, 18 April 1802, was set aside as a religious and national feastday. On that day, the great bell of Notre-Dame in Paris, silent for ten years, rang out and Napoleon, the other consuls, and reluctant republican generals, attended the solemn Mass. Archbishop Boisgelin, who had preached at the coronation of Louis XVI in 1775, preached again at the ceremony that re-established a united Church. Throughout France church bells pealed joyfully as the church doors were opened again and Catholics celebrated the full restoration of public worship. People could now freely go to Mass and hear the word of God, have their children baptised, be married in church, and have their dead buried according to the rites of the Church. Peace had finally been restored to the Church and the nation. In that same year of 1802, Viscount René de Chateaubriand, re-

---

35. Seven more out of the thirty-six resigned before the promulgation of the Concordat. The figures have been calculated differently by different authors. Simon Delacroix, *La réorganisation de l'Église de France après la révolution (1801-1809)*, vol. 1, *Les nominations d'évêques et la liquidation du passé* (Paris 1962), pp 110-114.

converted from the infidelity of the Enlightenment and published *The Genius of Christianity, or the Beauties of the Christian Religion*. This magnificent *apologia* for Christianity captured many hearts. The tide appeared indeed to have turned for the Church and the Christian religion.

What happened in Saint-Bonnet and the surrounding area during the period from the fall of Robespierre in 1794 to the coming into force of the concordat in the spring of 1802, insofar as it is documented, affords by its similarities and differences, an interesting comment on the overall picture. More than almost any other diocese, the diocese of Lyon had made enormous efforts to preserve and reactivate the faith and much of the credit was due to the indefatigable Linsolas, the vicar general. Ingeniously adapting the system evolved for foreign missions in the far east, he sent priests from parish to parish to catechise and administer the sacraments. In the parishes, leading lay parishioners helped the missioners. The method proved most successful. It is not clear how much contact Linsolas had with the area around Saint-Bonnet for it had not formed part of the diocese of Lyon before the Revolution. At the request of Marbeuf, however, he chose a vicar general for the Beaujolais section of the diocese and by March 1795 two missionary priests, Fathers Roux and Loron, officiated regularly in Saint-Bonnet, performing baptisms and marriages. Later that year Cabuchet, believing that the parish was returning to something akin to normality after the end of the first Terror, hastened back to his parish. He took over his old church and, defiantly pealing the bell, summoned the parishioners to the services. Preaching and officiating fearlessly, he engaged in a campaign of rechristianisation. 'He is luring to his sermons,' his republican enemies complained, 'neighbouring communes and even goes to their houses where he held the most incendiary speeches.' Given the difficulties elsewhere to persuade a cowed and ageing clergy even to celebrate Mass, what was taking place in Saint-Bonnet showed how courageous Cabuchet was and how strong a support the parishioners accorded him. In most parishes it was difficult for the Catholics to get back the use of the parish church and even more difficult to recover the bells because some had been melted down. Cabuchet and the parish were openly defying the government by rejecting the Republic's new 'week' of ten days, the *decadi*, pealing the bell on Saturday and Sunday. The pealing of the bell announced that the church was no longer a church of silence.[36] In January 1797, Cabuchet officiated at the marriage of Claudine Colin, the eldest of the Colin girls.

As elsewhere, the religious peace of the first few years of the Directory was

---

36. The pealing of the bell was more significant than may appear for the bell had always called the parishioners together. It pealed on Saturday to remind them of the possibility of confession, on Sunday to summon them to Mass, when a parishioner died and, also, when danger threatened the community. It epitomised community solidarity. Hufton, 'Reconstruction,' p. 28.

not to last in Saint-Bonnet. Cabuchet's open defiance no doubt caused resentment among his enemies and, immediately after the Directory's coup d'état of Fructidor, they denounced him to the authorities. He was sentenced to deportation to Guyana and the gendarmes arrived to arrest him. In vain, however, for although they returned again and again the police could not catch him. Finally, an embarrassed commissaire had to admit to the ministry of police that despite his efforts he could not track down the priest. He promised to keep trying. Sheltered by a friendly people, Cabuchet evaded the hulks and Devil's Island and, remaining near Saint-Bonnet, exercised his ministry at night-time.[37] It was this secret ministry during this period that formed the basis of Jean-Claude's reminiscences about the hidden cult during the Revolution.[38] He does not mention that two of his sisters got married but he had memories of secret Masses said in barns at dead of night. His first confession remained etched in his mind. It took place in a weaver's house, in the back room where the weavers kept their looms. Jean-Claude was so small that to get to the priest he could not climb over the looms but crawled beneath them instead.[39] The experience, perhaps the confessor's kindness, so enthralled him that he wanted to go to confession every day and the priest, probably Cabuchet, had to refuse him.[40] Cabuchet later became bolder and began to exercise his ministry more openly. It was he who again officiated, on 10 November 1798, at the second marriage of Claudine Colin, whose first husband had died within a few months of the marriage. The Catholics were evidently not cowed even by the new wave of persecutions and, particularly in the mountainous areas like Saint-Bonnet, the faith was strong and they could defy the authorities. The news of a concordat in 1801 and the great day of national and religious celebration on Easter Sunday 1802 signalled the end of persecution and harassment in Saint-Bonnet as it did throughout the country.

The period from the fall of Robespierre in 1794 to Napoleon's promulgation of the concordat was only eight years but many things had happened in France. Religious peace, which had appeared to have come in 1794, had been shattered two years later and the persecutions had come again. Much blood was still shed by both republicans and their adversaries. In some parts of France, dechrist-

---

37. OM, doc. 704, 11.

38. Colin's reminiscences relate almost certainly to this Fructidorean Terror rather than to the first Terror. See Coste's remarks, OM 2, p. 494; OM 3, pp 299-300.

39. Weavers, like Jacques Colin, kept their looms in the lower room of their house. This room would have been the safest place for a priest to administer the sacraments.

40. The whole epoch acquired a romantic charm for many of his generation. 'O, those beautiful midnight Masses we used celebrate then! One could call them a continual commemoration of the Saviour's crib! How strong was our fervour! Like the first Christians, we lived under the executioner's axe, and like them we derived from it an indomitable courage.' Hufton, 'Reconstruction,' p. 52.

ianisation had bitten deeply, but in other parts Catholics made a determined effort to revive their religion. At great risk to themselves, they rebuilt the church and planned for the future, particularly in attempting to get seminaries going again. Most of those who rebuilt the church were priests or lay people and it was the attitude of the people that made it clear to the government that religion was not going to disappear in France. The concordat was the logical result of the persistent demand of the people for a restoration of religion. Bonaparte, although a Jacobin and unbeliever, was convinced that, if peace were to be restored to France and a firm foundation laid for the state, the religious question would have to be solved.

In 1802, when the concordat was promulgated, Jean-Claude was eleven years old. Those eleven years were as traumatic as a child could experience. Child psychologists claim that, if a child loses a parent before the age of five, a lasting mark is left on the child's personality. Jean-Claude had lost both at one blow. This pain of loss remained. Those who had peopled his world at the farm in Barbery since then had been the kind, weak-minded uncle Sébastien, the conscientious but puritanical Marie Échallier, probably some neighbours' children and his brothers and, for a time, his sisters. By the time he was eight, his immediate world had become an almost completely male world. Of his sisters, Jeannette had been brought up in Poule and Claudine and Mariette had married, one in January 1797, the other a year later. The only woman in the household was Marie Échallier. This minimal female influence in his early years and the strict morality imposed by Marie Échallier may have affected, later on, his own attitude to women.

Another, and most important, influence on the young Jean-Claude was the religious conflict that was evident all round him. Religion had been the all-pervasive atmosphere in his home and cast shadows over his childhood pleasures. A disaster, unequalled in its history, had overtaken the French Church. Its priests had been divided, hunted, and executed. Its bishops had fled. The highest prelate in the land, the archbishop of Paris, had publicly renounced his sacred office, thrown off his bishop's cross and donned the red bonnet of the Revolution already soaked in the blood of innocents, only to die himself on the guillotine. Just south of Lyon, the unfortunate Pius VI, scoffed at as 'Citizen Pope', had died, a prisoner of the Revolution. Confessors of the faith had sprung up all over the country, like the Carmelite sisters – immortalised by Gertrud von Le Fort and Bernanos – who sang the *Salve Regina* in diminishing volume as each in turn mounted the scaffold and the guillotine silenced them one by one. These were the stories, this the atmosphere in the homes of fervent Catholics. In Jean-Claude's home his mother, father, and curé were included in the book of confessors or martyrs for the faith. Their words, like his mother's commendation of all of them to their heavenly mother Mary, were remembered and treasured. His abiding experience was of priests on the run, midnight Masses in barns, and clandestine confessions in the loom-room. The sermons of his hero-priest, Father Cabuchet, had so engraved themselves on his memory that he repeated them to the trees in the woods of Crest. Sébastien, Marie Échallier, and Sister Martha, each in their own way, heightened the fervent pervasive religious atmosphere in which Jean-Claude was reared.

At about the time of the signing of the Concordat Jean Colin, the eldest boy, now head of the family, decided to transfer the family from the farm at Barbery to the village of Saint-Bonnet itself. A new phase was beginning in Jean-Claude's life.

CHAPTER 3

Catechisms, Confession and Communion

The Concordat between the Holy See and France promulgated in 1802, finally brought peace, both religious and civil, to France. It was to regulate relations between the French state and the French Church throughout the turbulent years of the nineteenth century right up to 1905 when the law of separation finally abrogated it. As interpreted and enforced, the Concordat was the context within which the Church struggled to re-organise itself after the trauma of the revolution. This 'Church of the Concordat' was the Church for whose mission the students, including Jean-Claude, trained at the seminary. It was within the context of this Church, too, that, between 1814 and 1816, a group of them conceived and envisaged the Society of Mary which, they believed, would be a support of that Church in that final age of the world that many believed was at hand. It was from within this Church of the Concordat that the Marist project began, took shape and began to spread to many parts of the world.

The vast majority of the people warmly welcomed the Concordat. Once again they could hear Mass and be baptised, married and buried with the rites of the Church.[1] Apart from bringing peace between Church and State and ending the schism between Roman and constitutional Churches, the Concordat also solved many immediate problems. The first was the vexed question of the ecclesiastical property that had been nationalised by the State and acquired by private people. By the terms of the Concordat, the Church agreed not to question the new ownership. The State for its part undertook to hand back Church property that had not been alienated and also promised to compensate for the confiscations by paying the parochial clergy.

The reverse side of the Concordat for the pope was that it deprived the Church of much of its status. No longer was it the Church of the French nation; what privileged position it now had was as 'the Church of majority of the French people'. So-called 'organic articles', unilaterally added by Bonaparte to the Concordat in order to mollify anti-clericals, appeared to give the state more control over her than ever the kings of France had exercised.[2] In many

1. Some bishops, priests and laity rejected the Concordat as co-operating with the Revolution and a number of 'Little Churches' (Petites Églises) persisted in Lyon and elsewhere right up to the Second Vatican Council.
2. The 'organic articles' had been added to the Concordat after its signature, against the protests of the pope. They included government control over papal documents entering France, church synods, seminaries, processions, clerical dress, parish boundaries.

ways, then, the Church in France, as it emerged from the Concordat of 1801, was significantly different from the old pre-revolutionary Church. Yet marked and scarred though the Church was, through the crucible of the revolution, the changes in its structure, which the Concordat codified, did not touch on the essence of its nature and life. It could, indeed, be argued that the renewed connection with the state, attenuated though this connection was, nevertheless served to impede the emergence of a reformed Church that might have grasped the nettle of the criticism levelled against it by the Enlightenment of the eighteenth century. That criticism, which lay at the root of the revolt against the Church, would surface again. The Concordat did, however, permit the much-needed restoration, which the ravages of revolution had made necessary in the Church.

Much would depend on how the terms of the agreement, and, in particular, the restrictive 'organic articles' would be interpreted. Opposition to the Church existed among the prefects, the powerful heads of the departments, which had replaced the old provinces. Anti-clericalism was rife among the police under their minister-general, the anti-clerical Joseph Fouché, who bore much of the responsibility for the massacres of the prisoners in Lyon in 1793 and 1794. Quite early, however, a benevolent interpretation of the Concordat and the organic articles prevailed. This was largely due to the influence of the man whom Napoleon chose to implement the Concordat, Jean-Étienne-Marie Portalis.[3] Portalis, a lawyer of considerable ability, had played a major part in drawing up the revision of French law, the 'Napoleonic Code', which remains the basis of European law, outside the Common Law area, to this day. The interpretation of the Concordat was, however, his main achievement. He was appointed minister for religion in 1801 and quickly assumed full responsibility for the religious programme of France. Gallican in outlook, he accepted the secularisation of the state but he also saw the need to reorganise and strengthen the Church and committed himself to bringing that about. While insisting on full religious freedom for Protestants and Jews, he was largely responsible for the support the state gave the Church and it was his benevolent interpretation of the Concordat that gave the bishops the freedom and the means to re-build. What was of great significance was that his manner of interpreting the Concordat in those early years fixed the norms for all future interpretation. On several occasions, he protected the clergy from the interference of state officials. While the Church could no longer claim to be the official state Church of France, nevertheless, as a result of Portalis' sympathetic and authoritative interpretation of the terms of the Concordat, she became far more independent in her internal affairs. Napoleon, the very powerful First Consul who was soon to

3. Jean-Étienne-Marie Portalis (1741-1807) a chief architect of the Napoleonic civil code and of the Concordat; minister for religion, 1801-1807.

become Emperor, followed Portalis' advice and it is rightly said of him that he behaved like a Christian prince of old, according military honours to the Blessed Sacrament, re-establishing the Gregorian calendar – which the revolutionaries had abolished – and even allowing congregations of women to return to France.

One of the most obvious changes that the Concordat had brought was the re-drawing of the ecclesiastical map of France. Before the Revolution France had 140 dioceses of varying sizes, but in 1790, the revolutionaries, anxious to make the dioceses coterminous with the newly-created departments, which had superseded the older provinces, reduced the number to 83. The Church had not accepted this change, which meant that for the people of Saint-Bonnet they were still part of the diocese of Mâcon. Now, however, the Concordat reduced the number of dioceses to 60, coterminous with the departments but often consisting of up to three departments. At a stroke two-thirds of the dioceses in pre-revolutionary France had disappeared. For the future Marist project the change was providential, because it brought into the one diocese the villages of Coutouvre, Usson, Marlhes and Saint-Bonnet – the birthplaces of Jeanne-Marie Chavoin, Jean-Claude Courveille, Marcellin Champagnat and Jean-Claude Colin; the lives of those four Marist pioneers had been linked together. For the Gallican Church the abolition of scores of age-old French sees was a further blow. Although they had the advantage of eliminating the inequalities between the dioceses, the new diocesan boundaries created many short-term difficulties. The new dioceses were made up of sections of several older dioceses – the diocese of Nancy alone regrouped parts of no less than eleven older dioceses. All these older sees had their local customs, feast days and catechisms and their priests, too, coming from different traditions, were different in their approach to the people.

The relief that the Concordat brought was timely, for the Revolution had severely damaged the Church. When the Concordat was promulgated on Easter Day 1802, only 11 of the 138 bishops who had been there when the Revolution began, were still in France, one of whom was the bishop of Mâcon, Gabriel François Moreau, who had remained on in Mâcon right through the Revolution. Priests, too, were in short supply. In addition to the normal wastage of 10 per cent, some 3,000 to 5,000 had died violent deaths and from 15 to 20 percent had abdicated or married. In one badly-stricken diocese – Isère – the number of priests had fallen from 1,879 to 567.[4] The Revolution had also closed the 200 minor and major seminaries. Yet, even before the Concordat,

---

4. Some 52 bishops had died, 68 were in exile, 3 had abandoned the episcopate. M. Vovelle, 'C'est la faute à la Révolution', in J. Le Goff and R. Rémond, *Histoire de la France religieuse*, vol. 3, *Du roi Très Chrétien à la laïcité républicaine* (Paris, 1991), pp 264-66. S. Delacroix, *La Réorganisation de l'Église de France après la Révolution, 1801-1809*, vol. 1 (Paris, 1962), pp 1-6, 23-4, 134-44.

when the persecution had not ended, Catholics had begun to provide for the future and nowhere were more determined efforts made than in the diocese of Lyon. Already in 1795 a school to train young boys for the priesthood had been established in Bény, not far from Bourg-en-Bresse. In 1798, at the height of the Fructidorean Terror, another school was established at Saint-Martin-en-Haut, and in 1799 at Roche in the Monts du Forez.[5] In Saint-Bonnet, Cabuchet, too, was concerned for vocations and on the lookout for suitable candidates. Since the Colins had moved into the village he was able to take a more personal interest in Pierre Colin and, sensing in him a promising candidate, he began to give him Latin lessons. A year later, in the autumn of 1802, Pierre was ready to go to train for the priesthood at another of those little seminaries, Saint-Jodard, a hamlet fifty or more kilometres southwest of Saint-Bonnet. One painful event preceded his departure. On 23 June, Mariette, the second girl in the Colin family, who had married in 1798, died at the age of twenty-two, leaving a two-year old daughter who survived her by only a year. For Jean-Claude, who hated even temporary partings, his sister's death and his brother's departure were painful losses.

The move from Barbery to Saint-Bonnet carried its own significance. Apart from Jean-Claude, there were five others in the large house in the centre of the village next door to the church. Uncle Sébastien was still the guardian but by now the twenty-five year old Jean, Jean-Claude's eldest brother, had assumed the role of head of the household. Two other brothers lived there – Sébastien, aged twenty-one and Joseph, aged ten, the youngest in the family, while during the summer Pierre came home from the seminary. The housekeeper, Marie Échallier, was still the only woman in the household, for the two surviving sisters, Claudine and Jeanne-Marie, were in the process of setting up an educational and religious foundation in Belleville, some miles away, where Father Gabriel Captier had been named curé.[6]

Jean-Claude's environment, too, had changed. His home was no longer the isolated Barbery with its handful of farmhouses but a village where there were boys and girls of his own age. School and church were close by. He was able to attend Sister Martha's school more easily, if indeed he did not begin only then to attend it. Since the family house was right up against the church he could go and pray there. Instead of clandestine Masses and sacraments in hay-barns and loft-rooms, which had been his experience during his childhood, church-bells now punctuated the day and marked the week. Almost everyone in the parish went to Mass and to vespers. Instruction in the faith, neglected for so long, was reassuming its normal place in the life of the parish, and Jean-Claude, with some scores of other children, was attending the curé's catechism classes.

5. Dumoulin, 'Le réveil du recrutement', pp 187-197.
6. Claudine had married twice; her first husband had died and she had been divorced from her second.

The change in boundaries meant that he now belonged not to the small diocese of Mâcon but to the vast diocese of Lyon which extended from the Beaujolais country of his birth to Saint-Étienne in the south. The diocese comprising the three civil departments of Rhone, Loire and Ain with a population of 937,000 had become the largest diocese in France. One early effect of the change was that Jean-Claude had to travel to Lyon to be confirmed. The confirmation took place in the magnificent Cathedral of Saint-Jean, on the feast of the Holy Trinity, on 5 June 1803. This medieval Cathedral, lying at the foot of Fourvière and on the banks of the Saone, which had housed an ecumenical council in 1274, had been desecrated during the revolution when the 'feast of reason' was celebrated there and the revolutionaries had notched and marked its flagstones to bring in their horses. Now, in 1802 it had been reopened as the central place of worship for the archdiocese with the new archbishop, Joseph Fesch, taking formal possession of it in January 1803.[7] One of the first celebrations he held was the great ceremony of Confirmation, on the feast of the Holy Trinity in the summer of that year. The gaudy souvenir leaflet Jean-Claude received on his Confirmation day has been preserved and is the only existing record of this significant day in his childhood. For some reason, he did not make his confirmation with the children of his own parish, for the souvenir leaflet is signed, not by his own curé, but by the curé of a neighbouring village, Gabriel Captier, the curé of Poule.[8] How Jean-Claude enjoyed what was, probably, his first visit to the great city of Lyon and how he celebrated this joyful day of his confirmation is not known. More is known of another important religious ceremony of his boyhood, his first Communion, for it became the occasion of a personal crisis. The crisis arose as a minor consequence of the incorporation into the great new diocese of Lyon of the little parish of Saint-Bonnet. For the first year and a half Jean-Claude could see more of Father Cabuchet, whom the family and, no doubt, the whole parish venerated as a confessor of the faith. Cabuchet, in his turn, felt attached to the families like the Colins who had paid so heavy a price for helping him. In December 1803, however, Cabuchet was promoted from Saint-Bonnet to the more important parish of Mornant. To replace this well-beloved hero, came a priest of a different stamp – Father Thomas Gilbert. Gilbert was fifty-one years old and a native of Villefranche, the capital of the Beaujolais, which, even before the revolution, had been part of the diocese of Lyon. He, like the great majority of his brother-priests in the Beaujolais, had taken the oath to the constitution and had functioned as a constitutional priest up to 1798. At that time, like many other constitutional priests, he was reintegrated into the Roman clergy.

7. Joseph Fesch (1763-1839), Napoleon's uncle; ordained, 1785; took the oath to the civil constitution; joined the army; reconciled to the Church by Émery and returned to the priesthood, 1801; archbishop of Lyon and primate of Gaul 1802; cardinal, 1803.
8. The date of his confirmation was probably 5 June 1803, OM 4, p. 492.

Thanks to that great re-organiser of the diocese of Lyon, Joseph Courbon, vicar-general of the diocese from 1802 up to his death in 1824, we have interesting information on many of the Lyonese priests of the time, including the new curé of Saint-Bonnet. Courbon was an organisational man. He had been a key cleric in the opposition to the constitutional Church during the revolution. Being of a conciliatory nature, however, he was quite ready to accept constitutional priests and, on the national level, had played an important role in working out how they could be integrated into the newly constituted post-Concordat Church. Needing to know how far his diocese could count on the available priests, he drew up some notes on the priests of the diocese that often become fascinating little character sketches. Apart from a dismissive note on priests who had apostatised, his assessment of the others was, in general, generous which makes the few lines on Thomas Gilbert more telling.[9] Gilbert, Courbon noted, was of good moral standing, above average ability and a good preacher. He described his zeal and piety, however, as 'ordinary' and added that Gilbert was very sure of his opinions, arrogant and haughty towards his confrères, with a character which Courbon summed up as 'hard and eccentric'.

Gilbert's own impressions of the people of Saint-Bonnet were mixed, as an interesting report on the state of the parish, which he drew up in 1804 shortly after his arrival, reveals. This report was in response to a questionnaire that the diocesan authorities had sent out to ascertain the state of the various parishes in the diocese. His report revealed that the curé was not well off. 'I enjoy no salary,' he complained, 'the curé *(desservant)* of Saint-Bonnet has neither property, nor income.' Since the Concordat had solemnly engaged itself to provide the clergy with a salary to compensate for the confiscation of the Church's property during the Revolution, his complaint was not unreasonable.[10] In answer to the questions of how many were Catholic and how practising they were, he replied that all were Catholics and that most frequented the sacraments. The parishioners were assiduous, too, in coming to the offices such as vespers.[11] He had complaints about the church-wardens who controlled parish finances. He found them tight-fisted – 'to get them to part with money was like death itself'. The revolution, he believed, had made them imperious and patronising in their attitude. A firm attitude was necessary, for, if the clergy was

9. Tableau général des prêtres du diocèse de Lyon. Du 1er vendémiaire 1802. Archives de l'archevêché de Lyon. Copy in APM.

10. Gilbert, 19 Feb. 1804; Archives de l'archevêché de Lyon. État des paroisses 1804. Saint-Nizier-d'Azergues (Canton) Saint-Bonnet-le-Troncy. Gilbert was the *desservant* or priest in charge of the parish. The *desservant* had a higher status than an assistant priest or curate, but not as high as a curé or parish priest.

11. 'A Monsieur Courbon, Vicaire Général à l'archevêché, à Lion ... Gilbert, [prêtre desservant], Saint-Bonnet le Tronci, canton de Saint-Nizier d'Azergues, ce 19 février 1804'. Archives de l'archevêché de Lyon, État des paroisses 1804. Copy in APM.

to achieve any good at all, it must jealously retain its independence of them. The government, he added, should attach the clergy to itself by showing it more esteem and confidence.

When this independent-minded, hard and eccentric priest clashed with the dogged people of Saint-Bonnet who had not hesitated to defend their beliefs vigorously during the revolutionary period, trouble could be expected. It was not long in coming and arose over the innocent question of the children's first Holy Communion. Like every new broom, when the new priest arrived in Saint-Bonnet in December 1803, he swept older customs clean. To the children preparing for their first Holy Communion, Gilbert announced that the Mâcon catechism, which they had been using, would be dropped and the Lyon catechism used in its place. Gilbert's move was a sensible one. Since the Concordat redrew the diocesan boundaries grouping parts of different sees together, dioceses were plagued with a proliferation of catechisms – the diocese of Orleans had no less than eight different ones. Gilbert was merely 'rationalising', bringing Saint-Bonnet into line with the rest of the diocese, something that would have to come sooner or later. The response in the parish, however, was an angry one. The shocked surprise of the children and their parents can be gauged from the fact that forty years later people of Saint-Bonnet could still recall the commotion.

The thirteen year old Jean-Claude was also upset, though largely for another of Gilbert's changes. It had been the practice of the previous curé, Cabuchet, to allow the children to begin their general confession several months before first communion. This not uncommon practice was to give those preparing for communion every possibility of making a confession that was thorough and well remembered; they could come back after the first confession and confess again or perhaps only then receive absolution. It was in line with the rigorist approach of many dioceses, particularly in pre-revolutionary days. For whatever reason, Gilbert would have none of these long preparations. A conscientious, perhaps scrupulous, little Jean-Claude, who had geared himself for a long-ranging confession extending over a period of months, now realised that he would be making his communion in three weeks. Distraught, he complained so bitterly at home that Marie Échallier set off to ask the priest to allow the boy to begin his confession right away as he had been expecting. Gilbert, who had 30 to 100 children in his catechism classes and wanted no exceptions, would have none of it. His brusque reply to Marie Échallier was: 'he will do the same as everyone else'. Then, one bare week before the first communion, Gilbert announced that the children could begin their confession. For a thunderstruck Jean-Claude, who was convinced that Cabuchet's way of lengthy preparation for confession was the only right way, this was too much. In a remarkable revolt, he refused point-blank even to return to the catechism classes. He raised such a commotion at home that the family decided that something had to be done.

Three or four miles away, an hour's walk down the Roncon valley and up over the summit of La Croix Nicelle, lay the village of Saint-Nizier d'Azergues, the capital of the canton. The curé of Saint-Nizier since February 1803, was the forty-year old Antoine Odin, 'Le gros Toine', or Big Tony as he was generally called. Big Tony was an imposing, well-built priest with a frank and candid air that made an immediately favourable impression. Intelligent, shrewd and tactful, he was, above all, a man of great faith. He had been one of the great missionaries in the area during the revolution and was credited as being a key figure in keeping the faith alive in much of the province of Beaujolais where he had shown himself indomitable and courageous. Cattin, the historian of the Church of Belley and Lyon during the revolution, singled him out for special praise.[12] A strong resourceful character, well-beloved by all, and especially cherished by his fellow-priests, Big Tony had now become the curé of the canton and as such he was senior to the other priests in the area.[13] It was to this man that Jean-Claude's family and the other families in Saint-Bonnet now turned. For Big Tony, there was no problem. To calm the upset caused by the introduction of the new catechism, he offered to prepare the children himself for their first communion and to use the Mâcon catechism with which they (and he) were familiar. When Jean-Claude's crisis arose, he was willing, too, to accommodate the Colin family and to provide the boy with the long preparation for his first communion he had counted on and which appeared so important to him. At last Jean-Claude was happy, and it was no wonder he developed a lasting esteem for the warm-hearted curé of Saint-Nizier.

What Gilbert thought of being bypassed is not recorded. He was encountering difficulties as he awkwardly attempted to settle into his new parish. Since the majority of the parishioners had violently rejected the constitutional clergy, insisting that their diocese was Mâcon, it is not surprising that the ex-constitutional Lyonese priest, Gilbert, found them difficult, particularly when he was trying to assimilate them to the diocese of Lyon. As regards Jean-Claude and the Colin family, who had defied him, however, he had the last laugh. Jean-Claude completed his long preparation with Father Odin and duly made his confession but before he could receive his first communion, he fell ill and had to return home. The Colins had to come back to Gilbert. Gilbert was now able to show that he would not be pushed around for despite all the pleas made to him, he insisted that, before he would give Jean-Claude his first communion, he must remake his confession to him. Jean-Claude had to accept this condition and so for the first and the last time he made his confession to the

12. Cattin, *Mémoires,* p. 76.
13. The curé of the canton was of the same standing as a rural dean or vicar forane.

autocratic curé. Then, on his own, and in his own parish church, in the early summer of 1804, he received his first communion at the hands of Gilbert.

This is the account Jean-Claude gave of the first communion crisis.[14] Mayet, the Marist chronicler, always seeking more information about his hero, contacted Jean-Claude's nephew, Jean-François Colin.[15] He was in luck for Jean-François' written reply adds precious and revealing details. Since these details were probably supplied by Jean-François' father, Jean Colin, the head of the Colin household, who was twenty-six when the incident took place, they are trustworthy enough. According to this account, the lead-up to first Communion was a time of severe spiritual trial for Jean-Claude. Racked by anguish, imploring his school-mates to pray that the Lord be merciful to him before admitting him to Holy Communion, he wept continually during all this period. The altar of the Blessed Virgin in the church was his refuge and there he used remain for long hours. He needed to be alone. On the daily trip from Saint-Bonnet to Saint-Nizier to attend the catechism class, he scarcely ever walked with his school-mates and always returned on his own. If he saw women – *personnes du sexe,* as the French quaintly puts it – coming down the road towards him, straightaway he would retrace his footsteps and make a great detour to avoid them. To emphasise the accuracy of this unusual conduct, Jean-François added 'this was told to me as absolutely certain' and Mayet carefully underlined those words.

This drama of the catechism, confession and communion, together with Jean-Claude's unusual behaviour on the road to Saint-Nizier is revealing. On the larger canvas, the stir caused by Gilbert, a Lyonese priest, when he came to Saint-Bonnet, illustrates some of the organisational difficulties that the Church faced when the new dioceses were established. Since they were often a patchwork of many older dioceses, with different traditions, the priests and faithful now had to get used to different customs. Perhaps, too, the hostility of constitutional Church and Roman Church was not too far beneath the surface. The Colin family emerges as courageous, quite prepared to stand by their young boy against the authority of the priest who lived next door to them. The incident sheds most light on Jean-Claude and, as this is the only incident of importance that has come to us from Jean-Claude's boyhood, it is a convenient time to look at what it reveals of his character. He clearly had a will of his own and, when it came to matters in which he believed passionately, he would not be cowed. As he appears to admit himself later, he was narrow as most youngsters of that age

14. OM, doc. 548, 1-3.
15. Jean-François Colin (1818-1899) seventh child of Jean Colin. Entered the Hermitage, the mother-house of the Marist Brothers, 1844; left owing to bad health, 1847; mayor of Chapelle-de-Mardore 1858-70, 1875. His father, Jean, came to live with him and, in 1867, at Jean-François' insistence, Jean-Claude came to visit him there.

are, but his ideals were high and he was quite determined not to compromise them. His refusal to pass a woman on the road was certainly strange, all the more so since he was, it appears, the only boy of the group to behave that way. An admission he made to Mayet many years later is revealing. One day a sexual scandal had been mentioned in conversation probably when he was at Saint-Irénée. Blushing at his own naiveté, he told Mayet that at that time he used believe that if a man and a woman passed one another on the road and had the intention of marrying and having children, conception would result.[16] His sheltered life, his love of solitude and the absence in the family home of any woman, except the scrupulous Marie Échallier, may account in part for this ignorance. In his anxiety to prepare well for his first Holy Communion, he was especially anxious to avoid sexual sins and, given his strange idea concerning conception, it is no wonder that at the mere sight of a woman coming his way he hastily beat a retreat. He was not quite fourteen at the time.

This first communion incident shows the thirteen-year-old Jean-Claude, although shy and timid, as a plucky young lad with plenty of grit, who was determined to do things the right way and no other. With his high moral sense, he would take every step to avoid committing sin. A comment he made later in life when speaking of confession, was interpreted by Mayet as a clear indication that he succeeded in doing so: 'Oh, how happy one is at a certain age when, looking back, one sees that one has escaped contamination! How much remorse has one been spared.'[17] Given, then, his ignorance of human sexuality and his resolute determination to avoid sexual sin, it is scarcely surprising that he was never quite at ease in the company of women.[18]

Did this crisis cause a certain development in Jean-Claude's character? In a close study of his 'socio-personal development and religious growth', Gaston Lessard makes a strong case for such a development.[19] Although it is difficult to judge interior development, the quarrel with Father Gilbert, the necessity of taking a firm stand and accepting to live with the consequences were difficult, but marking, moments in his young life. There was more to the incident than this negative experience of standing up to his curé. Just as the little world of Saint-Bonnet expanded into a new world, when his trip down the valley and up over the mountain brought him to a peak, from where the wide valley of the Azergues opened out in front of him to the north, south and east, so, too, his entry into the household of Big Tony Odin broadened his spiritual horizon. To have sat in the class of this generous, kind, openhearted priest – perhaps to

16. OM, doc. 539, 2.
17. OM, doc. 540.
18. OM, doc. 512.
19. G. Lessard, 'Une crise d'adolescence: Première communion de J.-C. Colin' (Unpublished paper, 1976, copy, APM).

have lived for weeks in his household – was an experience in itself. It had influenced the impressionable boy who came to esteem the expansive priest. As a result, he decided to bypass the priest of his own parish, Father Gilbert, and took to walking the four miles along the stony path, along by the fir and hazel trees, over the brow of La Croix Nicelle and down the valley to Saint-Nizier to go to confession to Odin.

There was a certain irony in the crisis about catechisms, for despite Gilbert's determination to substitute the catechism of Lyon for that of Mâcon, a new situation had already developed, which made both catechisms redundant. Napoleon had decided on a catechism for all France and the bishops, conscious of the proliferation of catechisms, were well disposed. The first version was ready by September 1803 but it took until March 1806 before the papal legate, Archbishop Giovanni Battista Caprara, approved it. At Napoleon's insistence, the archbishop of Orleans, Étienne Bernier, included in the teaching on the fourth commandment, an elaborate section on the duties of Christians to the civil authorities, which the emperor took care to revise himself. To the question 'What are the duties of Christians to the princes who govern them and in particular to Napoleon 1st, our Emperor?', the answer was: 'Christians owe to princes … and we owe in particular to Napoleon 1st our Emperor, the love, respect, obedience, fidelity, military service, taxes necessary for the conservation of the Empire and of his throne; we also owe him fervent prayers for his safety and for the spiritual and temporal welfare of the State.' To the question as to 'what one should think of those who fail in their duty towards our Emperor?' the answer was: 'According to Saint Paul, they resist the order established by God himself and render themselves worthy of eternal damnation.'

Another answer portrayed the Emperor as God's very image on earth! Another reply was to the effect that God gave empires not just to a person in particular but also to his family! If these sections show Napoleon's view on the relationship he wanted between Church and State, the lack of reaction of the French Church is more revealing of the bishops' attitude, for although the Belgian clergy resisted all pressure to implement this catechism and some French bishops dragged their feet in introducing it, only Archbishop d'Aviau of Bordeaux refused to publish it. Like most bishops, Napoleon's uncle, Cardinal Fesch, made it mandatory in his see of Lyon in 1805. About the same time, a new feast-day was introduced into the Church's calendar. Since the Bourbon kings had a St Louis, why should not Napoleon have a saint of his own? A 'St Napoleon' was discovered – a martyr from the fourth century named 'St Naopole', whose name was, evidently the same as 'Napoleon'! In 1637, King Louis XIII had consecrated France to Our Lady of the Assumption whose feast was on 15 August. The new feast was attached to this great feast of the Assumption. It was also Napoleon's birthday and the anniversary of the publication of the Concordat. On that day, Vespers were to be sung and 'a discourse giving an historical analysis of the events which we are celebrating, considering them in the designs of Providence…' This was to be followed by a procession and a *Te Deum* of thanks for the Emperor and for peace.[20] Among the events being celebrated was Napoleon's recent victory at Austerlitz, where twenty thousand Austrians, Russians and French had been killed. Rome at first thought of condemning the catechism and the new feast but decided instead to send a private warning to the French bishops. The catechism and the institution of the feast of 'St Napoleon', show the lengths to which most French bishops went in their gratitude to Napoleon for the restoration of the Church. Napoleon, for his part, hankered after the legitimacy of the kings. Altar and throne had again drifted close.

If Fesch had introduced the catechism a little earlier, Gilbert would have saved himself trouble from his suspicious parishioners, Jean-Claude might not have to make his spirited little stand and he might never have ventured out of his tight-knit little village over the hill to the wider world beyond. His decision to trek over the mountain to see Father Odin led, in turn, to an important development in his young life which was not at all welcome to him at the time. One day, not long after his First Communion, when Jean-Claude went to confession to him, Odin, sensing that he had here a young lad of quality, asked him if he would like 'to study', in other words, to go for the priesthood.[21] Jean-Claude replied that he would but that perhaps his family would not wish it. The priest said that he would see to that. The family agreed. Immediately, a terrible fear took hold of Jean-Claude. The idea of the priesthood quite overwhelmed him. Back he went to his confessor to tell him he did not want to become a priest. The priest's reply was rather vague. Poor Jean-Claude had neither peace nor ease because, although he was quite sure that he did not want to be a priest, he felt he had, unwittingly, taken some steps towards becoming one. He had. While this torment was going on in his mind, Pierre came home on holidays from the seminary and Jean-Claude confided in him his great desire of withdrawing from the world. Pierre spoke to his guardian and between them they decided that he should go to the minor seminary. Surprisingly, Jean-Claude fell in with their decision and accepted to go to the minor seminary with Pierre who began to teach him some Latin.[22] As he insisted later, however,

---

20. Fesch's pastoral letter of 3 July 1806, runs: 'Rejoicing in the Lord for the birth and happy destiny of his Imperial Majesty … we implore Heaven to bless his enterprises … We invoke with a special cult Saint Napoleon: the Protector of our Sovereign should be ours also'. The letter explains that 'Napoleon or Naopole suffered at Alexandria during the persecution of Diocletian … and died of his wounds …' In Les petits Bollandistes, *Vie des Saints,* vol. 5, (Paris, 1878), p. 236, a martyr, St Néopole is commemorated on 2nd of May.
21. OM, doc 499, 1.
22. OM, doc 852, 2.

he took his decision to go to the seminary 'with no thought of becoming a priest'. So on All Saints Day, 1804, he set out, probably with Pierre, for the minor seminary of Saint-Jodard where he was to remain for almost five years. When he moved from there, it was only to spend a further seven years in similar seminaries training for the priesthood. Those twelve years, from the age of fourteen to almost twenty-six, filled all his adolescence.

It is said of seminary training that it only develops what is there before. What picture do we get of Jean-Claude before he entered? He was, by all accounts, a small, diffident boy with a stammer, yet determined and courageous, quite capable of standing up to that formidable person, his own brusque curé. He was pious. As one of the youngest members of a pious family, where his Uncle Sébastien and the housekeeper, Marie Échallier, set a strict moral tone, that was not unexpected. He was, however, embarrassingly strict on himself. At home he used rise at night to pray but, when Uncle Sébastien discovered it he made him go to bed. He would wait until his uncle was asleep and then rose again to continue his prayers. He also practised physical mortifications, possibly using hair shirt and discipline. Many years later he pointed out to Father David the shop near the cathedral in Lyon where he used to buy them.[23] By then a mature man, he regarded his youthful asceticism as imprudent and, warning his confrères to be very cautious in allowing anyone to practise such mortification, he more than once admitted that he had ruined his own health. Imprudent though these mortifications were, they were often the temptation of the pious and inexperienced, and in their youth many saints practised them. What is surprising is that his confessor allowed it, but Jean-Claude may not have told him.

He enjoyed serving Mass. Revisiting the old home at 85 years of age, he told his nephew, Eugène, how he and the other boys used to jostle one another to be first to be called to serve. He recalled, too, the time he abandoned the cows he was looking after in the field near the church to run to serve the priest's Mass. He confided the cows to the Lord and he was overjoyed when he rushed out after Mass and found that not a single one had strayed. He often used to pray at the statue of Our Lady of the Seven Sorrows in the parish church and this became a central devotion in his life. The words of his dying mother, 'the only mother you now have is your heavenly mother', had left a lasting impression on both Pierre and himself.[24] Mayet describes a moving scene forty years later: 'He spoke to us of the Blessed Virgin, and … ended with these words. "This is our mother!" Saying this, he looked tenderly at her statue, stopped and began to weep. That look, the silence, those tears, touched all our hearts like a rapier

23. OM, doc. 885, 1.
24. St Catherine Labouré (1806-76), the Vincentian sister with whom the devotion of the Miraculous Medal is associated, reacted to the loss of her earthly mother in a manner similar to

thrust.'[25] The never-forgotten childhood experience when his dying mother entrusted him to his heavenly Mother, can be sensed below the surface here. That incident, too, may have subtly influenced the reticence he displayed towards women of flesh and blood who crossed his path.

It also influenced another character trait. Apart from the mortifications and devotions, what marked out the thirteen-year-old Jean-Claude most in the eyes of the villagers and his own young companions was his desire to be alone, his withdrawal from their world. As a child, the world had proved a hostile one for him. When he was but five, it had taken away first his mother and then his father, leaving him with a sense of loss which Marie Échallier and Uncle Sébastien could never fill. As a young boy of seven or eight, he had watched open-eyed his family and friends and even that great person in the life of the community, Father Cabuchet, the curé, gather furtively behind closed doors for Mass, for confession, to anoint, perhaps to bury secretly at the dead of night. These events could not but affect the timid little boy. Abandonment and aloneness, secrecy and solitude, disposed him to seek God in silence. The pursuits of his companions held no attraction for him; less so when the age of puberty revealed the mutual fascination of the sexes and the possibility of sinning gravely. Only in silence before the ever-patient Mother of Sorrows, his heavenly mother, did he find comfort. Again and again in later life, he told his friends that his one desire had been to be alone with God and live like the fathers in the desert. 'All my thought,' he said, 'was to be a hermit and go to live in the woods, in order to be alone with God.'[26] No wonder his confessor's suggestion of the priesthood, with the public ministry it would involve, terrified him. Yet, para-doxically, it was also this desire for solitude that finally led him to the seminary. Almost in the same breath that he related his deep desire to live as a hermit alone with God, he added: 'It was this thought of going to live in the woods that made me begin my studies. I thought that in that way I would be able to do so'.[27] Conflicting though these assertions may appear, their association in Jean-Claude's mind was not a random one, nor a throw-away remark mis-interpreted by Mayet. Thirty years later, in 1868-9, Jean-Claude repeated in more detail 'that when he was quite young, before beginning his classical studies, he had the desire to retire alone to a wood, to live there far from the world, and that, not being able to realise this project, he went to the minor seminary of Saint-Jodard. He decided to follow this course because he did not see any other

that of Jean-Claude and Pierre Colin. On the day her mother died, she climbed up to the image of Mary and took the Blessed Virgin as her mother from then on.
25. FS, doc 115, 2.
26. OM, doc 499, i.
27. OM, doc. 499, j.

way to leave the world; he could not see how he could take refuge in the desert as he had for so long wished'.[28] Since he could not withdraw from the world, he would, as Pierre urged him, take refuge from it in an institution which was 'not of the world' and which for many years would shelter him from the world.

It was with these ideas of flight and solitude jostling in his head, that Jean-Claude now chose to share the life of some 120 other boys of his age in the close intimate atmosphere of a boarding-school that was Saint-Jodard. His aspirations and actions were not as contradictory as they first might seem, particularly in a young boy who had not yet sorted out the conflicting dreams of adolescence. Indeed, Jean-Claude would not be the only one to harbour such apparent contradictions. Eighty years later Saint Thérèse of Lisieux, Marie-Françoise Thérèse Martin as she was then, also wanted to fly to the desert but became convinced that the Carmelite convent was the desert to which God was inviting her to go and hide herself. Jean-Claude's desires were not dissimilar, but he had not yet reached the same conclusion. So while his superiors at Saint-Jodard believed, as the records show, that he would go on for the priesthood, Jean-Claude had no such fixed intention. Time and seminary training might alter that.

---

28. OM, doc. 819,7; J. Coste, *Une vision mariale de l'Église: Jean-Claude Colin; A Marian Vision of the Church: Jean-Claude Colin*, ed. G. Lessard (Rome, 1998), pp 38-48.

CHAPTER 4

Pope Pius VII in Lyon

'Nobody thought about the pope when he was in Rome. Nobody bothered with what he did. What made him important was my coronation and his appearance in Paris.' *Napoleon Bonaparte.*

On All Saints Day, 1 November 1804, Jean-Claude Colin arrived at the minor seminary of Saint-Jodard. Saint-Jodard was one of the minor seminaries that dedicated Catholics had founded during the Revolutionary period in a valiant effort to provide priests for the ministry. The Council of Trent saw the reform of the clergy as a key to all reforms in the Church for, if the faithful were to be nourished with the word of God and with the sacraments, well-trained and worthy priests were necessary. It decided that the best training ground for future priests was the seminary and enjoined on every bishop to set up a seminary in his diocese where they could receive specific training, spiritual, moral and intellectual, for the priesthood. In addition to this major seminary, preparatory or minor seminaries were set up. Those minor seminaries were secondary schools where youths from twelve years on would receive secondary education, benefiting at the same time from an ecclesiastical atmosphere and a spiritual and moral training that would enable them to go on later to the major seminary for their more specialised priestly training. In the course of the 16th and 17th centuries, the seminary system had proved very successful in producing good-living and well-trained priests but the revolutionaries had suppressed all two hundred seminaries in France, casting a shadow over the future of the priesthood. By the time that the Concordat restored religious peace, many had turned against the Church, ceased to practise or remained ignorant of their faith. It was evident that, if religion was to be renewed, the pressing need was to provide the parishes with priests able to catechise and to administer the sacraments. Portalis, the minister for religion, was prepared to take the necessary steps to enable the bishops to do it. Already in 1802 he permitted seminaries to receive bequests and gifts for their support. At first, ten metropolitan seminaries were to be maintained by the state and then, later, the government allocated bourses and semi-bourses to all seminaries. The seminary of Saint-Irénée, in the city of Lyon, was the metropolitan or major seminary for the diocese of Lyon. Saint-Jodard where Colin now found himself was one of a half dozen minor seminaries.

The government measures were welcomed by the bishops and no one was more assiduous in profiting to the full from these laws favouring seminaries than Cardinal Fesch, archbishop of Lyon. Fesch had no scruple in using his influence as Napoleon's uncle to obtain for his diocese the maximum resources possible. Within the Church structure, a change from the pre-revolutionary set-up further enabled Fesch to set about the re-organisation he had set his heart on. The Concordat and Portalis' interpretation of it strengthened the position of the bishop within his diocese. No longer did chapters and canons circumscribe his power as before. The bishop was in full control of the diocese and exercised his power through vicars general who were dependent on him. Because power was concentrated within the diocese and the state did not interfere in the internal affairs of the Church, a bishop could reorganise his diocese speedily and effectively. This was what happened in Lyon. Fesch was fortunate in the very effective vicars general he chose, first André Jauffret and then Joseph Courbon, Claude-Marie Bochard and Gaspard Renaud. Although deeply interested in reforming his diocese, Fesch was so often away on imperial business that he had to depend on his correspondence with his vicars to make sure that the work was going as he planned. It was they who effectively ran the diocese for the first twenty years of the Concordat and were responsible for carrying out the most effective restoration of any diocese in post-Revolutionary France. Impressing on Renaud the importance of his work in Lyon, Fesch told him solemnly: 'Remember that you are at the head of what is probably, after Rome, the most illustrious of all Churches.'

Fesch, too, was clear-sighted enough to regard the availability of priests as a priority and was determined to procure them. Yet the work of restoration was slow. Assessing the situation in 1805, after three years of uphill work, Fesch admitted to his friend and counsellor, Father Émery, superior-general of the Sulpicians: 'I have a shortfall of 250 priests and, each year, 60 more die.'[1] His seminaries became a priority for him. He wrote letter after letter to Father Claude Cholleton, his vicar in charge of seminaries, insisting that all his effort go to the seminaries: 'It is with your seminaries, my dear Father, that you must occupy yourself. There is your post of honour; it is only there that you will find the way to heaven. I dispense you from all other work, if you occupy yourself with the seminaries. Keep them in your mind all day long, dream of them at night, visit them as often as you can.'[2] Angry that Cholleton spent time in the confessional, to the neglect, as he believed, of the students, Fesch wrote sternly

1. Fesch to Émery, 1 June 1805, cited in J. Gadille, R. Fédou, H. Hours, B. Vrégille, *Le Diocèse de Lyon* (Paris, 1983), p. 211.
2. Fesch to Cholleton, 3 July, 1805; 3 Dec 1805; 12 Jan, 18 Feb, 7 Aug *1806,* J. Jomand, *Le Cardinal Fesch par lui-même* (Lyon, 1970) pp 55-9; D. J. Grange, *Le recrutement du clergé au séminaire de Saint-Irénée de Lyon de 1810-1815* (Lyon, 1955), p. 23. Claude Cholleton was the uncle of Jean Cholleton, one of the first Marists.

to him: 'For the love of God ... I beg you to hand over to Father Paul your work for the religious women, sisters, brothers, and all who take up your time in the confessional ... Were I back at Lyon, I would set fire to your confessional.'[3] So central were seminaries to Fesch's concerns that even his nephew, the emperor, made fun of it: 'Were Uncle Joseph to be put through a still,' he said one day, 'all that would come out would be seminaries; it's the essence of his constitution'.[4] Fesch had to fight hard for his seminaries. Warning his best-loved vicar general, Courbon, of the terrible war waged by some within the government against seminaries, he warned: 'At the very thought of priests being made, they behave as if possessed by the devil.'[5] Officious anti-clerical civil servants meddled and obstructed. Questioned by the very powerful Prefect of the Department of the Rhone about his new foundation at Argentière, Fesch vigorously defended his actions: 'It [Argentière] is a house I acquired, repaired, furnished at my own expense, and where I have placed priests, in whom I have confidence, to form, under my own eyes ... those young people of my diocese who show a disposition for the priesthood.' Brushing aside the Prefect's interference, he sharply pointed out:

> I would like to add that seminaries were one of the subjects discussed between Pope Pius VII and his Imperial Majesty and that it was decided that they would be confided to the care ... of the chief pastors ... I am well-informed of this matter since I myself was the mediator at these discussions.[6]

While Fesch and his vicars are rightly credited with founding or developing no less than six minor seminaries, they were building on the zealous work of many ordinary priests and laity. As regards the seminary of Saint-Jodard, while Fesch took it into his care after the Concordat, it had an older and heroic origin. In 1796, Father Barthélemy-François Devis, who had gathered a few boys to train for the priesthood at Neulise, brought them with him to Saint-Jodard when he was appointed there. According to a contemporary account, Devis took up residence, 'in a garret or wretched loft exposed to the elements which one climbed to through a trap-door which was then closed. It was there, on a bed of straw with but a miserable blanket that the poor superior slept. The room and the garret contained from 50 to 60 students and the same place served, at the one time, as dormitory, study and refectory.'[7] Two years later

3. Jomand, *Fesch,* p. 57.
4. J. Leflon, *Monsieur Émery, L'Église Concordataire et Impériale,* vol. 2 (Paris, 1946), p. 245. Grange, 'Recrutement', p. 26, citing R. P. Dudon, 'Le cardinal Fesch et les séminaires lyonnais', *Études* (July 1903) p. 517, gives a slightly different wording.
5. Fesch to Courbon, 16 Dec 1807, Jomand, *Fesch,* p. 80.
6. Fesch to the Préfet du Rhône, 7 May 1805, Jomand, *Fesch,* pp. 52-3.
7. Grange, 'Recrutement', pp 12-14.

another group joined his students. Shortly afterwards they were able to obtain a more suitable building which had been originally destined for a convent.

In 1803, on the death of Devis, the charge of Saint-Jodard passed to Philibert Gardette, a man who was already working in close co-operation with him since the day some five years earlier that he had come to join him. In the story of Colin, Gardette merits attention for he was Colin's superior during his five years at the minor seminary of Saint-Jodard and again at the major seminary of Saint-Irénée, during his three years of theology prior to ordination. Since many of the staff were quite young, Gardette, because of his experience and age, was looked up to by Colin and his fellow-students. A true confessor of the faith, he had suffered for his loyalty from the beginning of the Revolution. He was a deacon when, in 1790, the Constitutional oath was being enforced. Rather than be ordained in his own diocese of Lyon by Lamourette, the constitutional archbishop, Gardette secretly left the diocese and was ordained by the bishop of Le Puy. On the run from the police for four or five years, he finally gave himself up rather than risk the safety of those harbouring him. He was sentenced to be transported to Guyana. After nine months of imprisonment in Bordeaux, under appalling conditions, he spent a further even more horrific three months on a prison hulk at Rochefort, blocked in the harbour by the English fleet. After his release, his first aim was to seek out and train for the priesthood, young men who would be loyal to the Catholic Church. He had gathered a little group of his own in his parish but at the request of the far-seeing Linsolas, the organiser of the clandestine Church, moved to Saint-Jodard to join forces with Devis. It is difficult to exaggerate Gardette's importance in Saint-Jodard. A co-founder of the college to which he remained entirely devoted during all his life, he lived for it and the students. He it was who made Saint-Jodard the success it was in the first decade of the 19th century when, during his term of office, the number of its students increased to two hundred, despite the high standards he demanded. Years later, many decades after he had left, the college was destroyed in a disastrous fire. Gardette, vicar general of the diocese, exerted all his efforts in raising money to restore it. When its property was to be sold, he threw himself on his knees before cardinal de Bonald, archbishop of Lyon from 1839, pleading successfully for a reprieve. When he lay dying the words 'Saint-Jodard' were constantly on his lips. It was said of him that he had at heart only four things: 'God, the Church, the major seminary of Saint-Irénée and Saint-Jodard!'[8]

When Colin was at Saint-Jodard it was reputed to be one of the finest of

8. 'Les petits-séminaires', pp xx-xxi. *Martyrs, Confesseurs et Serviteurs de la Foi* (Bourg, 1892). At least, thirty-seven Marists trained at Saint-Jodard, including Étienne Terraillon, Bishop Jean-Baptiste Epalle, and three superior-generals, Jean-Claude Colin, Antoine Martin and Jean-Claude Raffin, ibid. pp 355-6.

the minor seminaries in the diocese. Claude-Marie Bochard, the vicar general of Lyon in charge of seminaries, visited it during the course of the scholastic year 1807-8, and paid it the highest praise.[9] It was the best he had seen, he reported. Its spirit was truly the spirit of the Church. It nourished a love for learning and a zeal for piety. It was serious, modest and sensible. The studies were all on a good footing from the first class to the last. Bochard reserved most praise for the superior, Gardette. He was a modest man, he reported, who ran the college energetically and firmly but also with a certain gentleness. Gardette lived austerely. As regards the rule, he permitted no laxity in himself and taught his students likewise. He admitted that for himself sanctity was achieved by strict obedience to the 'holy rule'. Many years later, Colin told Mayet: 'I saw only one properly-constructed rule, and that was the rule of Saint-Jodard, drawn up by M. Gardette; it … fitted on a page'.[10] Though austere, Gardette was respected and loved. This was the man to whose college Colin had come and who was his role model during almost all of his ten years in the seminary. He admired Gardette and valued his counsel.

One of two minor criticisms that Bochard made of Saint-Jodard in his account of his visitation was that there was not sufficient recreation. Saint-Jodard's timetable was, by modern standards, exacting. Rising was at five and, until nine o'clock in the evening, classes or pious exercises took up almost all the time. Even Sundays were not free from classes. On Thursday afternoon, however, the students went for a long walk. It must have been eagerly looked forward to, for this walk, often along the riverbank, was the only recreation the boys had. Games, apparently, formed no part of the curriculum. Even Bochard, in his enthusiastic report, noted the lack of sufficient recreation, but made no positive suggestions. Life, too, was very much in common – dormitory, refectory, class, and walks. It was far from the solitude that Colin had craved for, and getting used to living with over a hundred boys of his own age, many less sensitive, less modest than he, had its difficulties. The presence of Pierre, who was protective of his younger brother, was a help, but this shy young lad had to make his own way in the end.

Apart from Gardette, the other superiors were a prefect and nine teachers. A report on the staff in 1807-8 noted that almost all of them were pious, zealous and capable, although one was reported given too much to levity and another as too easygoing with the students.[11] As teachers they were satisfactory. Some were still seminarians, too, 17 or 19 years old, who had yet to finish their theology at the major seminary. Colin's teacher during the year 1805-6 was Antoine Jallon, a small farmer's son, who still had four years to go before ordination

9. OM, doc. 10.
10. OM, doc. 491.
11. OM, doc. 9.

in 1809. He was some eight years Colin's senior. Later, in 1825, Jallon was one of the first to join the little group of missionaries in the Bugey, which was operating from Belley and, in 1836, he was one of the twenty that made profession in the Society of Mary.[12] Later, Colin used to remind him jocosely of the Latin classes he gave him.

The committed teachers, the packed timetable, and the pious and studious atmosphere of the college provided Colin and his contemporaries with excellent conditions in which to acquire the education and training Saint-Jodard offered. Essentially, as the official name of minor seminaries indicated, they gave a secondary education, classical and Christian, geared toward preparing students for their priestly studies. During the nine years Colin spent there and in the other minor seminaries, he acquired the rudiments of French, Latin, Greek and other subjects such as History, Geography and Logic.

Religion was at the heart of the training for, important though the studies were, the exercises of piety played a greater role. Religious zeal and piety were the main traits which Bochard noted in the teachers and, with a superior as committed to the thorough formation of seminarians as Gardette was, the emphasis was on this spiritual training. Prayer had always been a part of Colin's life, whether alone with God in the woods of Crest or before the image of the Mother of Sorrows in the church of Saint-Bonnet. Now he had all day to pray, for life in the seminary revolved around prayer. From the time he rose at five o'clock in the morning to lights out at nine o'clock in the evening, the day was punctuated by prayer – visits to the Blessed Sacrament, meditation, Mass, rosary, examinations of conscience, spiritual reading, spiritual talks. There were classes in sacred ceremonies and in hymn singing to prepare the Sunday and feastday Mass; there were courses in the Catechism, Sacred History and History of the Church. Even mealtime was a time for instruction for while they ate, a student read aloud from an edifying book. It might be a spiritual classic such as the *Imitation of Christ* or a work on Church History such as Fleury's *Church History*.[13] Lives of the saints, too, were read in the refectory and one book was the life of St Francis Régis who had ministered in the area around Le Puy. There was little fear of the students' being starved of spiritual nourishment. One of Colin's teachers gave him a copy of St Francis de Sales', *Spiritual Directory*, which was a selection of the saint's letters. Colin always retained a great love for St Francis de Sales and came to know the book by heart. Gardette, too, as the man bearing most responsibility for the training of the students, gave them regular spiritual conferences. Colin liked spiritual reading

12. OM, doc. 871 and notes; OM 4, pp 300-1.
13. Claude Fleury (1640-1723), confessor to Louis xv; his twenty-volume *Histoire ecclésiastique* (Paris, 1691-1720) is balanced and thorough, if Gallican in tendency. The history had reached only 1414 by Fleury's death but it was brought up to 1778.

'I did not do any theology during the vacation,' he related, 'I read especially many books of piety; that was my joy.'[14] How long the vacations were and what other activity he engaged in, he does not tell us.

Throughout his life Colin had always a great respect for the pope and no doubt, the influence of Gardette was important here. Gardette, as a 'refractory' or 'Roman' priest, had, like Colin's own family, endured much suffering during the Revolution. It was strengthened by an event which coincided with his entrance into Saint-Jodard, and which was significant also for French Catholics in general. Because of its importance in transforming French attitudes towards the papacy, this event merits recording in some detail.

On 2 November 1804, a day after Colin set off for Saint-Jodard, Pope Pius VII set off on a longer journey, all the consequences of which could not have been foreseen. On 2 November, Pius left the palace of the Quirinal in Rome and left for Paris to meet Napoleon, now sole master of France and of the countries that had become part of the new French empire. Great political events were in the air. Napoleon Bonaparte, the heir of the Revolution, having brought order to a revolution-torn France, set about making himself a hereditary emperor. There were obstacles. For many of the countries in Europe and in the eyes of some Frenchmen, he had usurped the crown. 'I did not usurp the crown,' was Napoleon's sharp reply, 'I found it in the gutter and I raised it up on the point of my sword.' Yet he felt the need to give his claim to the crown of France a legitimacy that the sword alone could not provide. A thousand years before, on Christmas Day 800, Pope Leo III, in a dramatic but well-rehearsed ceremony, had turned his back on the legitimate, but distant and ineffective, emperor in Constantinople and crowned Charlemagne, king of the Franks, as the first 'Holy Roman Emperor'.[15] Napoleon presented himself as the new Charlemagne, who, like the Frankish king of old, had restored order and saved the Church. He, too, wanted the consecration of his throne that the Church alone could bring. This time instead of the emperor coming to Rome, perhaps the pope would come to crown him in Paris. Would Pius VII oblige him? The proposition immediately interested Pius. If the new Charlemagne needed the blessing of the Church to consolidate his empire, Pius hoped, for his part, to secure benefits for the Church – consolidation of the new understanding between the empire and the Church, the abolition of the 'organic articles' to the Concordat, the settlement of the German Church and the return of papal territories. There was opposition – the hidden jealousy of Austria and England, the open anger of the anti-Revolutionary, de Maistre, who exclaimed: 'The crimes of Alexander Borgia are less revolting than this hideous apostasy of

14. OM, doc. 569.
15. Strictly speaking the term 'Holy Roman Emperor' did not come into usage until some time after Charlemagne's death.

his feeble successor'![16] The Comte de Provence, brother of the guillotined King Louis XVI, who was claimant to the throne and later became King Louis XVIII, was furious and never forgave the pope. Regardless of protests, however, Pius VII clung to his decision. No one, least of all the two principal parties, the emperor and the pope, could foresee all the consequences.

Pius left Rome on 2 November 1804, travelled across the Alps at Mont Cenis and, passing through Savoy, reached French soil on 13 November. Accompanied by seven cardinals, he travelled up to Lyon, and entered that great city at the confluence of the rapidly rolling Rhone and sluggish Saone early on the afternoon of 19 November.[17] Since Pius was merely passing through on his way to the crowning of the emperor in Paris, his arrival in Lyon was in no sense a 'papal visit', nor had any popular reception been envisaged for him. Then something unusual occurred. Some young Catholics, in particular Benoît Coste and the members of the recently established *Congregation*, took an initiative.[18] They went to the vicar general Jauffret and, receiving a half-hearted permission from him to make their plans, they assembled, dressed themselves in their striking black and white confraternity robes, and with lighted torches, went to greet the pope at the Cathedral of Saint-Jean. Their action was catching; the great multitude of the people downed tools, closed shop and went out to welcome the pope enthusiastically in Saint-Jean's square. When evening came the city was illuminated. Two huge crosses, 15 feet high, had been erected on towers, signs of the triumph of the Cross and of Christianity. Church and State united to give the pope a magnificent welcome. The archbishop of Lyon, Cardinal Fesch, who had travelled to meet him, the Prefect of the Department and a score of notables greeted him with speeches of welcome. Fifty thousand people thronged Place Bellecour, the central square of Lyon, to receive the pope's blessing. His visit was an outstanding success. Two hectic days later he was on his way to Paris, passing through Tarare, Saint-Symphorien-de-Lay and Roanne, towns not too distant from Saint-Bonnet and Saint-Jodard.

16. Joseph de Maistre (1753-1821), Sardinian ambassador at Saint Petersburg, published *Du Pape* (On the Pope), 1819, powerfully promoting Ultramontanism.

17. *Rétablissement du Culte divin dans l'Église de Notre-Dame de Fourvière, et détails intéressans sur le passage de N. S. Père le Pape Pie VII, à Lyon, le 29 [sic] Novembre, 1804; ainsi que sur son séjour, dans la même Ville, les 17, 18,19 Avril 1805, à son retour de Paris* (Lyon, 1805).

18. Benoît Coste, 'Mes souvenirs de soixante ans', pp. 145-6, copy APM. Benoît Coste (1781-1845) cofounder of the Congregation, 1802. The Congregation, a secret lay association, founded Confraternities of the Blessed Sacrament, taught catechism and performed other apostolic works. It played a key role in transforming Pius's passage through Lyon into a 'papal visit' to the people. Cholleton, Colin's spiritual director and professor, was spiritual father for the Congregation. Alphonse Ozanam, later a Marist priest, and his brother, Frédéric, also became members. X. de Montclos, 'Benoît Coste', X. de Montclos, ed., *Dictionnaire du monde religieux dans la France contemporaine, 6, Lyon, Le Lyonnais, Le Beaujolais* (Paris, 1994), pp 125-8; H. Hours, 'Pie VII et Lyon', in *Les Papes à Lyon: Pie VII 1804-1805* (Lyon, 1986), pp [67-70].

Everywhere the crowds gathered to greet him. The coronation took place on 2 December 1804, in the great cathedral of Notre-Dame in Paris in the presence of all the dignitaries of Church and State where Napoleon, as pre-arranged, received the crown from the pope and placed it on his own head. Although unsuccessful in his efforts to obtain concessions for the Church, his four-month stay in Paris had other important consequences. Delegations from the provinces had come to be present at the coronation and, when in Paris, all of them came to pay homage to the pope. Every place he went, people flocked to see him and to receive his blessing. In part, this welcome was due to Pius' gentle kindness and personal goodness, but it was also a tribute to the head of the Catholic Church, particularly in his role of bringing peace and reconciliation. To underline the new warmth of relations between Church and State, it was envisaged that together pope and emperor visit the region of Lyon, Provence and the Vendée. 'No, no,' cried Napoleon after reflecting a while, 'the people would travel one league [4.8 kilometres] to see me, they would travel thirty to be blessed by the pope, and that is not what I want.' Jealous of the attention the pope was receiving when he went out in Paris, Napoleon took to humili-ating him when he could, even refusing to let him celebrate Christmas Mass in the cathedral of Notre-Dame. To the pope's request for the return of papal territory, which he regarded as the sacred patrimony of the Church, Napoleon replied evasively, promising to protect and support 'our religion' but in fact not giving anything. Craftily, he had the suggestion put to Pius that he abandon Rome and take up residence either in Paris or Avignon to which suggestion the pope, in turn, only gave an enigmatic smile. Finally, after weeks of efforts, Pius persuaded Napoleon to let him return to Rome and he set off on 4 April 1805. This time he took a different route which brought him through Troyes and Saumur. At Chalon, 'all Burgundy hastened to render him homage' and there he celebrated Good Friday and the feast of the Resurrection. At Mâcon, he could scarcely tear himself away from the crowds that pressed around him to see and greet him.

When he arrived at Lyon on 17 April, the reception he received surpassed all previous welcomes, astonishing even his own entourage. The visit of a pope, and particularly of one who had negotiated on equal terms with the emperor and brought religious peace to France, was the great talking-point throughout the country and many hoped that the sacring of the emperor in Paris might herald a new era in France and Europe. This was the feeling expressed even in the message of the secular authorities. The Prefect of the Department, addressing Pius as 'the common Father of the faithful', declared solemnly that 'the happi-ness to which France has been restored is all the more dear in that it feels that it is due in part to the example of Your Holiness.'[19] So great was the enthusiasm

19. *Rétablissement du culte,* pp 36-7.

that a boat trip along the Saone was organised to give more people a chance of seeing the pope.[20]

The next day it was the steep ascent to the sanctuary of Fourvière. On the hill of the Old Forum, 'Forum Vetus' from which the name 'Fourvière' originated, stood the oldest church of the Blessed Virgin in Lyon, built close to where Saints Blandina, Pothinus, and the first martyrs of Lyon met their death in the 2nd century. Fourvière's history since the Revolution had been a sad one but a determined Cardinal Fesch had managed to get it back for the Church. He now seized the occasion to have it publicly reconciled and opened by the pope. On 19 April, Pius VII reconsecrated the Church, said Mass there and went out on the terrace overlooking the city to be greeted by thousands of the faithful. Banners waved, bells tolled and canons boomed as the crowds roared their approval. It was a historic moment. It was from its reconsecration by Pius VII that historians of Lyon date the custom of young priests and missionaries of climbing to the sanctuary of the Blessed Virgin and there consecrating their missionary vocation and their willingness to accept martyrdom.[21] Later, in his report in secret consistory to the cardinals in Rome, Pius remarked that he would not forget how during his stay at Lyon, 'the very famous chapel of Fourvières [sic], dedicated to the Blessed Virgin, was reopened by me, to the unbelievable joy of all the people'.[22]

In Lyon, Fesch, with his keen interest in seminaries, made sure that Pius visited the major seminary of Saint-Irénée. It was an occasion of joy, and, above all, of encouragement for staff and students who kept the missal with which he had celebrated Mass at Fourvière as a treasured souvenir. 'Increase and multiply', Pius said to them and to this visit later archbishops attributed an increase in vocations. It is not certain if many of the 'minor seminarians' got to see him though probably many did. Whole parishes led by their priests travelled distances to greet him en route, and Saint-Jodard, where Jean-Claude and Pierre Colin were students, was eighteen kilometres or so from Saint-Symphorien-de-Lay, through which Pius had passed. It is possible that the staff and students from Saint-Jodard travelled to greet the pope on this quite unique occasion.

The five days the pope spent in Lyon were certainly memorable. The festivities, the speeches, the crowds were everywhere. The merchants of pious

20. Benoît Coste's first-hand account recaptures the enthusiasm of Catholic Lyon on the occasion. 'The river itself seemed to disappear under that multitude of gondolas, carefully decorated, which accompanied the barge which bore the successor of Saint Peter. The spectators made the whole area resound with the echoes of their repeated cry of 'Viva, the Holy Father' ... they threw themselves on their knees to share in his blessings. One only thought moved the hearts of all at that moment – that of paying homage to Jesus Christ, founder and preserver of the holy Church.' Coste, 'Souvenirs', p. 152.
21. H. Hours, 'Pie VII et Lyon', *Les Papes à Lyon*, p. [71].
22. Pius VII, 26 June 1805, ibid. p. [65].

objects did a roaring trade as no less than 30,000 rosaries, crosses and medals were brought to be blessed by the pope. Pius was the living symbol of the peace and reconciliation so much yearned for. The French people, and in particular the faithful of Lyon, for their part, showed the pope that religion was very much alive in their hearts and souls. On 20 April, Pius eventually set out for Rome where he arrived 14 May. Although never intended as such, his visit to France had been a magnificent public relations success. 'The devotion of this people is inexpressible,' avowed the severe and unsympathetic Cardinal Antonelli. The pope was quite overcome. To Fouché, the minister of police, who inquired as to how he found France, an astonished Pius replied, 'God be thanked, my journey was through the midst of a people on its knees.'[23]

Towards the end of his reign, Napoleon commented that nobody 'thought about the pope when he was in Rome. Nobody bothered with what he did. What made him important was my coronation and his appearance in Paris.' He could have added Lyon! Up to the Revolution French Catholics looked to the curé to administer the sacraments, to the bishops to run the diocese and to His Most Christian Majesty, the king, to protect the Church. The pope was respected as head of the Church but was a distant figure. Many French historians agreed that Pius VII's visit 'marked the beginning of that devotion to the pope which was to increase during the 19th century.'[24] France rediscovered the pope. Pius VII's visit and his part in consolidating peace brought the pope right into the centre of French Catholic and political life. Catholic Lyon had played a major part in bringing this about.

The papal visit marked an important stage in the manner in which the Lyon clergy saw the role of the pope in the Church, which the Church of France, Gallican in outlook, had for long played down. A few years later, even the vicar general Courbon, a close friend of Cardinal Fesch, Napoleon's uncle, warned the Cardinal against pressure being brought to bear on Pius VII:

The French clergy, especially those of Lyon, love the pope so tenderly and have such faith in him, that it would feel profoundly afflicted and indignant that one could suggest a plan to extort by threats from his Holiness what his conscience rejects.[25]

Colin would have shared in that enthusiasm for Pius VII.

After that exciting year of 1804-5, Colin's career at Saint-Jodard was one of steady progress. On both intellectual and spiritual fronts, he was proving a ready pupil, for the college records show that he was a very devout, bright and

23. J. Leflon, *Histoire de l'Église*, eds A. Fliche and V. Martin, vol. 20, *La crise révolutionnaire, 1789-1846* (Paris, 1949) p. 232.
24. Ibid., p. 232, citing L. Lanzac de Laborie, *Paris sous Napoléon. La religion*, vol. 4, p. 181.
25. Archivio segreto vaticano, Segreteria di stato, epoca napoleonica, Francia (Fesch Papers). Coste, *Marian Vision*, p. 74.

diligent student. In the year 1806-7, his rating for piety and progress were both 'excellent', a position he maintained in later years. His health, however, was proving less satisfactory. Whether the regime was too severe for Colin or whether he had undermined his health with excessive childhood mortifications, he fell ill more than once. The first illness came during the course of 1807-8, lasted some time and probably forced him to return home for, although always at the top of the class, he had to repeat 5th class in 1808-9. The repetition of a year brought him into the same class as Étienne Terraillon, a farmer's son from Saint-Loup, thirty kilometres to the east of Saint-Jodard. Terraillon, who was a year younger than Colin, became one of the first group of Marists. They were not long in the same class. During the latter half of that year Colin again took ill, this time quite seriously, and had again to leave the seminary and return home. This illness, together with the communion crisis, is one of the few well-documented incidents of his personal life in those early years, and they lift the veil on the adolescent Colin. Like the communion crisis, too, he never forgot it.

As he appeared close to dying, he made his will.[26] This document, dated 23 April 1809, beneath its legal terminology furnishes some precious information. Its terms state that Colin left his goods, insofar as he could dispose of them, to one brother, Jean, the eldest, who was also his godfather and guardian and who, the will testified, had advanced him 1,200 francs over a period of three years, to cover the expense of his studies and keep. The sober legal terms of the will mask the high drama of the incident for Colin. Sick as he was, he was to learn a number of lessons and, from the many references he made later to it, it is clear that the whole episode was a marker in his life. Since his sickness was so severe as to be life-threatening, Colin also left money for Masses to be said for the repose of his soul. Trained in the austere, unworldly school of Father Gardette and the priests of Saint-Jodard, the dedicated young seminarian saw his approaching death as a call to prepare to meet his God even more thoroughly than he had prepared for his first confession. He asked for the priest in order to make his confession. From seven o'clock in the morning until ten at night, he waited in vain. The priest refused to come although, as Colin pointed out later, he lived right next door to the church. 'That in itself was more than enough to kill me,' Colin admitted. The priest was the intractable Gilbert! When that night Gilbert did deign to come, poor Colin was so ill that, as he later admitted, he never quite knew what he did or what the priest said to him.

The dying youth tried to put his temporal affairs also in order. He owed the cobbler a sou and he insisted that he be paid that trivial amount. On Friday, when he was offered broth to eat, he refused to break the fast. On Sunday, however, a shock was in store for him. His own relations insisted that he call a notary to draw up an authentic deed of his will. He recoiled from breaking the

26. OM, doc. 13.

Sabbath. If, however, he was intent on putting in order his spiritual accounts, his relations' thoughts were on other, more immediate accounts and, Sunday or no Sunday, they insisted that a notary be summoned and that, illness or no illness, he get down to the business of making his will. 'It is very wrong,' was all he could interject. His relations had their way and the notary was summoned from Lamure-sur-Azergues. With the excitement that the will-making brought, the situation almost became too much for Colin. 'I beheld my bed under siege,' he recounted, 'the will, the notary, was all they spoke to me about; everyone was thinking of his own interests.' More distressing was the state of Uncle Sébastien who feared that the other relations might deal harshly with his stewardship. 'This poor uncle,' Colin told Mayet a quarter of a century later, 'came in tears to my bedside saying that, when the accounts would be arranged, he might be caused pain and asking me to make a declaration on his behalf.' While his uncle was weeping at his bedside and beseeching him to help him, the sick boy was trying to focus on the notary and the will he must make. Unwilling to cause his uncle the slightest pain, he did manage to insert into the will an ample declaration in his favour, testifying that his uncle had fed, lodged, kept and educated him to an extent that had more than absorbed the share of his parents' and uncle's patrimony due to him. For this reason, Colin enjoined explicitly that no further demands whatsoever were to be made on his uncle on this score.

He recorded another and more serious incident. One of his brothers was angry that he had left his elder brother half his inheritance (which, since he was a minor, was, according to the Napoleonic Code, the total of which he could dispose). Who this was, Colin never said but his twenty-seven-year old brother, another Sébastien, who was never a success in life, may well have been the villain of the piece.[27] This incident may be related to the strangest account Colin gave of the 'bedside siege' that is so astonishing that it merits citing exactly as Mayet noted it:

> The doctor having prescribed for young Colin a potion by which he hoped to cure him, someone who thought he had an interest in his inheritance, persuaded him not to take it, telling him: 'It is poison.' So he refused to drink it, without saying why. When his brother saw this, he began to weep. To please his brother, young Colin then took the potion. The loathing this recollection gave him for attachment to earthly things is understandable.[28]

The plain meaning of the text is that Colin was alleging that one of his own family was trying to hasten his death or was at least indifferent as to his recovery. It must be asked, however, if the young Colin, seriously ill with a fever, accurately interpreted what took place? Was his later recall of the incident accurate?

27. OM 3, p. 304, footnote 3.
28. OM, doc. 508.

Some such incident almost certainly took place; otherwise he would not have recounted it in such explicit terms. It remained rooted in his memory for years afterwards when, if it were incorrect, his brothers could have put him right on so serious an accusation. Since Mayet was a very reliable recorder, it must be concluded that the account is probably accurate. If this is so, the finger must again point to his brother Sébastien, as the one who tried to prevent him from taking the doctor's potion. The other brother, whose tears finally moved Colin to follow the doctor's advice and take it, was almost certainly his elder brother, Jean.

Another more positive impression from his sick-bed remained with him. Many years later, warning his confrères to be very careful not to say things at a sickbed that would upset the sick, whose sense of hearing often remained even though they could give no sign of consciousness, he related what happened him during his illness. After lapsing into a coma, he regained consciousness. He could sense people coming up to his bedside, turning away and saying 'He is dying'. One woman, however, after a close examination, disagreed completely and declared that he was not going to die. Although he could not speak, Colin heard all. 'I heard someone say,' he recounted, "he is not going to die." This one word, I recall, did me great good.'[29]

The whole sick-bed episode was 'a moment of truth' for Colin and taught him some sharp lessons. Thenceforth, he would be more aware of the forces of self-interest in the world. The worldliness his relations displayed as he lay dying surprised and sickened him. He developed a life-long loathing of greed of any type and he was severe in condemning any sign of it in others. Thirty years later, in 1838-9, he told his confrères that what most helped to detach himself from his family were these events – his sick-bed besieged, talk of nothing but notaries and wills, everyone thinking only of his own interests. He may well have gone too far in cutting himself off from his family. Father de la Croix, vicar general of Belley, who had taught him in the seminary and who was born a few miles from Saint-Bonnet, reproached him severely for neglecting his family. The reproach was apparently without success.[30] On one occasion, Colin went so far as to say: 'I admit that I am twenty times more concerned with what happens to one of the Society than what happens to one of my family. I give no thought to my family; I do not even know if I have a family.'[31] He was never at his ease in dealing with his relations and when his nephew came to him in Belley, he was unable to say anything to him.[32] The whole incident was a major influence in his abhorrence for cupidity, an abhorrence which he enshrined in

29. OM, 645, 1; 819, 133.
30. OM, doc. 752, 32.
31. OM 2, p. 706, note 4.
32. RMJ, doc. 126.

the strongest terms in the rule from the very beginning. The rejection of greed became one of the three important 'nos' that characterised his outlook right through life.

It was this illness, in all probability, which has been credited with sparking off in Colin another reaction. Father Benoît Lagniet, in his important 'Historical Notes on the Origin of the Society', written between 1878 and 1881, declared that after his sickness Colin made an important decision:

> ... from [the time of] his literary studies at the seminary of Alix, around the year 1810, and on the occasion of an illness believed to be mortal, he nourished the plan of devoting himself to the establishment of a religious congregation bearing the name of Mary.[33]

Lagniet does not give any sources for this claim. Yet it cannot be lightly dismissed, for Lagniet enjoyed Colin's confidence during his generalate, acted as his direct assistant or 'provincial', and was in line to be elected to succeed him as superior-general in 1854, when, in fact, Father Favre was chosen. Well-placed to gather information on the origins of the Society, he was a precise and careful man who would scarcely have made such an assertion if Colin had not given him some indication that this was so.[34] His statement raises the intriguing problem of the origin of the Society of Mary and of what part Colin played in it already in his minor seminary days. To Lagniet's assertion must be added the words of Colin's official biographer, Jean Jeantin who, on 29 May 1870, boldly asserted that, already at the age of 14, Colin had the idea of forming a congregation consecrated to the Blessed Virgin and set down his ideas in writing.[35]

Although Colin's remarks scarcely intend to reveal, as Lagniet and Jeantin hoped, the origin of the Society of Mary, they help us understand the growth and development of Colin's mind and personality over a period for which we have little contemporary evidence. He had entered the minor seminary a boy of fourteen in 1804 and now, five years on, he did not yet see clearly. Hesitant and indecisive, he hovered around the altar, plunged himself wholeheartedly into the preparatory studies for the ministry and yet had no commitment to taking holy orders. He craved a hidden life lived for God alone while he lived the rough-and-tumble of the boarding school at Saint-Jodard. The shock of his illness and the scenes of selfishness he witnessed, made him long for a style of life where such greed would have no part. Where or how could these desires of

---

33. OM, doc. 854, 3; OM 3, pp 731-2. Benoît Lagniet (1806-1884), superior of Belley, 1838-42; superior of Puylata, 1842-3; superior of Verdelais, 1843-6; 'provincial' or immediate assistant of Colin, 1846; provincial of Paris, 1852.

34. Coste, *Marian Vision*, pp 48-54.

35. Father Detours claimed that Jean-Claude had the idea at the time of his first communion. François-Auguste Detours (1837-95), Marist priest. His researches and notes are an important source for the early history of the society.

his heart find fulfilment, and how could they be answered? Prayer and spiritual reading provided an interior answer and by 1810 he had begun to steep himself daily in Henry-Marie Boudon's *God Alone,* finding perhaps in Boudon's
idea of a spiritual association or union for God alone, the type of association
he dreamed of.[36] He had always nourished a deep love for Mary, the yearning
of a child for his mother, and now he felt drawn to imagine the possibility
of a society dedicated to her where worldliness would not enter in, where he
could serve God alone and where his desire for solitude would be fulfilled.

36. For Boudon and Jean-Claude's discovery of Boudon, see chapter 5. Boudon states explicitly:
'I called this little discourse *God Alone or the Association for God alone,* ardently hoping to form
a holy union among Christians which would tend with one accord to serve God…', H. Boudon,
Oeuvres Spirituelles qui contiennent Dieu Inconnu…, Dieu Seul…, Dieu Présent Par Tout…, vol.
1 (Lyon, 1741), p. 163.

Minor Seminaries and Major Illnesses

Shortly before he was taken ill in the spring of 1809 and had to return home to Saint-Bonnet, Jean-Claude Colin had gone through another little drama in his tortuous journey to the priesthood. He was now nineteen and of the age to be conscripted into the army. Seminarians who had progressed to the major seminary were exempted but not those still in minor seminaries. For his own diocese of Lyon, Fesch, however, had persuaded his uncle, Napoleon, to exempt minor seminarians also. In December 1808, the authorities of Saint-Jodard had included Colin on the list of those for whom they requested exemption, as they had done for Marcellin Champagnat the year before. Immediately, scruples assailed Colin. Since he had not decided to go on for the priesthood, he felt that he had no right to an exemption. Off he hurried to Gardette, the superior, to have him take his name off the list. Gardette, he recalled later, received him well, listened patiently to him, gave him sound advice and, dismissing him, remarked humorously: 'Silly! you will have time enough to shoulder a gun.' The exemption duly came through on 26 January 1809, but with events later that spring Gardette's quip was almost prophetic![1]

After his recovery from the life-threatening illness in the spring of 1809, Colin travelled to the spa of Bourbon-Lancy, over a hundred kilometres north-west from Saint-Bonnet, to take the waters. All went well until he was half-way home. Passing through the town of Charolles, an administrative town in the Charolais, the police stopped him and clapped him in jail. Somehow he got news to his brother Jean surprisingly quickly. Jean, who was at the market in Thizy, dropped everything, hurried back to Saint-Bonnet, collected the necessary documents and rode the 50 kilometres to Charolles without ever pausing to eat on the way. He arrived that evening at the jail to Colin's surprise and delight. Tears of joy were shed by the brothers and there were more tears of joy and relief when the family saw them arrive safe and sound back in Saint-Bonnet.

The arrest of Colin in the little town of Charolles had to do with the great political events of the time. Napoleon needed more young men for his armies. The first modern universal conscription had come in 1798 in France, but it was during Napoleon's many campaigns that it became an indispensable part of

1. OM, docs 499, 3; 12.

state policy. All men between the ages of twenty and twenty-five, classified by year, came under this conscription law, and the government could call on them according as they were required. The war in Spain had gone badly, culminating in the battle of Bailén, in southern Spain, on 19 June 1808, where a whole French army had been forced to capitulate.[2] Desperate for recruits, Napoleon persuaded the Senate, in September 1808, to draft a further 160,000 young men. Even that was not sufficient, for during the course of 1809, on two occasions, the Senate was forced to draft even more recruits for the imperial armies and to reduce the age of conscription from twenty to nineteen. Since conscription was quite unpopular, many young men evaded it when they could, and the government enlisted the help of the clergy. The priests were under orders to preach on Sundays that the draft was a patriotic duty. Yet despite this enlistment of the clergy as 'recruiting sergeants', when the new war with Austria broke out in 1809, the number of draft-dodgers soared to 40%. The government reacted energetically and mounted a sustained and successful campaign to ferret out the draft-dodgers, sending special bailiffs, composed of hardened war veterans from other parts of the country, to stiffen the action of the local police. They were thorough. John Mary Vianney (the 'Curé of Ars'), a classmate of Colin, evaded conscription and spent over a year in hiding; pierced by a prodding sabre and suffocated by rotting hay, he barely escaped discovery when the police scoured the barn where he lay concealed.[3] Another draft-dodger was the down-to-earth, astute Étienne Déclas, also a classmate. Petrified when he noticed some gendarmes eyeing him as they approached along the road, Déclas resorted to some vulgar diversionary tactics so that the gendarmes hurried past calling him a disgusting pig.[4] Colin's arrest at Charolles was for suspected draft-evasion. Were it not for the prompt action of his brother he would have been despatched in chains – the punishment of draft-dodgers – to the Spanish front, to shoulder a gun, as Gardette had warned, in a never-ending and increasingly brutal war.

Colin's encounter with the police revealed how public affairs in France were impinging on the little world of the seminary and from this year on –1809 – it would obtrude even more. The great political events of the day had begun to involve first the pope in Rome, then the French bishops and Church and finally, touched the very life of the seminary. At the root of it were the constant wars that Napoleon had to fight from now on, up to Waterloo, in his attempt to maintain his dominant position in Europe. At first it was only the guerrilla-like

2. Jean-Baptiste Marbot (1782-1854), one of Napoleon's generals, in his *Mémoires,* estimated that, over a period of six years from 1809 on, 200,000 French and 60,000 of their allies had been killed in Spain.
3. Saint Jean-Marie-Baptiste Vianney (1786-1859), ord. 1815; curé of Ars, 1818.
4. François Yardin to Victor Poupinel and Claude-Marie Joly, 20 Aug. 1861, APM, VM 211.

war still dragging on in Spain. Then there were new wars in Germany and Austria. There were distant rumours, too, from Rome of some discord between pope and emperor, but as the full facts were not known, it was dismissed as being no more than a storm in a teacup. The origins of the dispute were simple enough. Pius had protested against the restrictive organic articles that Napoleon had unilaterally attached to the Concordat but he had been ignored. The pope feared that he would introduce the Concordat, together with obnoxious articles, into other states that now either formed part of the Empire or were tributary to France. Napoleon's introduction of the imperial catechism and his intrusion of a feast of Saint Napoleon into the Church calendar had also annoyed Pius but, since the nuncio had agreed to them, he was unwilling to disavow him. When a few years later, however, a problem arose when Napoleon's demands clashed with the sovereignty of the Papal State, the disagreement escalated into a serious conflict.

After the decade of revolutionary wars, Napoleon had brought religious harmony by the Concordat and international peace by the Treaty of Amiens, both promulgated in 1802. The coming of peace was welcomed eagerly in France and abroad. Four years later, however, Napoleon was again at war defeating Austria and Russia at Austerlitz and Prussia at Jena. He also enforced a 'Continental Blockade' which forbade all European ports from receiving British ships and so denying that 'nation of shopkeepers' its vital trade with mainland Europe. To his annoyance, Pius refused to take measures to exclude British ships from Roman ports. Napoleon sharply reminded him that 'Your Holiness is the sovereign of Rome but I am the emperor'. Pius replied that no emperor had any rights over Rome. Pius was but echoing the claim of all popes for long centuries that they were independent of the power of any temporal ruler, a claim which, in the eyes of most Catholics, made an independent papal state a necessity. Napoleon's response was to nibble away at the Papal State, until finally, on 17 May 1809, he annexed the remainder. On 10 June, Pius replied by excommunicating all who sacrilegiously violated the 'Patrimony of Saint Peter', that is the Papal State. In reply, the French army broke into the Quirinal palace on the night of 5-6 July 1809, and General Radet took Pius VII prisoner. 'It is gross folly,' Napoleon told Fouché, yet, while blaming Radet, he allowed the pope to be carried off, first over the Alps to Grenoble, then back again over the Alps to Savona, near Genoa, where, closely guarded and spied on, he remained a prisoner for three years.

The distant dispute between pope and emperor made, at first, little impact in France where the bishops, unwilling to oppose Napoleon, hoped that the dispute was not too serious and might soon be healed. They had reason to be well-disposed, for Napoleon continued to favour the Church. In September 1807, the state had created 24,000 bourses or half-bourses for the seminaries,

helped the foundation of minor seminaries and exempted seminarians from
military service. In 1808, it re-established faculties of theology. It authorised
congregations of women religious and gave them financial support. The
Brothers of the Christian Schools, the Sulpicians, the Vincentians, the Foreign
Mission Society and even the Trappists were also authorised. The sums expended
on the support of the clergy were increased to support not only the major
parishes but the chapels of ease, so that, by 1807, the budget for religious affairs
had been increased in five years from 1,200,000 francs to 17,000,000.[5]
Moreover, since Napoleon had brought the blessings of peace to the Church
and peace to the nation, many bishops, patriotic Frenchmen as well as pastors
of the Church, hailed him as the new Cyrus who restored the people of God.

By 1807, however, things began to change. The peace had collapsed and,
although Napoleon's victories appeared to restore it for the time being, many
of the bishops became more muted in their support of his policies. The brutal
abduction of the well-respected Pius VII changed the nature of the dispute. It
was no longer an abstract quarrel about territorial sovereignty in the struggle
against England; the head of the Church had been attacked. Pius VII, to whose
goodness French Catholics had paid ringing tributes four years earlier when he
passed through their land, now came once more on to French soil, but this time
as a tightly-guarded prisoner. As he was hurried along through Savoy and into
Grenoble, the plight of this ageing and good man aroused the sympathy of clergy
and faithful. René-François Rohrbacher, a contemporary in age of Colin and
like him studying for the priesthood, recorded the enthusiasm that the visit
awakened in him for the pope and for Rome.[6] It was to inspire his great life-
work - the *Universal History of the Catholic Church* - which was a successful
attempt to counter the Gallican interpretation of Church history or, as one
commentator put it, to put the pope back into history. Read during meal-time
in the seminaries, including Marist houses, it proved a major influence in moving the young clergy to turn more to Rome and the pope. The sympathy which
Pius VII received as he passed through France, showed that many Catholics
shared the sentiments of young Rohrbacher, and this unexpected side-effect left
an enduring impression on the attitude of French Catholics to the Papacy
throughout the 19th century.

The quarrel between pope and emperor escalated. In accordance with the
terms of the Concordat, the emperor could nominate the bishops but they then
had to receive canonical institution from the pope. Napoleon nominated bishops,
but Pius refused to give them canonical institution. The effectiveness of this
weapon became clear when, before long, some seventeen sees of the French

---

5. Thirty thousand 'cures succursales' (subsidiary parishes or chapels of ease) now received state support. R. Rohrbacher, *Histoire Universelle de l'Église Catholique ...*, vol. 12, (Paris, 1882), pp 28-9.
6. R. F. Costigan, *Rohrbacher and the Ecclesiology of Ultramontanism* (Rome, 1980), pp. 5-9.

Empire, including Paris and Metz, remained vacant. The situation had become serious. An angry Napoleon now feared that the religious peace of France, so painstakingly established by the Concordat, was in jeopardy. Failing to move the pope, he decided to bypass him and called a Church council in 1811. Since the Council was for the whole Empire, it included besides the French bishops, many Italian, Belgian and some German bishops. Most French bishops, including Fesch, were Gallican and some had put severe pressure on the pope to yield to Napoleon's wishes, alleging that Pius was not respecting the rights of the French Church. In the aftermath of the Revolution, however, the dread of a schism like the one only recently healed, affected all Church people from bishops to laity, and when the bishops assembled, the thought uppermost in their mind was the unity of the Church. This concern prevailed over their Gallicanism and their wish to please the all-powerful emperor and so they insisted that any measures they adopted must get the prior approval of the pope.

The bishops also expressed concern about the pope's captivity and sent a delegation to Savona to ask him to accept the compromise. Since Napoleon could not accept the pope's terms, the whole council was a failure. Furious, Napoleon placed those bishops who most supported the pope under arrest. The damage, however, had been done. The concern the bishops voiced over the conflict between pope and emperor, alerted clergy and faithful to the serious-ness of the rupture. Informed Catholics, like the influential Émery, superior of Saint-Sulpice, now took their stand – if a reasoned and moderate one – on the side of the pope. Even before this, Émery had shown signs of modifying his Gallicanism which, at the expense of the papal authority, exalted the power of the national Church and through it the control of the State over the Church – a view welcome to French kings and to Napoleon alike. The impact of the Revolution and his own reflection were moving him towards a more nuanced view of the position and authority of the pope, especially vis-à-vis the national state. In his seminary of Saint-Sulpice, the Gallican teaching in the treatise *On the Church* on this question was watered down.[7] In Lyon, where the Sulpicians were in charge of the major seminary of Saint-Irénée and where Gardette and the staff held Émery in high regard, the professors almost certainly followed Émery's lead. Napoleon's standing with Catholics had been damaged. The flow of obsequious flattery in the pastoral letters of the bishops dried up and some clergy began to see Napoleon in a new light. In the diocese of Marseille he was even called 'the Antichrist'. Seminarians, too, perhaps even less inclined

7. J. Audinet, 'L'enseignement 'De Ecclesia' à Saint-Sulpice sous le Premier Empire et les débuts du gallicanisme modéré', in *L'Ecclésiologie au XIXe Siècle* (Paris, 1960), pp 115-39; Coste, *Marian Vision,* pp 66-74.

towards Gallicanism than their teachers, began to turn against the emperor.[8] Rohrbacher, now a theology student in the seminary of Nancy, in Lorraine, described the heightening atmosphere: 'We studied the treatise on the Church: it was in 1810 and 1811, at the height of the persecution of Bonaparte against Pius VII … We studied this key treatise thoroughly, all the more because …we could expect to give one's life for the truths we were … studying.'[9] There was a similar reaction among seminarians in Paris. On 9 June 1810, a worried student in the seminary of Saint-Sulpice wrote an outspoken letter to a friend, describing what he and fellow-seminarians were thinking about recent government moves and of the impact on their parents:

> The ruin of religion and of its ministers, is all one hears talk of. That dreadful truth can no longer be hidden; dismay and fear are everywhere … The Holy Father will make no deal which will harm religion of which he is the august head; by his unchanging patience in the midst of the innumerable ills which overwhelm him and by his unparalleled resignation, he brings it comfort … All our young people have dread in their hearts; they fear the misfortunes connected with the priestly state. Their parents, furthermore, whose consent, according to new decrees, they must have, turn them away from it.[10]

Unfortunately for the seminary of Saint-Sulpice, Fouché's ever-vigilant police intercepted this imprudent letter and immediately brought it to Napoleon's attention. Furious, he approved laws against the seminaries. The first blow came in October 1810 when a decree excluded Émery and the Sulpicians from the seminary in Paris and dissolved the society. A worried Fesch pleaded to be able to retain the Sulpicians in his major seminary of Saint-Irénée at Lyon and, as a concession, was allowed to do so until Christmas, when he, too, was forced to dispense with these highly valued seminary staff. On 15 November 1811, another decree, aimed at eliminating the competition between the seminaries and the other secondary schools, restricted the number of minor seminaries. Fesch protested but was unable to persuade Napoleon to rescind the decree. What provoked a major break between uncle and nephew was again the question of unity of the Church. Worried that a schism might result from Napoleon's policy towards the Church, Fesch, in March 1812, brought his complaints to Napoleon. An angry emperor ordered him to return to his diocese and to stay there. In disgrace, Fesch arrived in Lyon on 24 March 1812 and was to remain in his diocese almost continually until January 1814, his

8. Leflon, *Émery*, vol. 2, p. 306. On Gallicanism during this period, see A. Latreille, 'Le gallicanisme ecclésiastique sous le premier Empire', *Revue historique*, CXCIV (1944), 1-22.
9. Costigan, *Rohrbacher*, p. 5.
10. J. Gosselin, *Vie de M. Émery, neuvième supérieur du séminaire et de la compagnie de Saint-Sulpice…*, vol. 2, (Paris, 1861) 268-9.

longest ever stay in his diocese. Concerned how to protect his precious seminarians, he visited Saint-Irénée, Alix and l'Argentière. Napoleon's decree limit-
ing minor seminaries to one for each diocese, had ordered all other existing
ones must be incorporated into the recently established Imperial Université. A
member of Fesch's episcopal council suggested that he accept Napoleon's plan
and argued that those in charge there were good Catholic people. Fesch rose in
an explosion of anger: 'No, no, I shall not damn myself; not for anything in
the world will I tie my boys to the regime of the Université; the Université, it
is like a great barracks; soldiers are formed there; priests are what I want.'[11] He
was able to use his influence to obtain, for his own diocese of Lyon only, the
postponement of the closure until the end of the academic year.[12] By the beginning of the school year in 1812, however, five minor seminaries in his diocese
had to be closed. They included Saint-Jodard, where Colin had spent five years,
and Alix.

It was to Alix, not Saint-Jodard, that Colin had returned the autumn after
his illness. Alix was a tiny village of some 200 inhabitants and the seminary
there was new. It was only in 1807 that Fesch, on a pastoral visit to the
Beaujolais part of his diocese, noticing a fine church and buildings that had
once belonged to a convent of the Canonesses Regular of Saint Benedict,
decided that it would make an admirably situated seminary for students from
the region. It was a successful move and by 1810 it had 128 seminarians on its
rolls. For the Colins, Alix, less than forty-five kilometres from Saint-Bonnet,
was closer than Saint-Jodard and near Villefranche, the district capital where
they would have business. Moreover, the Colins had a vineyard in the area.

The ill-health which Colin had experienced at Saint-Jodard may have been
another reason for transferring to Alix, for the family may have hoped that he
would fare better in the newer seminary. Since Fesch, with imperial funds at his
disposal, was able to dispose of far more money in 1807 than the pioneer
founders of Saint-Jodard could have dreamed of, Alix was probably better
appointed as a seminary. The change to Alix, however, did not save Colin from
further illnesses. On one occasion, he was so ill that when he attempted to rise
for Sunday Mass, he collapsed from weakness. When the prefect, who at first
thought he was malingering, came to see him, he was so taken aback that he
insisted that Colin make his confession right away and receive the last rites.[13]

11. Ibid., 2, p. 436. The Imperial Université, established over the years between 1806-1808, differed from universities in anglophone countries. Presided over by a grand master, appointed by
Napoleon, it controlled all education from the universities to the primary schools, and included
administration, university staff, schoolmasters, inspectors etc. At this stage, it was not opposed
to the Church; the grand master, Louis de Fontanes, a friend of Chateaubriand, regarded religion as the heart of all society.
12. Lyonnet, *Le cardinal Fesch, archevêque de Lyon...*, vol. 2, (Lyon, 1841), pp 365-77.
13. OM, doc. 852, 3. On Colin's illnesses during his studies see OM 4, pp 523-5.

This serious illness took place probably during his first year at Alix, in 1809-10. Apparently he was ill again that year and had to put hot plasters on his leg. Fathers Lagniet and Maîtrepierre related later that he was again at death's doors. These frequent illnesses made his seminary life both difficult and prolonged, and cast a shadow over his future health. At Alix, however, the superior was a young priest in his early thirties, Nicolas-Augustin de la Croix d'Azolette, who had studied medicine for a while at Paris, before entering the seminary. Ordained in 1805, he was appointed superior of Alix in September 1810, at the beginning of Colin's second year there. Noticing that Colin looked unwell he called him up and questioned him. Having cleared it with the rest of the staff, he took the decision that Colin was to attend only the New Testament class and that he was to come every morning to the kitchen for a cup of hot cocoa. On the days that he did not come, the cocoa was brought to him at the classroom door. More grateful to Father Azolette than he could tell, Colin never forgot this kindness. 'If I had followed my heart,' he told Mayet, 'I would have thrown myself around his neck and hugged him. But imagine the embarrassment of a poor young lad from the country, all shyness and timidity.'[14] As well as easing the burden of classes and giving him some more nourishment, Azolette, by taking his illnesses seriously, had given him the psychological support he needed with his superiors and classmates, when his illnesses were weighing him down and making him feel an exception. His health improved, things appear to have gone well for him and the following year he took the first prizes in his class of some twenty-eight students.

He recorded one embarrassing episode during his years at Alix. Although Pierre Colin paid for Jean-Claude's upkeep, it was Jean, the eldest brother, who advanced the sum to the seminary. For once, the money was late in coming. Urged by one of the professors, the superior reproached Colin and, perhaps, his family. Colin was mortified. Although just recovering from a severe illness, he set out on the nine or ten kilometres to the family vineyard at Gleizé, near the town of Villefranche. There he borrowed 200 francs, and returned with it to the superior saying: 'Here is the payment for my keep,' adding somewhat proudly, 'and if more is needed, I could get it.' The superior and the professor, in particular, were taken aback and ashamed that they had cast doubt on the ability or willingness of the Colins to acquit their debts and apologised again and again to the young Colin.[15]

It was at Alix that Colin took another hesitant step towards the priesthood. A decision of Fesch was responsible. Fesch knew that some parents, although they did not intend their sons for the priesthood and knew full well that their

14. OM, doc. 501. Nicolas-Augustin de la Croix d'Azolette (1779-1861), superior of Alix, 1810; director at Saint-Irénée, 1812-17; bishop of Gap, 1837; archbishop of Auch, 1840.
15. OM, docs. 752, 7; 852, 4.

sons had no such intention either, nevertheless sent them to the seminary to obtain a good education. Precious places in the seminary, often financed by seminary bourses, which should have gone to genuine candidates for the priest-hood, were thus taken up. In a burst of anger during a council meeting, Fesch decreed that once students entered 3rd class, that is three years before complet-ing their secondary studies, and had passed a year's testing in the seminary, they would have to take tonsure.[16] To put this measure into practice he drove out to Alix a few days later and, on 23 May 1812, conferred tonsure on twenty-seven students. Colin was among them. Although tonsure was but a small step on the road to the priesthood, it did confer the clerical state. So it came about that, despite his protestations earlier and, indeed later, Colin had taken an official canonical step towards the priesthood.

To save as many seminarians as he could from what he regarded as the unsuitable atmosphere of the lycées, Fesch, in a bold move, decided, on his own authority, to reopen one of the minor seminaries and to cram as many of the senior students into it as could possibly profit from the classes. The semi-nary he chose was in the little village of Verrières, in the extreme south-west of the diocese. Since the village was up in the hilly country of the Woods of Forez, its remoteness meant that it was less liable to come under police scrutiny. If the gendarmes came and asked questions, the college could be fairly presented to be an adjunct of the major seminary of Saint-Irénée, since already the students in it had advanced to the level of philosophy. They even wore the soutane, a sign that they were already on the way to the priesthood. If the seminary's remoteness kept it safe from prying eyes, its location on the side of a steep hill, and, more especially, the general state of the building, made it an austere train-ing-ground. Verrières is yet another indicator of the determination of French Catholics, lay and clerical, to provide priests for their Church. In 1804, Father Pierre Périer, who like Gardette had been imprisoned during the Revolution, had established a school to prepare young boys for the priesthood, in his pres-bytery of Verrières and its adjoining barn. The 'seminary' was primitive enough. 'An attic, beneath the roof of tiles, served as our dormitory', one student described it a few years earlier, 'we climbed up there on a ladder. The badly-fitting windows could only be closed with papers. We froze there in the winter and suffocated in the summer.' During the recreations they would go round to the neighbouring farms to beg a little straw to block up the gaping holes that the wind and the rain had pierced in the worm-eaten roofs.[17] A generous woman,

16. OM, doc. 18. In the French system of education 3rd year corresponds approximately to 4th form (United Kingdom), 4th year intermediate (Ireland), 11th grade (USA). In France students progress from 8th year up to 1st year whereas in the other systems it is the reverse: the students progress from 1st to 6th (if secondary school only is taken into account) or from 1st to 12th.
17. J. M. Chausse, *Vie de M. l'Abbé Jean-Louis Duplay...*, vol. 1, (Lyon, 1887) pp 78-9.

Antoinette Montet, concerned at the paucity of priests, gave Father Périer 23,000 francs with which he was able to buy, in 1809, the nearby castle of Soleillant to enlarge the seminary.[18] Yet the buildings were so inadequate that a few years later, in 1816, a new building was erected in their place. The food was also inadequate. So, too, was the training provided, for when Bochard visited the college in 1809, his report, in sharp contrast to that on Saint-Jodard, was severely critical of the staff, the studies and the general atmosphere. In that year, however, new staff had been appointed with Jean-Joseph Barou as superior and the college gained a good reputation in the area.[19] The year 1812 was a crisis year for the seminary. With the sudden closure of the other five seminaries, two hundred and thirty were crowded into these unsatisfactory premises. Fesch had decided to push them ahead as soon as possible lest he lose them in the Université or through conscription into the army. His decision meant bringing in students who had not finished their secondary studies, some having as much as two more years to do. The different standards of achievement of this large and motley intake made it difficult for Barou and his handful of young professors, many of whom were scarcely older than some of the students, to cope. It was during this year, too, that the seminarians, like the rest of France, learned of the disastrous retreat from Moscow as the remnant of Napoleon's Grande Armée of 600,000 men struggled home. Many of the hundreds of thousands who died in the snows of Russia would have been the same age as the seminarians in Verrières and some certainly would have been known to them.

For the Marists Verrières had another significance, for it was there that most of those who became involved in the Marist project met one another for the first time. Marcellin Champagnat, Philippe Janvier, Jean Pierre Perrault-Mainand, Étienne Terraillon, Étienne Déclas, Jean-Baptiste Seyve and Colin were all there in 1812. Jean-Claude Courveille, too, may have been there the year before, but had probably already moved to Le Puy. Perhaps the sympathy that Barou showed later towards the Marists dates from this time.

By 1812, when after a one-year stay Colin left Verrières, he had spent nine years at the minor seminary and was 22 years of age. He had entered Saint-Jodard when he was fourteen, an age when most of the boys at Saint-Bonnet would have started to work on the farms and at the looms. Nine years later, even those who had gone on for a career, such as teaching, would have long finished their training. Many of them would have gone off to Russia with rifle and pack. During that long period when he had changed from boyhood to manhood, Colin's youth had been passed in a totally different world. What had the minor seminary given him during this malleable stage of life that is one's adolescence? His last year in the minor seminary may be the moment to try to piece

18. Chausse, *Duplay,* vol. 1, p. 78.
19. Chausse, *Duplay,* vol. 1, pp 91-2, 104-5.

together and reflect on what had been happening to him, particularly in what for him was the most important area of his life – his 'vocation' or relationship with God. Of necessity, this account of the young man's development is as superficial as any attempt to gain access to another person's mind and soul must be. Since, moreover, Colin has left no full account of his life in the minor seminary, the attempt to reconstruct it must rely on whatever scraps of information he and others give us later in life and on what is known of the type of training given in minor seminaries.

What the seminary set out to do was to form him spiritually in readiness for the priesthood. It would have brought home to him that the cleric was a man apart whose first care was not this world. Austere superiors, like Gardette, strict observers of the rule, would have impressed on him the importance of a disciplined lifestyle, of obedience and piety. The rule was of central importance. Faithfulness to the rule has always been, since St Benedict's time, a hallmark of the devout monk and, when the Council of Trent decreed that seminaries be set up to train young men for the priesthood, this monastic reverence for 'holy rule' was made part of the training. Colin was a faithful disciple of that rule incarnate, Father Gardette. So exact was he that the seminary authorities appointed him 'censeur', a type of prefect or monitor whose unenviable job it was to supervise his fellow-students in the study-hall and the dormitory. In this difficult, often unpopular task, he was not severe – he was reprimanded for being too easy – but, on one occasion, he insisted that a student change his way or else he would inform his parents. Typically, too, he was cautious almost to a fault on matters of modesty and, morning and night, insisted on closing the windows and shutters despite the protests of his companions.

The daily regime was much the same as in Saint-Jodard, mass, spiritual reading, hymns, rosaries, edifying reading at every meal. Colin's reading influenced his spiritual development at that youthful and impressionable stage, when, for the first time, he had the opportunity to read, seek guidance and reflect on his spiritual life. For his personal formation, Colin would have been expected to go regularly to the spiritual director of the seminary, to discuss with him his spiritual development and listen to his advice and monition. As regards the spiritual books which Colin chose personally to nurture his devotional life, some evidence exists. His sisters sent him, when he was in 3rd class at Alix – which since he repeated that class twice could be anytime between autumn 1809 and spring 1811 – a present that was to mean much to him. It was a parcel of books. Two were the works of Henry-Marie Boudon, the well-known 17th century writer who had been archdeacon of Évreux.[20] Those were *God Alone* and *The Love of Jesus in the most holy sacrament of the altar.* His sisters had chosen well. There could be no more welcome gift for their pious and

20. OM, docs 574, 488, 499.

studious little brother. Together with Francis de Sales' *The spiritual director of devout and religious souls,* which one of his teachers had given him during the school year 1806-7, he treasured those books and for years they were his constant companions. Of Boudon's *God Alone,* he said later: 'I carried it on me for ten years; it never left me.'[21] This attractively written little book placed all its emphasis, as its title revealed, on God alone whom one should love for his own sake, in total disinterestedness. God's interests and God's will must always be placed first. Colin knew Boudon's two books by heart. Francis de Sales' *Directory* consisted in extracts from the saint's letters and this, too, Colin learned by heart. In addition to the New Testament, other spiritual works he knew inside out were *The Imitation of Christ* and *The Spiritual Combat.*[22] He was also very fond of *Meditations on the Passion of our Lord Jesus Christ for every day of the month* by Rebeyrolis. This was a manual of an association in honour of the passion of Our Lord that met in the church of the Joséphistes of Lyon.[23] He had wanted to use Rebeyrolis for meditation but the superior of Alix, Gilbert Durand, would not allow him. Probably, Colin disliked the somewhat mechanical fashion in which it was customary to read out points of meditation to the seminarians and would have preferred to continue his own meditation in an unbroken fashion, for he tells us that later at Saint-Irénée he found the seminary practice boring.[24] With those authors Colin was squarely in the tradition of Catholic spirituality. In general, the spirituality of these books is the theology of the cross and of self-denial. Not for them the expansive humanistic spirituality of the modern era.

The seminary was first and foremost a school for forming pious and obedient priests. Intellectual studies and especially personal human development were subordinate to that. In addition to spiritual matters, there was, nevertheless, much else that a nineteenth-century cleric was expected to acquire. A proper deportment, seriousness of manner and correct behaviour were all part of his training. There were also the 'secular' studies to enable the young student to lay the groundwork for his theology and to properly represent the priesthood. At Saint-Jodard, Alix and Verrières, the students would have acquired a good grounding in the classics, particularly in Latin. French grammar and carefully vetted literature were also studied. There were inadequacies, as Colin's comments

---

21. OM, doc. 499, addition l.
22. OM, doc. 499, l implies as much.
23. *Méditations sur la passion de notre Seigneur Jésus-Christ, pour chaque jour du mois, en forme d'élévations.* OM 2, p. 225, footnote 2. Figure 48 in OM 2, is a reproduction of the cover of the book. For a discussion of the influence of those and other works on Colin's understanding of humility, see C. Girard, 'On the Sources of Colin's Teaching on Humility', *Forum Novum,* 4 (1998), 257-93.
24. OM, doc. 499, addition p.

in 1846 on the teaching in the seminaries and the pressure to which the students were subjected reveal:

> In our minor seminaries, the attention paid to French grammar is not sufficient. What good is your knowledge if you drive people away by speaking badly … I know I make many mistakes and I do not set myself up as a model … I would have so much wished to be in your place! It was not possible, the Revolution was just over, and there was pressure, pressure on studies so as to provide priests quickly. Latin was everything.[25]

Colin's remarks, though at a distance of almost forty years, reveal the role he saw for secular studies and at the same time the pressure to shorten these studies that existed in his day. Yet although it was to be expected that, with the shortage of priests after the Revolution, some priests would be formed in haste, the period of nine years that Colin had spent in the minor seminary was a considerable amount of time. The Revolution, however, as he implies, had upset the schooling that he and others should have received before entering. Seminary staff, as was their wont, bemoaned the poorly-educated students they had to work with.

Despite his disclaimer, Colin always did well and in the class of humanity, took first place in French composition.[26] He was bright and worked hard and methodically. For each course he would write a summary and then use the summaries for revision work.[27] He had his priorities, however, and to make sure that his studies did not distract him from God, he used put little signs in different parts of the lesson to mark where he would make an act of love, or humility or abandonment.[28]

In the last year of his minor seminary training, at Verrières, Colin studied Logic. This difficult year was the beginning of philosophical studies and its aim was to teach the young men the art of thinking clearly and judging soundly. The Logic class was divided into two divisions. In the first were Marcellin Champagnat and Étienne Terraillon. The 2nd division of Logic, amounting to some 130 students, had among its ranks Déclas, John Mary Vianney and Colin. John Mary Vianney was a slow learner and admitted later in life that he had suffered at Verrières probably as a result of his difficulties in study.[29] Colin again proved himself very bright. Despite his many illnesses he had no diffi-

---

25. Colin to confrères, 20 Oct. 1846, Mayet, 'Mémoires', 5, pp. 546-8.
26. OM, doc. 739, 2.
27. OM, doc. 571.
28. OM, doc. 545, 3.
29. Gardette was one of those who arranged for him to receive help and Jean-Marie Mioland, the professor of sacred scripture and master of ceremonies, gave him lessons. Chausse, *Duplay*, vol. 1, p. 212; F. Trochu, *The Curé d'Ars: Saint Jean-Marie-Baptiste Vianney, 1786-1859* (London, 1927), p. 80.

culty in keeping at the top of the class.[30] His conduct was noted as 'very good' and his character 'good'.

There was a final part in the training provided by the minor seminary that Colin missed out on. It happened this way. Normally, students were expected to spend an extra year after Logic studying 'physics', which was more or less the equivalent of mathematics. With a view to making class-numbers smaller and standards higher, the seminary authorities exempted weaker students and older students from this second year and allowed them to go directly, after one year's Logic, to the major seminary of Saint-Irénée, there to begin the final years of theology. John Mary Vianney qualified for this exemption. Since Colin was such a bright student the seminary authorities intended him to take that extra year. For reasons that he never disclosed, however, he petitioned for an exemption and it was granted. It was an action that he regretted in later life for it left a gap in his education. When later he was in the college at Belley, he was unable to accompany students in mathematics. For the immediate future, however, his successful plea for exemption meant that after one year of Logic in Verrières, he went on, in 1813, to begin theology at Saint-Irénée. Willy-nilly, for at this stage, at the age of twenty-three and after nine years in a minor seminary, one cannot call it unwittingly, Colin was hastening to a new and sharper crisis in his hesitant and long-protracted journey towards his choice of life. He could temporise no longer. To enter a major seminary, whose only and immediate purpose was to prepare for the priesthood, meant that finally the moment of decision could not be much longer delayed. It was to arrive sooner than he expected.

30. OM, doc. 22.

CHAPTER 6

Saint-Irénée: Studies and Subdiaconate

'Then I went to the major seminary, I have no idea how; and then I found myself a deacon, and again I have no idea how.' *Jean-Claude Colin to Mayet, 'Mémoires' Mayet, 1838-9.*

At the end of that summer of 1813, Jean-Claude Colin, repeating his routine of the previous nine years, packed his bags and set off for the seminary.[1] He was happy as usual to leave a 'world' where he did not feel at home and, with perhaps insufficient thought to where it was leading him, to return to the seminary, his chosen place of solitude with God. This time, however, there were differences. The seminary he was now going to was the seminary proper, the major seminary of Saint-Irénée for which Saint-Jodard, Alix and Verrières were but preparatory schools. All studies here were directly geared towards the priesthood. The students, too, having survived the many years of minor seminary, where many were either weeded out or left voluntarily, were young men in their late teens or early twenties. They were now on the point of taking a mature decision to seek ordination.

The major seminary of Lyon was located in the capital of the diocese. Lyon was a proud city with a long history. Originally Lugdunum, the *dún* or fortress of the Celtic God, Lugda, it had been developed by Greek settlers and Roman invaders before the Christian era. Christianity had taken firm and early root there. It was in Lyon that in 177 the first martyrs of Gaul, the bishop Pothinus and the heroic slave-girl, Blandina, and their companions had died for the faith. A free city of the Holy Roman Empire during the middle ages, though governed in fact by its archbishop, Lyon had become a centre for bankers who came there from Florence. Later it became the silk-capital of Europe. Lyon had suffered much during the wars of religion when Catholic and Huguenot struggled for mastery. It suffered even when, in 1793, the Jacobin army had taken the city after a bloody siege of two months and executed many of its citizens in

---

1. Three important unpublished studies for this chapter are: D. J. Grange, 'Le recrutement du clergé au séminaire de Saint-Irénée de Lyon de 1801-1815' (Faculty of canon Law, Lyon, doctoral degree, 1955); L. Alonso, 'La formación intelectual de Juan Claudio Colin en el Seminario de S. Ireneo de Lyon, 1 nov. 1813-22 julio 1816' (Pontifical Gregorian University thesis, 1964) and G-M Bouchard, 'La Prédication morale de Jean-Claude Colin: période 1816-1829 (Pontifical Lateran University, doctoral thesis, 1973).

cold blood. The very name of Lyon was abolished. When the Jacobins fell from power, Lyon suffered a new terror, as the enemies of the Jacobins took their revenge on them. Not until the signing of the Concordat of 1801 did peace and prosperity begin to return to the city.

It was to this great city that Colin came on All Saints Day 1813 to spend the final three years of his training for the priesthood. The difference between Lyon and the tiny village of Saint-Bonnet, where he had come from, or Saint-Jodard, Alix and the backwoods hamlet of Verrières, where he had studied up to this, could not have been greater. Lyon was the metropolis of south-eastern France, second only to Paris in importance, with a population of 121,000. Situated on the confluence of two great rivers, the Rhone and the Saone, it boasted majestic buildings, banks, parks, churches, offices of the 'department' or local government, an archiepiscopal palace, walled-in gardens of the well-to-do Lyonese silk-merchants, traders and bankers. The high walls of these properties concealed the unmistakable signs of the renewed wealth of its business class, for Lyon was enjoying an economic revival. Napoleon had been generous to the city and its commerce had flourished, its silk industry, aided by new technology, had made rapid progress. The city resounded to reconstruction works including that of the restoration of the great central city-square, Place Bellecour, now nearing completion.

The seminary of Saint-Irénée was the largest in France. Its name was a reminder of the antiquity of Christianity in France for the Greek-born Irenaeus, the first great Catholic theologian, had been bishop of Lyon in the second century and was believed to have suffered a martyr's death about the year 200. The seminary, begun in 1659 by the Sulpicians, had been closed by the Revolution, but reopened after the signing of the Concordat in 1801. The Sulpicians, renowned as directors of seminaries, had again taken charge until Napoleon had suppressed them in December 1811. The archbishop of Lyon, Cardinal Fesch, then appointed Colin's old hero, Father Cabuchet, now curé of Mornant, as superior. Cabuchet found the position too burdensome and returned to his parish where he died a year later. Fesch replaced him in 1812 with Father Gardette who, after being superior in Saint-Jodard, had come to Saint-Irénée as bursar and lecturer in holy scripture. Gardette was to remain superior there until 1841 and to exercise an unparalleled influence on future generations of Lyonese priests. Some of the staff were young priests of the diocese, recalled from Saint-Sulpice in Paris, and, like Gardette, anxious to run the college on the Sulpician lines they knew and valued. The seminary had changed its location since Pius VII visited it in 1804 and was again on its original site at the Place Croix-Paquet, on the right bank of the Rhone, whose waves lapped its walls in earlier days. The building itself was not an elegant one for it consisted in a number of buildings joined together to form an irregular four-storey edifice with a mansard or courbed-roof attic. Since it was scarcely adequate for the number of students, Saint-Irénée's two hundred and fifty seminarians were crammed two or three to a room. Yet it was better than most seminaries in France, for, from the time he became archbishop of Lyon, Fesch had lavished care and money on his seminaries and especially on Saint-Irénée. Writing to his vicar-general in 1805 he explained his vision. 'The seminary of Lyon must be great, commodious, noble; we should not plan according to our present means; our hopes should be more splendid; our successors will make them a reality, perhaps even ourselves.'[2] A year later he made an urgent plea to his nephew, the emperor, for generous support for Saint-Irénée. 'Sire, seminaries are too important a matter for a … government that the outlay already made of 30,000 livres should deter you. You have desired to establish at Lyon a seminary that would serve as the model for others.'[3]

After Napoleon sent him home to his diocese in 1812, Fesch's enforced presence at Lyon meant that he was free to become more involved in the affairs of the diocese, particularly in the running of seminaries and in recruitment. This direct involvement, however, had its disadvantages. Anxious to build up the number of priests, Fesch accepted candidates too easily. He used to cite the words of the master, whose attitude towards the unwilling guests in the parable of the wedding feast, was: '*Compelle intrare*' 'Force them to come in'.[4] Even his admiring biographer cited him as saying: 'It is better to have donkeys labour in the Lord's vineyard than that it remain untended'.[5] He also took a decision on the calls to holy orders which was to create problems for the seminary staff and raise anxiety among the students. For Colin it was to become a full-blown crisis.

It arose over the simple matter of requests by some students asking permission to postpone their decision to go on for the priesthood. When these requests came up at a meeting of the episcopal council at Lyon on 18 November 1812, Fesch became enraged. There and then he decreed that seminarians entering Saint-Irénée from the minor seminaries must take holy orders the following Christmas or pack their bags forthwith. There was some justification for his precipitous action. Since 1808, the state provided 1,360 bourses of 400 francs each which could be, and often were, divided into half-bourses. As a result, up to one third of the seminarians benefited from government grants. The seminaries could compete with the newly-formed lycées or state secondary schools, and, if students who had no intention of going on for the priesthood were using them simply as a way of cheap education, and perhaps avoiding military

---

2. Fesch to Jauffret, 29 Feb. 1804, Jomand, *Fesch*, p. 44.
3. Fesch to Napoleon, 21 May, 25 June 1805, Jomand, *Fesch*, pp. 46-7.
4. S. Cattet, *La vérité sur le Cardinal Fesch, ou réflexions d'un ancien vicaire-général de Lyon sur l'histoire de son éminence par M. l'Abbé Lyonnet* (Lyon, 1842), p. 168.
5. Lyonnet, *Fesch*, vol. 2, p. 395.

service into the bargain, the government could react. Anti-clericals within the imperial cabinet viewed the progress of the seminaries with jaundiced eyes and, eager for any opportunity to discredit them, would seize this as an opening. Fesch's action reflected his unwillingness to jeopardise the future of his seminary as well as his determination not to waste the diocese's resources of money and manpower educating students who would never be priests. At the same time, since holy orders conferred an exemption from conscription, he was ensuring that they would not be drafted at a time when Napoleon, desperate to build up a new army to replace the half-million soldiers lost that winter in the snows of Russia, was only too ready to seize recruits wherever he could find them.

Whatever the reasons for Fesch's decision, it was unwise. Up to the Second Vatican Council, the major orders that preceded the priesthood were subdiaconate and deaconate. Once a student had taken those orders he was regarded as committed for life to the priesthood. A dispensation from subdiaconate was rarely given and more rarely still from the deaconate. By insisting that the students apply for the major orders almost immediately after their entry to the major seminary, Fesch was making it difficult for the staff of Saint-Irénée. Within the space of a very few weeks of his entry into the major seminary, they would have to assess a student's aptitude for the priesthood at what was the critical and sensitive stage of final preparation. For the student, too, it was unfair to be rushed into applying for major orders within a few weeks of his entry into the major seminary. As a student approaches such a decisive step, he is often beset by anxiety, fearing, on the one hand, that he may not be called, and, on the other, hesitating before the awesome finality of his choice. When a whole class in a seminary is called to ordination at the same time, group tension can take a grip and upset the more scrupulous student. Imprudent actions on the part of those responsible for the calls could intensify the tension. Inexperienced in dealing with seminarians and too imperious to listen to wiser counsels, Fesch, by precipitating them into a major life-decision immediately after entry into the major seminary, was placing them under undue pressure at a most critical moment. He was also antagonising his own experienced staff.[6]

Perhaps the staff put pressure on him, because Fesch apparently made concessions in that winter of 1812 and his decree was not rigorously applied. In the school year of 1813, however, the decree was strictly enforced. This was the year that Colin joined Saint-Irénée, blithely unaware of any problem. Within a short time of arriving there, he and his classmates were told of the archbishop's decision concerning sub-diaconate and they were summoned to apply for this major order by Christmas. Colin was aghast at the announcement. Up to this he had been able to bury his head in the sand and postpone a decision on the

6. Cattet, *La vérité sur Fesch,* pp 164-7.

priesthood, while remaining in the congenial atmosphere of seminary life to study and pray to his heart's content. Now the hour of decision had struck and there was no escape. As in the first communion crisis, and later when Father Odin asked him directly to begin studies for the priesthood, the imminence of the step appalled him. Again he panicked. How could he, who in his heart felt that he did not want to go ahead for the priesthood, take the subdiaconate? Was he not cheating the diocese of the funds spent on him? Desperate, he hurried to see his spiritual director to have him take his name off the list for ordination. His director, Jean Cholleton, a young priest barely two years older than him, advised him to let his name remain.[7] Colin was not satisfied. Then began a struggle. He came back no less than fifteen times to knock at Cholleton's door until, finally, his harassed director was forced to close the door on him. Thwarted there, Colin made his way to the superior, Gardette, who had known him since his days at Saint-Jodard. An agitated Colin threw himself on his knees before him to beg to be taken off the list. Gardette replied kindly but told him that if he did that, Cardinal Fesch would be furious with him, and reminded Colin that if he did not take orders, he might have to join the army. 'Well then,' replied an agonising Colin, 'I prefer to join the army!' Having failed with Cholleton and Gardette, there was only one last resource for Colin – an appeal to the master of ceremonies who was responsible for drawing up the list of those to be called by the bishop on ordination day. The master of ceremonies was Father Jean-Marie Mioland, a kindly man who cared much for the students, and to him Colin now had recourse.[8] Mioland listened to him and, to Colin's relief and joy, agreed to take his name off the list of ordinands. This euphoria lasted only two days. It was replaced by a period of self-blame as he began to reproach himself for acting for his own satisfaction. He had no rest until he went again to see his director. Cholleton was kind, did not reproach him but heard him out and then advised him to put his name back on the list. He did so and, on 6 January 1814, the feast of the Epiphany, Fesch conferred minor orders and subdiaconate on him and thirty-three others. It is to this traumatic episode that Colin referred when he told Mayet, a quarter of a century later, of his bewilderment: 'Then I went to the major seminary, I have no idea how, and then I found myself a subdeacon, and again I have no idea how.'[9]

The episode is revealing. Colin again found it difficult to take a decision.

7. Jean Cholleton (1788-1852), professor of moral theology and spiritual director at Saint-Irénée, 1811; involved in founding the Society for the Propagation of the Faith; vicar general of Lyon, 1824-40; Marist profession, 1841.
8. Jean-Marie Mioland (1788-1859) master of ceremonies and director at Saint-Irénée; first superior of the Missionaries of France at Lyon, 1816; bishop of Amiens, 1838; archbishop of Toulouse, 1851.
9. OM, doc. 499, 4.

Undoubtedly, since applying for subdiaconate involved a life's orientation, his hesitation was understandable, yet he must have seen the moment of decision approaching over the previous ten years. Why the hesitation even now at the comparatively advanced age of twenty-three? Was it a flight from reality or a timidity of character? Probably, that vulnerability which had pursued him from his orphaned and troubled childhood still persisted. He felt insecure. Yet when Mioland agreed and the decision was thrown back on Colin, and he knew that it was up to him to leave or stay, he took his decision maturely, unselfishly and decisively. He does not tell us how he felt after the decision was taken but implies that he regained his peace of soul. He never looked back. The die was cast, for from now on he was heading for the same career as his brother, Pierre, who had been a priest of the diocese of Lyon since 1810. Given the strength with which, over almost ten years, he had refused to take such a decision, its importance for his future cannot be underestimated. Later on he would implicitly see it as God's guiding hand.

Little enough is known about Colin's life in the seminary in Lyon except that he was often ill. The climate of Lyon was not healthy for it was one of extremes. A perpetual fog overcast the sky in the winter and the fog and mist, caused by the confluence of the Rhone and Saone, brought temperatures that could drop well below freezing point. In the summer the sun in a clear blue sky burned stronger than in the Riviera and the humidity bred mosquitoes in abundance. In the seminary, physical exercise and sports, especially, had a minuscule role in the curriculum. There was a pleasant, tree-lined garden in the seminary but it scarcely provided sufficient recreation ground for the huge number of students. On Wednesday afternoons they could go to the seminary's country house and, come Easter, they could go there for the whole day. When walks in the city were permitted they might wander along the tree-flanked banks of the two great rivers, the Rhone and the Saone, visit the many old and beautiful churches – the great medieval Cathedral of Saint-Jean, the sober Gothic church of Saint-Paul and the flamboyant Gothic of Saint-Nizier, perhaps the most lively parish in Lyon and a hotbed of religious fervour. They would have climbed the eight or nine hundred steps to the sanctuary of Our Lady of Fourvière – become since Pius VII re-consecrated it in 1805 a much-frequented place of pilgrimage – prayed before the statue of the Virgin – the Black Madonna – and enjoyed the panorama of the city stretched out beneath them. The seminarians would have been quite conspicuous as they walked in a long crocodile through the streets. All the while they would have worn the long, heel-length black soutane, which, despite a law forbidding it, Fesch insisted that they wear from minor seminary days on. These outings and walks, if monotonous and restricted, at least helped to keep them healthy.

The principal aim of a seminary was to produce pious priests and the spiritual exercises were the chosen means. Immediately after arriving in the seminary, Colin would have made a retreat that was intended to set the tone for the year. From then on the seminary followed an unchanging routine. The seminarians rose at 5 a.m. during the winter and at 4.30 a.m. from Easter on. The daily routine of devotion began with morning meditation which was read out point by point. Then followed daily Mass in Latin. Strict restrictions were imposed on receiving Holy Communion but, with their directors' permission, subdeacons could receive twice a week and deacons could receive three times a week. Only the very devout student would be permitted by his director to receive daily communion. After breakfast, the rest of the morning was occupied with class. Before the midday meal the seminarian made a quarter of an hour examination of conscience centring on a particular failing. This 'particular' examination was modelled on a much-esteemed work of the 17th century Sulpician, Louis Tronson, *Particular Examinations on Diverse Subjects,* which placed emphasis on the rule, regularity and separation from the world.[10] The Divine Office, recited – again in Latin – at different times of the day, would take an hour and a half. Subdeacons and deacons were under a strict obligation to recite it and to omit even a part of it was considered a serious fault. The Office, as its name implies, was seen more as a daily obligation than scriptural nourishment for the soul, although the recitation of the psalms could be for some an excellent book of prayer. Spiritual reading preceded the evening meal and that was followed by evening prayer at 8.30 p.m. 'Lights out' followed shortly afterwards.

More formal training in spirituality came from the conferences of the superiors. Gardette would have used them to insist on the virtue of obedience and, in the first instance, to the rule. In one conference he told the students:

> Obedience to the rule implies humility, self-denial, constant sacrifice of one's own interests, depriving oneself of a thousand things agreeable to nature. The practice of the rule is the equivalent of an incessant prayer and of faithfully relating all one's actions to God.[11]

For Gardette, as for many other directors, even the humble seminary rule partook to some degree of the dignity of the 'Rule' which for many great founders, like St Francis of Assisi, was regarded as an expression of the will of God and its observance was the asceticism that led to personal sanctity. During the whole period of his stay Colin would have been expected to observe the rule exactly and promptly, even to stop in the middle of forming a letter if the bell summoned him elsewhere. He would also receive personal guidance from a spiritual director to whom he went for counsel, to report on his spiritual

---

10. L.Tronson, *Examens particuliers sur divers sujets, propres aux ecclésiastiques...* (Lyon, 1690; revised edition, 1740). I. Noye, 'Tronson', *Dictionnaire de Spiritualité,* vol. 15, (Paris, 1991) cols. 1329-33.
11. Grange, 'Recrutement', p. 60.

progress and to draw up a rule for his hours outside of class. Colin went to Cholleton, whose advice he valued even during his early years as a curate. During their private study, the students were expected to read other spiritual works such as the works of Rodríguez, Olier and Tronson.[12] Colin used the long vacation to read a number of spiritual works and in Saint-Irénée he discovered a new favourite, *Treatise on self-contempt* by Giuseppe Franchi, an 18th century Italian spiritual writer.[13] Franchi's long list of humiliations that the follower of Christ is asked to accept could appear almost masochistic by modern standards. To take one example, Franchi wanted the true follower to desire that:

> Everyone should be in agreement in despising him and attacking him scurrilously so that there is no limit to the flagrant insults he receives, not only to his reputation and to the esteem … that the public had for him but also to the extent that his soul is loaded with grief, affliction, and bitter anguish, so that his body is violently beaten and countless times mistreated so that his health is markedly damaged, so that his wealth is attacked and his property is stolen until it is totally gone.[14]

Franchi's work, however, must be seen both in its totality and in the context of the time. Its overall aim is to give his reader the strength that comes from indifference to what other people think. Colin, some twenty years later, made two interesting disclosures on his character and the good effect Franchi had on it as he recalled the profit the book brought him:

> You know my character: great vivacity, great activity. Well, this book worked in me such restfulness in my nothingness, a joy of being nothing, such a peace, to such an extent that during my time at the major seminary I was seen as slow. I boiled over; but the contempt for myself was working on me, I saw myself as nothing. I am too fortunate, I reflected, especially when I suffered dryness, I am so happy that God should endure me in his presence.[15]

---

12. Alfonso Rodríguez (1538-1616), Jesuit, wrote *Ejercicio de perfección y virtudes cristianas* (Seville, 1609) which remained a favourite ascetical work until well into the 20th century. Jean-Jacques Olier (1608-57), founder of the Society of Saint-Sulpice, devoted himself to the training of priests. His spirituality highlighted the divinity rather than the humanity of Christ and emphasised the necessity of self-abasement.

13. OM, docs 471, 2; 550, 1; 726, 1. Giuseppe Ignazio Franchi (1712-1778), a member of the Oratory of St Philip Neri, seminary superior and spiritual director. The work Colin valued so highly was *Traité de l'amour du mépris de soi-même* (Lyon, 1803) which was a translation of the 3rd edition of *Sull'amore al proprio disprezzo* (Lucca, 1774). For its influence on Colin, see R. Struminski, 'Father Colin and the love of self-contempt', *Forum Novum* 2 (1992-94), 196-209; Girard, 'Sources', pp 257-93. As Charles Girard points out, a more accurate English version of the title would be 'loving acceptance of the status in which one is held in a well-deserved contempt', a description that sums up well the thrust of the work.

14. Franchi, *Traité de l'amour du mépris*, pp. 58-9.

15. OM, doc. 471, 2.

More intriguing still is the forthright self-criticism, which he made a few years later. 'People accused me of everything, that I was headstrong, opinionated … The good Lord gave me the grace of getting to know Franchi and in it I found a really great peace. In the major seminary I suffered; well, then I found peace. The love of contempt, now that is a mine of peace.'[16] What he meant by being regarded as slow or what he suffered in the major seminary he did not elaborate on. It could have been real or imagined slights or lack of recognition of his talents. Was it his fellow-students who regarded him as 'slow-moving' or did he imagine it? How fair his self-assessment was is also difficult to gauge. The indications one has point to a shy and retiring boy unsure of himself. The opinion of staff or students has not survived. Perhaps one can allow for some pious exaggeration in this self-portrait. Yet, much of his critical self-assessment reflected elements in his character that became evident enough later in life. Stubborn or tenacious he certainly was. His determination to pursue the project of a Society of Mary is an example. 'Opinionated' or, at least of strong opinions, he was also, and later in life he could erupt in anger when others supported ideas he disliked. His infectious vivacity was also evident from the sparkle and joy he brought to communities he visited. These traits may well have been there already in the seminary. His frequent reference to Franchi's book and his warm recommendation of it to others are proof of its influence on him. He wanted to be humble and Franchi brought him that peace and 'joy of being nothing'.

In teaching him to disregard other people's opinion of him, the ascetical practices recommended by Franchi could give him that inner self-confidence to cope with opposition and not let himself be daunted by criticism. If that were so, its influence would then be a liberating one. There was the danger, however, for an insecure young man living the enclosed, inward-looking life of a seminary, that the practices prescribed by Franchi, if followed too literally, could have had a crushing effect on his personality if not balanced by the rest of his spiritual life. Given the lack of first-hand evidence, it is not possible to go further than his own claim that it brought him profound peace. In later life, when he himself had matured and acquired more self-confidence, Franchi's influence helped him to free himself from human respect and allowed him to get on with the great task he had set himself. This is the impression that his many enthusiastic references to the book in the 1830s give.

Several priests closely supervised his training, over those three years. The man with the overall responsibility was the superior, the austere but well-loved Philibert Gardette, who had over a decade's experience of seminarians. Colin had great respect for him and, for his part, Gardette thought well of him for he encouraged him and gently pushed him forward when he panicked at the

16. OM, doc. 726.

thought of taking orders. An important member of the staff was Simon Cattet from whom Colin had classes every day. Fesch had sent Cattet in 1809 to study at the élite seminary of Saint-Sulpice in Paris but when the Sulpicians were expelled, he was recalled prematurely to Saint-Irénée, in November 1811. Ordained a month later at the age of twenty-three, he was appointed professor of dogma and immediately took up his teaching. As well as teaching dogma, Cattet would have taken his turn in giving the students the subjects for prayer. Gardette and Cattet, if one is to credit the over-critical vicar general, Bochard, were the two dominant members of the staff. Bochard complained that Gardette, despite his modest exterior, used to take control whenever matters did not go his way, and Cattet was both dour and stubborn. The two communicated their harsh manner to the rest of the staff.[17]

A man who had even more impact on Colin was a young priest, Jean Cholleton, who was his professor of moral theology, his confessor and his spiritual director. Cholleton's family was very much a 'Church' family; an uncle had been Fesch's vicar general and a sister a Benedictine abbess. Fesch had sent him, too, with his close friend Cattet, to study at Saint-Sulpice where the superior, Émery, and other professors had shown a high regard for his qualities. He, too, was recalled prematurely to Saint-Irénée, in November 1811, to take over the teaching of moral theology and was ordained a month later at the age of twenty-three. He immediately began teaching. Perhaps even more than the rest of the tiny staff at Saint-Irénée, he was overworked, preparing classes, providing spiritual direction for a great number of students, and giving conferences and retreats. At one point, in 1816, his health failed temporarily. Cholleton was an open, warm-hearted man, candid even to the point of naiveté. In a letter to Fesch in November 1814, in which he praised all the staff for their commitment, Gardette singled out Cholleton: 'Father Cholleton, in particular,' he wrote, 'succeeds perfectly in his area and has made himself beloved by all.'[18]

Jean-Marie Mioland, the priest in charge of ceremonies, was the youngest of the team. He had the disadvantage of having to lecture to his fellow-students for he was promoted professor just after he finished his course in Saint-Irénée. Yet, a kind man of distinguished manner, he was highly regarded by his fellow-students and colleagues for his intelligence and especially for his moderation and good judgement. Older than the others and more experienced was the director, Nicolas-Augustin de la Croix d'Azolette. He had been superior of the minor seminary at Alix, then promoted to the more important one at Argentière before being brought to Saint-Irénée in 1812. He had taken care of Colin at Alix and he continued to do so at Saint-Irénée. The sixth member of

17. Bochard to Fesch, 30 Nov 1814, Fesch Papers. Simon Cattet (1788-1858); vicar general, 1825; critic of Fesch and supporter of his successor, Archbishop de Pins.
18. Gardette to Fesch, 28 Dec 1814, fonds du séminaire de Lyon, lettres Fesch, OM, doc. 34.

the staff was the bursar, Father Mathieu Menaide, curate of Saint-Paul's in Lyon. A kindly and apostolic priest of considerable courage, he was – though a poor speaker – well read in the theology of the day and of sound judgement. These were the half-dozen who made up the staff with whom Colin came into daily contact. All in all, the members of the staff were pious, hard-working and talented and later gave signal service to the French Church.

What is striking about these men, selected to train young men for the ministry, is how young many of them were themselves. Apart, too, from Gardette, and perhaps Menaide and Azolette, none of these 'superiors' had real experience of the ministry or of the priestly life and its peculiar difficulties. The normal expectation in a seminary was that the professors would provide the young seminarians with the spiritual and theological equipment that would serve them for the rest of their lives. Here in Saint-Irénée, these young teachers were expected to counsel and direct the spiritual lives of students some of whom were older than they. Cholleton directed scores of students while teaching the full range of moral theology and then, after his illness, abandoned moral theology and, apparently without any special preparation, took over the teaching of doctrinal theology. Perhaps the zeal of these young men was expected to more than make up for their lack of experience; perhaps, too, they were a 'scratch' team got together after Napoleon had suppressed the Sulpicians. The fact that they came in after the well-liked Sulpicians generated criticism and added to their difficulties. Young and inexperienced though they were, they put their best efforts into their work, and Gardette could well tell Fesch that they formed a good and devoted team. Gradually, too, they won the esteem of the students.

Apart from the seminary staff, the archbishop, Cardinal Fesch, and the two vicars general to whom he confided most of the day-to-day running of the diocese, had a responsibility in Colin's formation. Fesch, who hoped to make his seminary the best in France, tended to take an authoritarian line from time to time, but he was seldom in Lyon. More annoying to the young staff was the constant interference of the vicar general charged with supervising seminaries, Claude-Marie Bochard. Deeply committed to his job, Bochard worked hard to re-organise seminaries in the diocese. For a while after the departure of the Sulpicians, which he welcomed, Bochard lived in the seminary and acted as superior. Later, after the appointment of a new team and new superior, he meddled in the details and, overstepping his supervisory role, interfered with the staff and criticised them to the archbishop, as being too 'Sulpician', too independent of diocesan authority, or too close to the students. He was conscious, too, of the needs of the diocese of Lyon, and set about forming a team of diocesan missioners, which he was to call 'Fathers of the Cross of Jesus'. While Colin was at the seminary, Bochard was casting around for likely recruits and he communicated his project to the students in the form of a leaflet, the *Pensée Pieuse*.[19] His jealous zeal for the success of his own diocesan scheme, together with his authoritarian temperament, made him sharply critical of any rival projects that might lure students away from service in the diocese. The other vicar general, Joseph Courbon, was a favourite of Fesch, and was able, by his good-humour and good sense, to deflect from the staff much of Bochard's interference and to allow them to get on with their demanding task.

Colin and his fellow-students were worked hard at their studies. After class, they were expected to go over together the ground covered, the so-called repetitions, and to make written summaries of the lessons. Even Sunday was not free, for on Sunday evening came the dreaded 'Dominicals' when certain students had to expound and defend theses. As if it were not daunting enough to stand up before the whole seminary, Cardinal Fesch habitually drove over, in full regalia, from his palace or summerhouse to listen to the young theologians. Napoleon, on one occasion, had scornfully but with some justification asked Fesch what did he know about theology anyway. This did not prevent the archbishop from demanding that his future priests give their full attention to their study of theology. Although the students' day began at 5 a.m. – after Easter a half-hour earlier – he wanted it to begin at four in order to pack in more study. The vicar general, Courbon, gently chided Fesch. With a nice sense of humour, he remarked that if a sleepy student were forced to study the ancient Fathers of the Church at that unearthly hour of the morning, he might let his candle fall and then the study of patrology would take place by the light of the cardinal's beloved seminary ablaze. Fesch dropped his idea.

Yet for all this drive for study, the majority of students were no theologians. Informing Fesch of the results of the end of the year examination in 1814, Gardette admitted: 'We were not so generally content with the examination of the first year students. Not from the point of view of study and application, but because very many are weak, some lacking the logic to reason things out, others the Latin to express themselves. Among them, however, there are from fifteen to twenty good subjects.'[20] Since Colin consistently had good marks, he would have been reckoned among the small band of 'good subjects'. Though he was often ill during his time in Saint-Irénée, he was a diligent student who scrupulously learned the class-work and made his own summaries which he carefully preserved. Some summaries that he made later survive and show with what care and thoroughness he worked. It is unlikely that he read any other textbooks, for such activity was not encouraged. Any further understanding of the 'revelation' that he acquired was probably through books of piety that depicted or imagined the lives of Jesus Christ and of the Blessed Virgin. The rather dry

19. The *Pensée Pieuse* is printed in OM, doc. 33. See, 'Bochard', OM 4, pp 198-200.
20. Fesch Papers, cited in footnote 1 to OM, doc. 25.

theology of his classes and the fervent devotional literature of his private reading were curiously juxtaposed. Perhaps having the same revered priest, Cholleton, as theology professor and spiritual director enabled them to retain the necessary balance and unity.

The studies, too, though demanding great application, good memory and sound logic, were not of a nature to stretch the mind of a bright student like Colin. Their purpose was not to stimulate him to serious theological speculation. Theology had become a vast rambling subject but the seminary course was rigidly narrow and whole areas, which would now be regarded as an integral part of the curriculum, were neglected. The history of the Church was ignored except insofar as the reading in the refectory filled in for it. Canon Law was also neglected. Liturgy was essentially a matter of rubrics and the correct celebration of the sacraments. Holy scripture fared marginally better. Yet there was no real exegesis of texts, the subject was regarded as a minor subject and carried no semestrial examination. Already in the minor seminary, Colin had classes in scripture. These were continued in Saint-Irénée by two classes a week given by Gardette or Mioland. Colin's grandfather used to tell the children stories from the Bible and Colin was attracted to the scriptures. When he was ill in Alix, Father de la Croix d'Azolette exempted him from all classes but made an exception for the class on the New Testament because, as Colin tells us, 'I asked him to leave me that.' More important probably than the classes was the private reading of the Bible. The student, on the advice of his director, was expected to read privately certain parts of the scriptures at a set time during the day and to learn by heart a chapter of the New Testament every week. Colin copied out in a notebook the passages that appealed to him and, later, these extracts were to serve him well when composing his rule.[21]

Catholic theology of the period had become static, closed and desiccated. The textbook dominated the studies, for it was assumed that all the knowledge a future priest needed could be contained in one book. In class, the professor was normally expected not to go outside it on the principle that teachers came and went but the textbook remained.[22] The comments of the professor, if he chose to add or omit, could change emphases or soften positions adopted in the textbook but, generally, the textbook remained the centre of the class-work and of individual study. The classes were not lectures, as in the modern university. The professor merely read the text, dictated an explanation in Latin, and questioned the students on it.

The theology textbook used was Louis Bailly's eight-volume work on moral

21. OM, doc. 501; Coste, 'De Societatis Spiritu', *Acta Societatis Mariae* (Rome, 1960-62), pp 501-7, 627-35.
22. C. Dumoulin, *Un séminaire français au 19ème siècle: le recrutement, la formation, la vie des clercs à Bourges* (Paris, 1978), pp 224-6.

and dogmatic theology, *Theologia dogmatica et moralis,* although in Colin's last year at Saint-Irénée the older, simpler, 'Poitiers manual' – which differed little in orientation, temporarily replaced it.[23] Bailly, a late 18th century theologian, with a reputation for holiness, owed his renown as a theologian to this manual of dogma and moral theology published in 1789. Written in a clear Latin style, his manual was popular with seminary staffs and widely used in seminaries in France and outside France up to the middle of the 19th century. In many ways it differed but little from theology manuals in use up to Vatican II. After introducing the subject, it gave the 'state of the problem', defined the proposition to be proved, listed proofs from scripture, patrology and theology, and finally answered a lengthy series of possible objections.

Theology occupied almost all the class and study time. All other subjects were ancillary to it. Moral theology had two classes a day and took pride of place, because dogmatic theology had been somewhat discredited by the endless arid disputes of the 17th and 18th centuries. Moreover, the Council of Trent, which regarded the establishment of the seminary system as one of its greatest reforming measures, directed that the future priest should study the sacred sciences in order to be properly prepared to administer the sacraments, especially to hear confessions and to preach. These were the primary aims of the textbooks. A confessor's life must be holy, the textbooks insisted, but then went on to describe him as 'judge, physician and teacher', with an emphasis on his judicial role.[24] Confession was a tribunal and the priest was a judge.

The great debate in 17th and 18th century France on moral theology had been between Jansenists and Jesuits, a dispute that spilled over into politics and embroiled king and parliament, French Church and Rome. The Jansenists, Catholic 'Puritans' with a pessimistic view of the human race, embraced a moral theology that was harsh by modern standards, and showed a preoccupation with sin. Bailly, like most French theologians, was no Jansenist, but he had inherited from Jansenism its pessimistic approach to morality and was 'rigorist' in his theology. An example – relevant because it directly determined Colin's attitude in Cerdon towards a penitent – may illustrate the point. Birth-control had become more frequent in France and a common method was onanism. Theologians denounced it as gravely sinful. What, however, of the frequent case where one partner practised onanism but the other partner, usually the wife, was opposed to it? Could she agree to the marriage act? Bailly tackles the problem head-on and poses the question where the husband tells his wife that, if she refuses to cooperate, he will seek another woman, may the wife then

23. Gardette to Fesch, 28 Nov 1814, OM, doc. 34; L. Bailly, *Theologia dogmatica et moralis ad usum seminariorum,* 8 vols (Lyon, 1810, 3rd edit); C. de la Poype de Vertrieu, *Compendiosae institutiones theologicae ad usum seminarii Pictaviensis,* 4 vols (Poitiers, 1708-09).
24. Bailly, *Theologia,* vol. 4, pp 354-7, citing *Institutiones theologicae Pictaviensis.*

consent? No, replies Bailly. What if her husband threatens to kill her, can she agree, to save her life? 'No, she may not', replies Bailly, 'because it is never licit to consent to acts which are in themselves evil.'[25] Bailly's attitude was no different from that of almost all French theologians and Cholleton taught this doctrine at Saint-Irénée. A few years later, Colin was confronted with a similar case in Cerdon and for six months refused the sacraments to an unfortunate woman. Finally, the insistent prayers of the poor woman, whom the Blessed Virgin herself encouraged by appearing to her, wrought a total change in the attitude of the husband. Then, but only then, was Colin able, as he told Mayet, 'to reopen the source of the sacraments' to her![26]

Other instances of severity abound in Bailly. He maintained that just as a judge in a court is not obliged to give immediate sentence, so the priest-judge in the tribunal of confession is not obliged to give absolution right away. He laid down eight rules when the confessor should postpone or deny absolution to the penitent and added to them many other instances.[27] A confessor would commit grave sin if he did not deny or postpone absolution to a habitual sinner who said he was contrite and promised to amend his life but showed no real hope of amendment.

This was the manual that Colin used for his moral theology and from which he made copious notes. How far did his professor of moral theology and well-beloved director, Jean Cholleton, follow this exacting theology? When Cholleton studied at Saint-Sulpice in Paris, his professor of moral theology was Jean Montaigne who also used Bailly as the class textbook. In the notes he gave in class, Montaigne showed a more compassionate attitude, as, for instance, in according absolution to a penitent but habitual sinner. Fundamentally, however, he followed Bailly's inflexible line. The twenty-three year old Cholleton, who was no original thinker, followed Bailly perhaps with the modifications made by Montaigne. Cholleton's friend and biographer, Cattet, who taught with him at Saint-Irénée, said of his teaching, not without some naiveté: 'He was the enemy of novelty in moral theology as in matters of faith' and chose 'the opinion most conformed to the practice of the Saints or to the views of the most serious Doctors.'[28]

Colin's many critical references to the strict moral theology which he learned in his seminary days confirm that Cholleton did follow Bailly.[29] Most striking was the memorable occasion many years later when Cholleton generously volunteered to give some conferences on confessional practice to the young Marists.

25. Bailly, *Theologia,* vol. 6, pp 273-4.
26. OM, doc. 542.
27. Bailly, *Theologia,* vol. 4, pp 308-19.
28. S. Cattet, *Notice sur la vie du R. P. Cholleton* (Lyon, 1852), p. 9.
29. OM, docs 542; 693.

Colin, despite the love and veneration he always retained for his old master and director, turned down his offer and appointed Father Barthélemy Epalle instead. Gently but firmly he made the point: 'I respect and venerate the method of the Sulpicians; but since they never exercised the sacred ministry, I think that a different teaching would be more useful for us'.[30]

Colin's remarks were to the point. Like the Sulpician professors from whom he learned his theology, Cholleton had had no pastoral experience, had not exercised the ministry of penance, but taught moral theology from the book which, as elsewhere in France, was rigorist. A comparison with Colin's saintly contemporary, John Vianney, the outstanding confessor of nineteenth century France, is worth making. Preaching in his church at Ars, the curé told his rustic congregation:

> I know eight reasons which force a priest to postpone absolution; it is the Church herself who has given these rules which the priest may not transgress; if he ignores them, then woe to him and woe to the person he guides: he is a blind man leading the blind and both will fall into hell.

On another occasion, alluding no doubt to a practice of 'shopping around' for an easier confessor, he condemned it as making for bad and sacrilegious confessions: 'Those who search for confessors in order to receive easier absolution. O, my God! how many sacrilegious confessions. O, my God! how many Christians damned!'[31]

John Vianney received some of his training at Saint-Irénée, some from friendly parish priests and the rest from the sermon books he read. What he learned was no different from what Colin learned. Both were marked by the same unsparing approach. The theology that Colin learned in Saint-Irénée, summarised and learned with care and used in the early years of his priesthood, lacked the essential pastoral dimension. Given the long and complex development of the sacrament of penance, one cannot expect to find in 19th century moral manuals a concept of confession as the sacrament of reconciliation. It was the rigoristic moral teaching of Bailly and of French theologians in general. The milder, more human, moral theology of Alphonsus Liguori, so much beloved later by Colin, was already coming across the Alps from Italy and was being embraced by some eminent priests working in the home missions, but it had not breached the gates of Saint-Irénée.[32]

30. FA, doc. 254.

31. M.-A. Delaroche, *Sermons du Saint Curé d'Ars, Jean-Baptiste-Marie Vianney* (Paris, 1925), vol. 3, p. 75; vol. 4, p. 298. Bouchard, 'La Prédication de Colin', p. 58. J. Genet, *L'Énigme des sermons du curé d'Ars* (Paris, 1961), points out, however, that the editors of the Curé's sermons made additions to the text.

32. G. Humbert, 'Jalons chronologiques pour une histoire de la pénétration en pays francophones de la pensée et des oeuvres d'Alphonse de Liguori', in J. Delumeau, ed., *Alphonse de Liguori, pasteur et docteur* (Paris, 1987), pp 369-401.

To the modern mind, the seminary influences that tended to shape Colin's outlook on spiritual and moral matters were legalistic, if not negative. Tronson's examinations of conscience forced him daily to check his own observance of the minutiae of the rule and Gardette's spiritual conferences reinforced this attitude. Bailly's *Theologia,* the main textbook, was unbendingly rigorist; Cholleton expounded and endorsed it totally. Colin devoured Franchi's *Treatise on self-contempt* in his personal reading; Cholleton, of whom it was said that 'he had a great fear of God's judgement and that his salutary terror communicated itself to those to whom he was speaking', was his revered confessor and spiritual director.[33] The other books he steeped himself in, such as Rodríguez's *Exercise of Perfection,* were similar in outlook. Most, if not all of them, had a severe view of life for this was an age when the concept of sin was strong.[34] This serious outlook on life penetrated the seminaries and one cannot but be struck by a certain joylessness, almost negativity, in the formal training Colin received. His docility, piety and his serious application to his books would have made him more susceptible to those influences. At Saint-Irénée, his devotional life, daily Mass, and, perhaps most of all, his warm devotion to the Blessed Virgin provided some balance to these sterner influences. Would he be able to shake off those attitudes as he came into contact with the daily life of the people, or would they permanently mark his life and work? Only time would tell.

The other important area in Colin's seminary studies was dogma or doctrinal theology. It also received two classes a day. Just as moral theology was geared towards hearing confessions, dogma was tailored towards preaching. The Council of Trent had insisted that the pastor give the faithful a sermon every Sunday and feast-day and for this purpose it produced a catechism that expounded the main points of Catholic doctrine. Bailly followed the main lines of this catechism and included treatises on the existence of God, the Holy Trinity, the incarnation and so forth. The only real mention the Blessed Virgin received in the eight volumes was a short article in the tract on the incarnation that proved that the body of Christ was formed of the Virgin by the power of the Holy Spirit! Within this wide range of doctrinal theology, apologetics was the principal area of study. The aim of apologetics was to show that the Catholic Church was the true Church and then, on the basis of reason and revelation, to establish its authority. This is what, in his first year, 1813-4, Colin studied in the treatise *On the True Religion.* Having established that the true religion is the Catholic Church, he would have gone on to the key tract, *De Ecclesia* or *On the Church.* The treatment of the Church was quite different from *Lumen Gentium,* Vatican II's rich and stimulating document, where the beauty and grandeur of the Church of Christ is explored and set out for its

33. Mayet, 'Mémoires', 4, pp 508 bis-509m.
34. J. Delumeau, *Le péché et la peur, la culpabilisation en Occident xiii-xviii siècles* (Paris, 1983).

members. Bailly's tract *On the Church* did not deal with this inner life. It spoke of a Church that defended and defined itself carefully. After speaking briefly of the four marks of the true church – one, holy, catholic and apostolic – Bailly moved quickly to what was the key point for all theologians of the time – the authority of the Church vis-à-vis non-Catholics and, especially, vis-à-vis the State. He refuted the errors both of Protestantism and of the deism of the eighteenth century Enlightenment.

When he came to the important question of the authority of the pope, Bailly taught the Gallican doctrine stressing the independence of the French Church.[35] The Revolution, in abolishing the monarchy and by promoting a schism, had dealt severe blows to Gallicanism. The Concordat of 1801, by which the pope had dismissed the whole French hierarchy and appointed a new one, was another sharp blow to the Gallican independence claimed by the French bishops. Gallicanism, however, was far from dead. Napoleon and his advisers revived political Gallicanism as a means of controlling the Church. Theological Gallicanism, too, lived on until well into the 19th century. As in pre-Revolutionary France, professors in French seminaries were obliged to take an oath promising that they would teach Gallicansim.

Although the textbook at Saint-Irénée – Bailly's *Theologia* – and the refectory reading – Fleury's *History* – were Gallican, the teaching there was not a thorough-going Gallicanism. From its re-opening in 1801 Saint-Irénée had been run by the priests of Saint-Sulpice and as early as 1809 Fesch complained that the priests coming out of it held what he called 'ultramontane and fantastic' principles.[36] In the college of Saint-Sulpice in Paris, the superior, Émery, who had moved away from strict Gallicanism, had appointed Pierre-Denis Boyer, a bright and very apostolic theologian, as professor of dogma. It was Boyer who taught Cattet, Colin's professor of dogma. Alert to the problems of the day, Boyer, though moderately Gallican, was attached to the papacy. When Napoleon, frustrated by Pius VII's refusal to institute new bishops, called the council of 1811 to decree that the metropolitan bishop could institute bishops without reference to the pope, Boyer took the dangerous line of denying the competence of the council to do so. When Boyer's pupil, Cattet, was recalled from Saint-Sulpice to teach the same tract in Saint-Irénée, he was not completely free to teach what he wanted, for Cardinal Fesch and his vicar, Bochard, kept a lively interest in their seminary and were committed to Gallicanism. The political authorities, too, had the duty to enforce adherence to Gallicanism. Yet

---

35. Bailly, *Theologia*, vol. 2, pp 486-508.
36. Fesch to Courbon, 26 July 1809, Fesch letters, cited in Alonso, 'Formación intelectual', pp 14-15. Ultramontane was the pejorative term used by Gallicans to denote those who promoted the centralisation of authority and influence in the Holy See. 'Ultramontanism' is often contraposed to 'Gallicanism'.

it is more than likely that Cattet, in his oral commentary on the textbook, taught the mitigated Gallicanism which he had imbibed from his master in the Saint-Sulpice that he loved. Later he wrote: 'All of us, attached as we are from the very depths of our soul and by our principles to the chair of Peter, are disgusted by the assertions … against the papal authority.'[37] Cattet wrote these words many years after leaving the seminary; yet it is probable that this is the view he held at Saint-Irénée at a time when the maltreatment of the well-loved Pius VII had aroused a strong feeling of support for the pope, especially among the Lyon clergy, as Courbon testified. It is interesting that Colin used the identical expression 'from the very depths of our soul', *('par nos entrailles')* in his rule, calling on Marists to adhere to the Holy See with all their strength and *ex totis visceribus*.[38]

The views of the highly-respected superior, Gardette, who with Cattet – if Bochard is to be credited – set the tone for the staff of Saint-Irénée, would also be important. They emerge from a fascinating statement he made just at the end of the student 'revolt'. That July 1815 when new deacons, among whom was Colin, and new priests were ordained, Gardette, in what would be his final words of counsel to the young men he had guided to the priesthood, said solemnly:

> Be on your guard against efforts being used nowadays to seduce France from the centre of Catholic unity. Keep your eyes all fixed on your bishop as long as he is in communion with Rome. In matters of doubt, his opinion is a sure rule of conduct, until such a time as the pope repudiates him.[39]

In its context, this is striking advice. The young priests were told by their revered superior to follow their bishop *as long as he is in communion with Rome*. The bishop's attitude was to be their rule of conduct, *until the pope repudiates him*. The solemn moment of ordination was normally an occasion to remind the young priests of their duty of obedience to their bishop, and a key tenet of Gallicanism was the minimalisation of the power of the pope over the French bishops. Gardette used it to alert them to the existence of a higher allegiance: loyalty to the pope. His own searing experience during the Revolution as a refractory or Roman priest, together with the moderate Gallicanism emanating from Saint-Sulpice, is sufficient to explain his loyalty to the pope and his dread lest division arise between the French Church and Rome. That Gardette

37. Cattet, *La vérité sur Fesch,* p. 302.
38. 'illique (Sedes Apostolica) ex totis viribus et ex totis visceribus semper et ubique adhaerendo.' J. Coste, G. Lessard and S. Fagan eds, *Antiquiores Textus Constitutionum Societatis Mariae* (Rome, 1955), fascicle II, p. 32. The force of the Latin expression *ex totis visceribus* like its French equivalent *par nos entrailles,* the literal meaning of which is 'from one's innards or guts', is difficult to render into English.
39. Fesch Papers; cited in Coste, *Marian vision,* p. 74.

was a moderate in his Gallicanism finds some confirmation in a comment Colin made thirty years later. Colin had been speaking at length about Rohrbacher's anti-Gallican *Universal History of the Catholic Church,* praising it highly for its attachment to Rome. Turning, then, to Fleury's Gallican *Ecclesiastical History,* which had been normal mealtime reading in the seminaries, Colin warned against it, adding significantly: 'M. Gardette, the superior of the major seminary of Lyon, used to say that, until one was properly instructed, one should not read Fleury after the 8th century!'[40]

The Marist vow at Fourvière a year after Gardette's ordination address echoed these sentiments of respect for the pope. Colin, too, was to make loyalty to Roman teaching the third end of the society, urging Marists to cling always and everywhere to the Apostolic See with their whole strength and their whole being. He had grown up in an underground Church that was persecuted by the state and supplanted by those who had taken the Constitutional oath. The catechisms of that underground Church taught the faithful to hold in horror the schism of the constitutional clergy. The attitude of Cattet and Gardette, which Cholleton and the other priests on the staff would probably have followed, were powerful influences in reinforcing his childhood horror of the evils of schism and his attachment to Rome.[41]

Stormy political events, not unconnected with the papacy, were to unfold dramatically over the next year and a half, events in which Colin and his fellow-seminarians at Saint-Irénée were to become involved. To these events we must now turn.

40. Colin, Dec 1847, Mayet, 'Mémoires', 6, p. 705m.
41. Coste, *Vision Mariale,* pp 66-74.

CHAPTER 7

A Seminary in Ferment

Rohrbacher's account of how he and the seminarians at Nancy feared, as they studied the treatise *On the Church,* that they might be called on to lay down their lives for the truths it taught, is a sharp reminder of the shadow which Napoleon's policies were casting even over the seminary.[1] This relationship between Church and State was no mere speculative scholastic discussion but the burning question of the day. Pope Pius VII and the emperor Napoleon were locked in conflict. Napoleon's determination to dominate both State and Church had its roots in French Gallicanism. The Sulpicians, Émery and Boyer, had lately made a theological case against strict Gallicanism but it was not theological argument but political events that began to alienate the French clergy from Napoleon. When the clergy saw the manner in which the highly respected Pope Pius VII was being treated, resistance to the religious policy of Napoleon began to grow. Even Fesch, the emperor's ever-loyal uncle, who celebrated his bloody victories with *Te Deums*, had dared to raise his voice in protest to his nephew only to find himself in disgrace and banished from Napoleon's presence. In the face of one of the most eventful periods ever in French history, the clergy slowly came to realise that France and the French Church were entering an ever-mounting crisis.

The French government's efforts to hide the gravity of this conflict had been successful at first. Although Pius VII had excommunicated the emperor and the bull of excommunication had been secretly posted overnight on the walls of the basilicas in Rome on 10 June 1809, Napoleon's police saw to it that it got no further. It was at this juncture that the Catholics of Lyon played a crucial role. In 1804 they had transformed the passage of Pius VII through Lyon into a warm and triumphal welcome by the faithful and had set the tone for the reception of the pope elsewhere during that visit. Since then the Church in Lyon had grown in strength and organisation. Some Lyonese Catholics now learned what had happened at Rome and, angry at the treatment meted out to the pope, published the documents concerning the contest between Napoleon and Pius VII.[2] They also published the bull of excommunication, and, to the fury of

1. Costigan, *Rohrbacher,* p. 5. See chapter 4.
2. *Correspondance authentique de la cour de Rome avec la France...* ([Lyon], 1809); A. Lestra, *Histoire secrète de la Congrégation de Lyon...* (Paris, 1967), pp 175-92; L. Trénard, 'Lyon sous le premier empire', *Revue de l'Institut Napoléon,* (1959-1960), pp 163-4.

Fouché's police, circulated it secretly not only throughout Lyon but through-out France. Their action not merely aroused great sympathy for the pope but opened the eyes of many Catholics to Napoleon's tyrannical behaviour and marked the beginning of a change in Catholic opinion towards him.

For almost five years 1809-1814 the pope was kept prisoner first in Savona, near Genoa, then in Fontainebleau, near Paris. At first, Napoleon had managed to play down the quarrel, and the French bishops, increasingly indebted to the government for grants to the Church, had ignored it. But the council of 1811, which Napoleon called in order to circumvent the pope's refusal to institute bishops, revealed how Pius was being ill-treated and gradually Catholics, and priests and seminarians in particular, began to turn against Napoleon. The council failed because the bishops, despite imperial pressure, refused to act without the agreement of the pope. The unequal contest between the impris-oned Pius VII and the emperor dragged on even after the abortive council of 1811. Relentlessly, however, Napoleon, aided by some of the cardinals, kept up the pressure on Pius, now a prisoner in Fontainebleau. Isolated and ill, the pope finally agreed to a new Concordat but Napoleon, breaking his promise, pub-lished it as a law of the Empire in February 1813. Pius, overcome by remorse, solemnly renounced the agreement in March. How matters would have pro-gressed one cannot tell, but by October, when Colin was preparing to enter the major seminary, events on the battlefield overtook Napoleon's religious policy.

Up to 1812 the continuing war was a series of glorious victories for the invin-cible emperor in distant Spain, Germany or Russia. Since Napoleon's retreat from Moscow in the winter of 1812, however, the news was no longer of victories but of defeats. By October 1813, the British general, Wellington, had expelled the French from Spain. More disquieting still was the news from the main battlefields in Germany where Napoleon was in personal command. Despite the slant put on it in the official bulletins, it became clear that Napoleon had suffered a catastrophic defeat at the battle of Leipzig in October 1813. On the 2 November, as class began in Saint-Irénée, 70,000 men, the remnant of the Grande Armée, were struggling across the Rhine back into France and, for the first time in almost two decades, foreign armies were menacing the home coun-try itself. The threat quickly became a reality. A few days before Fesch had driven to Saint-Irénée in all his episcopal glory to ordain the subdeacons on 6 January 1814, came the alarming news that the Austrians, in a surprise attack through Geneva, had crossed into Switzerland and would soon be in France heading in the direction of Lyon. As the bad news persisted, Fesch, who was living in the episcopal palace, a few hundred metres across the Saone from the seminary, packed and fled from the city to the safety of the convent of the Benedictine nuns at Pradines near Roanne in the Loire valley, fifty kilometres from Lyon. This was 15 January. Two days later the Austrians arrived outside

Lyon. Their dragoons, hearing of Fesch's flight to Pradines, closed in on him. Alerted just in time, the cardinal archbishop disguised himself as a lackey, and fled across mountains and woods with a single companion. The dragoons swooped on his hiding place and, finding the nest warm but the bird flown, compensated themselves for their disappointment by confiscating his fine stable of horses.

While the cardinal was dodging the Austrian cavalry in the mountains around Lyon, even more dramatic events were taking place elsewhere in France. Napoleon decided to send Pius VII, still in close custody, back to Savona. Anxious, however, that the pope should not come near Lyon and the valley of the Rhone where the people had received him so enthusiastically, he decreed that the pope would travel, under strict police guard, by a circuitous route through Orleans, Limoges, Toulouse, Montpellier, Aix and Nice. This only had the effect of making the pope better known in the southwest and southeast of France, for the populace flocked to greet him. In Toulouse, the seminary staff and students turned out to welcome him. To the people, bewildered in the confusion of a collapsing empire and living in fear and hope for the future, Pius was a saintly man who represented a force for good. To the clergy he was the silent martyr of a persecuting government. His escorting gaolers soon realised that the journey of the captive pope was rapidly becoming a triumphal procession through France. He would end his journey not as a prisoner in Savona, as Napoleon had intended, but as a sovereign in Rome. The month of March that year brought even more excitement, for events had quickly overtaken the emperor. The Duke of Wellington had crossed the Pyrenees into France, and on 12 March, his armies marched into Bordeaux. With Wellington's tacit connivance, the governor of the city, Count Lynch, supported by the Chevaliers de la Foi, a secret Royalist and Catholic association, active also in Lyon and rumoured to be linked to the *Congrégation,* hoisted the white flag of the Bourbons and proclaimed the Count of Provence king of France as Louis XVIII. The Count was the brother of the executed Louis XVI, whose son Louis XVII never reigned, for he died in captivity. The Bordeaux incident was the first and, as it proved, decisive step in bringing back the Bourbons to the French throne. On 6 April came even more sensational news that Napoleon, the invincible emperor, had conceded defeat and had abdicated. On 24 April, Louis XVIII disembarked at Calais. The old order had changed and a new regime had begun in France. When Fesch, who had returned to Lyon but left again when he found it would soon fall to the Austrians, learned that his nephew had abdicated and had been sent to the island of Elba, he decided to go into exile in Rome.[3] Louis XVIII had by now effectively installed himself in Paris and France had once more a Christian king. To many convinced Catholics the time

3. Chausse, *Duplay,* vol. 1, p. 229.

had come to restore things to what they had been before the Revolution of 1789.

In Saint-Irénée, the staff and especially the students were ecstatic at these developments, for disillusionment with Napoleon had grown over recent years. As early as 1810, the police in Lyon complained that the Lyonese clergy remained 'more loyal to the pope than to the emperor'. The young priests 'must be carefully watched; they speak of the glory of the Martyrs. It is the result of the education in the Major Seminary'.[4] When Louis XVIII was proclaimed king, the students saw and heard with approval the rejoicing of the populace, embracing, drinking and dancing as they celebrated the news. Some of them were probably present at one or other of the solemn *Te Deums* celebrating the fall of Napoleon and the restoration of the king that were sung in the Cathedral, to the annoyance of Fesch. The armies of the victorious allies were now installed in France. In Lyon, the Austrian soldiers were disciplined and their occupation of Lyon peaceful. On their walks, Colin and the students from Saint-Irénée would have encountered Austrian and Hungarian soldiers who patrolled the streets with the National Guard. The Austrians from the Tyrol, who wore their green uniform and tilted hat, attracted attention but even more fascinating for the Lyonese were the Hungarian grenadiers in their tightly fitting white tunic, sky-blue trousers and black boots. The greatest surprise the Hungarians provided, however, was when they addressed the seminarians in Latin, which had remained a common language for the educated in their country.[5] If they passed the great square of Bellecour, the students would have heard the army bands playing the haunting music of Vienna. For a short time, too, they would have seen the Austrian flag waving over the town hall, but the Austrians, who left after two months, soon hauled it down and the white flag of the Bourbon kings was raised instead. In the churches, the most perceptible change was that prayers for 'the most Christian king', the title the popes of old had accorded the French kings, replaced the prayers for Emperor Napoleon.

The year 1813-14 had been an *'annus mirabilis'*. When the students returned in November 1814 to settle down for the new school year, all seemed set for a period not unduly untroubled by events in the political world. And so it was for the first few months. Then, in early March 1815, came the electrifying news that Napoleon had escaped from his island prison of Elba and had landed in France with a small bodyguard of faithful followers. At Grenoble, ninety kilometres southwest of Lyon, the soldiers had defected to Napoleon. Along the route from Grenoble to Lyon, peasants and workers came out in favour of Napoleon and, when his army reached Lyon, the *canuts* or silk-weavers, who

4. 'Rapport de police', 12.11.1810, Alonso, 'Formación intelectual de Colin', pp 14-15, citing Charlety, 'La vie politique à Lyon sous Napoléon 1er', *Revue d'Histoire de Lyon*, (1905) pp 431ff.
5. A. Steyert, *Nouvelle Histoire de Lyon...*, vol. 3, (1899) 628-9.

formed up to a quarter of the population of the city, went over to him *en masse.* The soldiers, too, were carried away by the enthusiasm and group after group defected to him. MacDonald, one of Napoleon's generals who remained loyal to the king, confronted the imperial army on the quays of the Rhone, but as more and more of his troops deserted, he was forced to turn round and gallop towards Paris. At seven in the evening Napoleon, surrounded by soldiers and torch-carrying weavers, crossed the Rhone at the bridge of la Guillotière, then over the Saone, and entered Cardinal Fesch's palace. Lyon proved a turning point and Napoleon rightly said later: 'In Grenoble I was only an adventurer; in Lyon I had become emperor.' Next day, with a farewell speech, ending with the emotional words 'People of Lyon, I love you,' a much-strengthened Napoleon set off for Chalon where Marshal Ney, who had boasted to the king that he would 'bring him back in an iron cage!' deserted to his side. Louis XVIII headed into exile a second time. Again the world was turned upside down: Napoleon was back in Paris and his uncle, Cardinal Fesch, was back in Lyon.

The morning after his entry into the archbishop's palace, Napoleon came out on the terrace with the vicar general, Courbon, to greet the people. The crowd shouted 'Long live the emperor!' but some added ominously 'Down with the priests!' Napoleon turned to Courbon and said: 'It seems that you are not well liked in this town.' Courbon, hurt by the remark, replied: 'Sire, all you hear is the rabble.'[6] Yet, in Lyon, as in many of the cities, anti-clericalism experienced a sharp revival during Napoleon's 'hundred days' such as France had not witnessed since the bad days of the Revolution. Many Catholics had rejoiced in the unexpected return of the king, discerning in it the certain promise of a revival of religion; in the words of the renowned preacher, Nicholas de Mac Carthy: 'The [Bourbon] lilies have renewed their splendour in order that faith and piety may flower again together with them and our legitimate princes have been given back to us, with a heavenly mission – to bring us back to ourselves and to our God.' Denis Frayssinous, another renowned preacher, who had taught at Saint-Sulpice, and was later Grand Master of the Université, declared: 'It is the voice of Providence which calls back the Bourbons!'[7] Napoleon's triumphal return was for them a major tragedy. Bishop de la Porte of Carcassonne believed that the four months of interregnum after Napoleon's return, 'demoralised our unfortunate country more than the twenty-five years of Revolution' and the differing attitudes towards the Church assumed during this brief period

6. Chausse, *Duplay,* vol. 1, p. 236.
7. N. de Mac Carthy, *Sermons,* vol. 1, (Paris, 1835) p. 308. D. Frayssinous, *Défense du Christianisme ou Conférences sur la religion,* vol. 3, (Paris, 1825), pp 467, 470. Nicholas de Mac Carthy (1769-1835), b. Dublin, ordained 1814, became Jesuit 1816; Denis-Luc-Antoine Frayssinous (1765-1841); Grand Master of the Université, 1822, member of the Académie, member of House of Peers, 1822; encouraged Jean-Claude, 1822; minister of public education and of ecclesiastical affairs, 1824-28; bishop of Hermopolis. C. Guillet, *La rumeur de Dieu* (Paris, 1994).

were to remain long afterwards.[8] The seminarians at Saint-Irénée, who had shared in the hope that the return of the king had raised, were very angry at the turn of events and strongly opposed to Napoleon.[9] Before, according to Fesch's biographer, they had revered him as a hero, now he was 'the tyrant'. From the windows of the seminary, some of the more hot-headed took to shouting down to the passers-by 'Long live the king!' Others went so far as to enrol in a resistance group, the 'Hunters of Henry IV', who had organised armed resistance to Napoleon and controlled the area of the mountains of Forez outside Lyon. Marcellin Champagnat, too, was upset by the turn of events. Less militant or more pious than his fellow-students, he was moved to vow that 'if the king returns' he would undertake extra religious practices![10]

For the clergy matters came to a head over a question of 'liturgy'. An order came from Napoleon's government in Paris commanding the clergy to restore the prayer for the emperor that they had abandoned on the return of the king. The formula prescribed was: *'Domine, salvum fac imperatorem nostrum'*, 'God save our emperor'. This order occasioned a crisis for many of the clergy who felt it against their conscience to obey. Memories of the ill-fated oath of 1791 were still fresh. Throughout France there was widespread resistance. In the diocese of Lyon the vicars general issued a circular announcing the order but the majority of priests ignored it. Then, spurred on by Fesch, the vicars issued a more urgent one. This time many priests, despite their reluctance, accepted it as part of the obedience due to their bishop. The attitude adopted in Saint-Irénée would be important, for many clergy looked to the seminary to see what line it would take. The staff there, however, were perplexed. Father Mioland wrote for advice to Father Duclaux, the superior of the Sulpicians in Paris. The situation in Saint-Irénée was explosive: 'The whole of our house, possibly,' he wrote, 'would rise up against us on the very first occasion we would sing it, at least it would be deeply scandalised.' The students outspokenly and violently opposed praying for the emperor and the repeated efforts of the officious vicar general, Bochard, failed to bring them into line. On 28 May Fesch determined to come in person with the two vicars general, Courbon and Bochard, to drum sense into the students. Things had radically changed, however, from his visit sixteen months earlier when he drove up in state to confer orders on so many of them. Fesch arrived, now, not in his own magnificent carriage with uniformed outriders and lackeys, but in an ordinary hackney carriage. Instead of the deferential reception he was used to, far different was the welcome the imperious archbishop now received. When they saw his cardinal's red cassock the students simply bolted out of sight. Some turned away, others rushed to hide themselves

---

8. A. Latreille, *L'Église catholique et la Révolution française*, vol. 2, (Paris, 1950), p. 249.
9. OM, docs 37, 38, 531, 562, 767. Lyonnet, *Fesch*, vol. 2, pp 578-80.
10. OM, doc. 36, 7.

in their rooms. The vicars scurried around and finally with difficulty managed to round up a group of students to come and listen to the cardinal. Colin was one of them. The cardinal addressed them solemnly but the students were not to be placated. When he said something they did not like, they called out *'nego'*, 'I deny that', or *'distinguo'*, 'that is not the full story'! Colin sat tight and said nothing but inwardly he was quite thrilled at Fesch's discomfiture for, as he admitted years later, he was of the same mind as the other students.[11] Fesch and his party soon saw that they were wasting their time and left, though not before suffering a final humiliation which some attribute to Ferdinand Donnet, the future cardinal archbishop of Bordeaux and others to Louis Querbes, the founder of the Clerks of St Viator. According to some accounts, one of the seminarians removed the wheel from the cardinal's carriage; according to others he wrote or chalked *Vive le roi!* or the royal fleur de lis on the side of the cardinal's carriage. To the hilarity of the students, Fesch drove off through the city, not knowing that he was flaunting the royalist emblem which was treasonable, and indeed dangerous, in a city that had become intensely suspicious of any opposition to Napoleon.

A further incident took place in which Colin played an active role. The student designated to sing the *'Domine, salvum fac imperatorem'* on Sunday complained to Colin that this was an outrageous imposition. Colin suggested to him that instead of singing *'Domine, salvum fac imperatorem'*, 'God, save the emperor', he change it to *'Domine, servum fac imperatorem'*, 'God, enslave the emperor'. The delighted student took the suggestion and did just that. At the end of Mass, his admiring fellow-students crowded round him, shaking his hand and applauding his stand. But the authorities got to know of it, reprimanded the student and forced him to sing the correct version on the following Sunday. Colin, who claimed he had made his suggestion in fun, now feared that the superior would send for him. Nothing happened. Perhaps the student never told on him, perhaps the staff itself was ambiguous about the whole matter.[12] Gardette and his young staff were walking a tight-rope caught between a near-mutiny in the seminary on the one hand, and the obedience due to the archbishop on the other. Bochard, the vicar general for the seminaries, redoubled his efforts to bring the students to heel and by 16 June, two days before Waterloo, he reported to Fesch:

More actions were needed to smother the fire of contentiousness and the

---

11. OM, doc. 562.
12. The prayer for the head of state was seen in most countries as a question of loyalty and to refuse it was tantamount to treason. Students took it more light-heartedly. At about the same time that the seminarians at Lyon were singing 'Lord, enslave the Emperor', Irish seminarians at Maynooth were singing 'Lord, thrash the king.' They had replaced *'Domine, salvum fac Regem'* by *'Domine, salvum whack Regem'!* For this they were denounced to a Parliamentary Commission of Inquiry.

insubordination of mind that was agitating our young men. God has blessed our efforts and our firmness. It was the only way to prevent an explosion. The last measures were milder and so the oil helped the vinegar to produce its effect.[13]

Colin would have experienced – and perhaps resented – the measures that the vicar general took to end their contentiousness and temper their Royalism. How far the vicars general managed to smother the students' unrest is unknown but they were motivated by their loyalty to the archbishop and their anxiety to keep political strife out of the seminary. They were also only too aware of the dangers of the situation. Napoleon's supporters ruled Lyon with an iron hand, closing down 'seditious' cafés, clapping in jail as spies anyone suspected of Royalist activities, and building fortifications to prepare for any Royalist attack. The populace had smashed the windows of houses whose inhabitants did not respond quickly enough to their demand to illuminate in honour of Napoleon. Indeed, the reason Fesch gave for his return to Lyon was 'to impose silence on those who shout "Long live Hell! Down with the priests!" and to rescue those clergy who have been thrown into jail on account of their political opinions.'[14] The conduct of the students was imprudent. On one occasion they almost persuaded Gardette to abandon Saint-Irénée altogether. Their behaviour could easily have resulted in the confiscation of the seminary. By mid-June Courbon and Bochard were writing in alarm to Fesch to tell him that the authorities wanted to take over Saint-Irénée and to turn it into a military hospital. This was precisely what Fesch, Courbon and Bochard, and the staff wanted at all costs to avoid.

Many of the priests continued to disobey the archbishop's order to pray for the emperor, as Courbon reported to Fesch. When he called on them to conform, he said, they behaved like the guests in the gospel invited to the wedding feast. Some said they were under threat of losing their congregations. Others replied that it was a matter of conscience for them: the contest between king and emperor, they claimed, was not yet decided – 'adhuc sub judice lis est', that is that 'the jury was still out on whether king or emperor would win'. Others ignored the invitation altogether preferring to follow the royalist counsels of certain priests in Chambéry, the capital of French Savoy, for, as Courbon remarked tartly to Fesch: 'They have great, indeed too great, a trust in the haughty Sorbonne of Chambéry and its dictates.'[15] One of those Chambéry priests, François-Marie Bigex, later became bishop of Pinerolo, and was to play

13. Bochard to Fesch, 16 June 1815, Fesch Papers, Archivio Segreto Vaticano, epoca napoleonica, Francia II; copy in APM.
14. Lyonnet, Fesch, 2, pp 563-4.
15. Courbon to Fesch, 14 June 1815, Fesch Papers.

an important role in the early years of the Society of Mary. Yet the danger to those priests and the seminary was real. On 15 June, Courbon reported to Fesch that 'The Prefects [of the Departments] and the Police Commissioner are treating the refusal to say the prayer [for the emperor] as treason.'[16] Three days later, before the imperial police could deal with recalcitrant priests or seminarians, the emperor was defeated at Waterloo on 18 June 1815. Yet despite the decisiveness of this defeat on 18 June, Lyon was a long time returning to order, for Napoleon had many supporters – mainly the weavers and artisans, but also some of the bourgeoisie. During a whole month after Waterloo, those in control refused to accept Napoleon's overthrow and the danger of a backlash against Royalists, including the clergy, remained. On 24 June angry bands raced through the city tearing down notices of allied victories, shouting *'Vive l'Empereur!',* insulting and mistreating any who did not appear to share their Napoleonic fury.[17] On 12 July, almost all the population of La Guillotière poured into the streets of Lyon shouting: 'Long live the Emperor! … Death to traitors! Let's burn their houses!'[18] Some wanted to massacre the imprisoned royalist prisoners. In July a rioting mob took control of the city and for a few days confusion reigned. Yet the end-result was inevitable. The Austrians and Piedmontese had swept down from the Alps, defeated the Bonapartist army and were at the gates of Lyon. It was only when the Austrians entered Lyon on 17 July, however, that a peaceful transition of power took place. This time they were to remain a full five months, and the citizens had to bear the heavy burden of an occupying army. Napoleon, exiled to St Helena, returned no more. France was again under the rule of 'the Most Christian king', Louis XVIII.

On 23 June of that summer of 1815, while angry mobs roamed the streets of Lyon, Colin received the diaconate. He had reached his twenty-fifth year, a quarter of a century that was undoubtedly the most troubled period ever in the history of France and of the French Church. One pope had died in captivity, another had been dragged up and down France. A king, defender of the faith, had been executed, an emperor had conquered half of Europe, had lost, won back and lost again. On the streets of Lyon, Colin had seen two hostile French armies confronting one another and had twice seen foreign soldiers coming in as conquerors – Austrians, Hungarians, Cossacks. The autocratic archbishop who had given him minor orders and subdiaconate had been forced to go on the run, like his predecessor, and was finally definitively exiled from his diocese. The world had been turned upside down, not once but many times. If he ever reflected on the ups and downs of life, the kaleidoscopic changes of which he

16. Courbon to Fesch, 15 June 1815, Fesch Papers, cited in Alonso, 'Formación intelectual de Colin', p. 22.
17. P. Gonnet, 'Les Cent Jours à Lyon', *Revue d'histoire de Lyon* 7 (Lyon, 1908), 290-6.
18. Ibid. p. 295.

had been a witness must have left a deep impression on this impressionable young man. It may well explain why, later on in life, he warned his fellow-Marists to keep out of politics, reminding them that 'saving souls not changing governments was their business!'[19]

Colin had originally come to the seminary to find that desert he sought in the woods of Crest, for a seminary of its nature kept the wicked world distant. Now for months, as political and military events rocked the city, the world had invaded the seminary and caught up the seminarians in its dramatic events. The students longed ardently for the return of the Most Christian king and believed his coming would herald the revival of the Church to its rightful place. The explosive mixture of religion and politics burst in on the peaceful atmosphere of the seminary. The few seminarians who supported Napoleon, the 'Corsican' as he was derisively called, were the subject of vexations and practical jokes. In a state of near-mutiny for up to four months, the students had argued with the superiors, with the vicar general, and even with their bishop. They had even wanted to abandon Saint-Irénée altogether. Heated political arguments and armchair military prognostics replaced spiritual and theological discussions. As soldiers drilled, citizens built barricades, and armed bands roamed the streets, how much serious study the students engaged in, is conjectural. The silence that Gardette's rule imposed would probably have gone by the board, for recollection was not easy when passions ran high and the city prepared for a siege.

Who were those students with whom Colin was thrown into closer contact as the political crisis continued? Colin would have known many of them from the minor seminaries – Saint-Jodard, Alix and Verrières. The rest, in general, came from other seminaries and sometimes the rivalries between them sprang to the surface. With so many recruiting stations, Saint-Irénée was a major seminary bursting at its seams when Colin arrived there in 1813. The previous year of 1812 had seen the intake rise from a previous high of 69 recruits, to an unprecedented 105! In Colin's year a further 80 had entered, some of whom may have been dodging the draft and quite a few drifted away over the following years. The high intakes swelled to two hundred and fifty the number of students in the old, rehabilitated seminary. They came from all over the vast diocese which covered three civil departments, Loire, Rhone and Ain. These mostly rural departments, especially Rhone and Ain, although roughly equal in population, were unequally represented among the students. The department of the Loire, the most westerly of the three departments, contributed well over half the students. The department of the Rhone, which now included all the region around Saint-Bonnet, contributed a third. The department of Ain, the most easterly of the three departments, one of whose principal towns was

19. FS, doc. 31, 7.

Belley, was very much in the third place, with a mere 14 per cent of the students coming from there. The mountainous area of the Bugey, near Belley, where the first Marist missions would take place, gave scarcely any vocations. Most of Saint-Irénée's students – 58 per cent – were sons of the soil, from families of comfortable farmers, many of whom were also engaged in weaving. Others – almost a third – were the sons of small traders and artisans. The working class, the richer middle classes and the professions furnished very few recruits. This pattern of post-revolution recruitment was a reversal from the Church in the first half of the 18th century, before the Enlightenment and the Revolution had taken their toll. At that time very many came from the higher middle classes and few from the 'peasant' classes. At Saint-Irénée, the number of bourses indicates that most came from families that were not wealthy; half of the students received a full bourse and most of the others, like Colin perhaps, a half bourse or more. The disruptions caused by the Revolution meant that they were less well-educated than their predecessors of the 18th century. To some extent the social origins of the students aspiring to the priesthood fit the sociological pattern of an upwardly mobile class. They often came from large families where the parents were happy to see a son embrace the priesthood, for it guaranteed a respected future for him. The religious fervour of Catholic families in the era following the persecutions endured, however, played a significant role.[20] The great majority of the students were of much the same age as Colin, that is, in their early twenties, but there was a sizeable number of students in their late twenties or early thirties.[21] The average age of ordination was about twenty-four or twenty-five.

The final years before ordination saw a number pack their bags and go, some voluntarily, others forced to go by the staff who judged them unfit for one reason or another. The departure of a fellow-student was usually a sobering occasion to the student-body. One day, at the end of the first semester in the school year of 1813-14, to the shock and sorrow of his comrades, it was the turn of John Mary Vianney, whom, as one of them, Étienne Déclas later con-

20. In 1810, the bishops' council noted: 'Since the Church of France no longer offers families the hope of fortune and advancement which the pre-Revolution clergy offered, the majority of young people who consecrate themselves to the Sacred Ministry belong to the class of people in straitened circumstances', cited in Grange, 'Recrutement', p. 88. Yet the picture Stendhal paints in his novel *The Red and the Black* of socially climbing peasants who entered priesthood, entering the seminary to avoid conscription or the hard life of the farm, derives from an anticlerical prejudice rather than from strict observation. Y. Essertel has shown the crucial role of the family, parish, school, seminary and religious congregations in awakening vocations. 'Réseaux et vocations missionnaires dans le diocèse de Lyon de 1815 à 1962', *Revue d'histoire ecclésiastique* 90 (1995), 49-70.
21. Grange, 'Recrutement', pp. 68-88.

fessed, students regarded as a saint. Committed though John Mary Vianney was to becoming a priest and highly-esteemed by all for his piety, he was so weak in Latin, the medium of instruction, that Mioland, the kindly professor of liturgy, gave him special lessons. Even then he did not make sufficient progress and Gardette and his council finally felt obliged to send him home. His perseverance despite this crushing blow and his later career in the little hamlet of Ars form a glorious page in the history of the Catholic Church in the 19th century. His support for Jean-Claude Colin and his project brought many good vocations to the Marists.

As always, the contact with one's fellow-students is of no small consequence in a seminary, for formation, that mysterious concept, does not come merely from lectures in theology and the admonitions of the staff. The stories, the projects, the dreams of one's fellow-students are equally, if not more, influential. The experiences open to a student in Saint-Irénée at this period, after two decades of the most traumatic change ever in France, were rich and varied. All had grown up during the Revolution and many, like Colin, had childhood experiences of the Terror.[22] Others like Marcellin Champagnat would have no such traumatic experiences of revolutionary persecution but would have felt loss of proper training brought about by the disruption of the education system. Some would have told of the dechristianisation that had taken hold of parts of the country. Others again recalled what their elders had told them about the magnificent Church of France before the scoffing of the Enlightenment and the persecutions of the Revolution brought it crashing down in ruin. In one such discussion on the Enlightenment, when a student was holding forth on the achievements of that 'Age of Lights', Gardette made the tart comment: 'Yes, and it was the Devil who held the lantern!' Others had stories of miracles, of the cult of the Sacred Heart, of the intervention of local saints. All, staff and students alike, would have felt the need for a great renewal of their Church and were enthused by the fact that a Christian king and a Christian parliament again ruled France. The Church was entering into a phase of religious renewal.

Before the scholastic year began again on All Saints Day 1814, a newcomer came to Saint-Irénée who had his own story to tell. This young man had already completed part of his theology studies at Le Puy en Velay in the diocese of Saint Flour, but since the Concordat had transferred his native parish of Usson-en-Forez to the diocese of Lyon, the Lyonese diocesan authorities insisted that he join the seminary at Saint-Irénée to complete his priestly training for the Lyon diocese. In all likelihood, he came there first during the summer, and

22. Claudine Thévenet (1774-1837), foundress of the Religious of Jesus and Mary, and Mayet's aunt, witnessed the brutal massacre of prisoners, including her own brothers, in the quarter of the city known as Les Brotteaux, after the siege of Lyon. J-M. Horny, *Claudine Thévenet, Lyon, 1774-1837* (Rome, 1993), pp 22-4.

returned to join the class of second theology in November 1814.[23] Newcomers arriving into a closed community of a seminary automatically attract great attention because they often bring something fresh and interesting, and this newcomer was no exception. At twenty-seven years, he was older than most of his new fellow-seminarians but, apart from his seniority, his lively personality was such as to provoke a stir. Fervent and pious, he was also outgoing, articulate, and the ardour of his eloquence would win him an immediate following. The dream of a restored 'Most Christian king' whose reign would foster the renewal of religion was one he fervently shared. He nourished, too, a secret project. At some time during the school year, probably towards the end, he broached it to one of the students and his fervour won him over immediately. Before long a large group of fellow-students would come under his influence and his message would change their lives forever. The newcomer's name was Jean-Claude Courveille.

23. OM, doc. 27.

CHAPTER 8

From Our Lady of Le Puy to Our Lady of Fourvière

'It was from this room and from this meeting that Father Déclas went out one day to find little Colin, as he was called.'[1]

The new school-year of 1815 had not long started when, one day during recreation, a fellow-student whom he had known since they entered Verrières together three years before, approached Colin. It was Étienne Déclas, the simple, sincere former horse-groom. Déclas had come straight from a meeting, where he, Jean-Claude Courveille and possibly Étienne Terraillon had been discussing a new project and considering whom they should invite to take part in it. Jean-Claude Colin was mentioned as a good candidate and Déclas, who was friendly with him, hurried out to find 'little Colin', as they called him, and bring him along. Déclas had an exciting story to tell little Colin of how he got involved in the project. One Wednesday during the previous school year when he was cutting Courveille's hair, Courveille had confided in him his own hopes and dreams. The reading in the refectory was the life of St Francis Régis, a saintly Jesuit missioner of the 17th century, who had spent himself on pastoral missions in the region around Le Puy and whom the local people venerated as the apostle of all of Velay and Vivarais, regions south-west of Lyon.[2] Courveille said to Déclas:

> What if, like St Francis Régis, we gave missions in the country. We would go on foot, simply, eating the food of the peasants. We would drink the milk and eat the bread of the country folk. We would instruct them and those people would be able to go to confession to other priests besides their own curés! Would Déclas join him? Courveille asked. 'Yes', replied Déclas.[3]

From time to time during the rest of the year, Courveille reminded him of their plan. Then one day, shortly before the end of that school year of 1814-15, Courveille went further. He assured Déclas that this was quite a serious project

---

1. OM, doc 868, 2. François Detours' report of what Déclas told Father Georges David. François-Auguste Detours (1837-95); wrote 'Histoire chronologique de la Societé de Marie, 1782 à 1852' (unpublished).

2. Jean François Régis (1597-1640).

3. OM, doc 868, 2. Déclas gave other accounts: OM, docs 551; 591; 869. Doc 868 is more detailed on this section. In his statement of how he learned of the project, Colin does not say that Déclas came to fetch him, but merely that Courveille told him of the project. The two versions are not mutually exclusive. Terraillon's account is in OM, doc 750.

and that an order like the Jesuits would be founded whose members would be called Marists. Courveille and Déclas kept in contact during the vacation and when, on All Saints Day 1815, they returned at the beginning of the school year, they, with the permission of the superiors, set about recruiting others.[4] Cholleton, the professor of moral theology, who knew and approved of the project, had lent them his room for their meetings and it was from there that Déclas went out to find Colin. Colin agreed to go along and take part. There Courveille recounted a deeply moving experience he had had, a story which he told Déclas, Terraillon, Champagnat and all those whom he invited to join his group. The story was so fascinating that years later Terraillon still recalled the stunning impact it made.[5]

Jean-Claude Courveille was born in 1787 in the small town of Usson-en-Forez in what is now the department of the Loire. His father, a merchant, died when he was eighteen. During the persecutions of the Revolution his parents saved and kept hidden in their house the miraculous statue of Our Lady of Chambriac and before this statue young Courveille often prayed. In 1812, when he was already a young man of twenty-three, he had an intense religious experience in which he felt urged to found the Society of Mary. It was to result in Courveille winning over a large group of senior seminarians to the idea during the year 1815-16 and in the pledge they took, in July 1816, to found the Society. Because of its importance it is necessary to record chronologically, as far as possible, the accounts that have been preserved of this experience.

The first written account occurs in a letter of Pierre Colin dated the 9 October 1819. This recently-discovered letter was written to Bishop Bigex of Pinerolo.[6] Pierre wrote it in the name of 'all his confrères'. The account he gave is what he received from Jean-Claude, for Pierre had left the seminary before Courveille came and did not know about the Marist project until Jean-Claude told him a year or so before he wrote the letter. Since it was an important letter to a bishop, however, it was more fitting that it come in Pierre's name since he was the parish priest. This important document merits citing in part:

About twelve years ago a young man, now thirty-four or thirty-five years old, and a priest this past three years, after receiving a particular grace at Our Lady of Le Puy in Velay, felt himself moved to establish a society of religious under the name of the Society of Mary. Fearing he might be deceived, he kept silent for two years but feeling interiorly an ever more pressing urge to do this work, he felt obliged to speak to his confessor and

4. OM, doc. 868, 2.
5. OM, doc. 750, 3.
6. Marist Brothers, Paul Sester and André Lanfrey discovered this important document in July 1996. François-Marie Bigex (1751-1827), bishop of the diocese of Pinerolo; archbishop of Chambéry 1824.

to many other wise and learned persons. Finally, in the year 1816, when he was in his last year of theology at the seminary of Saint-Irénée in Lyon, with the permission of his directors, he chose twelve to whom he communicated his aim and the plan of his Society.[7]

Earlier by twenty to thirty years than any we had possessed up to now, this account is only three or four years from the time that Courveille first communicated his plan to his fellow-students at Saint-Irénée. The 'young man' of 34 or 35 can be no other than Courveille who was thirty-two in 1819 and Our Lady of Le Puy in Velay is explicitly mentioned. The key words are 'after receiving a particular grace' which indicate some interior spiritual experience. The letter adds that Courveille was reluctant to speak about this experience until compelled to do so, a circumstance that is found in later accounts.

Courveille left the group in 1826. Champagnat, the two Colins, Déclas and Terraillon remained as Marists and all except Pierre Colin had formed part of the original band to whom Courveille revealed his experience in 1815-16. Three of those – Colin, Déclas and Terraillon – make reference to Courveille's account. Colin, who for decades was reticent about mentioning Courveille by name, throughout his life from 1837 to 1870 repeated that Mary had spoken of her role in the early Church and at the end of time. In 1837, Colin reported Mary as saying: 'I was the support of the new-born Church; I shall be the support of the Church at the end of time,' adding significantly: 'It is some thirty years since this was said to a priest.'[8] Then in 1844 he said: 'The Blessed Virgin has said to it [the Society of Mary], "I was the support of the new-born Church; I shall be the support of the Church at the end of time".'[9] The letter to Bigex in 1819 makes it clear that the priest he was referring to was Courveille.

Déclas also refers to Courveille's experience. One day, in October 1842, he was at recreation with Mayet and others. Mayet was always on the look-out for details of the early history of the Society and, possibly in answer to a query from him, Déclas remarked that the person to whom the first idea had come was Courveille. Mayet, who might have expected Déclas to answer 'Colin', was astonished. He had never heard tell of Courveille's role. It was probably at Mayet's instigation, then, that, in 1844, the Marist Father, Charles-Alphonse Ozanam persuaded Déclas to write a full account. Ozanam passed this on to Mayet. In his account Déclas confirmed that the first to have the idea of the society was Courveille at Le Puy. He added that Courveille had tried in vain to put the thought aside but finally told his confessor and that later, when forced

7. Colin to Bigex, 9 Oct. 1819. G. Lessard, 'An unpublished letter of Pierre Colin', *Forum Novum* 4 (1997), 87-94. A. Lanfrey, 'Commentaire critique de la lettre du 9 Octobre 1819', ibid., pp. 94-123.
8. OM, doc. 422 c. J. Coste, 'Mary in the newborn Church and at the end of time; analysis of data in Jean-Claude Colin', *Forum Novum* 3 (1995-6), 246-7.
9. OM, doc. 690, 1.

to transfer from the seminary of Le Puy to Saint-Irénée, he told Bochard of the 'work of Mary' which he hoped to do.

Étienne Terraillon, another of the first four recruits, recounted substantially the same story.[10] The first idea of the Society of Mary, he related in 1841-2, is due to Our Lady of Le Puy. He told how Courveille was cured of his semi-blindness by Our Lady of Le Puy and of his unbounded gratitude to the Blessed Virgin. He then went on to recount how Courveille reflected that everywhere Jesus had altars, Mary had her own little altar, too, and that just as Jesus had his Society, so Mary should also have her Society.[11] In his brief account Terraillon does not mention that Courveille had a supernatural revelation or mystical experience.

Ten years later Courveille himself gave what is the most detailed account of this experience. In 1851-2, he replied to the persistent questioning of Mayet in two letters. The two letters have disappeared: in 1853, Mayet gave them to Julien Favre, the provincial, and since then no trace of them has been found. Before parting with the letters Mayet, however, used them to write a full account of the events as detailed in them. This was probably in 1853. Fifteen years later, Mayet rewrote his account and destroyed the earlier version. It is on this 1868 text that we depend for Courveille's own description of his spiritual experience at Le Puy in 1812. In his 1868 version, Mayet, as, unfortunately, in other texts which he transcribes, prefers to give his own description rather than let the witness speak for himself, although on occasions he indicates by parentheses or otherwise that the words are Courveille's own.

According to this account, when Courveille was only ten years old, an attack of small-pox left him with such severe lesions to the cornea of his eyes that his eyesight was gravely damaged. This severe handicap kept him from many normal activities of boys of his age. He had hoped to study for the priesthood but this now proved impossible. The doctors to whom his mother brought him pronounced the damage incurable. Twelve years later, in 1809, responding to a powerful inner urge, he went on a pilgrimage to the shrine of Our Lady of Le Puy, in the cathedral town of Le Puy-en-Velay, capital of the department of Haute-Loire. The pilgrimage to Our Lady of Le Puy was one of the oldest in France, dating back to the thirteenth century. Every year, on the feast of the Assumption, thousands of pilgrims converged on this little town of ten thousand inhabitants, to climb up to the cathedral perched on a volcanic rock, there to venerate Our Lady of Le Puy. In 1809, probably also on the feast of the Assumption, the twenty-two year old Jean-Claude Courveille joined the other pilgrims and, as was the custom, he took some of the oil from the lamp before the statue of the Madonna which he then put on his eyes. Suddenly, to

10. OM, doc. 750, 1.
11. OM, docs 750, 1; 705; 798.

his amazed delight he found that his sight was totally restored. Gazing around the cathedral, he discovered that he could make out perfectly even small objects. The cure, for so it was, proved no temporary one for from that moment, for the rest of his life, he never experienced the slightest difficulty with his sight. The following year he returned to pray before the same statue and made a promise to the Blessed Virgin to devote himself totally to her and to do all for the glory of the Lord, her honour and the salvation of souls. He decided to become a priest, intending through that ministry to fulfill this promise. On the feast of the Assumption, 15 August 1812, while he was renewing this promise before the statue, he had an intense spiritual experience. At this point Mayet appears to cite Courveille's own words from the lost letters:

> He heard, not with bodily ears, but with those of the heart, interiorly but very distinctly … Here … is what I want. As I have always imitated my divine Son in everything, and have followed Him even to Calvary, standing at the foot of the cross when He gave up His life for the salvation of the world, now when I am with Him in glory, I imitate Him in what He does on earth for His Church, of which I am the protectress and I am like a powerful army for defending and saving souls. Just as at a time when a frightful heresy was to convulse all Europe, He raised up His servant Ignatius to form a society that bore His name in calling itself the Society of Jesus and its members Jesuits to combat Hell unleashed against the Church of my divine Son, so too, I desire, and it is the will of my adorable Son, that in the last age of impiety and unbelief, there also be a Society consecrated to me, which bears my name and calls itself the Society of Mary and its members Marists, to combat against Hell …[12]

Confronted with this claim and anxious to settle once and for all the precise nature of Courveille's experience at Le Puy, Mayet wrote back to ask him outright: 'This interior word of Mary, was it a real revelation, like some that occur and which are very certain, even though one hears nothing with the bodily ears, or was it solely a strong interior impression?' Courveille responded: 'I heard no word. All happened interiorly in my heart.'

Courveille went on to tell Mayet how he went to the seminary of Le Puy to study for the priesthood but that he was so frightened by what happened that he told no one, fearing it might be no more than an illusion. The interior urging he experienced at Le Puy, however, would not go away and he seemed to feel the Virgin Mary reproaching him for his hesitations and telling him: 'Speak to your directors, disclose the matter to them and you will see what they will tell you.' Plucking up courage, he spoke to two of the seminary directors, one of

---

12. OM, doc. 718, 5. The suspension points are in Mayet's text but probably do not indicate omissions. OM 4, p. 509, note for p. 581, 2.

whom was his confessor. They took time to consider his extraordinary disclosure and then told him that 'the matter appeared good to them, that it might well come from God, and be pleasing to Him, and that it should not be despised.' Heartened by this advice, he was casting round for suitable co-workers for the project when the vicars general of Lyon ordered him to leave the seminary of Le Puy for that of Lyon. There he revealed his secret to Cholleton whom he had chosen as his spiritual director.

This is the story, according to Courveille's account in 1852, that he told Colin and the others at Saint-Irénée which won over more than a dozen of his fellow-students. How is one to assess its accuracy since it dates forty years after the events it describes? Courveille's account contains the elements found in one form or another in the accounts independently given by his earliest companions – a special spiritual experience at the shrine of Our Lady of Le Puy; Mary spoke to him urging him to start the Society in her name; the parallel between her work in the early Church and in those last times; a parallel between the Society of Jesus and that of Mary.

The essential elements are the same. What is different are the two parallels Courveille draws: the first between the evils that followed the Reformation and those that followed the Revolution of 1789 and the second between the future role of the Marists and that of the Jesuits. When Courveille was growing to manhood, the calamity that the Revolution brought recalled to many that earlier upheaval of the Reformation. There was a feeling among religious people that a society like that of the suppressed Jesuits was necessary to uphold the Church in this new hour of trial. Noteworthy, too, is the nuance Courveille makes when describing his experience. He heard, he said, 'not with the ears of the body, but with those of the heart: interiorly but distinctly'. In his second letter he added: 'I heard no word. All happened interiorly in my heart.' The distinction is almost word for word what Saint Theresa of Avila wrote in her autobiography. Probably he had read her works, whether, as is more likely, after he became a Benedictine or earlier, is not quite clear.[13]

In assessing the reliability of his account, several other factors must be considered. Courveille was sixty-five years old when he wrote it and by this time, munity of the Benedictine order at Solesmes where he proved himself a successful missioner. It is unlikely that, at this stage of his life, he fabricated or distorted his story. Taken together with the other documents, the least that this shows is that over the long time-span from 1815 to 1852 Courveille was consistent in his claim of his spiritual experience at Le Puy in 1812.

Mayet's attitude to these various accounts is significant. Although interested in apparitions of the Virgin, such as the one at La Salette in 1846, he was a

---

13. OM, vol. 1, p. 581, footnote 2.

painstaking researcher. Determined to discover all he could about the origins of the Society, he sought out information from as many of the early Marists as he could: Déclas, Terraillon, Pierre Colin, Séon and Colin. Three times he contacted Courveille. Although he did edit Courveille's written replies, he was such a careful recorder that his account can be presumed to be accurate. At the end of his investigations, he accepted Courveille's claim at face value. His assessment must be taken seriously.

Of importance, too, is Courveille's subsequent action which is consistent with a genuine conviction of the truth of his experience. It was this certainty that Mary wanted him to work on the project of a Society dedicated to her, a conviction that refused to go away although he prayed and offered Masses that it would, that drove him first, although unwillingly, to seek the counsel of his spiritual guides. Strengthened by their advice he sought to gain recruits from his classmates. He was successful. His transparent conviction and evident piety won them over. When these factors are taken together, it is difficult not to accept the story Courveille told Mayet in 1852 that he had a spiritual experience at Le Puy in 1812.

Since Courveille's 'revelation' at Le Puy was so important in the history of the Society of Mary and was to mark the whole course of Colin's life from then on, some analysis is necessary. In this account Courveille shows Mary as revealing a clear wish. Mary, he tells us, does this by drawing twin parallels. The first parallel is between the way she imitated Jesus when he was on earth, particularly when he was dying on the cross for man's salvation, (which theologians regard as the moment of the Church's foundation) and what she does now which is protecting the Church and saving souls. The second parallel is between the action of her Son at the time of the Reformation, when to defend the Church he raised up a society bearing his name, and her own action in these latter-days of impiety and unbelief when, to combat the modern forces of evil, she wants to raise up a society bearing her own name. A society bearing her name with a mission to support the Church, was then the message of the Virgin Mary. The 'active' role is interesting for whereas in other revelations Mary is either silent or contemplative, here she is shown as an active participant in her Son's work and wants a society with the same active mission. Striking, too, is the vivid language used especially in reference to the Reformation which is described as 'Hell unleashed'. As Courveille heard no actual words, the expression he used came from his own understanding of the evils that accompanied the Reformation, reflecting the attitude of Catholics in an age that was far from ecumenical.

When Courveille told his story to his companions at Saint-Irénée the effect was immediate and electrifying. Terraillon described the impact it made on Déclas to whom Courveille revealed it first and then on the others:

This disclosure struck this seminarian [Déclas] singularly and left him profoundly impressed ... he enthused about the project, and his sole thought
was of communicating it to others ... He spoke first to M. Colin or to me
.... This message struck both of us to the supreme degree and left us quite
stunned.[14]

The spiritual experience Courveille had, and the conviction with which he
related it to his early companions, were key factors in the beginning of the
Marist project. Terraillon wrote: 'We determined to give ourselves resolutely to
the realisation of a project which enraptured us from its first presentation to
us.' The Blessed Virgin herself, they were convinced, had asked for a society
dedicated to her with its own specific mission. 'Here is what I want,' was quite
significant in the creation of the Society of Mary. The impression that this call
of Mary and her choice of them made on the young seminarians evoked an
eager and wholehearted response.

Some time during the scholastic year of 1815-16, perhaps as early as
Christmas 1815, fifteen had enrolled themselves in the project. Who were that
chosen band? The names of four who persevered to the end in the society of
Mary are known. Déclas was the first Courveille approached and, dazzled by
what Courveille revealed at that unforgettable moment when he was cutting
Courveille's hair, the simple horse-groom turned seminarian remained committed to it all his life. Then there was Étienne Terraillon, a farmer's son from
Saint-Loup, thirty kilometres east of Lyon. Terraillon maintained a tenuous
relationship with the group but then later occupied positions of trust in the
young society. One of the most significant of all Courveille's recruits was
Marcellin Champagnat, an energetic warm-hearted merchant's son from
Marlhes, twenty-three kilometers south of Saint-Étienne. Marcellin was a
straightforward, courageous and determined young man of twenty-six. He had
identified a pressing pastoral need, that of the education of the neglected youth
and was very willing to join Courveille's group if he could undertake the founding of a branch of teaching brothers. This was agreed to.[15]

A fourth was Colin. Why he was chosen is not clear. Déclas, with whom he
was always friendly, may have suggested him and Courveille, possibly on the
advice of Bochard and Cholleton, saw him as very suitable for the project. He
was a bright and steady student but it was probably his piety that recommended him to them as a suitable candidate. His great love for the Virgin Mary

14. OM, doc. 750, 2-3.
15. [J-B. Furet], *Life of Blessed Marcellin Joseph Benedict Champagnat, 1789-1840, Marist Priest*,
Bicentenary Edition (Rome, 1989), p. 28. Coste downplays too much the importance of this
mandate given by the group to Champagnat. 'Le mandat donné par ses compagnons à Marcellin
Champagnat en 1816. Essai d'histoire de la tradition', *The Study of Marist Spirituality: a collo-
quium held in Rome, September 24-28, 1984* (Rome, 1984), pp 1-16. See OM, docs 416, 1; 820, 10.

would have been evident to his fellow-seminarians. Later, the Curé of Ars, who was with him at Saint-Irénée for a short time, said of him: 'Oh, how he loves the Blessed Virgin!' Whatever was Courveille's reason for telling him of Mary's desire for a society dedicated to her, Colin accepted to be part of it with joy in his heart. He had rejected many other enticing offers but this time something clicked. He had always pined for a life removed from the world in which Mary, his heavenly mother, would play a major role. Yet, by remaining in the seminary and accepting diaconate, he was moving inexorably and rapidly towards the very public work of a priest in a parish. Now, on the threshold of ordination, came this revelation of a call by Mary for a society doing the work of salvation under her leadership. In such a society his fears would vanish. As he told his close associate, Julian Eymard, 'terrified by the … dangers of the priesthood, he consoled himself with the thought of a Society of Mary … to which the priesthood would give him entrance.'[16] The call promised to fulfill all he dreamt of from his boyhood on. 'This suits you,' he told himself and, without hesitation, he threw himself into the project with all the enthusiasm and suppressed energy of a man who had finally found what for him was 'the pearl of great price'. He never turned back.

Although Colin welcomed Courveille's invitation, he claimed later that he had the idea of a Marist project before ever Courveille spoke to him. The alacrity with which he accepted Courveille's invitation shows at least how ready, perhaps pre-disposed, he was for it. After Courveille left in disgrace, Colin never mentioned his role until, in the 1860s, dissensions about the rule arose and spilled over into a controversy as to who was the founder of the Society. Colin affirmed that others – by which he meant himself – had the idea before Courveille. He made this claim in 1865 and 1868, and then in 1869-70, in a statement to his secretary Jeantin, he repeated it categorically. All Courveille did was to manifest the idea or to make it public. He had already jotted down, he claimed, some notes on the subject. He stuck consistently to this statement. Since, however, this claim was made fifty years after the events and in an atmosphere of controversy when Colin's own role was under challenge, its reliability needs to be examined.

Apart from Colin's longing since boyhood for a hidden life in which Mary figured largely, which accords well with his claim, there exists a letter written decades before the controversy of the 1860s which provides more positive confirmation. In the course of the year 1824, Mgr de Pins, the apostolic administrator of Lyon, had been dealing with Courveille as superior of the Marist group in Lyon. He knew little of the other group of Marists in Belley for they were in a separate diocese. From Belley, however, the two Colins took pains to write to him promising to put him right as regards the Marist society and its

16. OM, doc. 741.

rules and aims and clearly intimating that they, more than any others, were in a position to tell him about the society and about 'those people who ... had conceived the project before anyone had thought of it'.[17] The meaning of this phrase is clear – the Colin brothers are affirming that Jean-Claude had conceived the idea before ever Courveille had told them of it. Colin's claim, then, predates by decades the controversies of the 1860s, and even predates Courveille's retiral from the Marist scene in 1826. Yet Colin's indebtedness to Courveille was great as he himself admitted to Jeantin in 1870:

> Later, Father said that it was not quite the same project. He had, before he came to the seminary, the project of a society consecrated, it is true, to the Blessed Virgin but he did not have the name of the Society of Mary; that name came from Father Courveille.[18]

To concede that the name was Courveille's, not his, was a major concession on Colin's part because for him the name of the Society was of the greatest importance and became the first and one of the finest articles of his final rule.

Because Colin and the first Marists said so little about the early days, the resulting vagueness may have given rise to the suggestion, discussed by some early Marists in 1830, 1846 and 1860, that the society owed its origin to a Jesuit priest of Le Puy or to a proposal, circulating in Spain during the Revolutionary period, to found a Society of Mary. Courveille denied this out of hand.[19]

In 1996, in a major attempt to throw fresh light on Marist origins, André Lanfrey put forward the hypothesis of 'the Society of Mary as a secret organisation', that is, as emanating from a secret devotional society, the *Association des Amis* – Association of Friends – the so-called 'Aa's or kindred organisation.[20] There are many merits in this attractive hypothesis. It could explain the secretiveness of Colin and other Marists on the early history, and such formulas as 'of one mind and one heart', or 'unknown and, as it were, hidden'. It encounters, however, the major difficulty of the absence of proof. No convincing evidence of the involvement of an Aa or a kindred society in the origins of the Society of Mary exists. Since Aas were vowed to secrecy, a scarcity of evidence is not unexpected but the silence concerning them in the relatively abundant surviving Marist documents is total. Courveille, Déclas, Terraillon, Champagnat,

---

17. OM, doc. 117, 4. See, too, OM, doc. 753, 1. Later documents make the claim more explicitly. OM, docs 804, 7; 813, 2, 819, 5-39.
18. OM, doc. 819, 6a.
19. A. Lanfrey, 'The Legend of the Jesuit of Le Puy', *Marist Notebooks*, no. 10 (1997), 1-16; Coste, *Lectures*, pp 18-19; Coste, *Marian Vision*, pp 96-8. Coste has also disposed of suggestions that Courveille took it from the writings of Maria of Ágreda or Grignion de Montfort. For Maria of Ágreda see below, chapter 10.
20. A. Lanfrey, 'La Société de Marie comme Congrégation secrète', *Marist Notebooks,* no. 9 (July 1996), pp 15-92; Idem, *Marcellin Champagnat et les Frères Maristes: Instituteurs congréganistes au XIXe siècle* (Paris, 1999), pp 47-9.

Colin were all deeply involved in the early days of the Society and left some account of the origins of the Society but nowhere does a trace of Aas emerge. Since Courveille was the first to speak of the Society of Mary, what he related is crucial. While he willingly gave a detailed account of the origins and allowed Mayet to question him closely, he never once suggested the influence or existence of an Aa either for the period at Le Puy or Saint-Irénée. Early researchers on the origins of the Society, Mayet, Jeantin, Lagniet and Detours, who knew the early generation of Marists well, never allude to a secret society, even when baffled by the mysterious reticence of Colin. This is all the more telling since the question of the origins of the society became a burning issue in the 1860s when claim and counter-claim were put forward in the bitter dispute that arose.

Yet André Lanfrey's hypothesis concerning the Aa and similar secret devotional societies is helpful in that it alerts us to a significant truth. The Society of Mary did not spring up from nowhere. It grew and flourished in a rich spiritual tradition that stretched back to a period long before the Revolution and which was still motivating Catholics. During this Restoration period, zealous Catholics were anxious to roll back the secularisation of the Revolution, to restore the Church to its former glory, and to proclaim the gospel with new vigour. In Lyon the Catholic revival was strong. Benoît Coste had organised the 'Congrégation' or 'Society of Young People'. This was a devout lay organisation which engaged in many apostolic works. It founded the Society for the Propagation of the Faith which largely financed the Marist and other foreign missions. Pauline Jaricot, whose role in that Society was a leading one, had been converted by a sermon preached by Father Würtz, assistant priest in the parish church of Saint-Nizier, a kilometre or two from Saint-Irénée.[21] This parish was a centre of renewal and Ultramontanism.[22]

It was an age of secret societies, from Carbonari to their Catholic equivalents like the Chevaliers de la Foi who had played a role in restoring the 'Most Christian king' to France. This was an age of 'Enthusiasm', of ferment, an age when prophecies flourished in many countries of western Europe and when religious circles abounded in apocalyptic millenarianism, that is the imminent return of Christ to begin his thousand year reign as foretold in the Book of Revelation. Many religious people believed that the world had reached its final age as foretold in the New Testament. The new religious orders that sprang up re-echoed this pre-occupation with the 'last times' and geared their mission to

21. Pauline Jaricot (1799-1862) founded the *Living Rosary,* 1826.
22. Jacques Besson, the parish priest, assisted de Maistre with his work *Du Pape* (1819), a book which helped launch Ultramontanism. Among those associated with Saint-Nizier were Claudine Thévenet's family and the Ozanams, including Frédéric (1813-53), founder of the Society of St Vincent de Paul.

it. Like religious reformers generally, they wanted a return to the supposed ideal Christian community of the early Church.

Seminaries, with their young idealistic students, were hotbeds of those enthusiasms. Zealous seminarians formed pious groups and associations. The students for the priesthood, now only a few years from ordination, believed that before long it would fall to them to re-evangelise the neglected people. In Saint-Irénée, as Colin related later on, many plans and projects were formed. Visions were floated of a new evangelisation, a new dawn. Outside agents were ready to stoke the fire of the students' enthusiasms. Advocates of congregations and societies, old and new, hoping to reap some of the rich harvest of vocations that had sprung up in Saint-Irénée, eagerly spread attractive apostolates before the seminarians. The Sulpicians, suppressed by Napoleon, had resumed their work in 1814, and their influence was strong in Saint-Irénée. The Jesuits, re-established in 1814 by Pope Pius VII, were enticing many, including the talented contemporary of Colin, Louis Querbes, who, however, went on to establish his own society of the Clerks of St Viator attracting many generous young Lyonese students.

The allure of heroic work in the foreign missions of Asia, America and Africa, was attracting other seminarians; the Congregation of the Mission (Vincentians or Lazarists) and the Paris Foreign Mission Society, re-established in 1814 and 1815 respectively, had restarted their pioneering evangelisation in all parts of the French colonies and were calling out for recruits. Louis-Guillaume Dubourg, the bishop who was to ordain Colin and his colleagues in 1816, came to Lyon seeking young men willing to return to work with him in his vast diocese of New Orleans, which covered the whole of Louisiana from New Orleans to Saint Louis. Dubourg was but the first of the many vicars apostolic of mission dioceses who came to Saint-Irénée hoping to get recruits. A buzz of excitement pervaded the seminary. Colin, solicited from all sides, later recalled those exciting times: 'how many times people tried to enrol me sometimes in this work, sometimes in another!'[23]

Members of the seminary staff were caught up in the general enthusiasm. Cholleton was a member of the *Congrégation,* others appeared willing to join new religious societies. The vicars general, Courbon and Bochard, were aware of these movements and of the attraction they held out to the best students and young priests of the diocese. 'The way the students are now inflamed,' Courbon warned Fesch, 'if we do not force each one to remain at his post, before long we will not recognise ourselves any more.'[24] To stop the haemorrhage of subjects, the archiepiscopal council decided that any ecclesiastic leaving the

23. OM, doc. 819, 9.
24. OM, doc. 29, 2.

diocese without permission would be suspended *ipso facto*.[25] Bochard, the other active vicar general, felt that the diocese should take a positive step and set up its own diocesan missionary society. Accordingly, he drew up a leaflet that he distributed to the students in Saint-Irénée, entitled *Pensée Pieuse* (Pious Thought). As a serious contribution by the vicar general in charge of seminaries, and a comment on the situation in Saint-Irénée in the year 1814-15, it merits citing in brief:

> In the sad state of desolation of the Church after a century of impiety ... who cannot but recognise that today the whole of society is more irreligious than Christian! In this difficult situation which ... shows no sign that it will soon end well ... so profoundly corrupted is ... public opinion, what will things come to if ... Providence does not soon give us one of its wonderful works ... when Luther appeared, did not Ignatius of Loyola come with his pious ... priests? And after ... the horrors of religious wars, did not Vincent de Paul come with his zealous missioners? O Lord, is ... nothing which can restore the depraved human race ... reserved for our time? And you, my brother who reads those words, what does it mean to you? ... if perchance the Lord now chose you as one of his apostles ... what would your astonished soul say? ... If the angel of God knocked at your door, if he offered you such a sublime apostolate: oh, then, learn how to reply to him, following the example of the Queen of Saints ... be it done unto me according to ... the holy will of God.[26]

Bochard went on to propose the setting up of a group of diocesan missioners to work in the most dechristianised areas and invited the students to join, promising them a varied and fruitful apostolate. Bochard had the support of other members of the staff. De la Croix d'Azolette, director at the seminary, helped organise the group and it was in his room they used to meet. Mioland, the professor of liturgy, was part of it. André Coindre, a zealous assistant priest at Bourg, joined the group in 1816.[27] The result was the forming of a new diocesan congregation called 'the Priests of the Cross of Jesus' of which Mioland was superior.

The concern and fervour expressed by Courbon and the reaction of Bochard reveal something of the background in Saint-Irénée at the time when the first Marists were beginning to meet. From the outset Courveille's group had the blessing of the vicar general Bochard, who hoped to take them over.

25. OM, doc. 30, 1.
26. The *Pensée Pieuse* is printed in full in OM, doc. 33.
27. André Coindre (1787-1826). At Saint-Irénée about the same time as Pierre Colin. In 1817, he felt called to work for poor girls and for this helped to found the Sisters of the Sacred Hearts of Jesus and Mary and the brothers of the Sacred Heart. Associated with Claudine Thévenet in the foundation of the Religious of Jesus and Mary.

They told Cholleton of their project. After celebrating Mass about the matter, he went along with it. At first, Gardette, despite his strict control of the seminary, knew nothing about it, but he soon learned from Déclas, who refused to take part without the express permission of his spiritual director who was none other than Gardette. When Déclas came and asked his permission to join the group, Gardette, surprised that no one had consulted him before this group began meeting, immediately asked whose authority they had. Déclas indicated obliquely that Bochard was the authority. Gardette, whose relations with the vicar general were not always easy and who may well have had misgivings about the altruism of Bochard's support, hesitated. He walked ten times around his room and finally turned to Déclas and said: 'Yes'!

During that school year, from probably as early as December 1815 to July 1816, the group met secretly in Cholleton's room. Many of the meetings were held at the seminary's country house, situated at La Croix Rousse in Lyon, again in Cholleton's room or, more usually, as Terraillon recounted, in the groves.[28] At the beginning the group devoted time to deciding whom they should invite to join and before long the group had increased to fifteen. Their meetings became a source of mutual encouragement, for they stimulated and fired one another with their dreams and enthusiasm. Decades later, the un-romantic Terraillon, no less than the simple Déclas, recalled those fervent early days with affection. 'We used these meetings,' Terraillon recounted, 'to inflame our desires, sometimes by reflecting that we had the good fortune to be the first children of Mary, sometimes by reflecting on the great need of people.' In this blend of personal piety and missionary zeal, they had grasped from the outset that the sense of being children of Mary and the sense of missionary zeal were interwoven and interdependent.[29] Courveille, who was a pious and a moving speaker, set the pace. His passionate sermons inspired them as Terraillon and Déclas recalled later: 'M. Courveille spoke … ardent words to us generally on the necessity of imitating Mary particularly in her indescribable humility.'[30] The content of the revelation he had received at Le Puy would have been central to their discussions, what was meant by every word that the Virgin uttered – the comparison with the foundation of the Jesuits, the name of the new congregation, the evils of the times and other ideas that the enthusiastic Courveille had made his own, such as the reign of a most Christian King.

As the year drew to a close and ordinations were just around the corner, the little group knew that they would soon be scattered to the four winds. To ensure that the project would have a follow-up, they decided to draw up a pledge to be signed by all. Four copies of this pledge have survived, all in the

28. OM, doc. 750, 5.
29. J. Coste, *A Certain Idea of the Society of Mary: Jean-Claude Colin* (Rome, 1990) pp 21-2.
30. OM, doc. 750, 5.

handwriting of Pierre Colin.[31] It was signed by twelve, for according to Déclas, three of the fifteen did not sign. Those who did included Courveille, Déclas, Terraillon, Champagnat, and Colin. The wording of the pledge is important for it reveals the thinking of the group and the ideals to which they vowed to devote their lives:[32]

> In the name of the Father and the Son and the Holy Spirit. All for the greater glory of God and the honour of Mary the mother of the Lord Jesus. We the undersigned, striving to work together for the greater glory of God and [the honour] of Mary the mother of the Lord Jesus, assert and make known our sincere intention and firm will of consecrating ourselves, as soon as ever it is opportune, to founding the most holy congregation of Mariists [sic]. That is why by this present act and our signatures we irrevocably dedicate ourselves and all we have, insofar as we are able, to the society of the Blessed Virgin Mary, and we do this neither childishly nor lightly, nor from any human motive or hope of temporal gain; but seriously, having taken timely counsel and weighed all before God, solely for the greater glory of God and the honour of Mary, mother of the Lord Jesus. We pledge ourselves to endure all sufferings, labours, inconveniences, and, if needs be, torture because we can do all things in him who strengthens us, Jesus Christ: to him we promise faithfulness in the bosom of our most holy mother, the Roman Catholic Church, and adhering to its supreme head the Roman pontiff with all our force; also to our very reverend bishop, our ordinary; that we may be good ministers of Jesus Christ, nourished by words of faith and wholesome doctrines which, by his grace, we have received; confident that under the reign of our most Christian king, which is favourable to peace and to religion, this special institute will see the light of day. We solemnly promise that, under the most august name of Mary and with her help, we shall spend ourselves and all we have in saving souls by whatever way possible; all this is, however, subject to the wiser judgement of our superiors. Praised be the holy and immaculate Conception of the Blessed Virgin Mary. Amen.

This is the pledge, full of youthful fervour and zeal, that Colin and his companions signed. While re-affirming their faith in Christ in the bosom of

---

31. In his letter to Bigex, in 1819, which includes a copy, Pierre referred to it as containing in 'summary form the aim and plan of the Society'. Was this 'plan', which Pierre, earlier in the letter, said that Courveille had communicated to the group, a more complete written plan than the summary? There is no evidence of it and, if a more complete plan existed, which is unlikely, it has not survived.

32. The text translated here is that edited by G. Lessard from P. Colin's letter to Bigex. It differs in some minor details from the text in OM, doc. 50. G. Lessard, 'An unpublished letter', *Forum Novum* 4 (1997), p. 90; Lanfrey, 'Commentaire critique', ibid., pp 111-13.

the Church to whose head they vow to be true, the young men promise in the most solemn way to do all they can to found a congregation of Marists. Then follows a statement of their mission, surprisingly high-minded and far-reaching for a group of inexperienced young men: they vow to spend themselves and all that they have to save souls 'by every possible means'. The mysterious reference to the reign of the most Christian king is an indication of their belief that they were entering into an exceptional time, perhaps the 'end-times' of the world. The word 'special' as applied to the institute, translates weakly the Latin, *eximia* which has the meaning of outstanding or exceptional, and should perhaps be understood as a reference to the special role of the Society in these last times.

It is a generous and courageous statement by twelve young clerics. This pledge in its exalted piety, heroic commitment and romantic language bears the trace of the fervour of young neophytes emerging from the hothouse of the seminary which at that time Saint-Irénée certainly was. Nevertheless, its fervour, sincerity and openness of spirit are moving. The Fourvière pledge is a key document towards understanding the Marist venture. Although not mentioned in the pledge, the project was to consist of four branches: priests, brothers, sisters and laity.

The pledge was probably drafted and re-drafted. Courveille, from whom the original thrust came, played a major role in its composition, for his influence can be seen in the heading of the pledge and in the reference to 'the Christian king'. Cholleton probably looked over it and it may be to him it refers when it speaks of taking timely advice. Over what period the text was drawn up is uncertain but it was ready for the great day of their ordination. That day called for special preparation and, together with the continuing study, took up much time. Fesch was an exile in Rome but the Sulpician, Bishop Louis Dubourg, newly ordained for the diocese of New Orleans, was in Lyon and he ordained the fifty-two ordinands. Courveille first received minor orders and then he and most of the others received the priesthood on 22 July 1816. It must have been a frantically busy but happy day.

The following day was the day they had set aside for publicly making their pledge and the place chosen was the shrine of Our Lady of Fourvière. Fourvière, always a place of pilgrimage, had become even more so since Pius VII rededicated the shrine in 1805. Priests, royalist supporters and other groups went often in procession there. New priests also went there after ordination. On that morning of 23 July 1816 the twelve Marists, dressed in their black cassocks and round hats, set off, crossed the Saone and climbed the steep hill of some 800 steps to Fourvière. There in the small chapel of Our Lady, next to the great basilica erected later in the century, the newly ordained priests and clerics gathered at the altar. Courveille alone celebrated Mass, with Terraillon assisting him. The others did not celebrate but received communion from the hands of Courveille. The reason Terraillon gave for this was that they were reserving their first solemn Mass for their home town. It is also a symbolic gesture similar to the one that marked the founding of the Society of Jesus almost three hundred years before, when on the hill of Montmartre in Paris, six Jesuits received communion at the hands of Blessed Peter Favre. Courveille was the head of the group; it was he who had taken the initiative and it was fitting that they all receive communion from his hands. During the ceremony, they placed their pledge on the altar or, according to another account, under the corporal, the square piece of linen on which the consecrated bread and wine is placed. At the end of Mass, they read it aloud. It was all moving and dignified. They could not have chosen a more memorable day nor could they have made it in a more solemn fashion nor at a more appropriate shrine. They had made their vow. Within the next day or two, all of them parted to take some vacation at home and then the newly-ordained would go to the posts which the bishop had assigned to them. Their priestly ministry had begun. Their Society of Mary was still to be realised.

CHAPTER 9

Cerdon transforms Colin

'At first when I was curate …from all sides they complained that I was cold, that I was dead. I have indeed greatly changed.' Colin.

After his ordination and the memorable morning at Fourvière, Colin went to Salles, a little parish in the Beaujolais part of the diocese, not too far from his native Saint-Bonnet, where his brother Pierre was curé. There he celebrated his first Mass on 26 July, the feast of St Anne, the mother of the Blessed Virgin. The following day, 27 July, Pierre was officially appointed curé of Cerdon. He had asked to have Colin as his assistant and his request was granted. The prospect of being curate to his brother had frightened Colin when he learned of it and, as usual, he hurried off to consult his confessor, Jean Cholleton. 'You know my plans,' he said to him, 'I fear that the love I have for my brother may prove an obstacle to realising them.' A smiling Cholleton, used to Colin's scruples, replied: 'Go ahead and have no fear; your brother will be your first companion.'[1] He spent six or seven weeks in Salles, during which he may well have visited his relations in Saint-Bonnet, passed a few days at Saint-Irénée, and then, accompanied by his brother, in or about the second week of September, travelled to Pierre's new parish in Cerdon. He was to remain there over eight years and that stay was to prove pivotal for his personal development and for his mission.

Cerdon was in the Bugey, a region in the south-west of the department of Ain. In 1816 it constituted the eastern part of the diocese of Lyon. A picturesque little town nestling at the meeting point of three valleys where the foothills of the massive south Jura mountains began, Cerdon's importance and its history were closely linked to its position and its roads. From Roman times a road joining the important centres of Lyon and Geneva passed through it. By the new road built in 1763, the little town was some seventy kilometres north-east of Lyon and about the same distance south-west of Geneva before which the road became more mountainous. The journey from Lyon to Cerdon in Colin's time took the stage-coach twenty hours. The Cerdonese made good use of their position on this route. From time immemorial their town had been a staging-post for the mail. The *Statistique Générale* of 1805 noted that the town had 'a fairly considerable industry: the relay of horses which the inhabitants provide

1. OM, doc. 821, 18.

for climbing the four kilometres of mountainous road, is one important part.' For a franc and a half, the Cerdonese used to hire out a trace horse to pull the mail coach, and any other carriage, up the mountainside; the horse would then return of its own accord.

They made good use, too, of their natural resources. The slopes of the valleys were well suited to producing an excellent grape and the *Statistique* described Cerdon as 'a wine-growing country' with an extensive trade in wines.[2] A stream flowed through the town and the Cerdonese had harnessed it to drive two mills and a paper factory. The population in 1820 was 1,470 and by 1826, the year after the Colins left, it had increased to 1,719. The people in the town were probably little different from those of other towns in rural France. The marriage certificates in Cerdon give the professions of parents of the couples and so make it possible to reconstruct the social mix.[3] The great majority of the population described themselves as cultivators, a term which could include both farmers and wine-growers. Others described themselves as engaged in paper manufacturing, proprietors, or wine-makers. The rest were the usual mixture to be found in any country town of the period: tailors, weavers, masons, bakers, carpenters, coach-makers, wheel-wrights, stone-cutters, hatters, saddlers, cobblers, shopkeepers and inn-keepers. There was also a midwife, a doctor and, since Cerdon boasted a police station, a few gendarmes. There was a little convent, too. Three sisters of the congregation of Saint Joseph of Lyon, Sisters Etiennette, Françoise and Pierrette, formed a little community in the town and taught the children. A few wealthy landowners had survived the Revolution. One of those was the new mayor, Jacques-Robert Bajollet, who had been appointed shortly before the arrival of the Colins. He and his assistant, Jean François Moiret, and a notary formed, together with the commune or town council, the administration of the village.

The biographer of Bishop Devie (who was to play an important part in Colin's life) claimed that, at that time, the diocese of Lyon was more wretched than other dioceses, and that within the diocese, the most abandoned part was, without question, the department of Ain, where Cerdon was located. 'The department of Ain,' he wrote, 'became ... a sort of Siberia for the clergy of Lyon, to the point that to be sent to the Bugey ... was considered by the priests as a disgrace'.[4] Cardinal Fesch and his vicars general had shown themselves devoted pastors, very active in rebuilding and improving the church in Lyon. It is true, however, that within the diocese of Lyon, the department of the Ain

2. M. Bossi, *Statistique Générale ... Département de l'Ain,* (Paris, 1808), p. 119.
3. Actes des mariages, 1816-1825, Archives communales de Cerdon, Registres d'état-civil. Copy put at my disposal by Father Pierre Jacolin, s.m.
4. J. Cognat, *Vie de Mgr Alexandre-Raymond Devie, évêque de Belley,* vol. 1, (Lyon-Paris, 1865), pp 182-3.

fared least well for it sent far less of its sons to Saint-Irénée to train for the priesthood than the other two departments in the diocese, the Loire and the Rhone. As a result it had fewer priests and this in turn meant that the restoration, spiritual and material, went ahead more slowly. In Cerdon, according to the report in 1804 of Jean-Claude Carron, the first curé to arrive after the signing of the Concordat in 1801, and that of Pierre Colin twenty years later, the people there were not excessively irreligious nor was the material state of the church quite dilapidated. During the Revolution, the Church had certainly suffered in Cerdon as elsewhere. On 10 December 1793 a violent crowd rushed to sack the church and when the mayor and some leading citizens opposed them, they threatened to clap them in jail.[5] The mob smashed the altar and tabernacle, and burned the great cross over the altar and any objects of devotion they could find. The high steeple offended the revolutionaries' ideal of 'equality' and so they hacked it down. The church itself was transformed into a temple of reason and the revolutionaries used the pulpit to harangue their hearers. An eyewitness, Charles-Gabriel Clerc, detailed worse sacrileges:

> These profanations, however revolting, appeared tolerable when one saw baptised Christians give themselves over to sacrileges infinitely more horrible. We saw those monstrous Christians running through the streets of Cerdon … disguised as priests, thurible in hand, vested in cope and chasuble and incensing a donkey, rigged out also in a cope.[6]

In all these manifestations, the revolutionaries in Cerdon were merely imitating the antics of extreme revolutionaries throughout France. Many, if not most, of the Cerdonese remained attached to the Catholic religion. When, in 1797, the second great wave of persecutions deported the priests to Devil's Island or forced them into hiding, the laity took the law into their own hands. They decided that they would sing the office and hymns in the church themselves and accompany the funerals to the cemetery. They maintained these practices for four years until Napoleon finally restored freedom of religion. When the Concordat became law, the municipal council, in April 1802, publicly thanked those who were prominent in aiding the priests loyal to Rome and providing rooms in their houses for the celebration of Mass.[7] One of those families singled out for praise was that of the mayor, Bajollet. A new bell was named after him.

Yet, the Revolution had brought changes in the attitude of the people to the Church. From Father Carron's report of 1804, it appears that most of the Cerdonese came to the services in the church and every home had its crucifix,

5. A. Janichon, *Monographie de Cerdon,* (Bourg, 1926), pp 126-9.
6. C.-G. Clerc, 'Annales [de Cerdon] depuis l'an 1770 – jusqu'en 1832', pp 15-16, unpublished mss in APM. Charles-Gabriel Clerc (1766-1839).
7. Janichon, *Cerdon,* pp 186-7.

holy water and, generally, an image of the Virgin Mary. On the other hand, although most of the women went to confession, very few of the men frequented the 'sacred tribunal of penance'. This reluctance on the part of the men to confess their sins to a priest had become a common feature in post-revolutionary France. Often it was human respect or peer pressure – the men did not like it to be known that they confessed their sins to the priest.[8] A further deterrent would have been the strictness of the confessors. Most were schooled in the rigorist moral theology common to the French Church. To add to the difficulty, even after the Concordat, some confessors, too, were refusing absolution to anyone who did not restore church and other property seized during the Revolution.

Cerdon had seen something of Napoleon's wars. In 1814, the Austrians had descended from Geneva and occupied the town, damaging the police barracks and exacting support. They subsequently retreated before the French army but returned again in a few weeks. War compensation had to be paid to the Austrian commander, Count Bubna. When Napoleon returned in 1815, much of the Bugey was overjoyed and, even after his defeat at Waterloo that summer, many continued to support the Bonapartist cause hoping that the emperor would return once again. As late as May 1816, royalist forces had to march on the not-too-distant city of Grenoble to suppress the Bonapartists active there. Shortly before the Colins arrived, the authorities had seized 264 army guns in the area around Cerdon including 48 in the town itself. The local Bonapartist leader, César Savarin, was hiding in the mountains, but Cerdon's new mayor, Bajollet, a zealous supporter of the restored monarchy, denounced him, and he was arrested at Poncieux, five or six kilometres to the south of the town. Savarin was executed at Bourg, the capital of the department, on 24 October, a few weeks after the arrival of the brothers Colin at Cerdon.

Apart from political unrest, that year of 1816 was climatically a disaster. So bad was it that Clerc, the local chronicler and schoolmaster, declared that it should be erased from the Christian era.[9] Wet, windy and cold weather had destroyed the crops. Though he could not have known it then, the year 1816 had been an appallingly bad year everywhere, and scientists now trace the cause to an immense volcanic eruption the previous year on Mount Tambora on the island of Sumbawa in Indonesia! The atmospheric dust the eruption produced in the stratosphere circled the earth and, reflecting sunlight back into space, reduced the amount of it reaching the earth. The disastrous effects on the weather were felt across America and in western Europe. Geneva, the city nearest to Cerdon, recorded its coldest summer on record from 1753 to modern

---

8. P. Boutry, 'Industrialisation et déstructuration de la société rurale', in J. Le Goff and R. Rémond, *Histoire de la France religieuse*, vol. 3, (Paris, 1991), p. 283.
9. Clerc, 'Annales' p. 31-2.

times.[10] In Cerdon, during the first nineteen days of May, snow and hail devastated the crops and the incessant rain rotted the hay and even the plants. In the autumn showers of hail again brought more damage. By 21 October the mountains were snow-covered! The effect on the area was a disastrous failure of the harvest, affecting the grape, the grain and the potato. In the major town of Poncin there was the usual profiteering that accompanies shortages and famines. As the price of provisions soared out of the reach of the poor, many began to go hungry. Spurred to action by the distress, Bajollet, the mayor, called a meeting of the town council on 4 December to consider how to provide help, and the curé, Pierre Colin, was invited to come and take part. Throughout the department relief was being organised, the mayor told the meeting, and something must be done in Cerdon where the need was greater because of 'the bad weather, the frosts in the spring and autumn which have destroyed the hopes of three quarters of its inhabitants, who have no other resources except agriculture and the vine.' The report of the meeting adds that 'the curé and the members of the council' agreed and an emergency fund was set up to which was diverted a sum due to the church committee for repairing the bell-tower.[11] How effective these measures were it is impossible to gauge but the appalling results of the bad harvests that winter became evident early in the new year. For several months in early 1817, people were reduced to gathering and eating the grass of the fields or consuming the fodder destined for the animals. Some of the worst off died of want. Remarkably, there were no outbreaks of violence for, although the people daily witnessed the carts of grain grinding up the mountain side in convoys en route for Switzerland, they made no attempt to seize them. A better harvest in 1817 brought relief at last.

The involvement of the curé and, no doubt to some degree, his younger brother, speaks well of their acceptance in the town. The mayor, Bajollet, welcomed them warmly; the schoolmaster and chronicler, Clerc, spoke of both brothers as 'virtuous priests with the spirit of their calling'. Bajollet and Clerc represented the upper echelons in this little community. There is no evidence, however, that the Colins experienced any ill-feeling or opposition from the poorer people who made up most of the parishioners. The two brothers settled in, were happy there and were well-liked. Later in life Colin always spoke kindly of the Cerdonese, those 'good people' among whom he first ministered. They were not paragons of virtue. Clerc, after describing in detail the dreadful winter of 1816-17, decided, as he put it in his annals for 1818, to add to his comments on the changing climate some comments on changing customs. Morality had changed, he was convinced, and for the worse:

10. H. Stommel and E. Stommel, 'The Year without a Summer', *Scientific American* 240 (1979), 176-86.
11. 'Registre municipal de la Commune de Cerdon', 4 Dec. 1817, Archives Municipales de Cerdon, copy in APM; OM, doc. 91, observation 3.

For some years now, this generation has made unmistakable progress in godlessness, luxury and depravity. The young people, and especially those recruited for Napoleon's recent wars, manifest a degree of malice, pride and arrogance, which is afflicting for society and disastrous for the future. The women, for their part, share this contagion; they carry this luxury and impertinence to its highest level. Both one and the other vie in exalting themselves above their birth, families and station. Religion, its holy maxims, its duties, its practices are disregarded and abandoned …[12]

Clerc went on to condemn perverse and scandalous writing and the government's inability or unwillingness to put it down. His comments are on French society in general, and so what he has to say cannot be taken as a precise portrait of the Cerdonese in 1817. Nevertheless Cerdon and its people would have provided the setting and the substance for his remarks. These are the criticisms of an intelligent and upright schoolteacher, whose habit of keeping a journal gave him the opportunity of reflecting on the town he undoubtedly loved. It should be noted, however, that a report on schoolmasters, which Father Champion, the curé of Poncin, made in 1809, depicted Clerc as zealous, even preachy.[13] A generation gap had opened between the world Clerc had known and the younger people, and his criticisms reveal his frustrations at the new world that the Revolution ushered in. His comments have to be carefully weighed.

Clerc's comments can be compared with those of the curés of Cerdon. In 1804, Jean-Claude Carron, the curé from 1803 to 1809, replied to a questionnaire from the diocesan office in Lyon. Carron commented favourably on the people. Carron reported that most houses had family prayers and most appeared to have come to the services – Mass and vespers. There were three congregations or religious sodalities of lay people there – those of the Sacred Heart, the Rosary and the Blessed Sacrament in 1804. On the negative side, Carron noted the men were not coming to confession. His main complaint concerned alcohol. Taverns abounded, he said, whereas three would be quite adequate and he wanted measures taken against those who supplied drink while the services were taking place.

In 1823, the recently-appointed Bishop Devie, determined to assess the state of his diocese, sent to each of his curés a list of 156 questions. The questions were mainly concerned with the material state of the parish buildings but a few touched on the conduct of the people. Pierre Colin had few complaints to make. One reproach he made concerned the Sabbath, for he acknowledged

---

12. Clerc, 'Annales', p. 33
13. 'Renseignements sur les Maîtres d'Ecole du Canton de Poncin transmis par M. Champion, Curé de Poncin, 21 avril 1809', Dossier Fesch-De Pins, Enseignement primaire et secondaire, Archive Archevêché de Lyon, Cerdon. Copy APM.

that during the harvest time, and in particular during the wine harvest, they worked on Sunday. A second complaint was that the taverns were not always closed during the Sunday services. Dancing was the only other abuse he noted. On the 8 September the parishioners went to the chapel of our Lady in the little village of Préaux a few hundred yards from Cerdon itself. Besides the devotions, there was dancing, and merriment followed for this was the town's feast day. The townsfolk, Pierre had to admit, 'behaved badly: the dancing continued sometimes for days on end even during the services at the parish church'. All three of Pierre's complaints figured in Colin's account of his pastoral activity at Cerdon. Those abuses were common enough in post-revolutionary France; the young people wanted to have fun, and dancing and drinking were essential ingredients. The tavern was, as always, the preserve and refuge of the menfolk. As for Sunday work, although for some it was purely to make more money, for others it could be an economic necessity, especially for labourers who were paid by the day. Apart from these faults, the Colins were loud in their praise of the people of Cerdon. There were no superstitious practices of note in the parish and the people were reasonably devout. The confraternities of the Sacred Heart and of the Rosary continued to thrive but the confraternity of the Blessed Sacrament had disappeared. The impression that emerges is that the Cerdonese were certainly no worse and perhaps a bit better than the people in many another parish in the diocese at that time. Colin gave his own impression of them some twenty years later: they were cowards, he said, and you had to be bold with them, for if they thought you were afraid they would be bold but if you took a stand they retreated.[14] Yet the Cerdon of Colin was probably not much different from the Ars of John Vianney and other villages. The systematic programme of dechristianisation had made an impact, if in differing degrees, across the country. Colin's comment later in life was not dissimilar from Clerc's: 'The great Revolution has left deep traces upon our France, we are given over to indifference, to pantheism, to materialism.' Like all the clergy of the Restoration period, this was the reality he and his brother had to face in Cerdon.

The reports of 1804 and 1823, together with another by Father Champion, the curé of Poncin, in 1809 give interesting data on the state of education in Cerdon. The revolutionaries, in attacking the Church, severely damaged the existing education system without providing something in its place. The replies of the curés of Ain to Devie's questionnaire of 1823 reported that only a quarter of the population were adequately educated.[15] In 1804 Carron believed that most people in Cerdon could read. There was a school for boys and one for girls taught by some pious parishioners. According to a report of 1809, there

---

14. OM, doc. 541, 6-7.
15. *Pratique religieuse dans l'Europe révolutionnaire*, p. 502.

were three teachers in the school for boys. One of them, Benoît de la Salle, was suspected of having liberal views. Another, Joseph Bolliet, a younger man, appears to have been employed only in a temporary capacity. The third was the annalist, Clerc, a committed Catholic and royalist, but so full of zeal that he frightened both parents and children. He was probably the longest serving of the teachers, for he was still there in 1815.[16] Fourteen years later, in the Colins' time, a regular schoolmaster paid by the commune taught the boys, and nuns looked after the girls. Yet Pierre was not at all happy with the level of education the sisters provided and he felt that the boys' school was beset with problems. Some time around 1823 Pierre Colin had to get rid of a new teacher for possessing an 'abominable book', and the inspector reported that his successor was no better and would have to be dismissed too.[17]

The reports of 1804 and 1823 give more information on the state of the church, sacristy and church property. Despite the ravages of the Revolution, Father Carron was able to report that the church and its furnishings were in reasonably good order, though repairs had to be made and furnishings bought. 'My church is decent, my sacristy, too,' he wrote, 'but both lack furniture, decoration and embellishment … the altars, except one, are decent and fairly clean and I can say the same for the vestments … I have no sacred vessels except a pyx for viaticum …' There was also a garden, which 'although small was adequate'. When Pierre replied to Bishop Devie's questionnaire nearly twenty years later, he was able to report that the church was in quite good order. It was now better furnished with a chalice, paten, ciborium, statues, lamps and sacred vestments. The most important improvement had been the presbytery itself. Bajollet, the mayor, had taken the initiative. In 1818, fearing that one of the presbytery walls might fall down and ruin the whole building, the mayor had begun repair works. These repairs proved more extensive than expected and finally in July 1820 it became necessary to demolish the whole building. For the next year and a half, up to January 1822 the Colin brothers had been lodged at the house of a notary in the Swiss quarter of the town, so called because the road to Switzerland passed by there. Jeanne-Marie Chavoin probably accompanied them. The new building was a solid presbytery that is still standing.

Colin's work was that of an ordinary country curate – saying Mass, preaching, baptising, confessing, marrying, visiting the sick and burying the dead. Already on 19 September, a few days after arriving in Cerdon, he had his first marriage which was the validation of the civil marriage a couple had contracted thirteen years before. His first three burials were all of little children, the oldest of whom was five months – a stark reminder of the high rate of infant mortality. Baptisms averaged one a week and funerals a little more frequent. Despite his

16. 'Renseignements sur les Maîtres d'Ecole par Champion'.
17. OM, doc. 85.

initial shyness, he adapted himself to this part of the ministry without any apparent difficulty. Scruples, however, did trouble him. On occasion it took him up to 11 o'clock in the morning to bring himself to say Mass. Hearing confessions posed an even greater anguish as he recounted years later:

> For nine years I never left the confessional without throwing myself at the feet of Mary and saying to her: 'Oh, my good Mother, what have you exposed me to?' My confessional was in the chapel of the Blessed Virgin. The ministry of the confessional is a terrifying one; I have never gone to it without trembling.[18]

Caught between the strict teaching on confession which he had received at the seminary and the realities of the pastoral situation, the pious young priest was overwhelmed and frightened. His first reaction was to run to Cholleton, his director and professor of moral theology, for help, and the kindly professor generously gave him counsel and comfort. Before long, however, he gently pointed out to Colin that he could not remain in leading strings for ever and it was time to stand on his own feet. This proved excellent advice, as Colin admitted later. He had an invaluable advantage, which few other new curates had – the presence and support of his well-loved brother. Pierre Colin was able to guide Jean-Claude's first steps during the difficult early years of the ministry, for he had by now almost six years of parish experience. Yet as regards curing him of a rigorist approach in the confessional, his brother would be of little help, for he had undergone the same training in moral theology. The tragic case mentioned earlier merits citing in full for it shows the extent to which Colin was ruled by the moral rigorism of the time:

> A good and pious woman was the victim of the bad conduct of her husband and the crime of onanism. According to the principles he had received, Father Colin could not let this pass and give her absolution, although she had serious reasons for permitting such a crime to take place, and although she detested it, and despite all she did to avoid it. This poor woman wept at being banished from the sacraments she loved, and good Father Colin suffered even more than she did … One night, this poor woman saw the Blessed Virgin, who, showing her a rosary, told her that with that weapon she would be victorious. She then devoted herself to Mary, prayed to her, and from that time, her husband never made her any criminal proposal, respected the holy laws of marriage and Father Colin was happy to re-open the source of the sacraments to someone whom, for six months, he had kept away from it by an innocent mistake.[19]

In telling this story later, Colin denounced 'the rigorous, far too rigorous

18. OM, doc. 506, 3.
19. OM, doc. 542, 4. See chapter 6.

teaching' given in the seminary and the terrible embarrassment it caused him. Those principles that seemed so logical when Cholleton expounded them in class, were proving an enormous obstacle for him and a burden for his congregation. No wonder confession was such a terrifying experience for him. Yet, harrowing though it was, this experience had the effect of bringing the hitherto sheltered and shy young priest to a better understanding of the difficulties ordinary people faced in their daily life. It may well have helped him, too, to cope with his scruples.

If it is not possible to trace accurately a change in his approach to confession, the change in another part of his ministry was apparent for all to see. At Saint-Irénée, the students were taught to read aloud on one tone or *recto tono,* and, in Cerdon, when Colin preached on Sundays, he read his Sunday sermon in like manner. 'When I was first a curate,' he admitted later, 'during two months I never said one word more loudly than another … From all sides they complained that I was cold, that I was dead.'[20] Then one day, why he does not say, he let go. The people sat up and took notice. Seeing the effect it had, Colin abandoned his monotonous moral lessons and spoke from the heart. The men of the parish were delighted. They had found him so boring before, now they whispered delightedly among themselves when they saw that he was going to give the sermon. 'It's the curate, the curate', they exclaimed![21] Pierre, apparently, did not preach with the same vigour, but he recognised his brother's talent as a warm and powerful preacher, as the following incident shows:

> When there was some great blow to be struck, his brother, the curé who undoubtedly recognised the gift God had given him … pushed Father Colin to the fore. One day, the latter had thundered forth in the pulpit; he came down and said to his curé: 'It is always me you put forward; I'm not the curé.' 'Don't complain …,' his brother said to him, 'after your talk, a man who had not been at confession for ten years came to see me.'[22]

Pierre's modesty in accepting a lower profile and his shrewdness in making use of his brother's talent to drive home an important pastoral point is impressive. Colin was also an excellent impromptu speaker and effective too in devising stratagems to make his point:

> On another occasion, he was in the pulpit about to speak, when he changed the subject, abandoning the one he had prepared and improvising. This sermon made a terrifying impression … I think he took as his theme the abuse of grace and perhaps that was the day he caused the funeral pall to be carried through every quarter of the town.[23]

20. OM, doc. 487, 2.
21. OM, doc. 745, 8.
22. OM, doc. 541, 8.
23. OM, doc. 541, 10.

This sermon made such an impression that people came to Jeanne-Marie Chavoin, the foundress of the Marist Sisters who was now looking after the presbytery, begging for a copy, but since it was improvised she had none. The most dramatic success he had in the pulpit was on another occasion when he came to the support of his brother. One Sunday Pierre had met some parishioners working on Sunday and had remonstrated with them. His remarks were met with murmurs and insults. Colin determined to act, and the following Sunday, speaking with righteous indignation, he turned towards Pierre who was presiding at the mass and said:

And you, pastor of this parish, is it not true, that last Sunday, you came among your people and that, like Moses, you suffered the pain of seeing them worshipping at the feet of the god of avarice. Then, your soul was shattered, your eyes filled with tears and like him you wanted to oppose this evil. But like Moses, were you not greeted with the insults of this people? And now, O pastor of this parish, what else can you do except climb again the holy mountain and cry to God: pardon them this sin or blot me out from the book of life.

A later account added a dramatic climax: As Jean-Claude spoke those words, Pierre rose, weeping, from his stall and in tears came up to the altar-step and threw himself down to pray. The congregation was moved to tears. The Sabbath, according to Colin, was better kept in future.[24]

If Colin could make a terrifying impression on the people by the force of his eloquence, he could equally twist their hearts by his warm compassion. 'After speaking like rolling thunder in the pulpit on the previous days,' Mayet reports, 'one day he began to speak in a fatherly tone and to speak to their hearts. Everybody cried.' Another instance reveals his ingenuity in moving his audience. He was concerned at how ill-instructed the children were and once when people were present in the church, he began to examine the children on the most basic articles of the faith. 'Who is God, what is the Trinity?' he asked them one after another. He got no reply, for deliberately he had questioned only those children who knew no catechism. Then he walked up and down without a word; his face contracted and a deep sorrow came over his countenance and he cried out: 'Poor children, poor children! If you took dangerously ill and someone came to find us (and one should) we could not in conscience absolve you because you are ignorant of the things necessary for salvation. Poor children! Poor children! You are on the edge of an abyss.' The effect was immediate. In tears, people came to him immediately after the lesson, offering to go round the families and to teach the children their catechism. His goal was attained.[25]

24. OM, docs 543; 885, 4-5.
25. OM, doc. 745, 5.

Knowledge of the catechism was, in the eyes of Colin, an essential part of his Cerdon ministry. One young lad hid in the cemetery instead of coming to class, but one can only imagine his horror when straightaway Colin went to his home to reproach the father for not sending his son to catechism. When the angry father took up a stick and rushed at the lad, Colin had to come between them and disarm the father. On another occasion, he took a more direct method. A young lad 18 years old was so careless about the catechism that over many years he could not be allowed to make his first communion. Colin resolved to put an end to this. 'He questioned him on the catechism and when the youth made no reply, he pulled out a cane from under his habit and said to him: "Hold out your hand." The young man held out his hand, received the salary of his laziness and, during the course of the year, he finally made his communion to the satisfaction of Father Colin.'[26]

Other incidents reveal how he used his ingenuity for the service of his pastoral ministry. The village feast with its dancing, drinking and disorders set alarm bells ringing for the French clergy of the time and Colin and his brother were no exceptions. That Cerdon had its annual village fête was normal and acceptable enough. When one year, however, the mayor agreed to have a second fête, Colin decided to act. Going over the head of the town council he travelled some forty kilometres to Bourg-en-Bresse, the departmental capital, to speak to the prefect, a very senior figure in the governmental system. There, instead of voicing complaints against the mayor or the council, he ingenuously assumed the role of submitting a matter for the prefect's advice: 'Look, Monsieur Prefect, this fête, during which disorders are to be feared, can we permit it to be established?' The prefect was embarrassed. Next Sunday, the priests told their parishioners all they had done, putting to the fore the civil authority. The ploy succeeded. The fiesta was abandoned.

'At balls and dances, purity is under attack from all sides,' wrote a famous eighteenth century French preacher and this suspicious attitude towards dancing was representative of the feeling of the French clergy before and after the Revolution.[27] While admitting that dancing was in itself innocent, what the clergy feared was that sexual sins could accompany it. Trained in this tradition, the two Colins viewed dancing with horror as corrupting the morals of their people. Colin used humour and a little ridicule to counter the abuse. To one young woman who confessed her liking for the ball, the penance he gave was that she should dance on her own before her barn-door! 'She thought, at first, he was joking,' Mayet recorded, 'but she said that this little indirect lesson,

26. OM, doc. 745, 4, 12.
27. J. Delumeau, *Le Péché et la Peur; la culpabilisation en Occident: xiii-xviii siècles* (Paris, 1983), p. 488. The preacher was Hyacinthe de Montargon. Grignion de Montfort wrote in a similar vein.

more than anything else, made her realise how ridiculous dancing was.' He used the same ridicule to combat another 'evil' – the latest fashion which, the clergy believed, was not always sufficiently modest. To one young woman he bowed low in the street, ironically congratulating her on being so attentive to the advice of her pastor.[28] A girl, dressed in the latest fashion, passed him in the street. He gazed after her, with pseudo puzzlement, then turned to a passerby and asked, 'Who is this woman?' When told it was not a woman but a young girl, he repeated in a stunned fashion: 'It's a girl!' His mock astonishment circulated quickly and killed the fashion dead.[29] The ridicule may appear heavy-handed, the irony somewhat hob-nailed, but Colin was convinced it was his duty and that his methods were effective.

To a more liberated age, Colin's campaign against fairs, dancing and women's fashion sounds narrow, even puritanical. The village feast, however, usually resulted in a number of unwanted pregnancies, as Gustave Thibon, the French philosopher, born in the neighbouring department of Ardèche testified in his memoirs.[30] Colin's action appears in better perspective when compared to that of St Jean-Marie Vianney, who in the little village of Ars, fifty kilometres away but in the same department of Ain, was thundering in the pulpit Sunday after Sunday against the dance:

> There is not a commandment of God which dancing does not cause people to break … Mothers may indeed say: 'Oh, I keep an eye on my daughters.' You keep an eye on their dress; you cannot keep guard over their heart. Go, you wicked parents, go down to hell where the wrath of God awaits you, because of your conduct when you gave free scope to your children; go! It will not be long before they join you, seeing that you have shown them the way so well … Then you will see whether your pastor was right in forbidding those hellish amusements.[31]

And the saintly curé backed up his words with actions. One Sunday a ball and pageant were beginning in the village square. Suddenly he was seen emerging from his house. Fear seized the people and, as the saintly curé said later 'They fled like a flock of pigeons'! Over a period of eight years, he refused absolution to a girl who went to one dance a year. As for a girl dressed immodestly, the curé thundered from the pulpit: 'Her extravagant and indecent dress proclaims her to be a tool by means of which hell seeks the ruin of souls. Only at the judgement-seat of God, will such a one know the number of crimes of which she has been the cause.'[32] At much the same time, further to the south

28. OM, doc. 541, 4, 5, a.
29. OM, doc. 745, 10.
30. G. Thibon, *Au soir de ma vie* (Paris, 1993), p. 126.
31. F. Trochu, *The Curé d'Ars: St Jean-Marie-Baptiste Vianney: 1786-1859* (London, 1927), p. 146.
32. Trochu, *Curé d'Ars,* pp 147; 155.

of France, that other saint, Eugène de Mazenod, founder of the Oblate Fathers, was organising meetings of young women who would then publicly renounce dancing and walking out with young men.[33] Colin did not take such strong measures but relied on the power of his word and persuasion. It says much for his strength of personality.

These episodes, which reveal Colin as a decisive, warm-hearted and talented young pastor, were, for the most part, narrated by Colin himself to Mayet twenty or more years later. Yet even though they are a type of self-portrait of the young Father Colin, good reasons exist for accepting them as accurate. Apart from Colin's innate honesty, when Mayet wrote other witnesses were alive – especially Pierre Colin and Jeanne-Marie Chavoin, who lived with him in Cerdon – able, if called on, to pronounce on their accuracy. Those accounts fit in well with Jeanne-Marie's own briefer description of events in Cerdon. Certain characteristics of Colin that emerge in the episodes correspond well with traits his contemporaries noted in him later in life. Given again the consistency with which Colin retold those stories much later again, with only minor differences, it is fair to assume that they give a true account of episodes in his first years of ministry, which remained etched in his memory.

Remote though Cerdon was from cultural centres, Colin was fortunate to be able to keep up some intellectual study. Bajollet, the mayor, invited him to use the library in his chateau at Mérignat and Colin often studied there until two o'clock in the morning. According to one account, the library had been left to the mayor by his uncle, a learned priest, and it was well-stocked, especially with 18th century works.[34] Among the books he studied there was a theology book based on the catechism of the Council of Trent. The library was probably the first one in which Colin had read that was not exclusively religious. What journals he was able to read at the chateau is not known but the Colins, like most priests, subscribed to *L'Ami de la religion et du roi*, 'The Friend of religion and the king', a journal which appeared twice a week on Wednesdays and Saturdays. It had a broad coverage of the affairs of France and of the Catholic Church both inside and outside France. As its name implies, the paper was clerical and royalist and appealed to his political as well as his religious sentiments, for, like most Restoration clergy, he accepted the alliance of throne and altar. His reading would have put him in touch with the main currents of thought during these years. It was probably at this time that he wrote an article for a journal, to which he referred later but gave no details.

Bajollet or other notables used invite the Colins to dinner and during the meal religious matters often came up for criticism. Colin prudently decided

33. J. Leflon, *Eugène de Mazenod*, vol. 2, (Paris, 1960), pp 107-8. P. Boutry, *Prêtres et Paroisses au pays du curé d'Ars* (Paris, 1986), p. 381.
34. OM, doc. 648, 2

that the dinner-table was not the place to argue out such ideas, but bided his time. On the following Sunday he refuted them from the pulpit without fear of contradiction.[35] These table discussions made Colin realise that the Revolution and its ideas had not vanished totally on the battlefield of Waterloo. Rousseau, Voltaire and other Enlightenment authors had left their mark and their works were now experiencing a revival of interest.

The Colins did not like to visit homes unless they were needed, for visiting might have involved drinking a glass or two of the wine for which Cerdon was famous. Later, however, Colin confessed that were he to start again he would have visited all his parishioners. Visiting the sick, however, and the reconciliation of the dying, were high priorities for him:

> When he had sick people, he never left them before giving absolution. If, for fear of tiring them, he could not do it right away he preferred to keep walking around in the neighbourhood for two or three hours; he returned three or four times, if necessary, and never left them until he had reconciled them with God … Not one of his sick died without absolution.[36]

Occasionally, too, he visited hardened sinners and was prepared to use forceful tactics to have them put their lives in order. One man, a carpenter it seems, who had not been to confession for forty years, saw him come to his house one day and said immediately: 'I know what you want but it is useless, useless.' Colin had him bring him into another room, and then the dialogue began:

> 'Kneel down,' he said to the man. He objected. 'Come on, friend; do me this favour.' He knelt. 'Make the sign of the cross.' He did. 'Start off.' And he started off, he made his confession and since then he has been a good Christian …[37]

The incident is extraordinary and can only be explained by the force of Colin's conviction and personality. His combination of warmth and force appears to have left no rancour. He and Pierre, as Colin testified later, worked perfectly together; indeed, according to Jeanne-Marie Chavoin, the only time they disagreed was when, from mutual regard, they vied with each other as to who should take the more difficult visitations. They gave of their best to the parish. Their zeal, holiness, and style of life had begun to transform the parish. Jeanne-Marie Chavoin rendered this testimony:

> When the Fathers Colin were at Cerdon, they were revered by all the inhabitants. Had they remained there, the whole parish would soon have been like a religious community; already a fervent group of 30 men used to meet in

35. OM, doc. 541, 13.
36. OM, doc. 744.
37. OM, doc. 481, 1.

the presbytery like children. Their [the Colins'] domestic set-up was so poor and they lived in such poverty that everyone in Cerdon was astounded.[38]

It was a fine tribute. If the Colins transformed Cerdon, Cerdon had transformed Colin. The change that the years there wrought in Colin is remarkable. Gone is the retiring, young student, day-dreaming of a hermit's life, shunning the world. He now emerges as a powerful preacher who can twist a whole parish around his finger, whose eloquence can coax and terrify by turn. The timid young man, with a slight stutter, had emerged from his shell and found that he could speak and act decisively. He could move people by his warm-heartedness, and shake them by his righteous anger. Gone is the hesitant, inde-cisive student who could not make up his mind whether to enter the seminary or not, whether to remain or not, whether to receive holy orders or not. Here is a mature man who knew what he wanted done and determinedly set about getting it done, even if it meant treading on a few corns to do so. He could irrupt into people's lives and take over. Gone is the callow young neophyte whose ignorance of the facts of life gave him fantastic notions about women and marriage, in whose presence Pierre had to shush some fellow-priests lest their outspokenness shock his innocence and prudishness. Here he is now con-fronting young women and older matrons in the street and driving his pastoral message home with homespun but telling irony. Undaunted by prefects, mayors or other figures of authority, he was not afraid of taking initiatives when he needed something done. After a few years Colin bestrode the scene at Cerdon. No wonder he was able to say later on with apostolic pride 'we were the masters there'!

When and how did this transformation come about? Many years later, Colin told his close associate, Julian Eymard, that during the first twenty-five years of his life, that is up to about 1816, he was overwhelmed with spiritual suf-fering, scruples and anguish.[39] A number of factors wrought a great change. The need to deal with people's problems, the belief that he had accomplished something worthwhile for them, the feeling that he was successfully guiding them along the right path – a normal satisfaction for the good pastor everywhere – brought him great joy. Cerdon had proved providential. The little town pro-vided the ideal environment, for the people, despite a blustering exterior, proved warm and kind. The attitude of his curé is crucial for a newly-ordained priest. In having Pierre as his curé, Colin could not have been more fortunate. Pierre, who had contributed towards the cost of his training, had asked for him as assistant and guided his first steps in the priesthood. There were no jealousies between them. They shared the rectory work and shared the ministry. Pierre was a well-esteemed confessor but, unlike some curés, he shared his penitents

38. OM, doc. 513, 1.
39. OM, doc. 546.

with Colin. When Pierre noted how successful Jean-Claude was and how he outshone Pierre himself in preaching and touching people's hearts, he showed no resentment but rather pushed him forward. This humble and loving elder brother created the warm, receptive atmosphere in which Colin could open up and blossom forth.

There was something else. Despite his trouble with confession, Colin often said in later life that his stay at Cerdon was a blessed time, for during all those years he experienced extraordinary serenity of soul. He had told Pierre that he would have communications which he could not share with him, and Pierre reassured him that that was acceptable to him. Living in one house, however, and sharing the same work with a younger brother whom he loved and had always protected, Pierre soon realised that something very unusual was taking place in his brother. He noticed how Jean-Claude's face was so often radiant as with some extraordinary joy and could only guess at some spiritual preoccupation or grace. What that was became clear to him when Jean-Claude, less than a year after their arrival in Cerdon, opened his heart to him and told him of the pledge of the twelve at Fourvière the previous year. As Cholleton had foretold, he gained his first recruit, for Pierre immediately asked to be allowed to join. A beginning had been made. Pierre was to remain his most constant support for the rest of his life. Before exploring the source of the radiant joy Pierre noted in Jean-Claude, the activity of the other signatories to the pledge must now be examined.

CHAPTER 10

The Six Years of Consolation

'If I went back to Cerdon, I would go and see the small closet five feet square which was at the foot of my bed. That is where I spent the nights and where I wrote the first ideas on the Society'. Jean-Claude Colin to Jeantin, July 1870.

For the Marist aspirants ordained that July, came the joy of their first Mass in their native place and then the anxious yet eager journey to their new parishes to take up their assignments. Seminary life, with its close companionship and sharing of dreams, was over and life on the ministry, with all its pressing demands, had opened out before them. They would have much to learn and to do in these first years. Déclas related their parting:

> We said to each other ... that each of us would go wherever Providence sent him, until the moment came to come together and to go to Le Puy, where the first idea of the Society had been given and where we would be well received.[1]

To go to Le Puy or to set up a new congregation, however, they needed the permission of the diocese and so, although Marists hold the 23 July 1816 as the date of the foundation of the Society, the event of that day was one without any immediate aftermath. Archbishop Fesch was permanently in exile and a year later, on 1 October 1817, the pope was to withdraw all jurisdiction from him. The vicars general – Bochard, Courbon and Renaud – now ruled the diocese. Since Bochard had welcomed Courveille and his project when he had come from Le Puy and had assisted him to choose members for his group, the group had some reason to expect his support. Before long, however, it became clear that Bochard had a different objective from Courveille. If Courveille hoped for a Society of Mary with its base in Le Puy, Bochard wanted a diocesan society in Lyon along the lines he had sketched in his *Pensée Pieuse*. His plan involved absorbing Courveille's group into his own diocesan congregation. He was totally opposed to the idea that more young priests be allowed to leave the diocese to go to other dioceses or to found new works. Courbon, the senior and more kindly vicar general, poked fun at the Marist project. A shortage of priests for the diocese was his excuse for not favouring their plan. There was no question of the Marist aspirants being released to gather as a group in either Le Puy or their own diocese.

1. OM, doc. 591, 10.

The eyes of the aspirants were turned to Verrières, the tiny village in the south-east of the diocese where Courveille had been posted as curate. Courveille, however, found that Jean-Joseph Barou, the parish priest and superior of the seminary, was a member of Bochard's society. Although he made an effort to found a third order of Mary, Courveille was able to accomplish little. He was transferred to another parish and then, in August 1817, to Rive-de-Gier, near the large town of Saint-Étienne. Despite the opposition of the parish priest, he recruited some women-teachers as Sisters of Mary. By 1820, he had a similar group at Saint-Clair. Both groups merged at Saint-Clair.

The efforts of Courveille to begin branches of sisters and a third order indicate that the Marist project was not to be confined to priests alone. What the group envisaged was a society which, like traditional orders, would have a 'first order' consisting of priests with brothers assisting them in their work, a second order or sisters' branch and a third order or lay branch, often referred to as tertiaries. Marcellin Champagnat, who had joined the Marist group on condition that he could found a branch of teaching brothers, had been appointed curate in the parish of La Valla, 56 kilometres south-west of Lyon and not far from Courveille's parish of Rive-de-Gier. When he found that a dying youth of seventeen had not the slightest knowledge of religion he had persuaded two men, Jean-Marie Granjon and Jean-Baptiste Audras, to come and help him instruct the youth of the region. The date they came together, 2 January 1817, marks the beginning of the Marist brothers. Champagnat respected Courveille, who often came to see him and, in 1817, helped him buy a house close to the presbytery at La Valla. In November Champagnat opened a school at Marlhes, his native village. Courveille, however, was transferred in 1819 to Épercieux, some 75 kilometres west of Lyon. There he began a little community of brothers. Although no progress had been made as regards the priests' branch, part of the Marist project was taking shape in the south and west of the diocese, thanks to the zeal of Champagnat and Courveille.

Away in the east of the diocese, at Cerdon, the third area where the hope of a new Society of Mary was alive, Colin rejoiced at such success. 'When I heard a piece of news,' he told Mayet later, 'I glowed all over, my face became radiant.'[2] His brother Pierre witnessed this radiance and wondered what was happening. Many years later Colin revealed that, at the end of every day, the thought of the pledge to establish a Society of Mary was sufficient to console and reassure him. 'Over a period of six years, I experienced extreme sweetness when thinking of this society,' he said in 1838-9, and a year or two later he told Mayet '… I experienced tangible comfort just at the thought of it.'[3] There was no doubt in Colin's mind but that the dream would be realised. He was, he said later in

2. OM, doc. 519, 7.
3. OM, docs 447, 1; 519, 7.

his carefully dictated note to Brother Jean-Marie, his secretary, 'filled interiorly with a lively confidence that the project came from God and would be realised in the end'.[4] 'During the first six or seven years I had not the shadow of a doubt or of discouragement.'[5] This spiritual experience at a time when he was coming into his full powers as a pastor, gave a definitive direction to his life. In committing himself totally to the project of a Society of Mary, he was convinced that he was doing what God wanted him to do.

It was in the light of this conviction of God's designs that he took a momentous step: he began to write down what he saw as the central ideas for the Society of Mary. By penning the rule, Colin had assumed responsibility, perhaps unconsciously, for the spiritual orientation of his fellow-Marists for through it he was attempting to have them share his spiritual experience and to bring them along the same itinerary he was travelling. Yet he wrote because he felt impelled to write, not knowing, he admitted later, whether it would ever be of any use.[6]

Colin's decision soon after coming to Cerdon to write the rule was an astonishing development. A year before, when the twelve made the promise at Fourvière, Courveille was seen as the charismatic leader, and in the background, Cholleton, their professor of theology and spiritual director, was the group's protector and advisor. Yet it was neither of these but the hesitant little Colin who so soon afterwards assumed the mantle of spiritual mentor of the group. Few, if any, parallels exist in other religious orders.[7] How did the timid young priest, with the oils of ordination still fresh on his hands, without any first-hand knowledge of religious life, take on himself this formidable task of writing the basis of the rule for his colleagues? He himself made the point: 'Do you think that I would have put myself forward on my own accord to make a rule? I would have acted like a madman.'[8] The decision is so remarkable that it merits further investigation.

It could be that Colin had a mandate to write the rule. While they were all still at Saint-Irénée or when they used meet in the years following their ordination, Courveille or the group could have asked him to write it. Certainly, no one appears to have accused him of taking on an unwarranted responsibility. Courveille gloried in being regarded as superior general of the group yet there is no indication that he complained of Colin's action. Courveille may have realised that his own education was inadequate – an inspector at La Valla found several spelling and grammatical mistakes in a notice he had put up in the school – and, as long as his own position as superior was not questioned, he

4. OM, doc. 815, 3.
5. OM, doc. 819, 42.
6. OM, doc. 816.
7. Most 19th century religious orders based their rules on existing rules.
8. OM, doc. 842, 11.

may willingly have accepted that the rule be written by someone better able to commit ideas to paper. If someone were mandated, Colin's scholastic achievements would have made him a good choice. Against this, however, is the absence of any mention of a mandate. Furthermore, Colin's own explanation does not support this interpretation.

It is not clear either when the others learned of Colin's initiative. Later, the Colins claimed that they kept much of their activity at Cerdon, particularly the correspondence with Rome, a secret from the authorities and even from Déclas but they did not say that the writing of the rule was kept secret from the group. Moreover, in the years immediately after 1816 the group kept in contact, for the Colins told Bishop Bigex that 'although separated from one another, they have all kept the most intimate union between themselves'.[9] The registers of Saint-Irénée show that Courveille, Champagnat, Déclas, Terraillon, the two Colins and other members of the group came there for annual retreats during this period and Terraillon later recalled their meetings:

> Always united among ourselves, we used act in perfect accord. Our little meetings were never interrupted. They took place sometimes in Belley, sometimes in Lyon, but more often in Lyon. Normally, we made use of the pastoral retreats to concert our efforts and to inflame ourselves more and more.[10]

Because of this closeness to one another, it is likely that Courveille and probably the others learned of Colin's project quite early on. The letter which the Colins wrote to the pope in 1822, refers explicitly to the Cerdon rule. Since Courveille signed this letter it is evident that by then, at least, he knew and accepted Colin's rule as the expression of the aim of the Society.

When Colin spoke later of his duty to give the Society 'the early ideas' this could mean that he did not intend to write a complete rule. Yet there is no indication that he confined himself to a few ideas. What he wrote was probably based on what he had jotted down even before he met Courveille at the seminary for he asserted later that what he envisioned in Cerdon was not the same as what had been mooted at Saint-Irénée. Yet he could not but have been influenced by Courveille's account of the Le Puy revelation and he was part of the enthusiastic group who, over the following months, discussed, prayed, exchanged views, listened to Courveille's fervent exhortations, consulted Cholleton and finally made their collective promise at Fourvière. His later statement was probably a deliberate attempt to distance himself from Courveille and to emphasise that the Cerdon rule owed nothing to him.

Were Colin's own early ideas, as matured in his experiences of 1815-16, the

---

9. Pierre Colin to Bigex, 9 Oct. 1819, *Forum Novum*, 4, p. 93.
10. OM, docs 51; 750, 8.

only source of his rule? The letter to Bigex referred to the Fourvière pledge as a summary of 'the Society's aim and plan'. This could mean that Courveille or the group had a written 'plan'. Yet there is no other mention of such a written plan and no trace of it remains. Moreover, Colin again and again denied that he had used any other rule. During later controversies, other possible sources were suggested but no evidence was produced for them.

For Colin, the explanation for his extraordinary step of writing the rule, with its consequence of determining the direction in which, spiritually, the whole Society was to go, did not lie in any mandate from his colleagues nor arise from a personal choice. Its origin was totally different. It was, he believed, from above. That is what he indicated clearly in the letter to Pope Pius VII in 1822 and what he declared more openly in 1869:

> From the first years of my priestly ministry, I found myself engaged in working for the Society of Marist Fathers and even in preparing its first Constitutions. The impulse which led me to do this was less a voluntary impulse of my own choice, than an inner impulse, I would say an almost irresistible one, with the conviction that the Society was part of God's plan, that it would succeed, without knowing how or by what means, nor whether my work would one day be of some use.[11]

To the chapter of 1870 he declared categorically that those first ideas 'are not from me'. This confidence that the work he was doing was Mary's, revealed itself in his simple childlike way of turning to her to help him in the work. Denis-Joseph Maîtrepierre, the Society's novice-master, gave the following account:

> When drawing up the rules, he was sometimes overcome by the feeling of his unworthiness and incapacity: then he would throw himself on his knees before the image of Mary and, with his eyes ardently fixed on her, he would cry out: 'Who am I, who am I to do your work?' And after that, feeling his soul melting into a kind of confidence, he used to say to her, 'Speak, Holy Virgin, say what should be put here.' Filled with this holy emotion he would stand up and rapidly write down the ideas which characterise so well the spirit of the society.'

With a naiveté which Maîtrepierre says concealed a rich simplicity of soul, Colin, when baffled by the work, would go further:

> On other occasions, uncertain as regards ideas, decisions and expressions, I cast my eyes on the little statue of the Virgin, I placed the pen in the little hand she held out to me, and I said to her: 'Write it yourself, Holy Virgin.' She did not write, but after that I used write more easily.'[12]

11. OM, docs 69, 4; 816.
12. OM, doc. 752, 44. Denis-Joseph Maîtrepierre (1800-72); master of novices, 1844-64, during which time he wrote this account.

This conviction of an interior, almost irresistible impulsion is the reason why certain intuitions and phrases in the Cerdon rule remained sacrosanct for him. This is why he later dismissed out of hand the rule of his successor, Julien Favre, as 'a human work … made in a human way … no longer the original work.'[13] The natural sense of the words Colin used is that he received some type of divine impulsion. 'People consider what I have done as my work,' he remarked, 'I was no more than the instrument, the pen.'[14]

It was decades later, when Mayet, Jeantin, David and others tried to pin down exactly what this interior impulse was, that difficulties arose. To some extent the problem arose from Colin's oblique manner of expressing himself. While denying any divine revelation, he said more than once that he would not say that he had not had 'special graces'.[15] It is not surprising that his eager confrères found his words tantalisingly ambiguous. When Colin, in an allusion to another aspect of the origins, spoke in embarrassed and mysterious tones, a puzzled or exasperated Mayet wrote, 'What should one take from all that? I don't know. I don't judge. I just quote.'[16] Yet the problem lay with his interlocutors as much as with Colin. Their questioning of Colin took place, for the most part, at the time of Colin's dispute with Favre when they wanted to dispel unwelcome gossip about the origin of the rule. They were already convinced that Mary had appeared to Colin at Cerdon. If they could be assured also that the Blessed Virgin had spoken directly to Colin in that little room at Cerdon as he wrote the rule, they felt that the Society would be that much more solidly based. As Colin's official secretaries and supporters, they were anxious to prove that his rule alone was divinely inspired.[17]

The account that he dictated to his secretary, Brother Jean-Marie in 1869, describes simply how he saw his action fifty years on:

> Filled with an inner and total confidence that amounted to a kind of certainty that the project came from God and in the long run would be realised, he used the free moments which the sacred ministry left him to prepare for its success by jotting down the first ideas that were to serve as the basis for the constitutions.

Not knowing if his work would be of any use, yet convinced that this is what he had to do, he spent his nights working on it, sometimes until four o'clock in the morning.[18] Nostalgically, he recalled later on: 'If I went back to

13. OM, doc. 803, 1, 8, 10-12.
14. OM, doc. 819, 164.
15. OM, doc. 819, 111.
16. OM, doc. 425m.
17. Later a cult began to develop of the 'room of apparitions' in the presbytery of Cerdon. It has no historical foundation. OM 3, pp 897-8, note 4.
18. OM, docs 815; 816, 1; 827, 6; 819, 42.

Cerdon, I would go and see the small closet five feet square which was at the foot of my bed. That is where I spent the nights and where I wrote the first ideas on the Society.'[19]

A possible scenario might be the following. Here is a young man, just ordained, idealistic, enthusiastic, prayerful. He is totally devoted to the Blessed Virgin Mary, who is for him a living person with whom he talks daily, in whom he confides, and whom he trusts as a mother. For long he has cherished a dream of a society vowed to her and has jotted down some ideas. It is only during his last year in the seminary that this dream finds unexpected and most welcome embodiment in the Le Puy revelation. From it he learns what was the 'work' Mary asked for and to this he pledges himself at Fourvière. He is totally caught up in the vision of a society dedicated to Mary. He goes to Cerdon where he has a profound spiritual experience, which brings him affirmation, peace and consolation. Though he proves a good pastor and gifted preacher, he lives impatiently for the day when 'the work of Mary' – the very thought of which brings him transports of joy – will eventually begin. He is confident that God wills it and feels impelled by God to play an active part in the project. He begins to draft the charter of that society, that 'House of the Virgin', as he describes it in his rule. He can now develop and expand the ideas he had written earlier. During those years, he receives further graces, one of which would be 'hidden and unknown' as the most apt way of living and of winning people for God. He envisions the ideal Society of Mary and gives free rein to his idealism. At all times talking to and consulting the Blessed Virgin as a child his mother, night after night he takes up his pen and attempts to put on paper the ideas that come to him from this intimate communion with God and the Blessed Virgin. Reflected on, prayed over, left on the altar sometimes for more than forty days, the articles are written down and his rule takes shape over a period of three years. The result of his labour, his vision of the congregation dedicated to Mary, is undoubtedly coloured by the culture he lived in and conditioned by his own mindset. As a result there is much that is human in the rule. There is also much that is inspired. Over the years, his own experience and that of his confrères and the wisdom of the Church will sort the one from the other, the wheat from the chaff.

God, theologians believe, normally works through natural means and so this explanation may provide a simpler answer to the question of Colin's inspiration. Though Jeantin, and especially David, hoped to be told that Mary dictated the actual words at Cerdon, Colin refused to go along with this. Jean Coste, after many years of study, concluded that the 'graces' of Cerdon do not consist in something that is mysterious and miraculous but rather in a 'grow-

19. OM, doc. 839, 36.

ing cluster of those convictions regarding the Church, the world, the Society of Mary' which came to him during those years of grace.[20]

When Colin took up his quill to write, he wrote in French in a *cahier* or exercise book. This exercise book has not survived, perishing, apparently, when he burned his papers. In 1822, he presented a Latin text, based on the original French, to the papal nuncio in Paris. The Latin text also went up in flames. By chance a copy of two small sections was preserved.[21] Since those sections were those that the nuncio asked Colin to change, they were not up to the standard of the others. Yet, since they are the only complete sections to survive, they merit examination.

Colin wrote as a visionary attempting to catch on paper the intuitions that gripped him. The 'Society of Mary' was envisioned by him as the 'House of Blessed Mary'. What he saw in his mind's eye, what he 'imagined', was a community of dedicated Marists living together a life of total commitment. The rule was to describe their ideal way of life. The Marists would form one tightly-bound body and would allow nothing to distract them from the total service of God and his holy Mother. If they did slip from this ideal, the rule would be there to raise them up and strengthen them. A few examples may help to reveal his vision of the 'House of Mary'. It is a place where covetousness and pride may never enter in. 'To repel this covetousness from the House of Blessed Mary, who always during her whole life abhorred this spirit of covetousness,' every necessary means must be taken. Should the superior, one of his counsellors or anyone else, retain this spirit of covetousness for more than a quarter of hour, he must confess his fault, and how long he harboured it, to the whole council, called together specially for that purpose.

The same applied to the spirit of pride. It, too, had to be kept away by the same resolute measures. A series of seven articles described the ideal way the superior should act towards his council. Colin insisted that the superior should speak last in council and, if the voting is divided, he should prefer the view of those opposed to his own! For Colin the reason was as simple as it was crystal-clear: 'Mary always followed the will of others rather than her own.'

More disconcerting for a modern generation where personal fulfilment is so prized, were Colin's articles on discipline. 'On Thursdays and Saturdays, the religious will wear the iron hair-shirt; they will give themselves six strokes of the discipline on Tuesday.' The coadjutor brothers got off lighter with just two hours a week of the hairshirt and five strokes of the discipline. If a priest committed a private fault, he had to wear the hairshirt for from two to three weeks

20. Jean Coste perceptively describes Colin's vision in *A Marian Vision of the Church*.
21. J. Coste, G. Lessard, S. Fagan, eds, *Antiquiores textus constitutionum Societatis Mariae*, fascicle I, primae redactiones: 1816-1833 (Rome, 1955), pp 5-8, 19-24. J. Coste, 'The two oldest fragments of the Constitutions', *Acta SM* 3 (1954-55), 468-79.

and take the lash of the discipline three times a week. The punishment to be meted out to rebellious subjects was severe:

> If the guilty religious be rebellious … and unwilling to submit to the punishment laid down, he will be shut up in a cell, in which there is a chair, a straw pallet with two blankets in winter. In summer, however, no blanket will be given and the guilty person will sleep in his clothes … There will be three such cells in the House [of Mary] for locking up the guilty.[22]

The idea of a prison in a convent or religious house is strange for today's world. All Colin knew of religious communities, however, was gleaned from his reading about medieval monasteries, for when he wrote religious orders had only just begun to return to France. Since those monasteries were 'total institutions', quasi-independent units, they would have a prison cell for recalcitrants. The new 'House of Mary' that Colin envisioned was to have a similar structure to the old monastery, the only model he knew.

The two sections, which the nuncio singled out as too strict, were softened into counsels of perfection or abandoned altogether as the advice of those consulted on the practicalities of life showed Colin how unworkable they were. The more liberal one, asking the superior to follow his council rather than his own view, was the only one Colin insisted on keeping. If, as the Sulpician Pierre-Denis Boyer, who examined it in Paris, commented, the rule was made 'for angels rather than for men' at least it reveals Colin's lofty views. In Cerdon, as a young newly-ordained priest he had written down the ideal of the 'House' or Society of Mary. From now on he had to confront this ideal with the insight of Church people experienced in both religious rules and in the ways of humankind. The wonder is not that they found his rule too idealistic but that they found it so good – a firm basis from which to work.

His rule must be seen in the light of the times in which it was written. Colin lived in a society where life was harder than in the modern advanced world and in a religious world where mortification and self-denial were more acceptable than in the post-Vatican II era with its emphasis on human fulfilment. In Restoration France, particularly after the atrocities perpetrated during the Revolution, the wickedness of society, like the coming of the 'last times', was a common theme. Many pious Christians felt the need of making atonement to an outraged God; reformers pined for the mythical golden age of Church in the time of the apostles; others believed that the end of time was imminent.

Colin was a child of his time and full of youthful fervour and zeal; he pictured the ideal type of 'House of the Blessed Virgin' where every member would be completely dedicated and committed. The rule was no more than a description of how he believed that those whom Mary chose for her work for

---

22. *Antiquiores textus,* fascicle I, pp 19-22.

the Church in the end-times should act. They were to form an ideal family which would cheerfully welcome the demanding conditions for becoming true sons of Mary, imitating her in her selflessness, her humility, her devotion to God. That way they could be one with her in the great work of the salvation of souls. Colin's vision has been described as utopian. The description is not inapt insofar as Colin, reacting against the imperfections of the present state, boldly imagined a radically different and better world.

Jean Coste, applying textual criticism to Colin's later writings and comments, discovered between two hundred and three hundred other fragments of the Cerdon rule.[23] Three of the more valuable fragments can be cited here. One is the maxim 'unknown and hidden'. Colin said on one occasion: 'When God speaks to a soul he says a great deal in a few words. For instance, unknown and hidden.' While at first this attitude represented for Colin his boyhood dream of being alone with God in the woods of Crest, he came to see in it, too, the Virgin's own manner of being and acting in the Church of her Son. Gradually it became for him a way of describing how Marists should live and how they should conduct their apostolate. More than any other intuition, those few words have proved an inspiration for Marists from the beginning and much ink has been spilt in advancing different interpretations and applications of the maxim.

A second important intuition dating from the Cerdon period was that Marists be simply instruments of God's mercy just as Mary their foundress was. This idea was to be a central one in his mission work in the Bugey. 'Let the missioners take care to become … apt instruments of divine mercy', Colin wrote in that important summary of his rule, the *Summarium,* which he presented at Rome in 1833. 'Do not complain of the time spent with sinners,' he added and 'Marists should leave to others the care of souls who are doing well. It is for sinners that they have come.'

A third fragment concerned Mary's role which was always central to his thought. He spoke of it in terms of what she did at the time of the apostles and in these latter times. He told his confrères in 1848:

> Yes, Messieurs [here his tone became solemn], I do not mind repeating it here once more: the words 'I was the mainstay of the new-born Church; I shall be again at the end of time', served us, in the very earliest days of the society, as a foundation and an encouragement. They were always before us. We worked in that direction…[24]

His words, 'the very earliest days', is indication enough that this intuition

23. Coste, *Marian Vision,* pp 110-63; G. Lessard, 'L'ultima fatica di Coste: une vision mariale de l'Église', conference given at Collegio S. Giovanni Evangelista, Via Livorno, Rome, 15 Nov 1998.
24. FS, doc. 152.

can be traced back to Cerdon and perhaps to his final year in the seminary. To those key points he would add others such as fidelity to the Church of Rome. The lost Cerdon rule would also have contained many practicalities – the aim of the Society, the vows, practices of devotion and so forth such as Colin embodied in the *Summarium*. The recovered fragments of the rule taken together with the surviving three articles, offer some view, however inadequate, of what Colin wrote at Cerdon. From it emerges how Colin envisioned the Society of Mary. Mary would be its centre. Like her its life would be hidden and unknown and its apostolate unobtrusive and compassionate, open to all and directed to those most in need.

Colin's decision to write was to have lasting effects. Revised, commented on and prayed over, this text was to provide the basis for the definitive rule of the Society fifty years later. The rule and his relationship with it help us to understand the man. It was to retain a central place in his life right up to its approval by Rome two years before his death. To preserve the ideas he first jotted down he was ready to engage in the fiercest of battles. Judging from the final constitutions, in which he retained as much as he could of that early rule, one can but wonder that this young priest could write so inspiringly. For him there was no doubt: it was the result of the graces he received. The rule was Colin's major achievement at Cerdon.

Because of the centrality of Mary in Colin's thought, this may be the place to mention a work on Mary which influenced him profoundly. It is *The Mystical City*, written by a seventeenth-century Spanish nun, Maria of Ágreda.[25] His borrowing from this book explains why again and again throughout his life he spoke with authority on how Mary would act in a way that implies a familiarity with many details of her life. One revealing remark in 1843, among many others, will suffice. He said: 'I also read in these days that the Blessed Virgin never raised her eyes to look at anyone. When she went to visit the sick in the hospitals, she did it with such a modest air that she did not even see those she was visiting; without doubt she saw them by the interior vision she had, but she never looked at them exteriorly.'[26] Colin did not glean this 'knowledge' of how Mary acted from theology nor from the New Testament, for the apologetic theology and superficial scripture courses of the seminary scarcely mentioned her. He took it from *The Mystical City* made his own by study and meditation. Mayet, reporting in 1843 that Colin quoted sections of

25. Maria Jésus, (1602-65), b. Ágreda, Old Castille; professed as Discalced Conceptionist, 1620; abbess, 1627-52; cause for beatification introduced, 1672; *The Mystical City*, published five years after her death, containing an account of her visions was criticised by Bossuet, the Sorbonne and the Roman Inquisition but praised by St Anthony Mary Claret, Dom Guéranger and the universities of Spain, Louvain, Vienna, Toulouse and Perpignan.
26. Mayet, 'Mémoires', 5, 657-8; See Y. Mathieu, 'L'usage colinien de la Cité mystique de Dieu de Marie d'Ágreda', *Forum Novum* 3 (1996), 449.

it to his confrères, added: 'This book gave him the greatest, the sweetest ideas about Mary…'[27] It became a treasure house from which he drew his understanding of her life.

While Maria of Ágreda in *The Mystical City* describes how Mary lived, what she did, even how she dressed, her major intuition was to take the apocalyptical vision of the Book of Revelation – the new Jerusalem descending from heaven – and identify it with Mary herself. She is this 'Mystical City of God'. Although she was in heaven, Mary chose to come down to earth to be the support of the apostles and the early Church. From *The Mystical City* Colin drew his understanding of the life of the Virgin and her role in the Church as he assimilated it and interpreted it according to his own insight. His painful childhood experiences and his temperament had made him seek to be alone with God. Now contemplating the life of the Virgin Mary in the early Church he became convinced of her hidden presence yet powerful support. Mary, he believed, continued her quiet work in the Church throughout the ages and was continuing it in his day too. Going a step further, he believed that she would continue her work through him and through others who were called to be members of her society. Through them, Mary would still be the support of the Church in these latter tempestuous days. She was the originator, the ideal set before each member and the model of their apostolate. Like her its life would be hidden and unknown and its apostolate unobtrusive and compassionate, open to all and directed to those most in need. They would live and act in the Church of this final age, in a manner that reflected the way she lived and acted in the Church of that first age. Mary, the Mystical City of God, unobtrusively active still in the Church, was the vision in his mind's eye as night after night he took up his pen to describe what the 'Marists' of the new congregation devoted to her would be. Maria of Ágreda profoundly influenced the manner in which he saw the work of Mary when in the struggles of the early Church she gave it her quiet yet powerful support and as she now, through her Marist sons and daughters, supports the embattled Church of the final age.[28] Mary was the city, descended from heaven, whose twelve gates would be open to all at all times. From this Colin took his idea that the whole world would be Marist, an idea which caused him to insist that the lay branch of her society be open to everyone. Mary was the mother embracing all to her bosom because she wishes to save all. Neither would her Society have any limits, for the Marists would be ready to help all peoples in whatever distant land. For Marists, then, Mary was the originator, the ideal set before each of them and the model of their apostolate.

27. OM, doc. 554, 1.
28. Coste, *Marian Vision,* pp 76-92; G. Lessard, 'Un trésor pour ces derniers temps', *Forum Novum* 3 (1995-6), pp 457-72.

In the rectory with Colin was his brother Pierre. Although overshadowed by Jean-Claude, Pierre was as strong-minded and as shrewd as his brother, as his letters to the vicars general defending his rights as curé of the parish reveal. Later he was a much sought-after confessor. There is little record of what he thought at first of his brother's nightly vigil scratching away with his quill pen until early morning. Pierre was soon to find out. Sometime in 1817, probably before the annual retreat at Saint-Irénée which began on 27 August, Colin let him into his secret project. Pierre said immediately: 'I'll be part of it; I knew something was afoot.'[29] When asked how Pierre came to suspect something, Colin admitted: 'I experienced an extraordinary contentment, internally and externally.' Seeing his brother enraptured in some vision, Pierre was moved if not awed and it made him gladly take second place. Intelligent, straightforward and totally loyal, his adhesion was of the utmost importance. From a practical point of view as well as emotionally, his support was invaluable to Colin. His position in the diocese as a respected parish priest of some six years experience lent weight to the letters that Colin wrote appealing to the authorities for support for the project. The support he provided at Cerdon was providential, for Colin could never have had such a free hand in any other parish. They worked very closely together. Colin wrote later: 'The first year that we lived together … we consulted one another, not doing anything without one another.'[30]

Not only was Pierre an invaluable acquisition in himself but very quickly he made a move that enriched the whole Marist venture enormously. It was Pierre who in 1817 took the initiative in bringing Jeanne-Marie Chavoin and Marie Jotillon into the project.[31] Given Colin's earlier diffident approach to women, it would probably have been more difficult for him to take that initiative which was to prove of capital importance for the project. Pierre had known both these pious young women during the four years he was curate in Coutouvre, the little village in the department of the Loire where they lived. Both Jeanne-Marie and Marie were attracted to religious life but had not as yet found what they wanted. Jeanne-Marie had turned down no less than four invitations to join a convent and, finally, her director, Father Jean-Philibert Lefranc, had told her that 'you are not meant for an existing community, but for one which is to come into existence'. Marie Jotillon had spent some time with a group that included Pierre's sister Jeanne-Marie Colin and it was she who kept some contact with Pierre after he was transferred from Coutouvre. In a bold proposition that reveals his enthusiasm for the new-found vision that inspired him, Pierre urged the two of them to come to Cerdon to begin the Marist sisters there.

29. OM, doc. 819, 43.
30. FS, doc 25.
31. *Correspondence of Mother Saint Joseph; foundress of the Marist Sisters, 1786-1858* (Rome, 1966), pp 21-35.

Jeanne-Marie came first to assess the situation and then the two women accepted. For them it showed no small trust in Pierre and great faith, to leave their native village in the Beaujolais, travel to a remote part of the diocese and take part in a nebulous project with little to indicate that it would succeed. They came towards the end of 1817 and stayed. For a year or more they lodged with the Sisters of Saint Joseph. Towards the end of 1818, Marie Jotillon went to Saint-Clair, a village near Vienne, to help a group of Courveille's sisters. About the same time, since the Colins had lost their housekeeper, Jeanne-Marie moved in to the rectory at Cerdon to replace her. Her two nephews, Theodore and Jean-Marie Millot, joined her later.

The presence of Jeanne-Marie and two young children, one about ten, the other four, must have changed considerably the nature of the rectory and it may have been the closest thing to a normal family life that Colin experienced. The Colin brothers became very attached to the children, particularly to Jean-Marie. A quarter of a century later Mayet, who knew Jean-Marie, now a Marist priest, recounted that he could be regarded as 'the child of Father Superior General, whom he loved as a father, with the strongest possible filial tenderness.'[32] Colin taught the child to love the Blessed Virgin and to pray to her, with such simplicity and tenderness that, as he told Mayet, he used to speak to Mary as familiarly as he would speak to his aunt, Jeanne-Marie. The little child was brought into playing a part in the work for the Society during those early years at Cerdon as Mayet recorded:

> How many times, he [Jean-Marie] said to me one day in 1842 (18 March), did Father Colin at that time give me letters which I was to place on the altar during mass and to take away afterwards. At other times, he sent me to bring them to the feet of the Blessed Virgin and I left them in a little hiding place that he had shown me.[33]

These happenings at the rectory reveal a different side of Colin, a tenderness that one might not have expected.

Of greater significance was his relationship with Jeanne-Marie Chavoin. Jeanne-Marie was a tailor's daughter, a 'robust and auburn-haired peasant woman of thirty-one, with large expressive brown eyes, a warm smile and a determined chin', as her biographer describes her.[34] She spoke with the accent of her countryside, sometimes using its dialect. A straightforward woman, outspoken and direct, she knew what she wanted and did not hesitate to say so. Her warm-hearted generosity was remarked on by many. François Morcel, a

---

32. OM, doc. 534, 1.
33. OM, doc. 534, 4.
34. J. Leonard, *Triumph of Failure: Jeanne-Marie Chavoin, foundress of the Marist Sisters* (Slough, 1988), p.26.

Marist priest, said of her later that she was 'intelligent, lively, very kind and large-hearted, ready to render service'.[35] Above all she was a woman of deep faith, deeply devoted to the Blessed Sacrament and with a practical love of her neighbour. In Coutouvre she had helped and counselled many of the villagers, organised a prayer association and acted as sacristan. She wanted religious life but something simpler than existing congregations. She believed she found what she wanted in the project the Colins put before her, for, as she told Devie in 1823, when rejecting his attempt to enrol her and Marie Jotillon in an existing congregation: 'My Lord, ... we left our home and family to begin the Society of the Blessed Virgin.'[36] The first year at Cerdon which she had spent with the Sisters of Saint Joseph had been painful. During it she had lived as a nun in all but name and, generous as she always was, had, no doubt, done much good and so the villagers would not have thought it strange that she moved in to supply the part of a housekeeper for their two well-esteemed priests. Now she looked after the children, the two priests, and much of the affairs of the parish. Her presence made the rectory a welcoming home, a place from which Colin could draw energy and where a group of thirty fervent male parishioners could meet.[37] If Colin was transformed from a timid creature to a mature man, able to face his people and speak confidently to them, some of it may be attributed to the influence of this open, enthusiastic and deeply spiritual young woman. As for his Marist project, Jeanne-Marie brought a new dimension and a new dynamic. Having won Colin by her commitment to the work of Mary, she brought out hidden strengths in him. She gave him confidence, assurance of his role and courage to go forward. She read his soul and told him how he had saddened the Holy Spirit by his lack of trust. Jeanne-Marie, like Colin, received internal graces which they shared with one another. Some of those graces, both she and he were convinced, were intended for the progress of the Society. Since she shared his vision of the Society, 'the work', as they called it, of the Blessed Virgin, he had great trust in her. He told Cardinal Odescalchi in 1834 that she 'has been favoured by grace from childhood ... The Lord has imparted to her many lights concerning the Society and the virtues of Mary.'[38] A spiritual intimacy developed between them. If she, Jean-Claude and Pierre, shared the same vision at Cerdon, Jean-Claude admitted that she had more Marist spirit than either of them. It was no accident that the pivotal intuition in Colin's understanding of the religious life and the apostolate, 'unknown and hidden', first surfaced in a letter of Jeanne-Marie to Bishop Devie in 1824, indication enough of how one in mind and heart she and Colin

35. RMJ, doc. 265, 1.
36. OM, doc 513, 7.
37. RMJ, doc. 101, 1.
38. Colin to Odescalchi, CMJ, 10, 2.

were.[39] She was convinced, and repeated it more than once, that it was he that Mary had chosen to guide her Society. Her letter in 1849, when Colin doubted whether he should provide a rule for the sisters, seems to arch back across the years to that time at Cerdon when the greatest spiritual intimacy existed between them. She was determined to remind him of his appointed role:

> Who other than you … can know that you have been chosen by God and Mary our Mother in a special way, to rule her Society, and to rule it in its entirety, without there being question of cutting away branches from the trunk and without interfering with the rights of their of Lordships the Bishops?[40]

Jeanne-Marie's rhetorical question, 'who other than you can know?', would appear to be a reference to the spiritual experiences that both she and Colin had or shared with one another at that time. Her conviction that he was the instrument, divinely chosen, to guide the work of Mary forward was of supreme importance in making Colin gradually take a more central role. This shy, almost prudish young priest, trusted her and could speak to her about personal matters.[41] It showed a new openness in the man who felt ill at ease in the presence of women. Despite difficulties, misunderstandings and rejection, Jeanne-Marie was to remain faithful till the end to Colin, whom she later described as knowing better than anyone that 'the Society of Mary is not the work of men but of God alone', for from the beginning it was to him that it was manifested.[42] At Cerdon, together with Pierre, they hoped and prayed that the society they dreamt of would soon take shape. When they became discouraged, they supported one another. Jeanne-Marie gave a touching description of their ups and downs:

> When the fathers were almost overwhelmed by … annoying difficulties, I felt full of courage and cheered them up. At other times, when they were untroubled, my turn came. Ah! Those were our finest hours. One day they received a letter that upset them very much and the same post brought an important answer. The fathers were discouraged. I said to them, 'Let's go to the church. We all three went. We prayed for an hour or an hour and a half, and we came out feeling peaceful and contented.[43]

What the bad news was that Jeanne-Marie mentions or from where the letters came is not known. What she describes, however, conjures up the atmosphere of tremulous expectation, of what might be called 'holy hope' in the presbytery at Cerdon, as the three waited with longing for the day when

---

39. OM, doc. 118, 1.
40. CMJ, doc. 40, 5.
41. OM, doc. 296.
42. CMJ, doc. 40, 2-5.
43. RMJ, doc. 101, 2.

their dream of a society dedicated to Mary would finally be realised. Jeanne-Marie's account recalls the recurring disappointments of the years from 1816 to 1822 as they watched with hope and fear the arrival of the postman to see what news he would bring. It recalls, too, the deep spiritual life they lived together and the confidence they shared. Letters were their main means of contact with Courveille and Champagnat, for to travel to Lyon would take the best part of a day and Courveille's parish of Rive-de-Gier was further still. Only a few of those many letters have survived and none of the very early ones. Courveille probably wrote to relate the difficulties that the diocesan authorities were making and sometimes to ask for money. There were letters, too, from the vicars general of Lyon but they were usually discouraging refusals. A hopeful initiative came in February 1819 when one of the Marist aspirants, Jean-Antoine Gillibert, now professor of theology at Saint-Irénée, promised to have a request delivered to Pius VII. He had been in Rome as secretary to Cardinal Fesch and knew people there. It proved a further disappointment, however, for nothing happened and nothing further is known of Gillibert's letter. Yet the very fact that the Marist group was approaching Rome directly may indicate their frustration at the lack of progress and their loss of confidence in the diocesan authorities of Lyon.

Courveille, according to Colin, wanted to go ahead regardless of the bishops. Colin, respectful of Church authority and assured inwardly that the society was in God's plan, was dismayed and began to distance himself from Courveille. With little confidence in Courveille's judgement, he feared that the whole endeavour would be compromised and realised that he would have to take a more active part. He was caught in a dilemma. The very reason he had opted for the Society was because within it he could remain anonymous:

> It was at the time I saw myself obliged to take charge of the Society's affairs … I suffered very much. There was in me such strong resistance against doing that; I would have gone I don't know where to escape. My soul was all confused. Yet I kept saying, My God, your will be done! I forced myself to say it, but it seemed to me that it was not said wholeheartedly.[44]

Distressed, he was angry with the Blessed Virgin, even distrustful of her because she left him in charge of those things. In anguish of soul, he confessed to Cholleton, his spiritual director: 'I do tell God I want nothing but his holy will, but everything rises up in me when I say that.' Cholleton reassured him that by doing just that he was submitting to God's will. An incident took place, probably at this time, that stuck in Colin's memory. While he was saying Mass

---

44. OM, doc. 519, 2-4. Mayet believed that Colin was referring to his election as superior in 1836 but in an unpublished article on number one of the Constitutions in 1999 Gaston Lessard makes a good case for connecting it with Colin's vow.

he felt discouraged about the project. Afterwards, he related: 'A soul to whom God alone could have revealed what had gone on inside myself told me that on that day I had saddened the Holy Spirit very much.'[45] This was Jeanne-Marie.

In or about 1819 Colin decided to make a vow 'to occupy himself with it [the setting up of the Society] until he could go and place his project at the feet of the Holy Father in Rome and know what the Holy See thought.' This solemn promise to God was to have important consequences for him and the society, for it sustained him in difficulties in the years ahead.[46] It had the further effect of involving him more deeply in actively working for the approval of the Society and was a step that brought him imperceptibly to the position as head of the society. Colin had developed since he left the seminary. As well as the steady support of Pierre, there was the sharing of his vision and the affirmation of purpose which Jeanne-Marie gave him. The six years of consolation had brought him strength. He would need it, for little did he know when he made his vow that it would take fourteen or fifteen years and many battles before he could realise it.

It was in October 1819 that the Colins wrote to Bishop Bigex for advice. This letter in Pierre's handwriting and signed by him was addressed not from Lyon or Courveille's parish but from Cerdon. As well as outlining the story of the revelation of Le Puy, the letter included a copy of the Fourvière pledge of 1816 and added interesting information on the situation of the Marist aspirants three years on:

> Although separated from one another, they have all conserved the most intimate union between themselves, persisting always in their resolution and only waiting the moment marked in the decrees of divine providence and for the permission of their ecclesiastical superiors.[47]

Pierre adds that he wrote the letter in the name of all, an indication that all or most were still committed to the ideal expressed in the pledge. Although the continuing interest of the group that the letter suggests could fit in with Déclas' claim that 'We used write, we used visit sometimes, and we even gained a few recruits', yet there is no other evidence that they had sustained their commitment.[48] Pierre concluded that they were anxious to see the pope but in the meantime they sought Bigex's advice as to which cardinal they should write to in Rome. If Pierre, as parish priest, wrote the letter it was Colin who gave him the details of both the Le Puy revelation and the Fourvière pledge. Bigex was encouraging. In November 1819, a letter, signed apparently by the Colins and

45. OM, doc. 454.
46. G. Lessard, 'Jean-Claude Colin makes a vow to go to Rome', *Forum Novum* 2 (1992-4), pp 277-88.
47. P. Colin to Bigex, 9 Oct. 1819, *Forum Novum*, 4 (1997), pp 93-4.
48. OM, doc 591, 10.

Courveille, was sent to Rome, this time to Cardinal Pacca, Prefect of the Congregation of Bishops and Regulars. It is not known if Pacca, who had supported Pius VII during the Napoleonic period and had suffered for it, ever received the letter, for no reply came.

Early in 1820, the Cerdon group attempted a new initiative. They wrote to François Richard, vicar general of Le Puy, which as the place of Courveille's revelation had always maintained an attraction for the group of Marists. Jeanne-Marie travelled there and spoke to Richard. She followed this up with a letter on 19 November 1821 and, although this letter has also been lost, the vicar general's reply a few days later reveals both the purpose of her visit and the content of her letter.[49] Jeanne-Marie had asked Richard about the possibility of the Marists coming to Le Puy, while informing him that the Marists had approached the Holy See, hoping evidently for the vicar general's encouragement. Richard, although not opposed to the Marist project or to their eventual coming to Le Puy, was guarded in his reply, urging the Marists to pray, to consult their ecclesiastical superiors and to take counsel. He mentioned, too, that the priests had written to him a year and a half earlier. He had not replied but now explained to Jeanne-Marie why he did not and why he could not take any decision:

> I would have replied to your priests were it not that we were busy preparing for the reception of our Bishop of Saint-Flour, and as we are now expecting from day to day the arrival of the Bishop of Le Puy, I thought it more fitting to leave to them the honour of admitting you and the priests into their diocese.

The priests were almost certainly Jean-Claude and Pierre although it is possible others were also involved. Richard's hesitation is understandable in view of complex developments involving Church and State. The Concordat of Napoleon had suppressed the diocese of Le Puy. After Napoleon's downfall, the Church and the government signed a new Concordat in 1817 which re-established many of the suppressed dioceses including Le Puy. A hitch arose, for parliament refused to ratify this Concordat. Le Puy had to wait until June 1823 to receive its own bishop. In the meantime Richard was in charge of Le Puy and was understandably unwilling to admit a new group before the question of diocesan boundaries and their bishops was resolved. He did offer, however, to take in the Marist priests as missionaries for a year, provided they had the permission of their ecclesiastical authorities. That is where the matter rested. It was another setback for the group.

Although almost certainly Colin was behind the move, the important role played by Jeanne-Marie is noteworthy. Perhaps she was freer than the priests

---

49. CMJ, doc 1.

were but her courage is remarkable and their trust in her complete. This initiative, like the previous one, originated in Cerdon. The next effort also originated
there. The new initiative, although more promising at the start, became
enmeshed in the same high politics of Church and State. It had the effect, however, of bringing Colin, strengthened now by the years of consolation he had
experienced at Cerdon and powerfully supported by Jeanne-Marie and Pierre,
more centre-stage than before.

CHAPTER 11

Colin takes the Initiative

'Today the little Society of Mary begins!'
Pierre Colin to Devie, 29 October 1824.

By 1820, four years after their Fourvière promise, the little group of priests had made scant progress towards forming a Society of Mary. Some of them, discouraged perhaps by the lack of progress and the opposition in the diocese, drifted away. In October 1820 Joseph Verrier finally yielded to Bochard's pressure and the following December Pierre Pousset followed suit. Both had been at one time interested in the Marist project. Perhaps they felt that Bochard had something concrete to offer, unlike the apparently unrealisable Marist dream and decided that they could best realise their desire for missionary work by joining his group which had taken the name of the 'Fathers of the Cross of Jesus'.

Yet the sweetness and consolation that Colin experienced over the six years at Cerdon, assuring him that the project was from God, sustained his and Pierre's courage. No sooner were the two brothers back in the newly-refurbished presbytery after lodging for a year and a half at the notary's house, than they set about making a fresh approach to Rome. On 25 January 1822, they wrote to Pius VII.[1] This letter, in Pierre's handwriting, was sent from Cerdon and was signed by both brothers. Courveille also signed it, probably some days later. Both Colins added the word 'priest' after their names, Courveille, who signed above them, added 'spg' after his name, which can be taken to indicate 'superior general'. After mentioning the earlier efforts to bring the project to the pope's attention, the writers raised the possibility that they might soon come to place the plan of the Society before His Holiness. They also set out the aims of the society: to seek the glory of God and the honour of the Blessed Virgin, support the Roman Catholic Church and undertake mission work at home and in every part of the world. They promised that the constitutions, containing those aims, would be shown to the Holy Father and assured him that they came from no book or from any existing rule whatever. They concluded with the somewhat mysterious promise to tell the pope from whence those rules truly came. This last claim marks the letter out as the work of Colin,

---

1. OM, doc. 69, commentary and notes; see also OM, docs 819, 40 and addition d; 845, 43; 887, 2-3.

for it is an allusion to his conviction that the rules had no mere human origin but were traceable to the Blessed Virgin.[2]

When it arrived in Rome the letter went to Mgr Giuseppe Antonio Sala, a datary at the Sacred Penitentiary, who dealt with French affairs. Sala was well disposed towards the new missionary organisations that were springing up in France and commended the project of the Marists as a splendid offer and one that should be kept in mind. He praised their excellent intentions and their obedience to the Holy See. In view, however, of the opposition of the vicars general in Lyon, and the shortage of priests in French dioceses, he recommended prudence. The Holy See should pass no judgement on the project until it had seen its rules and had received testimonials from the bishops, in particular from the bishop in whose diocese the Marists hoped to begin their work. The group, Sala suggested, could be told to take the matter up with the nuncio in Paris. On 9 March 1822, a reply along those lines, approved by Pius VII, was sent. It was addressed to Courveille but since the address on it was Cerdon the letter was delivered to the rectory there. One can only guess the excitement of the Colins and Jeanne-Marie Chavoin when the papal letter arrived. Repressing their eagerness, however, they first went to the church to pray. Only then did they open it. If it did not contain the full papal approval they hoped for, it was nonetheless a public and positive acknowledgement by Rome of the existence of the group calling itself the Society of Mary and praise for its stated aims. It gave them all new heart. It was to lead to new developments and to push the rustic young curate – for so Colin still felt himself – further into the limelight.

The group now prepared to take the pope at his word and go to see the nuncio in Paris. Significantly, it was decided that neither Courveille nor Pierre Colin but Jean-Claude Colin alone, should undertake this important mission. Colin was the obvious choice for it was easier for the curate than for either curé to absent himself and, given the hostility of the vicars general to the project, this was crucial. Furthermore, the rule would have to be presented to the nuncio and Colin could explain it and its origin better than either Courveille or Pierre. Furthermore, since Courveille was publicly displaying the papal letter and boasting of his new society, Jean-Claude and Pierre were probably pleased to distance themselves from his pretentious ways and pleased that he would not make the official approach about the project.

Difficulties arose immediately. The vicars general did their best to block the move. Three times Colin asked the vicars general for permission to travel and three times his letter was ignored. In the end, despairing of a satisfactory reply,

2. A half-century later, in a solemn declaration to the General Chapter of 1872, he re-affirmed this claim, explicitly referring to the 1822 letter to the pope. OM, doc. 848, 5.

the Colin brothers decided to write to Bishop Bigex to ask what they should do. Bigex was explicit:

> As the Holy Father has referred you to Monsignor the nuncio to make your religious project fully known to him, it appears to me that your immediate superiors would not have the right to stop you fulfilling those orders or intentions of His Holiness and that, if the permission is not forthcoming, you can lawfully go to see the nuncio …[3]

While advising the brothers not to overstay the normal diocesan time-limit for absences, Bigex did not hide his strong support for their project and assured them that their action was in line with canon law and that their project was part of God's providence. Encouraged, the brothers decided to press ahead. A news item, which appeared in *L'Ami de la Religion et du Roi* in early November, may have spurred the group to act quickly. A change in diocesan boundaries appeared imminent.[4] Both the pope and the French Church were convinced that more dioceses were necessary. Despairing of the stalled negotiations between Rome and Paris about increasing the number of dioceses through a new Concordat with the French parliament, Pope Pius VII now announced that with the agreement of King Louis XVIII, he had decided to create some thirty new dioceses. Among them was a new diocese of Belley that would include Cerdon. If this happened, the Marists would be divided between two dioceses. No bishops for the new dioceses had, however, been appointed and there was no guarantee that this plan would not peter out like previous arrangements. The Marists might still obtain approval while they were all in the one diocese.

By the time that all difficulties were overcome and preliminaries were completed, it was towards the end of November 1822 when Colin was able to board the coach at Cerdon for the eighteen-hour journey to Lyon. There he took the coach to Paris. He spent three days and three nights travelling, perched on the overhead seat of the coach. The chill of winter was already setting in as he started this long journey. It was also a major challenge for him for he had never before travelled so far from home nor come near that great world capital, Paris. Over twenty years later the thrill of the trip was still fresh in his memory. 'Me in Paris! Imagine it! … I had a nerve … but it did not come naturally to me. Ah, I was well aware of it, me a poor country curate.'[5]

He stayed at the Foreign Mission house in Rue du Bac and from there he went to see the nuncio, Archbishop Vincenzo Macchi; the archbishop of Paris, Hyacinthe-Louis de Quelen; the recently appointed grand master of the Université, Monsignor Denis-Luc-Antoine Frayssinous, and the superior-general

---

3. OM, doc. 76.
4. *L'Ami de la Religion et du Roi,* 33 (no. 859) p. 390, 2 Nov 1822.
5. OM, doc. 602.

of the Sulpicians, Antoine du Pouget Duclaux. He would have called on the king, Louis XVIII, but he was advised that it was not opportune. His determination is striking; the inner impulsion was driving him on. His meetings were positive. Duclaux was friendly and helpful and Colin revered him ever afterwards. He left him a copy of the rule. The nuncio, who was the main object of Colin's visit, was also welcoming. The nuncio had to act prudently for ecclesiastical affairs in France were at a critical stage, and nowhere more than in the diocese of Lyon where efforts to replace the exiled Fesch had angered some Gallican-minded clergy. The nuncio liked the rule, apparently, but expressed reservations about some of the more severe articles in it. Colin went on to meet Frayssinous and a satisfying exchange took place:

> Mgr Frayssinous listened to me, he let me say everything, never interrupted once; only at the end he said to me: 'You say that you feel in your heart a very strong feeling which impels you to commit yourself to this work?' 'Yes,' I told him. He told me to be patient, that the administration in Lyon was about to change …'[6]

The blocking tactics of the vicars general were evidently preoccupying Colin's mind. The conviction of an internal impulsion to commit himself to this work, however, impressed Frayssinous who appeared sympathetic. Within two weeks Colin was back in Lyon. What is amazing is the courage he showed. He certainly had nerve, this timid little country curate, to embark on such a mission to Paris and to call on all those distinguished persons. What is only a little less surprising is the warm welcome they gave to this little curate. His total conviction and his modest but strong personality impressed them all.

If he was hoping to similarly impress the vicars general, he was mistaken. As the Colins told the nuncio, when they asked the vicars general to free the Marists to carry out their project, 'we could get no other reply from them except the one they have been giving us for more than six years: that they need priests and that they cannot permit us to leave.'[7] A month after Colin's return what they most feared seemed imminent. The department of the Ain, which since 1801 had formed part of the diocese of Lyon, was now to be split off from it and erected as a separate diocese of Belley. Since Cerdon was in this new diocese, the Marist group would be split in two – one group in Belley and the other in Lyon. Furthermore, since the department of Ain produced few vocations, its erection into a separate diocese would result in a shortage of priests. This would make it more difficult for the Marist group at Cerdon to obtain permission to leave the diocese. If Marists did not get approval to set up their congregation before the new decree was implemented, the likelihood of their

6. OM, doc. 603.
7. OM, doc. 82, 4.

project becoming a reality would be even more remote. Panic-stricken, Colin and his brother wrote to the nuncio on 8 February 1823 imploring him to fix matters for them before the new bishop of Belley took over his diocese. In the same letter they assured him that, in consequence of his criticisms, they had softened sections of the rule. They felt, however, that they could not change the section that invited the superior to follow the advice of his councillors in preference to his own. This letter to the nuncio was followed by other initiatives. Pierre travelled to Le Puy – from where the group still longed to launch the society – to see if he could build on the initiative of Jeanne-Marie. He suggested to Richard, the vicar general, that the Marists be permitted to set up in Le Puy even without the approval of their own Lyonese diocesan authorities. It was asking too much, for a new bishop – Louis de Bonald – had already been appointed to the diocese, though he had not yet taken possession. Richard, understandably enough, could not pre-empt the new bishop's decisions. He did write favourably, however, to de Bonald about the Marist project.[8]

Then, in a final effort to avert the inevitable, Colin returned to Paris in the spring of 1823 to see the nuncio. While there, he received a one-page critique of the rule which Pierre-Denis Boyer, the Sulpician theologian appointed to examine it, had drawn up. Boyer praised it highly but added that it was 'made more for angels than for men', for he doubted whether it could be observed by a large group.[9] Colin also spoke with de Bonald, the new bishop of Le Puy, of their desire to begin in his diocese, but though the bishop expressed great interest, he could promise nothing. De Bonald no doubt felt that he could not well begin his career as bishop by poaching priests from two other dioceses. Colin did not see the new bishop of Belley, Devie. It is doubtful if Devie were in Paris but, in any case, Colin was not anxious to see him though Duclaux, the superior of the Sulpicians, was at pains to assure Colin that Devie appeared to be a good and pious bishop. Most significant of all for Colin was his interview with Macchi, the nuncio. The nuncio had kind words for him, but told him that to get approval of the rule he would have to bring it to Rome. He added that since Cerdon was now in the new diocese of Belley and Devie was its bishop, he was handing the whole Marist file over to him. This was the news Colin dreaded to hear. Just as he had feared, the Marist group was split into two, and his own group fell into the smaller and more needy diocese of Belley. Colin returned crest-fallen to Lyon. It was at this stage that he began to wonder if he had not over-reached himself and began to fear that the dream might have been a mirage. For the first time ever, he began to have serious doubts about the enterprise. It was while he was having those doubts, shortly after his return to Lyon,

8. OM, doc. 819, 47-8.
9. OM, doc. 819, 46 a, b and footnote 1.

that he had an extraordinary experience which, as told by his biographer, Jeantin, had all the trappings of the miraculous:

Alone and in pensive mood, he was walking along one of the quays of Lyon when suddenly a respectable woman approached him and said to him: 'Father, could you come to my house for a moment?' He accepted that invitation. After seating him, she said to him without any preliminaries: 'Father, the thoughts you are running through your head just now greatly displease God. His goodness has given you three great graces in your life …' Immediately she entered into the details of the three extraordinary favours. The poor curate, seeing that this woman knew so well inner things which he had never told anyone, could not get over his surprise; 'God who gave you such great graces can give you even greater ones. Have courage and confidence then.' So she told him all he must do to respond at that time to the holy will of God. 'See how it was for me then,' cried the humble servant of God, sobbing. 'I did not say yes or no to her but simply "Thank you, Madam" and I went away.'[10]

In another account that he gave of the incident, Colin revealed that the woman was Pauline Jaricot, a devout wealthy young Lyonese, who among other initiatives had been deeply involved in promoting the highly successful Association for the Propagation of the Faith.[11] Pauline, a woman of deep faith and an indefatigable worker for the poor, especially for young women, was also a mystic who heard the voice of the Lord.[12] Although Jeantin's account leads one to believe that when she approached Colin on the riverbank Pauline Jaricot was unknown to him, the incident can have a simpler and a more plausible interpretation. When Colin was in Paris, Pauline's brother, Philéas, was staying in the seminary of Saint-Sulpice and very attached to his saintly sister. When Colin was returning to Lyon after his first visit, Philéas asked him to bring a package to Pauline who lived not far from the coach stop for Cerdon and wrote to her to tell her to expect a visit from Colin. It is not impossible that Philéas made a similar request when Colin was returning after his second trip. In any case Colin had met Pauline before and probably had heard her own brother and others speak of this remarkable woman. Jeantin, by recounting the sudden approach of a woman, whom he does not identify as known to Colin, wants to supernaturalise the incident as he does with other events in Colin's life. Nevertheless, Colin also saw what took place at the meeting as extraordinary, for he spoke of it often and marvelled at her ability to read his thoughts. Yet he refused to go to see her again, although she invited him. Pauline, how-

10. J. Jeantin, *Les très révérend Père Colin* (Lyon, 1895-1898), vol. 1, pp 100-1.
11. OM, doc. 819, 114 and b, c, d.
12. D. Lathoud, *Marie-Pauline Jaricot*, vol. 1, (Paris, 1937), pp 75-7.

ever, had rekindled his conviction of God's intervention in his life and given him fresh courage.

He immediately set about continuing his efforts for the society and so approached Bishop Devie, who had just been installed in Belley. As Duclaux had told Colin, Devie was a good and holy bishop, but this did not make him any less energetic in pushing his episcopal claims and wanting to control closely all ecclesiastics, priests, brothers and sisters, in his diocese. It was while he was on his way to see Devie that Colin had an experience more extraordinary than the meeting with Pauline Jaricot. One day towards the end of July 1823, shortly after the bishop's arrival, Colin set out for Belley. He left the presbytery of Cerdon to walk the twenty kilometres to the little town of Ambérieu where he would catch the coach. It was still night. Outside Cerdon he turned off the main road to take a short-cut along an old Roman road, which locals called La montée de la Coria, or Coria Ascent, for it passed through the hills of Coria towards the castle of Mérignat. He had walked about twenty minutes from the time he left the presbytery and had begun the ascent when suddenly he found that he could go no further. Fifteen years later he described what happened to him:

> On one of the journeys I made for the Society, I felt that all the demons were after me to stop me making it. Yes, I really believe it was so. I was weighed down! … I could not hold myself up. I felt an invincible repugnance! … After twenty minutes walking, I threw myself on my knees in the moonlight, in the middle of the road, and I said: My God, if it is not your will, then I shall not do it. But if you want it, give me back my strength, and so show me that it is your holy will. Suddenly, I felt myself uplifted, happy, light-hearted; I went ahead like a hare …[13]

That was the account of the episode he gave at table during Holy Week of 1838. Over thirty years later, in April 1869, dictating to his secretaries, Jeantin and David, an account of the origins of the Society, he gave an almost identical version of the incident. In 1853, however, he had also described what had happened, this time very briefly to Father Julien Favre who was about to succeed him as superior-general. Favre reported it to Mayet who noted it down. Although in accordance with the other versions, what Colin told Favre adds a vital detail:

> He was overcome with a very great moral lassitude, a profound ennui … When he prayed, then the Blessed Virgin appeared to him and he felt himself filled with a heavenly joy and a superhuman courage. He told me so.[14]

13. OM, doc. 425, 10; OM 4, *Synopse historique,* section 322.III. J. Coste, 'L'apparition de la Sainte Vierge au Père Colin sur le chemin de Mérignat', unpublished mss, 1956, APM, Fonds Coste, Cerdon, Belley.
14. OM, doc. 717.

A Marian vision was in keeping with the times – it was the age of Rue du Bac, La Salette, and Lourdes – and was just what many wanted, for it would confirm for them the supernatural origin of the society and also the divine inspiration of the constitutions. Zealous confrères, hungry for the miraculous, wanted Colin to speak again about the vision and relate all its circumstances. When, in 1868, Colin, in his dictation to Jeantin and David on the origins, mentioned the event at the Coria – though with no allusion to a vision – Victor Choizin, the Paris provincial, anxious to build a chapel at the place of the 'apparition', put pressure on Jeantin to worm the details out of him. Humorously he wrote:

> There are questions to which we must at all costs have an answer: we must know where the Virgin appeared to Father Colin … But we must use all possible finesse with the venerable old man. Father David and you, one the dove, the other the serpent, that's what Father Mayet says, you are more able than anyone to find the secret. If you don't, I'll try myself.[15]

Given the importance of the matter in the eyes of many Marists, Choizin was justified in seeking information. The 'serpent' and the 'dove' tried but failed to get much more. 'The ferret', as Jeantin called Choizin, decided to try himself. He came on Colin suddenly in Sainte-Foy and, button-holing him, straight away asked: 'Is it not true that all that concerns you belongs to your spiritual children?' 'Oh, certainly, certainly.' 'Well then, is it really true that the Blessed Virgin appeared to you the day you went to take the Ambérieu coach and your legs were bound?' Disconcerted, Colin let slip the words, 'Yes! well, yes,' words he regretted…'[16]

Of these two accounts of the 'apparition', Favre's account is the more significant. Favre, the superior-general of the Society from 1854 to 1885, was a clear-headed man, who knew his theology and was not given to enthusiasms. It is most unlikely that he would embellish Colin's account. By adding 'He told me so' to Colin's account, he appears to want to underline the strict accuracy of his report. Jeantin suggests that the very plausible reason why Colin told Favre was because Favre was about to take on the difficult role of general and Colin wanted to encourage him by recounting the apparition of the Virgin confirming her approval of the Marist project. In the second episode, the elderly Colin was surprised by Choizin into making an admission that goes into no detail. His 'Yes! well, yes,' was dragged out of him by a smart manoeuvre and could be interpreted as the old founder's effort to evade further annoying questioning. When, however, on two occasions later, his admission came up, Colin,

15. OM 3, pp 257-8, footnote 2.
16. OM 3, p. 407. This episode is reported in the lithographed text of the conferences Jeantin gave at Paignton, 1887.

although complaining of Choizin on one occasion and maintaining an unbreakable silence on the other, did not withdraw his words. Like his reticence on the impulse to write the rule for which, despite pressure from eager interlocutors, he claimed no divine biblical-style inspiration, this reserve is in keeping with his determination to avoid invoking supernatural intervention. There is a consistency, however, in his accounts that makes it clear that something quite unusual happened him that for him was of great significance. It gave him ' a heavenly joy' and 'a superhuman courage'. No wonder, then, that he dashed forward unstoppably, allowing nothing to stand in the way of the great project. This is the only supernatural vision to which Colin admitted and then only to encourage his successor, Favre. A vision was something he was not interested in speaking of, but what happened that morning was for him a sign of divine approval of the project.

In March 1824, returning from one of his many trips to Belley to see Devie, he had a very different though frightening experience in which Mayet again detected the intervention of the Blessed Virgin. It had been a long winter and the road between Belley and Ambérieu was icy. It was nightfall and the coach was within four kilometres of Tenay, which is twenty-five kilometres from Belley, and was passing along the shores of Lac des Hôpitaux, when it went out of control and overturned into the lake. Colin was thrown free. 'How astonished I was to find myself on the water's edge!' he recounted later, '…my umbrella and my little case near me, totally unhurt and unshaken, not knowing how I had been ejected there, with the thought: 'the Blessed Virgin has saved you' as if a voice had told me.'[17] One woman was not so fortunate. She was tossed into the lake and clung to the wheel of the coach. As she desperately clutched the wheel it continued to turn so that sometimes she was above the water, sometimes under the water. Every time she came up she would cry for help before sinking again as her weight dragged the wheel down and brought her under the freezing water of the lake. Seeing her plight Colin ran for help to the coach driver, only to be told by him that he had his hands full saving his horses. Colin returned to the drowning woman, took hold of his umbrella and held it out to her. She grabbed on to it and he managed to pull her ashore to safety. Even that was not the end of the story. They were four kilometres from the nearest village and it was night time. They set off on foot and Mayet describes a scene which would be hilarious were it not so serious:

> The unfortunate woman had no strength left and was petrified with the cold; soon her clothes froze and became as stiff as boards. They were about one league from Tenay … It was night time. There ensued a struggle between the holy founder's purity and his charity. He proposed to this woman that she walk in front of him and he helped her by pushing her. But

17. OM, doc. 425, 11.

soon this means proved inadequate; he was forced, despite all his repugnance, to give her his arm and to drag her, not lead her, to the village. Some distance from it, he met ... some people to whom he promptly abandoned the poor woman ... The woman herself ... attributed her life to ... [his] charitable care ...[18]

At this point, except for adding that in the village they were well looked after, Mayet's narrative concludes. Mayet, although faithful in telling the details, makes sure to underline the modesty of Colin and how it was only by sheer charity that he linked arms with the unfortunate woman to drag her along the road that terrible night. Interestingly, Mayet places this story immediately after his account of Colin's admission that, as a young boy, he believed that if a man and a woman simply passed one another by, and had the intention of marrying, they would conceive a child, and so he used turn aside when he saw a woman coming towards him. Some time after the accident, Colin was again travelling past the same spot, people in the diligence began to talk about it and recounted how, were it not for a priest who was also in the carriage, two women would have perished. Colin held his tongue.[19]

All Colin's visits to Devie were not as dramatic as those two proved to be. When he met Devie for the first time, the bishop welcomed him: 'Ah! the curate from Cerdon! the nuncio told me of your plan.' This was the auspicious beginning of a relationship that was to prove stormy but also fruitful. Pierre wrote to Devie asking permission to send Jeanne-Marie to him so that she might open her heart to him. The bishop agreed and the meeting was apparently a success, for at this time Jeanne-Marie took steps to begin the sisters' branch. With some difficulty, she persuaded the authorities to allow Marie Jotillon, who had gone to help Courveille's sisters at Saint-Clair-du-Rhone, to rejoin her at Cerdon to begin the first community of Marist sisters. The account book of Jeanne and Marie states laconically:

> Jeanne Marie Chavoin and Marie Jotillon came to live together on 8 September 1823 in the parish of Cerdon, in the department of the Ain, with the approval of the bishop of Belley, in order to begin under his authority and the direction of the Fathers Colin, curé and assistant of the said parish, the Congregation of the Daughters of Mary.[20]

Their example attracted Marie Gardet, a niece of Marie Jotillon. It was to prove a difficult winter but decisive for the founding of the sisters' branch. Devie came to Cerdon on his first visit and did his best to persuade the sisters to merge with the Sisters of Saint Joseph or those of Saint Charles. Jeanne-

18. OM, doc. 539, 3, 5, additions.
19. OM, doc. 654, 2.
20. *Recollections: Mother Saint Joseph* (Rome, 1974), doc. 110.

Marie refused and 'spoke out boldly like St Peter' that they 'left home and family to start the Society of the Blessed Virgin.' Devie allowed them to take a habit. In December the first postulant arrived, Jeanne-Marie Chavoin of la Grêle, cousin of Jeanne-Marie. The four young women suffered severely in their poor lodging during the winter with a bad floor over a stable with a horse. Jeanne-Marie related that she often thought that the horse was better lodged. Their perseverance was heroic and was a source of encouragement for the Colins who were being looked after now by Jeanne-Marie's mother, Jeanne Verchère. When the long hard winter of 1823-4 was over – a heroic year for the sisters – the first fruits were appearing. Colin's concern for the sisters emerges in an eloquent request to Devie to grant their wish to take the first steps towards becoming religious and to have some religious garb. They were impatiently awaiting his coming, Colin told him, wanting 'to shed the profane dress of the world in order to dress themselves in the holy habit of the Blessed Virgin.' His request became an impassioned plea as he continued:

> Those poor children of Mary raise their suppliant eyes and hands to heaven, and it is high time that they, and the world too, be able to recognise publicly that it was not in vain that they trusted in the powerful protection of that august Queen of Heaven.[21]

Moved no doubt by the pleas of the sisters and Jean-Claude, Devie came on 6 June 1824, the feast of Pentecost. The sisters had bought some light blue material and fashioned simple dresses and, in a little ceremony, Devie blessed them for the postulants. It was another small but satisfying step in the 'work of Mary'. The sisters moved into a larger house. The question of religious dress was important if the Cerdonese were to see them as religious. Over that summer a number of young women of the town, attracted by the example of the little group, came and were admitted as postulants. This was an encouraging beginning and a source of great hope to the entire group. There was movement, too, in the priests' branch. That July, Colin reported eagerly to Devie that Étienne Déclas and Étienne Terraillon had expressed their deeply-felt desire to join the Cerdon group. As Terraillon, unlike Déclas, was not in the Belley diocese, Colin asked Devie's permission to encourage him to ask for an *exeat* from the Lyon diocese.[22]

In Lyon, the old order, as Frayssinous had hinted to Colin, was giving place to the new. Fesch, Napoleon's uncle, in permanent exile in Rome, would not resign the see. Pius VII died in August 1823 and, in December, the new pope, Leo XII, appointed Jean-Paul-Gaston de Pins, bishop of Limoges, as apostolic administrator of Lyon. Although de Pins had not the highly-coveted title of

21. OM, doc. 100.
22. OM, doc. 107, 1.

Archbishop of Lyon and Primate of the Gauls, he was in effect the archbishop.[23]
Clergy of 'Ultramontane' views hailed his appointment but Bochard protested
publicly, left the diocese of Lyon and retired to the diocese of Belley. Despite
his earlier efforts to block the Marists and his threats to impose canonical
censures on Champagnat, Bochard now wrote to the Colins to re-establish
good relations with the Marist group and promised to send them recruits.
Courbon died on 8 February 1824. Significantly, too, one of the vicars general
that de Pins appointed was Jean Cholleton, who had helped the young Marist
aspirants during their time at Saint-Irénée.

The first contacts the Marists had with de Pins concerned the schools. De
Pins was keenly interested in providing schools. For Champagnat, who had
met only opposition from Bochard, from the local parish priests and others in
the diocese, the arrival of de Pins was a godsend. Gardette, his former superior
at Saint-Irénée, and Cholleton were strong supporters. De Pins praised
Champagnat's work and gave it a generous subsidy of 8,000 francs that,
according to Colin, caused quite a stir in the town. On 13 May 1824, he authorised Courveille to leave his parish and to help Champagnat in his work for the
brothers of the schools. On the following day, Courveille and Champagnat
bought land eight kilometres north-east of La Valla on which they built The
Hermitage, which became the mother-house and novitiate of the brothers. It
was a major step. Generously and tirelessly, Champagnat took part in the actual
building. Two months later, on 19 July 1824, Courveille and Champagnat published a prospectus of the 'Little Brothers of Mary' which advertised for recruits
and offered the brothers' services to parishes wishing to benefit from the
education they provided.

When de Pins' council authorised Courveille to join Champagnat, it indicated that Champagnat was in charge. In the prospectus, however, Courveille
placed the letters, 'P S G L' after his name, meaning 'Priest, Superior General'.
Champagnat, concerned only with the success of the work of Mary and the
welfare of the brothers, raised no objection, but Courveille's claim to be superior general was not acceptable to the others. Perhaps it was at this time that the
simple Déclas warned Courveille and reminded him that there was as yet no
superior general and that one would be chosen later when the project got under
way. Courveille's further contacts with de Pins and his administration masked
another ambiguity. De Pins apparently understood that in dealing with him,
he was dealing with the Society of Mary as a whole and he was unaware of the
group at Cerdon.

De Pins was only two weeks in Lyon when Colin decided to see him to

23. Jean-Paul-Gaston de Pins (1766-1850) born into a family of the nobility in southern France,
nominated bishop of Béziers 1817 but unable to take possession, because of the non-ratification
of the new concordat; bishop of Limoges, 1822; apostolic administrator of Lyon, 1823-40.

inform him about the whole Marist project. He went to Lyon no less than three times to try to see de Pins only to find that he was absent. He spoke instead to the three vicars general one after another. In a long report to Devie, he related how he found all the new vicars general well-disposed.[24] Jean-Joseph Barou, the second vicar general and soon to become first vicar general, had been Colin's superior at Verrières. He advised that the society begin in Lyon. Colin replied that they had originally hoped to begin in Le Puy, but since the pope had sent them to the nuncio and both the nuncio and Bishop de Bonald of Le Puy, had sent them to the bishop of Belley, he had to accept that it was God's will that they begin in Belley. He also dismissed the suggestion that the Society begin with a house in both Lyon and Belley, because the two houses would not develop the same spirit. Colin went on then to tell Devie that Cholleton, the third vicar general, was very favourably disposed but could not say so openly because, as Colin confided to Devie: 'We spoke to him openly about accepting the position of superior general.' It is noteworthy that Cholleton does not appear to have rejected this proposition. Whether Colin acted on his own initiative in making this offer, or whether others were involved is not clear. The use of the plural 'we' would seem to involve at least Pierre and probably Déclas. Jeanne-Marie may have known, though probably not Champagnat who was working with Courveille. In this decision to set up Cholleton as the first superior-general one can see that Colin had taken on himself the task of getting the society off the ground. He esteemed Cholleton highly and wrote later: 'He was always our father, our guide, our light in the midst of the difficulties of the newborn Society ... this Society ... is more his work than ours.'[25] He certainly wanted him as general, as his vote in 1836 and his proposition later to retire in his favour were to show. He told Devie that if Cholleton came to his diocese as superior-general of the society, he would bring a number of the priests with him, a proposition that could not fail to interest the bishop. It was astute diplomacy.

Colin had another interview with Barou in July 1824.[26] Barou now accepted that the society begin in Belley and believed that de Pins would not object to the transfer of a few of his priests if Devie asked him. He was mistaken for when Terraillon went to de Pins asking for his *exeat* he was turned down, de Pins rejecting all Terraillon's arguments and warning, somewhat mysteriously, against proceeding in too human a manner. He made it clear to Terraillon that the society should begin in Lyon. With no hope of getting any further, Terraillon was left wondering if Cerdon was really the place to begin, although,

24. OM, doc. 100.
25. Colin, circular letter, 10 Feb. 1852, APM, 233.71 cited in OM, vol. 4, p. 233.
26. OM, doc. 107.

Jean-Claude Colin
Oil Painting by Fr Antoine Philipon,
Marist.

Mother St Joseph (Jeanne-Marie
Chavoin): 'We left home and family to
start the Society of the Blessed Virgin.'

St Marcellin Champagnat: 'As your
wills should form one with the Fathers
of the Society of Mary, so I desire that
your hearts … may always be one in
Jesus and Mary.'

Cardinal Joseph Fesch: 'Were my uncle
Joseph to be put through a still, all that
would come out would be seminaries!'
— Napoleon's comment on his uncle.

Cardinal Vincenzo Macchi: As nuncio in
Paris he received Colin well and later
encouraged him to come to Rome where
he obtained the papal audience for him.

François-Marie Bigex: 'This saintly
bishop … encouraged us by his letters
and, over four years, willingly guided us
by his counsel.'

Jean-Baptiste-François Pompallier, first
Bishop of Auckland: 'the obtaining of a
brief of authorisation … for the Society
of Mary is uppermost [in my mind]. If
that takes place, I shall be quite content
to go to the ends of the world, to the
islands of the Pacific Ocean.'

Pope Gregory XVI: 'The salvation of all
mankind … makes us ever more
vigilant to leave nothing untried so that
from the rising of the sun to its setting
the name of the Lord may be praised
and the Catholic faith … flourish and
shine forth in all the earth.'

Alexandre-Raymond Devie, Bishop of Belley:'He tried us sorely … but when he saw the approbation coming he said to a curé, "The finger of God is here."' – Colin.'

Archbishop Jean-Paul-Gaston de Pins, apostolic administrator of the diocese of Lyon, supported Champagnat and later warmly recommended the Marists to the Holy See. 'He is a true St Francis of Sales.' – Étienne Terraillon in 1824.

Cardinal Castruccio Castracane: 'So the whole world will be Marist?' 'Yes, the whole world, yourself, if you want to. And the Pope too.'

Gabriel-Claude Mayet, chronicler of the Society: 'I have collected only the facts that deal with Father Colin or the history of the Society.'

Fourvière: The Chapel at the beginning of the nineteenth century.

Interior of Fourvière chapel: 'And there, after celebrating the Holy Sacrifice of the Mass, they consecrated themselves, by unanimous consent, to this project.'

Ruffieu church in the Bugey. From the window in the loft Father Humbert relayed Colin's sermon to the large crowd outside who 'were as moved as those who were inside.'

La Capucinière: The chapel of the first Marist house, blessed by Bishop Devie in 1835. On 24 September 1836, the first Marists made their profession here.

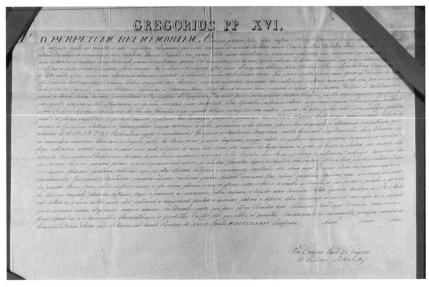

Omnium Gentium: Papal brief of approbation of the Society, 1836.

Frieze in Basilica at Fourvière: St Marcellin Champagnat, St Peter Julian Eymard,
Jean-Claude Colin and the Missions of Oceania.

The Cathedral of Our Lady of Le Puy where the Blessed Virgin told Courveille that she wanted a 'Society of Mary' whose 'members would be called Marists'.

Belley College: The Statue of the Virgin in the background was the one Colin had placed in a niche overlooking the courtyard during an elaborate ceremony in 1833. The pupils, 42 musicians, and an 'immense crowd' were present. In the foreground the statue of St Peter Chanel.

Cerdon: The three valleys. The church and rectory in the foreground.

A mission in nineteenth-century France: blessing the mission cross.

as he told Colin, he was so attached to the set up at Cerdon, that, were he allowed, he would come there hot-foot.

After the hopes that the conversations with Barou had raised, the reaction of de Pins was a setback. The Colins decided to make a major effort to win him over and, at the same time, to set the record straight. On 10 November, they wrote him a long, carefully argued letter:

We believe that your Excellency cannot as yet have more than an imperfect knowledge [of the project], for it is only to the bishop of Belley and our director that we have given all the information. The Society has already started in the diocese of Belley. Before it takes on any new increases, we regard it as absolutely necessary to give your grace a full account of all that concerns the work; to speak to you of the Rules, which are in the hands ... of the bishop of Belley; of the people who, without having worked exteriorly at the project, conceived the idea before anyone thought of it [and] of the steps already taken ...[27]

The Colins were making it clear to de Pins that his knowledge of the Marists was imperfect because whoever he was dealing with in Lyon – and they clearly had Courveille in mind – was not the central person in the project. By 'people who conceived the project before anyone thought of it' they meant Colin, who was the true originator and repository of the Marist project. They would willingly give him full information of the Society's origin, rules and progress which, up to this, they had told only the bishop of Belley and 'our director'. The society, they pointed out, had already been founded in the diocese of Belley and only later could it spread out to make new foundations. To drive home the point that the Society had already begun but to keep De Pins' good-will, they added: 'If the Society, which is already born, is blessed by God and your Grace is agreeable, it will not be long before it comes to the diocese of Lyon.' The Colins concluded that such a return to Lyon, their home diocese, would be a consolation to which they looked forward. Tortuous though the language was, the letter represented a determined attempt by the Colins to reclaim for the Belley group the central role in the affairs of the Society and to make sure that de Pins knew that only by dealing with them, and not with Courveille, would he be able to know the society properly.

Whether de Pins completely understood the undertones of this complicated letter, he was now alerted to another dimension of the society. He consented to see Colin. The meeting took place towards the end of November 1824. De Pins refused point-blank to allow any of his priests to join the group in the diocese of Belley. He nursed a grievance against that diocese on account of the Sisters of St Joseph, for when Belley was hived off from Lyon to become a diocese in

27. OM, doc. 117, 3-4.

1822, Devie erected the branch of those sisters living in what was now his diocese into a separate diocesan congregation. Three times de Pins raised the matter with Colin. He was not pleased when he learned that the Marist group, which like the Sisters of St Joseph had originated in Lyon and which he had supported financially, was also being taken over by Belley.

De Pins' position was understandable – he was pleased to have the brothers providing much-needed education in his diocese, but he had no intention of releasing any of his priests to join a new religious congregation in the diocese of Belley. De Pins had made his position so clear that Colin did not approach him again for some five years. There was no hope of reuniting the two groups in the immediate future. Although the interview dashed the hopes Colin had built up from his discussions with Barou, he did not lose heart. In his extensive report to Devie, he reconfirmed his attachment to him and his reliance on his help.

Colin also wrote to Courveille to give him a summary of what took place with de Pins but he did not give him the full report he gave Devie. He expressed his surprise that de Pins did not know of the Cerdon side of the project, a remark that was probably a reproach to Courveille for not having properly informed de Pins. The letter indicates a certain distance between the two men, for whereas Terraillon had addressed Colin as 'Dear beloved friend,' Colin now addressed Courveille formally as 'Monsieur'. He certainly did not refer to him as superior general which Courveille would have liked. It is significant, too, that he did not invite Courveille to preside or take a major role at the ceremony of the clothing of the sisters – an event of major importance – but merely invited him to be present at the ceremony. Taken with what he said in the letter to de Pins, it is apparent that Colin no longer accepted Courveille's claim to leadership.

Colin's eight-year stay in Cerdon was coming to an end. They had been years of growth when his character began to emerge in greater relief. His mission in the project of a Society of Mary had become clearer. Yielding to an inner urge, which he believed was divinely inspired, he had drafted an idealistic rule for an ideal society. Then over the next four years he had ventured to propose his rule and seek approval for the project from Church authorities. Once Bigex had reassured him that he was not disobeying Church authority, the young country curate bypassed the Lyon authorities and bravely set out for Paris where he skilfully conducted negotiations with very senior churchmen. To put himself forward in this way was not natural to him and showed great courage. Difficulties and doubts came his way. Unusual events, however, which he read as so many signs – the meeting with Pauline Jaricot, the incident at the Lac des Hôpitaux where he believed that the Virgin saved his life, and, above all, his remarkable experience on La Coria Ascent – confirmed his belief that the work he was doing was that of the Virgin. Strengthened by Jeanne-Marie Chavoin in his resolve to push ahead, he continued negotiations with vicars general and bishops in Belley and Lyon. With Devie, whose appointment he had first seen as a catastrophe for the project, he had overcome his initial disappointment and had worked towards establishing a good relationship. In his negotiations at Lyon, he had shown courage and skill, and kept his primary objective – a society worthy of Mary – clearly in focus. De Pins' rejection had not discouraged him. Colin emerged as a man who knew what he wanted and would keep working for it. His vigorous activity and steely resolve is surprising in a country curate so young and inexperienced. He drew the strength for this activity from prayer; he often told his confrères that he never engaged in any important task without serious prayer.

Despite de Pins' refusal to release priests, the year 1824 was an encouraging one for the Society. It was now in two clusters – one in the diocese of Lyon around the Hermitage, the other in the diocese of Belley around Cerdon. With Champagnat and Courveille at the Hermitage there were twenty brothers and ten postulants and by October the building was well on the way to completion.[28] In addition, there were some twenty-four brothers teaching 1,300 boys in eleven schools. At de Pins' request, they had taken on a large school at Charlieu in the department of the Loire. In November they had opened another school at Chavanay in the department of the Rhone.

In Belley, too, the group had made progress. Devie had permitted Déclas to join the Colins at the presbytery and so at Cerdon there were the three priests. More significant were developments among the sisters. They had attracted so many vocations that the house they had acquired in June was too small and for this reason, and because the Cerdon recruits were too close to home, Jeanne-Marie wrote to Devie in November 1824 to ask that they might go elsewhere. This remarkable letter shows not merely Jeanne-Marie's concern for the sisters but the important role she was taking in the whole Marist project. She refers to the Marists as 'the happiest of your children' and she revealed to Devie, a 'light' she received after Communion indicating what the Colin brothers should do. This was the letter that has the first mention of the formula: 'unknown and as if hidden'.[29] Two weeks later, on 8 December, a major event took place. Jeanne-Marie was elected superior of the sisters and took the name

28. OM, docs 754, 27; 757, 14. S. Farrell, *Achievement from the Depths* (Drummoyne, New South Wales, 1984), pp 96-106; F. McMahon, *The Story of Marcellin Champagnat and his fellow Founders of the Society of Mary* (Rome, 1994), pp 36-53; A. Lanfrey, *Marcellin Champagnat et les Frères Maristes: instituteurs congréganistes au XIXe siècle* (Paris, 1999) p. 85.

29. CMJ, doc. 2. Jeanne-Marie's actual words are 'We have seen and most warmly appreciated the way traced out for us by your Lordship *(nous a fait tenir)* of remaining hidden and unknown in the eyes of men.' What role that attributes to Devie in the formulation is unclear.

Mother St Joseph.[30] Then in a ceremony in the parish church of Cerdon, with up to a hundred parishioners present, nine sisters, one of whom was already close to death, took the habit. Pierre presided and Jean-Claude and Déclas were present. The ceremony, performed according to a well-elaborated Marist ritual, was a joyful occasion for all. The joy was well founded. It was the formal recognition of the sisters' branch of the Society of Mary as a religious congregation. The sisters were the first Marists to take publicly the canonical vows of religion.[31]

The coming of Déclas to the rectory had prompted Pierre Colin's enthusiastic letter to Devie on 29 October but his ecstatic comment could apply to the whole society at the end of 1824: 'Today,' he had written, 'the little Society of Mary begins!'[32]

30. According to the custom of the time, she would be addressed from now on as 'Mother St Joseph'. It was thought more convenient, however, to retain the name 'Jeanne-Marie Chavoin' for the rest of this volume.
31. The brothers were living as a religious congregation but had not taken the canonical vows.
32. OM, doc. 114, 1.

CHAPTER 12

Belley and the Bugey Missions

'I especially want there to be in the Society some record of our beginnings, not just so that we shall be talked about ... but so that in the future people will conform to our way of acting and imitate the simplicity that God has blessed. Later, when the Society has grown and certain people will be tempted to reject this way of acting, the written records will serve as a rallying-point.' Colin to Mayet, June 1844. (OM, doc. 581, 1).

The crowded year of 1824 was to be the Colins' last year at Cerdon. In his letter of 29 November 1824 to Courveille inviting him to the clothing ceremony and relating his unsuccessful interview with de Pins, Colin added almost casually that Déclas had joined them and that in January they would begin to make some 'apostolic forays'. These forays were to become an important turning point in his life and that of the society. They were the beginnings of the Bugey missions which Colin always remembered as the early heroic years. These missions would not have come about, however, were it not for Alexandre Devie, the first bishop in the newly-reconstituted diocese of Belley. Something must now be said of this bishop who was to play an important role in the life of Colin and in the beginnings of the society.

Alexandre Devie was born in the year 1767 in Montélimar, a town on the Rhone, some 140 kilometres south of Lyon, not far from the large city of Valence.[1] During the Revolution he had refused the oath and had to go on the run. He had become a professor of philosophy and superior at the seminary of Viviers. In 1813, the bishop of Valence had made him vicar general of the diocese. The bishop died in 1815 and for the next four years, until a new bishop was appointed, Devie played the major part in running the diocese. While there he helped re-establish religious congregations and encouraged the active apostolate. He was ascetic, charitable and intelligent. Well-versed in theology, and with an understanding of the needs of the people, he had written books and published articles on pastoral practice which were modelled on the moral theology of Alphonsus Liguori. Devie was an indefatigable worker, sleeping only six hours a night and taking his recreation by changing from one job to another. His prime objective was the re-organisation of his diocese. He wasted no time. Within a few months he had held two meetings where he met all his

1. Alexandre-Raymond Devie (1767-1852) bishop of Belley, 1823-52.

priests. A detailed questionnaire, sent to all parish priests, briefed him on the state of each parish. Then he set out to see conditions for himself, travelling to every part of the diocese. The calash or four-wheeled carriage in which he travelled, he had fitted with a shelf for books and for writing so that he could work while travelling. He often travelled in wintry conditions, along roads that were no more than dirt-tracks and sometimes he was forced to finish the journey on foot, struggling through the mud. Seven times in twenty-nine years he visited all his parishes, so committed he was to a renewal of his diocese. This was the earnest, zealous, fifty-six year old man who, on 23 July 1823, had taken possession of the diocese of Belley.

Missions to the people were one of the principal methods Devie conceived for reviving the faith in his run-down diocese. Already as vicar general in the diocese of Valence, he had promoted the missions and seen their worth. When Devie came to Belley he invited several groups of priests, including the Capuchins, to give missions. He also hoped to set up his own group of diocesan missioners. He soon became aware that the little group of aspirant Marists longed to be released from parish work in order to live as a religious community and towards the end of 1824, he proposed to them to preach missions and retreats in the hill country around Cerdon. They accepted the invitation. Devie's move was important. By taking them out of parish work and grouping them as a mission band, he contributed powerfully to making them a unit.

Colin decided that the best place from which to launch their missions would be the capital of the department, Bourg-en-Bresse, which was a large town, centrally situated, and the site of the major seminary. He went to Bourg to acquire a house for the group, while the Marist sisters, who were to move out of Cerdon, too, had some women there make inquiries for a place for them. Both plans came to nothing, however, for Devie, who was installing a group of diocesan missionaries in Bourg, told the Marist group to come to Belley.[2] Belley was a small town of some 4,000 people – less than half that of Bourg – in the extreme south-east corner of the department. Colin later called it 'a little hole in the middle of the mountains' and 'a wilderness' where 'the grass grew in the streets'. Yet Belley was a picturesque and historic town that since the Middle Ages had been the capital of the Bugey and the seat of the bishop. It was to be the home of Colin for the next fourteen years.

Belley was the base from which the little group organised their main mission work but even before they went there, while still involved in the parish work of Cerdon, they began with two nearby parishes.[3] On 9 January, at

2. OM, docs 821, 37; 118, 2.
3. For the missions see Coste, *Lectures,* pp. 69-80; C. Whelan, *The Marist Story, (3) The Bugey Experience* (Sidcup, 1996); P. Jacolin, 'Apports sur les premières missions Maristes dans le Bugey', unpublished article which gives the findings of Bernard Bourtot and Pierre Jacolin during their tour of the Bugey in the winter of 1996-7.

Bishop Devie's request, Colin and Déclas went to give a mission in the parish of La Balme only two kilometres from Cerdon. Access was difficult for it was 283 metres higher than Cerdon and the mountain path that ran between the two villages was quite steep. It was a typical hamlet of the Bugey, with a population of some 400 people, but had had no resident priest for some years. The Sabbath was not observed and the instruction of the children neglected for, to learn the catechism, they would have to travel to another village.

If Colin was delighted that the bishop had accepted that they could come together as a religious group, nevertheless, as he prepared to begin the mission, he experienced a crisis which he described as 'the most violent possible'.[4] This unusually strong language from Colin many years later indicates how it was for him. What was surfacing again was his old dilemma. His deepest wish was still to be alone with God, to converse with him, to lead a hidden life. A public mission was the very antithesis of this desire. One can sense the agony this new challenge posed to the young priest, whose whole instinct from his boyhood in Saint-Bonnet to his old age in La Neylière was to lose himself in prayer. Earlier it was the vision of a society dedicated to Mary, working in an unobtrusive manner, that had made his yearning for solitude compatible with the ministry of the priesthood. Now, as he prepared for the first mission, he was only too well aware that it would lead him into a more public life. In between, however, had come the years of consolation and prayer at Cerdon and they made a difference. They had brought him conviction and courage regarding the project and, despite the personal crisis he experienced, he did not hesitate. He remarked later: 'I had to plunge into it, since we were beginning with the missions.' The missions, he was convinced, were to be, in God's plan, the beginnings of the society and, though he suffered in being pushed into the arena of a public mission, he accepted it willingly.

On a practical level, the preparation was difficult for he had never preached a mission before. Neither could he count for much help from his companion, Étienne Déclas. Déclas, the first to join the two brothers at Cerdon, was a holy man but poorly instructed. He had little *savoir-faire,* poor manners, and made atrocious errors in French. Narrow in outlook, he suffered from nervous tensions and, convinced that he was pursued by demons, he drove them away by making faces at them. Mayet commented that 'in his conduct, on account of the temptations he suffered and the unbelievable grimaces he then used to make, he could be taken for a madman or a demoniac.'[5] When Colin had asked Devie for him, the bishop could not hide his surprise and exclaimed 'what will you do with M. Déclas; he has no talents'.[6] When they wrote to

4. OM, doc. 433.
5. OM, doc. 537, k.
6. OM, doc. 819, 56.

Rome, the Colins told him nothing, for as Pierre Colin said, 'his imprudent zeal and lack of judgement would have compromised everything'.[7] He was, however, a most generous, simple and humble priest. Above all, he had a zeal for souls. From the time at the seminary, he had been a friend of the Curé of Ars and went to stay with him on occasion at his parish. Together they would prepare a 'gala' meal:

> Between the two of them they succeeded in making an omelette and reheating the potatoes which the curé left in his mess tin ... soup after the manner of the Trappists and fruits from the garden – this was the complete menu.[8]

They would talk about how best to save sinners. There was a clear affinity in zeal and asceticism between the saintly curé and 'the apostle of the Bugey' as Déclas was called.

Colin, however, found him an exasperating companion on the first mission. Unwittingly this rough-hewn diamond of a man said such extraordinary and inexact things in his sermons at La Balme that Colin could not listen to him without pain.[9] That mission began on 9 January 1825. Every day Déclas and Colin walked up the steep mountainside, each with his little black bag containing sermons and breviary slung across his shoulder. It was nightfall when, after catechising children, preaching, hearing confessions and visiting the sick, they descended the same steep incline. They continued this for three weeks. Of great support was the generosity of Pierre Colin who looked after the parish on his own and came up to La Balme a few times a week. He may have brought provisions but he certainly brought support and no doubt news of the sisters and parishioners. The long mission, outwardly at least, appears to have been a success. The account Pierre wrote to the bishop was a glowing one.[10] The people of La Balme, he told him, came willingly and diligently. All of them went to the sacrament of penance, including many who had been away from confession for a long time. A report appeared in *L'Ami de la Religion et du Roi* some time later, which confirmed Pierre's account:

> Two little missions which took place recently in the mountain of the Bugey ... have proved that the country people feel the need for this special preaching as much as the towns-folk. These two missions were given during the months of January, February and March in the parishes of Lab[alme] and Corlier ... The leading families there gave the good example, especially in one of the parishes where one saw the de F. family, who are rightly esteemed in the locality, distinguish themselves by their assiduity and their zeal.[11]

7. OM, doc. 689, 4.
8. Dossier J. M. Vianney, APM (undated mss), cited in J. Coste, 'The Curé of Ars and the Society of Mary', *Acta SM* vol 5 (1959), pp 388-91.
9. OM, docs 468, 469.
10. OM, doc. 131.
11. *Ami de la Religion et du Roi*, 44 (14 May 1825), 10. Jacolin, 'Apports'.

The family referred to as 'de F' was the family of Louis de Finance, who owned forests, a glass factory and a chateau in the area. The report, compiled possibly by the vicar general, Claude-Joseph Ruivet, reflects the social distinctions of the time, when the richer classes were expected to give example and were lauded for doing so. The report also represents high praise for the two untrained Marists on their first mission venture.

Those three long weeks, during which the profound reaction of the people to their ministry unfolded, could well have been the period when the difficulties Colin experienced at the outset of the mission began to dissolve. Behind Déclas' odd preaching and gesticulations, Colin came to see how his zeal won over sinners of long standing and even learned people. A man of prayer and mortification, Déclas reconciled people who had made bad confessions over thirty or forty years. Although later Colin would never allow him to preach in the towns, or even say a public Mass in Belley, he declared that of Marists, Déclas would have most souls around him on judgement day.[12]

The second mission *L'Ami de la Religion et du Roi* referred to was the mission to Corlier. No sooner had Colin and Déclas finished in La Balme than they were asked to undertake a mission in this parish. Although as the crow flies, it was only six or seven kilometres in distance from Cerdon, it too was high in the mountains and had to be reached by circuitous routes. Corlier had no more than some 250 inhabitants, and since 1823 it had no resident priest. It was looked after by the parish priest of Izenave – the hard-working Antoine Jallon – who may have invited the missioners. For whatever reason, Déclas did not accompany Colin, at least at the beginning of the mission. Jallon, however, came to Corlier to work with him. Unlike at La Balme, the people were slow in answering the church bell calling them to the mission. In the morning only one person was in the church when Colin preached and it was the same that afternoon for Jallon. A laughing Colin said to Jallon: 'You're lucky to be short-sighted; you preach before a single person like you preach before a crowd; … it is all the same to you. But I would like you to see yourself in my place.'[13] In June 1825, Colin gave a mission in Jallon's own parish of Izenave and commented that nowhere else did he find the children so well-instructed.

When these missions ended, Colin returned to Cerdon. There was much tidying up to be done for it was time for all the Marists to pack their bags and go to Belley, as Devie had decided. The people were sad to see them go. Jeanne-Marie reported that there were regrets and tears. The annalist, Charles-Gabriel Clerc noted simply: 'On 22 June 1825, our worthy pastors, the Colin brothers, left this parish after eight years and ten months of ministry and went to Belley,

12. OM, doc. 537, 7-9.
13. OM, doc. 819, 62.

taking with them the first religious sisters of the Congregation of Mary'.[14] The sisters badly needed new accommodation. The thirteen had been packed into a tiny house and when the vicar general, Ruivet, saw how cramped they were, he had written urgently to the bishop on their behalf. Devie offered them the house of Bon-Repos in Belley. So it was that five days after the fathers left, the sisters, a number of whom were natives of Cerdon, also took their leave to the distress of the villagers who had hoped that they would remain. How the three priests got to Belley we do not know. The sisters set out on foot behind a horse-drawn cart that carried their belongings at midnight of 27 July to arrive there at midday on 29 July. Both groups were now installed in Belley.

Colin engaged in renting a house for the priests. Devie agreed at first but, fearing perhaps that the little group of three would become too independent, changed his mind and told him they would have to live in the minor seminary, or 'the college', as it was called. The superior of the college, Father Jean-François Guigard, had been at Saint-Irénée with Colin and Déclas and had been ordained in April 1816 just three months before them. Yet he did not give the three Marists a good welcome. Their lodging was quite unsuitable – a cold corridor at the top of the house beside the trapdoor leading down into the gallery of the chapel. Years later Colin, admitting that they suffered greatly in the college, described their living quarters:

> I saw again today the little corner we occupied in the beginning. It was up there on the third floor in the corridor behind the glass door ... So you could hardly call it hot and we were not well off there. I do not say this for myself because I did not notice it.[15]

Worse still was the hostility of the teachers who engaged in cruel raillery against the newcomers, poking fun at their desire to be a new religious group who called themselves Marists. 'They cast jibes at us from time to time,' he recounted, 'and they were right. Who were we? We were hardly fit for anything except to be trampled underfoot. People would willingly have spat on us.'[16] Some denounced them as Jansenists, others called them 'volume two of the Jesuits bound in ass-skin'. Sadly, the teachers doing the jeering were fellow-priests or seminarians. The students, taking their cue from the teachers, joined in. The superior made no effort to stop the raillery.

The food, too, was bad. Jeanne-Marie claimed that the fathers would have gone hungry were it not for the sisters. Mayet, at first, and Maîtrepierre were somewhat sceptical of this claim but there seems no reason to doubt Jeanne-Marie's statement for she had been there at the time. Later, she repeated her

14. OM, doc. 136.
15. OM, doc. 514, 4.
16. Ibid.

comment.[17] She recalled, too, that once when Colin was sick the sister in charge brought him a bowl of broth in the morning which was to do him for the whole day. 'No one bothered any more about him than about a dog,' was Jeanne-Marie's comment.[18] The sisters at the college were the Sisters of Saint Joseph and they may have been under orders or also taken their cue from the attitude of the teachers. One can readily believe that Jeanne-Marie, strong and straightforward woman as she was, and accustomed to look after the Colins at Cerdon, did not hesitate to bring them food when she could.

What with the merciless jeering, poor food and total absence of heating during the cold winters, it was a relief to go on the mission. Despite the hard work and rough conditions in the Bugey mountains, there was the shared joy of apostolic endeavour and the appreciation of the people. Pierre suffered more, as Colin pointed out, for he stayed at home in charge of the sisters. He replaced Déclas as priest-in-charge of the nearby parish of Bons five kilometres away and there, too, conditions were primitive.[19] There was no presbytery and he either ate at the inn or was served a potato stew by the church-warden. Pierre's courage and humility are striking. He had left his fine rectory of Cerdon where, as curé he was in charge of the parish, and had come to live in a makeshift draughty 'cell' subject to the mockery of teachers and students. As at Cerdon and throughout his whole life, he proved an unfailing source of strength for his dynamic younger brother.

The resentment of the teachers may have arisen from the fact that the little group were not engaged in the work of the college, were inexperienced as missioners, and appeared to set themselves apart as members of a congregation. Devie, in appointing them and granting them special faculties for the missions, referred to them officially as 'our missioners called Marists', thus designating them as diocesan missioners. Already before he left Cerdon, Colin had many contacts with Devie and, with a surprising openness, had confided in him the ups and downs of his beloved project. Over the next fourteen years, from June 1825 to November 1839, they lived almost side by side in the little town of Belley. As his bishop whom he esteemed, Devie began to play a most important role in the life of Colin. Perhaps, of all the bishops Colin came into contact with, Devie had the greatest impact on him and it was while he was still Devie's subject and in his diocese, that Colin organised his beloved Society of Mary and had it officially recognised. Devie's decision to accept the little group at Belley as missioners meant that over the next four years they gave some twenty-eight missions. Colin, who was the leading spirit in those missions and, from 1825, officially in charge, took part in all but three or four. This totally new

17. RMJ, docs 100, 6; 101, 12.
18. Ibid., doc. 101, 12.
19. OM, doc. 513, 12.

experience transformed his outlook. To it he constantly referred back as to a golden age. It is of importance then, to examine those Marist missions in the Bugey and how they fitted in to the context of the day.

Parish missions had become a principal means of evangelisation and conversion, particularly in times of upheaval. In France they began largely in response to the Protestant Reformation. During the 17th century Vincent de Paul, Jean-Jacques Olier, John Eudes and the several religious orders – Oratorians, Capuchins and Jesuits – were active in mission work and this activity continued into the 18th century up to the Revolution. Recommenced after the Concordat of 1801, Napoleon forbade them when he fell out with Pius VII. They began again in real earnest with the Restoration of the Bourbon king, Louis XVIII, and became the chief means of the French Church in its effort to re-evangelise France. They were to be a key instrument for repairing the damage inflicted on the Church of France by the Revolution. The period from 1816 to 1830 was one of the great ages of missions.

The Restoration period in France, usually dated from 1815 to 1830, was a time when the French Church recovered much of the ground it lost during the upheaval of the Revolution. On the other hand, this renewal cloaked an ambiguity. Religious and royalist restoration appeared to go together. The very name of the twice-weekly paper that most priests, including the Colins, read – *L'Ami de la Religion et du Roi* (The Friend of Religion and of the King) – is revealing. The mission movement took on the general tone of the restoration of throne and altar, understandable enough since it was the return of the Most Christian King that permitted their resumption. While inviting the people to faith in Christ, the missioners also preached loyalty to the Bourbon kings. Some of the hymns proclaimed this twin loyalty:

Vive la France!	Long live France!
Vive le Roi!	Long live the king!
Toujours en France,	For ever in France,
Les Bourbons et la Foi!	The Bourbons and the Faith!

'To bring France back to God and God back to France' was the missioners' avowed aim. The period from 1816 to 1830 saw at least 1500 missions in France which was an enormous effort by any standard. By 1821 they were at their apogee with hundreds of missions taking place all over France.

By then, however, they were encountering increasingly bitter opposition. The ideas of the Enlightenment, which had played a part in launching the Revolution, were regaining popularity. In the seven years from 1817 to 1824, twelve editions of Voltaire – whose motto had been 'crush the Infamous One' (that is, the Church) – and thirteen editions of Rousseau were published. A reaction by Liberals, many of whom were anticlerical and impatient of being excluded from power, against right-wing policies had begun by 1819 but it was only after the accession of Charles x in 1824 that it became formidable. Charles firmly believed in the union of throne and altar and his first act was to have himself anointed king in Rheims cathedral in the manner of pre-Revolution kings. A year later his government enacted a law which imposed the death sentence for sacrilege. The law was impracticable and served only to generate opposition to the regime and to the Church. Together with the Catholic schools and the religious orders, the missioners constituted a prime target for Liberals who controlled much of the press.

Yet these years, too, brought a fresh impetus to the work of missioners, the new inspiration coming from a somewhat different source. In Rome Leo xii, pope since September 1823, had begun a determined effort of renewal. His first encyclical, which Colin would have read in *L'Ami de la Religion et du Roi,* appealed for a religious restoration and also reminded princes that they defended their own cause when they defended the authority of the Church.[20] Enthusiastically, the pope proclaimed a jubilee in Rome for 1825 – the only Holy Year in the 19th century. The jubilee was an assertion of the renewed vigour of the Church, the sacred nature of the Holy City, and a universal call to conversion and renewal. As was the custom, the jubilee was extended to the rest of the Catholic world for the following year – 1826 – and bishops and pastors throughout the Church used it as a powerful call to their people to conversion and reconciliation. Apart from the pastoral situation in France, the papal jubilee formed the pastoral context for Bishop Devie's request to Colin and his little group to preach missions in the Bugey.

Devie was pleased to have the tiny group in Cerdon, despite their inexperience and small numbers, for he saw in them a kernel around which he could build his own diocesan missioners. This was not Colin's view. In his mind, as he had written in his rule, willingness to give missions in any part of the world was a key characteristic of the society to be formed. Yet he saw Devie's request as providential, for it was the first coming together of the Marists as a group for mission and he realised that it was there the society had to begin. So, although in providing the spiritual renewal that the missions brought to the people of the Bugey, the aims of Devie and Colin coincided, in the long-term their outlooks differed. For Devie they were diocesan missioners who styled themselves Marists; for Colin they were Marist missioners who were working now for the diocese but would, when the opportunity came, spread themselves elsewhere, wherever there was need of them, as their letter to Pius vii had stated. The little group of missioners was now three in number. Déclas had asked Jallon outright would he not think of joining them and he agreed. Jallon was born in the department of the Loire in 1782 and so was older than the other two. His

20. *L'Ami de la Religion et du Roi,* 40 (3 July 1824), 241-50; P. Boutry, 'Léon xii', *Dictionnaire Historique de la Papauté,* ed. P. Levillain (Paris, 1994), pp 1031-5.

parents were so poor that, to support the family, he had become a horse groom. His master, noticing his talents, persuaded him to take up studies, and he went on to Saint-Jodard where as a senior student he had taught Colin Latin. Jallon had been ordained in 1809 and had left the seminary long before the Fourvière promise. After several earlier appointments, he had been named curé of Izenave on 20 July 1816, a week before the Colins were appointed to nearby Cerdon and a relationship had developed between them. Colin used to go to him for confession and Jallon came for confession to one or the other of the Colins. A careful, methodical man, he was simple, humble and zealous and proved a valuable addition to the little band. By October 1825, he was able to leave his parish and join the two Colins and Déclas in Belley.

The missions Devie assigned to the other groups of missioners were either in the towns or in the more prosperous regions of his diocese. He sent the Marists to the area called the Bugey. Geographically, the Bugey is divided into the Bas Bugey, the lowlands near Belley and Haut Bugey, the highlands around Cerdon. It was to the Haut Bugey that the Marists were sent. The Haut Bugey was a plateau with many valleys. Although its green slopes and valleys provided pasture for cattle, the countryside was poor and people eked out a living in what was a harsh climate. Spiritually, too, it was a neglected area. Although most of the priests in whose parishes the Marists evangelised were welcoming, one or two had problems. Six of the parishes had no resident priest. Most of the villages were from 500 to 1,000 metres above sea-level and snow-covered from November to March. Yet those winter months were the time for missions for it was only after crops and grapes had been harvested, and the snow and bad weather prevented outside work, that the farmers had time. For the missioners, the cold and damp conditions in the churches, the confessionals and rectories could be punishing. Every place had to be reached on foot amid snow and mud. When one morning, the short-sighted Jallon sank his feet into a pool of water which the snow had covered, his only reaction was to say quietly to the others: 'There's water here'.[21]

Almost immediately after Jallon's arrival, he and Colin and Déclas set out on the first of a series of missions. These winter missions of 1825-6 took them to seven different parishes in the northern part of the Haut Bugey near Cerdon. The first mission was in Lacoux, high up in the mountains and some twenty odd kilometres north-west of Belley. Attached to it, a little further down the valley, was the parish of Chaley. The priest in charge of both parishes was friendly and 'the ardour with which the people abandoned their work to hear the word of God was unbelievable' according to the report in *L'Ami de la Religion et du Roi*.[22] At the end of the mission a cross was erected. The mis-

21. OM doc. 639, 5.
22. *L'Ami de la Religion et du Roi*, 46 (21 Dec. 1825), 186-7.

sioners also went down the valley to give instruction at Chaley. To give some permancey to the mission's results, confraternities of the Blessed Sacrament and the Holy Rosary were then established.

The other parishes evangelised that winter were in the same area though slightly further north. Châtillon-de-Corneille, which they first visited in November, proved eventful. It was there that Colin and Déclas lodged in the Hôtel du Nord. Despite its pretentious name it had only one bed for guests and that was in the same room where the proprietors, husband and wife, slept. At bedtime the husband and wife went outside to leave the priests some time to themselves. While they were out, Colin locked the door and would not let them back in, telling them to find a bed somewhere else.[23] The mission itself got off to a bad start. Not a soul darkened the door of the church. Colin and his companions took a hand-bell and went around the village ringing it. They were ignored. A widow, Antoinette Bouché, was sick, so Colin went to visit her. She refused to receive him. Rejected, the missioners moved on to the nearby parish of Poncieux, high in the mountains. It, too, had no resident priest. The mission here was apparently a success. The inhabitants, through their mayor, petitioned to have a priest for the parish, increased their efforts to make provision for his support, and at the end of 1826 had the satisfaction of seeing their request granted. Another event marked their mission at Poncieux. While they were there the widow Bouché at Châtillon died and Colin came back for the funeral. The whole parish had come to the church for the funeral. As Colin said later 'Now I had got them!', so he mounted the pulpit and preached a 'vehement instruction' on the eternal truths. At the graveside he preached again. Overcome by remorse the parishioners, so lately hostile, all repented.[24] Sometime later Colin took ill on another mission and had to pass through the village of Châtillon on his way to Belley. When the villagers saw him, they shouted 'Here's the bishop, here's the bishop.' They beat the drum and hurried to the church where he preached to them. He was hearing confessions half the night. He was so taken by it all that on his return to Belley he begged the bishop to allow him to return to Châtillon. Devie needed him and refused.[25] When these missions were completed the group returned to Belley where the set-up was as miserable as ever. When Jallon arrived, Colin gave him his own little room and set himself up in another room which was no more than a passage way for everyone to pass through. He put up with it. 'They passed through my room to go to the chapel,' he later recorded, 'and when I was asleep they woke me up early. Well, I stopped sleeping. That is all.'[26] On New Year's Day 1826

23. OM, doc. 819, 61.
24. OM, docs 686, 2-7; 819, 60-3.
25. OM, doc. 686, 2-7.
26. OM, doc. 514, 4. The text can be understood that they 'passed by' Colin's room or 'passed through' it. It seems more likely that they actually passed through it.

they received a visit from the curé of the cathedral. He was shocked to find that in such cold weather and in such exposed a position their rooms had no heating. He protested to the bishop who ordered that a new partition be erected to form a little room where a stove was to be placed. There at least they could warm themselves when it was too cold in their rooms.

In December or January, they again went on the mission to Saint-Jérôme and again to Châtillon, both of which, with Poncieux, formed part of the one commune. This time the bishop also sent Father Antoine Montagny, whom Colin knew from seminary days. At the end of the mission they erected a twenty-five foot cross. The next mission was to Vieu-d'Izenave. This time Déclas and Jallon went on ahead. When Colin set off to join the other two, the bishop gave him a sealed letter, addressed to them, naming him superior of the mission band. He was mortified when he learned the contents and did not know where to hide himself. It was the first time he had ever been called 'Father Superior'.[27] It was probably one of the other missioners who recommended the move to the bishop, but certainly Colin never forgot the incident which so embarrassed him. The mission in Vieu-d'Izenave ended in March. Another mission followed immediately in Aranc during which it is recorded that Déclas celebrated two weddings. This mission ended in April and concluded the first full mission season of the missioners. They then returned to Belley for the summer months.

During this summer of 1826 a momentous event affecting the whole project took place. Early in June Colin paid a visit to the Hermitage. There a perplexed Marcellin Champagnat sought his advice concerning a letter he had received. The background to the letter was complex. Living at the Hermitage, the novitiate of the brothers, were Champagnat, Courveille and Terraillon and some brothers in training. Trouble arose with Courveille who saw himself as superior-general of all Marists but who wanted also to be local superior of the brothers. Brother John-Baptist Furet, the biographer of Champagnat, who had come to join Champagnat at La Valla in 1822, relates that in 1825 Courveille insisted on the election of a superior of the community, hoping that the brothers would elect him. Instead almost all voted for Champagnat. A second election brought the same result. When, however, at Christmas 1825 Champagnat fell ill, Courveille took over. His rule was strict and weighed heavily on the young brothers. He also wrote to the diocesan authorities denouncing Champagnat's manner of training the brothers as too lenient, and as a result the vicar general, Cattet, came on official diocesan visitation and made severe criticisms.[28] In May 1826, however, Courveille went to the Trappist monastery of Aiguebelle on what he described as a pilgrimage, on retreat according to Terraillon. It was from there that he wrote the letter to the community at the Hermitage which

27. OM, doc. 687.
28. Furet, *Life of Champagnat*, p. 144 and footnote 4.

Champagnat now showed Colin. It was long and complicated but contained the following statement:

> If you believe ... that I am only a stumbling block in the holy Society of Mary, more harmful than useful ...I pray that you tell me so simply and then I will be able to live in the holy house where I am, to make sure of my salvation.

Elsewhere in the letter, however, Courveille makes it clear that he hoped that Champagnat, Terraillon and the brothers would call him back for 'it is most painful for me to see myself excluded'. Why he felt he might be only a stumbling block, and why he believed he needed to be invited back to his own community, Courveille did not say. The anxious scene that took place when Courveille's letter arrived was described by Terraillon in his account of the early years of the society some fifteen years later:[29]

> My opinion was to accept this resignation. M. Champagnat was of a contrary opinion because M. Courveil [sic] was involved in his financial affairs. I insisted all the same. I had serious reasons for that. M. Champagnat would not give in. We could make no further progress.

The very next day Colin arrived. Champagnat saw him first and won him to his point of view. Terraillon, however, stuck to his guns and made this extraordinary appeal to both of them:

> You are missing out on an excellent opportunity that may not come again. In this area M. Courveil has the reputation of a saint. If we are forced to exclude him later on, as could happen, all the odium will fall on us. By availing of this opportunity, he will have excluded himself. He will appear to be fickle and we will be sheltered from any blame. Trust me, accept this resignation. I'm convinced that later on you will congratulate yourselves for what you did.

Amazingly Terraillon now produced a reply to send to Courveille, which he had already written, needing only their signatures. At first Champagnat and Colin were shocked and a little scandalised at Terraillon's insistence, but finally sensing an urgency in his passionate appeal, which he may have backed up by hinting at those 'serious reasons', they came round to his point of view. Champagnat, Terraillon and Colin signed this reply which accepted Courveille's resignation and, since he was content at the monastery of Aiguebelle, advised him to remain there. Terraillon moved fast. The very next day he personally posted the letter at Saint-Chamond, the large town nearby, and went on that same day to Lyon to see Barou, the first vicar general.

---

29. OM, doc. 750, 10-11. Coste and Lessard date this first account by Terraillon between 1840-42; he gave a second account in 1859-60, OM, doc. 798, 6, 7.

Unknown to Champagnat and Colin, Terraillon had already been to see Barou and to him he had revealed his 'serious reasons'. In his account later, Terraillon avoids going into detail, merely saying that he told Barou that Courveille's presence in the brothers' house was harmful. When he gave Barou the proofs, the vicar general exclaimed bitterly: 'How can you count on anyone's virtue now!'[30] When Terraillon came again with the news of the reply they had sent to Courveille, Barou thanked God that the matter had been arranged quietly without scandal. When within a few days Courveille left Aiguebelle and came to him asking that he might return to the Hermitage, Barou replied categorically: 'Neither to the Hermitage, nor anywhere else; there is no place for you in the diocese.' Although Terraillon went on to say that Courveille went to his native place, Apinac, 'where he gave a great scandal', he never said what Courveille's actions were. John-Baptist, however, in his *Life of Champagnat* accused Courveille of scandalising young people by a shameful fall, a charge which John-Baptist made more explicit later when, in the information he passed on to Colin, he accused Courveille of immoral behaviour with a young postulant.[31]

Colin's role in the withdrawal of Courveille has been questioned.[32] Did he arrive by chance on that day or had he been alerted? There is no way of knowing. The groups in Belley and the Hermitage visited regularly and Colin did

30. OM, doc. 798, 6, 7, 8.

31. Furet, *Life of Champagnat*, pp 144-46. OM, doc. 819, 23-7.

32. It has been suggested that there is no real proof of immoral conduct by Courveille. This assertion takes on a significance for the character of Colin when it is linked with the suggestion that the whole affair was a coup intended by the Colin brothers, with the assistance of Champagnat, to get rid of Courveille (C. Rozier, 'L'ancêtre dans le placard', pp 23, 25-6, 42, copy in APM). Given the nature of the charge against Courveille and the secrecy in which it was normal to envelop such scandals, direct proof is not available. Certain indications, however, exist. The first is the determined attitude of Terraillon. Terraillon esteemed Courveille, and it is most unlikely that he would have twice denounced him to the diocesan authorities if he had not had good grounds for doing so. Apart from Champagnat and Courveille, he was the only other priest in the Hermitage at the time and so, perhaps as spiritual adviser, in a position to obtain information. He repeated his allegations more openly in 1859-60 almost twenty years later. The second indication is the evidence of John-Baptist Furet. He explicitly accused Courveille of immoral behaviour with a young postulant. Although his evidence is weakened by the fact that he did not like Courveille, whom he accuses of being unkind to his hero, Champagnat, and was not resident at the Hermitage in that year, in such a matter it must be taken seriously. He had joined in 1822 and would have known the brothers in the Hermitage. Later he became Champagnat's trusted right-hand man. It is unlikely that he would make such a serious accusation in his published book and enlarge on it later, were he not certain of his facts. A third pointer is the evidence of Benoît Lagniet, a serious and well-informed witness, who recounted later episodes where Courveille was even more explicitly accused of pedophilia to the point where his scandalised priest-uncle would not let him say Mass. See OM, doc. 819, 27-30. Terraillon, John-Baptist and Lagniet were religious men of integrity well placed to know the facts. To their evidence must be added the record of the deliberations of the episcopal council of the diocese of Bourges in 1833 and again in 1835 which

not appear to have any knowledge of the affair until Champagnat spoke to him. If he did sign the reply to Courveille as appears most likely, the question can be asked whether he was right in agreeing to the exclusion of Courveille from the project he initiated.[33] What is noticeable is the gradual change in his attitude towards Courveille. In the letter to Bigex in 1819 Pierre Colin had mentioned Courveille's central role. By 1822, however, it appears that a wrangle had developed over who should keep the pope's letter. Colin was at pains to tell de Pins that Courveille did not speak for the project. He did not want Courveille to be superior general for he regarded him as having poor judgement. Yet there is no evidence that he tried to oust Courveille and he certainly did not seek the position himself. His choice was Cholleton.

For Colin as for Terraillon and Champagnat, however, Courveille was the pious youth to whom the Blessed Virgin had chosen to reveal her wishes at Le Puy, the fervent young deacon who had enthused them all at Saint-Irénée and the presiding priest at the founding ceremony at Fourvière from whose hands they had all received communion on that great day. All three must have agonised at the thought that this man was to be excluded from the society. For the little group of Marists, the affair at the Hermitage was a severe setback and a scandal at a time when they were working hard for recognition. Champagnat lamented it bitterly in letters to the Lyon chancellery. Colin probably saw it first and foremost as a threat to the project of a Society of Mary, although since he distrusted Courveille's judgement, his departure may have brought some relief. It was another lesson for him in human nature and he may well have repeated Barou's acrid comment: 'Now can you trust in anyone's virtue!' For forty years the only times Colin ever mentioned Courveille's name were in two letters to Champagnat.

So passed from the scene a key figure in the early years of the society. If Colin had misgivings about Courveille's judgement, Champagnat trusted him, and even after the accusations made against him, Déclas and Terraillon regarded him as a good man. He had not spared his time, his energy and especially his money in promoting the Marist project. Later in life he became a well-esteemed Benedictine monk and retreat-preacher. He never lost his love for the Society which he did so much to bring to birth.

mention allegations made against Courveille's morals. See OM, doc. 407, 3, 7. The sum of this evidence indicates that the accusations levelled against Courveille were well-founded. The suggestion that the whole affair was a coup to get rid of Courveille is quite unsubstantiated. Father Rozier's illness prevented him from completing the account in 'L'ancêtre dans le placard', the precise meaning of which is not always clear.

33. Brother John-Baptist Furet and Déclas mention only Champagnat and Terraillon as signatories and, in a somewhat indeterminate reply to Jeantin in 1870, the ageing Colin accepted the account of John-Baptist as accurate (*Life of Champagnat*, p. 146; OM, docs 551, 11; 844, 1). Nevertheless since neither John-Baptist nor Déclas was present or saw the reply, whereas Terraillon drew it up and waited for it to be signed, his version, which is earlier, includes Colin as a signatory, and is to be preferred.

CHAPTER 13

'Speaking to the Heart'

'May the grace and peace of God our Father and Our Lord Jesus Christ be with you! … It is to help you, to encourage you, to retain … increase, this treasure of grace and peace, or to recover it … that God … sends us into your parish as the most unworthy instruments of his mercy for you.' Colin's opening talk for a mission.[1]

Early in 1826 Jeanne-Marie Chavoin, concerned at the miserable circumstances of the Marists in the college, had gone to see the bishop. She begged him to appoint Father Jean-Félix Pichat, who was her spiritual advisor, as superior in the college of Belley. Devie replied that he could not, since the man was in poor health. Jeanne-Marie was not to be outdone. Sister Anne was terminally ill and as she lay on her death-bed, Jeanne-Marie asked her to obtain three favours for her when she went to heaven, one of which was that Pichat be appointed superior. Sister Anne died on 16 March and, sure enough, some time later, Devie decided to appoint Pichat. He took over the college in September 1826. Pichat, an able and likeable priest, had been in the diocese of Lyon before Belley was set up, but Devie, aware of his value, had recalled him to Belley and made him a canon of the diocese. Pichat had a great devotion to the Blessed Virgin and was very well disposed towards the Marists. His appointment that autumn of 1826 transformed the attitude in the college towards them. The persecution ended and they were now assured of a warm welcome when they returned home. Pichat appointed Pierre Colin as spiritual director of the college. The change, moreover, meant even more than a better set-up for the little group. 'As for us, my dear friend,' an overjoyed Colin told Champagnat, 'we are happy; the college is in the hands of the Society; we are quite united to Father Pichat, who is more than ever committed to the project.'[2] For Colin, Pichat was a Marist.

The hard-pressed Champagnat needed some good tidings, for 1826 had been a terrible year for him. His health had been bad, a number of his first and well-loved brothers had left and there were debts on the house. The affair of Courveille added to those worries. Since he and the brothers had accepted Courveille's claim to be superior general, the set-back was all the greater. Then, in October, the only other priest in the Hermitage, Terraillon, left what he

1. Manuscript sermons of Colin, fascicle 36: APM 241.51, pp 1-2.
2. OM, doc. 169, 2.

probably saw as a sinking ship. Champagnat was now on his own as he told the diocesan authorities:

> The unfortunate matter of Father Courveille and the departure of Father Terraillon, place me in a false position with regard to the public, who always talk without knowing the whole story ... I am alone; despite that, I do not lose courage, knowing how powerful God is and how his ways are hidden from the most far-seeing of humans ... I still firmly believe that God wants this work, in this age when unbelief makes such frightful progress ... I have explained to you simply my position ... it is in the Lord and his most holy Mother that I take my repose and I bless their Holy Names.[3]

Champagnat's strong faith alone saved him from discouragement. There were financial problems, too, and since some of Courveille's money was invested in the Hermitage, it became necessary to attend to that matter, too. Fortunately, Courveille did not raise difficulties and an arrangement was made. Courageously, in this difficult year, Champagnat opened three more schools. Neither did the diocesan authorities raise difficulties. Instead, appreciating the value of Champagnat and his work, they appointed, at his request, the newly-ordained Étienne Séon to the Hermitage the following year. Séon was to become one of the pillars of the early society. Colin, too, although away in the diocese of Belley, proved a source of strength for Champagnat during that difficult autumn and winter of 1826. He wrote to him encouragingly in December and his letters were to become more frequent. Colin's role became more important now that Courveille was gone.

Colin was busy about other matters that year. The summer months provided him and the others with the time to reflect on their experiences in the missions and plan the coming winter session. Many years later, both Colin and Jallon gave detailed accounts of how they conducted them. They set out on the mission under the protection of Mary, carrying on their backs the bag containing 'our treasure' as Colin called the sermons, their breviaries and everything else they needed for the mission. On reaching the parish boundary they would kneel and pray for sinners. Then they went to see the curé. They began the mission with the children. In addition to the preaching, confession and the mission Mass, which constituted the kernel of the retreat, special ceremonies punctuated the three-or-four-week stay. They held a service for the dead of the parish, with a sermon on death and another on purgatory and after Mass processed to the cemetery, with four of the most prominent men in the parish carrying the funeral pall. If there were two palls, one was used as a banner. Another day they preached on trust in Mary and then processed carrying her

3. OM, docs 173, 6, 7, 8, 9; 286, 1.

statue and singing the Litany and hymns. On the next morning all the children came to Mass and the missioner asked them if they wanted to choose the Blessed Virgin as their mother. He reminded them that Mary only wanted obedient children, and made them ask their parents' pardon for all their sins of disobedience. In turn the parents were invited to bless them. The renewal of baptismal vows took place on another day. As the missioner explained each article of the Creed, he asked the congregation if they believed it. Each replied 'I believe', lifting up the lighted candles they held in their hands. Atonement for sin was coupled with adoration of the Blessed Sacrament. The priests prostrated themselves and an act of reparation was read. Sinners were at the top of their list of priorities. If their first act on reaching the parish was to kneel and pray for them, one of the last acts towards the end, if many still had not come, was to renew prayers for them. The bell would be rung at eight o'clock every evening and each family was to say five Our Fathers and Hail Marys for the conversion of sinners. A missioner would leave the confessional and recite the prayers aloud.

Comparing these ceremonies with those practised by missioners of the period, one can see that they are quite similar.[4] Renewal of baptismal vows, procession to the cemetery, act of reparation, consecration to the Blessed Virgin, procession of the Blessed Sacrament, combined with the core mission practices, sermons, confession and communion, were standard parts of the mission. The one ceremony that neither Jallon nor Colin mentioned was the erection of a mission cross, often a very large one which required up to eight men to carry it in relays. This final act of the missions and the elaborate ceremony that accompanied it was the culminating part of the missions, for it symbolised placing Christ again as Lord of the parish. Some missions also uprooted the tree of liberty planted during the Revolution and so the ceremony of raising the cross in its place assumed a political significance. Either from liberal and anti-clerical sentiment, or fearing civil disorder, from time to time authorities discouraged the ceremony of erecting a cross. Generally, however, for the Restoration missions, it was an essential part of the mission. Some Marist missions did conclude with the erection of a cross, but Colin left it to the choice of the curé. Nowhere is there mention of the uprooting of a tree of liberty nor of any protest against the missioners.

It was probably during the summer of 1826, though it could have been earlier, that he drew up his 'Instructions for Missioners'. He gave them to Pichat, the superior of the college, asking him to present them as his own. They so

4. E. Sevrin, *Les missions religieuses en France sous la Restauration*, 2 vols, (Paris, 1948, 1959); *Précis historique de la mission de Riom* (Riom, 1818); *Relation de la mission d'Avignon, en Mars et Avril 1819* (Avignon, 1819); L.J.M.R., *Précis historique de la mission de Marseille, en Janvier et Février 1820* (Marseille, n.d.).

impressed Pichat that he showed them to Bishop Devie who also admired them. They became the Marist mission guide. Although the document of the 'Instructions for Missioners' is no longer extant, Jean Coste has reconstructed much of the content and the result reveals a series of directives and counsels that one can justly call Colinian or 'Marist'.[5] They give a glimpse of Colin's reflections on missions.

Many of the 'Instructions' were the common practice of all missioners: place God's interest first, put prayer at the centre of your work, remember that zeal for souls is the priority. Colin's 'Instructions', however, are marked by an approach that is considerate, gentle and humble. Do not take over from the curé. Do not present yourselves as great missioners but come unobtrusively as teachers of catechism. Go first to the children. Win the people gradually by your gentle approach before placing the difficult choices of the gospel before them. Forestall concerns about cost by making no demands and avoiding expense. Be quite content with missions to the poor and the rustic. Spend little time with the pious but give full attention to sinners. Since sinners need prayers, the moment you reach the parish boundary begin praying for them and have all families pray with you for them. Prepare yourselves, through diligent study of theology and holy scripture, to give solid spirituality, not tawdry showy emotional stuff. Through the practice of solid virtues, become instruments of God's mercy.

The modesty in approach, which runs throughout these 'Instructions', appears to have been followed by the Bugey missioners. They made few demands for themselves, and their style of life on the mission was as much a sermon as their preaching. Sixty kilometres away that great pastoral priest, the Curé of Ars, was moved by what he learned of their methods:

> The Marists, theirs is a work according to God's own heart because there is humility, simplicity, and contradictions; they are setting about it in the right way, beginning their missions by teaching the catechism and first communions … the Marist is more hidden. Were I more talented, I would become Marist.[6]

Later in life, speaking of his companions, Déclas, Humbert and Jallon, Colin commented:

> They were humble, straightforward and simple souls. See how the good Lord blessed them. Everything in their lives reflected poverty. We ate with peasants, we slept all together. Their preaching was utterly simple, and the peoples of the parishes surrendered. We were overwhelmed in the confessional.[7]

5. J. Coste, *Studies on the Early Ideas of Colin* (Rome, 1989), p. 18; Lessard, 'L'ultima fatica di Coste'.
6. OM, doc. 419, 3-4.
7. OM, doc. 846, 33.

If they were overwhelmed in the confessional, the new approach that Colin was gradually adopting towards penitents was probably responsible. For centuries the fear of God was deeply rooted in the religion of western Europe. For Catholics, recognition of the evil of sin gave prominence to the sacrament of penance and the confession of one's sins. The spiritual classics, Thomas à Kempis' *Imitation of Christ* and Ignatius of Loyola's *Exercises* included meditations on sin and death. In the theology of the day, whether in Protestant England or in Catholic France, the God of the theologians was a demanding God of justice and atonement rather than a God of love and infinite mercy. This rigorist approach then in vogue in France was what Colin had learned at Saint-Irénée and one of its characteristics was either to delay giving absolution or to refuse it altogether. At Cerdon Colin had dreaded hearing confessions because of the uncompromising stand that he felt he had to take especially on moral issues. It was not during his stay at Cerdon, as Jeantin suggests, that Colin's conversion to a more merciful approach, associated with Alphonsus Liguori, who had been beatified in 1816, took place. It seems likely that during the first Bugey missions the Marists took a rigorist approach. Colin recalled how he consulted Déclas and Jallon on cases, and found them quite severe but he added:

> Since I was the youngest, I followed their decision, mistrustful of myself, although deep inside my opinion was different ... Later on I recognised that, in those cases, we paid too much attention to the law and not enough to the fragility of human nature.[8]

His gradual conversion to Liguorism probably dates from 1826. A number of events around that time would have pushed him in that direction. It was the year of the jubilee and, in February and March, *L'Ami de la Religion et du Roi* published a French translation of Pope Leo XII's encyclical *Caritate Christi* of Christmas Day 1825 extending the jubilee to the whole world. The pope, while encouraging people to reconcile themselves to God, had an unusually strong message for confessors. They must be gentle towards penitents, he insisted. A priest who refused absolution to someone who admitted a serious crime or was stained by every kind of sin, was going against the Roman ritual, the official service book containing the prayers and formulas for the administration of the sacraments. Leo reminded them of the words of Jesus: 'It is not those who are well but those who are sick who need a doctor'. The deferring of absolution should be quite exceptional. The confessor must go out of his way to help. Even if the penitent is not at all prepared or properly disposed for receiving the sacrament, he can acquire the proper disposition, if only the priest, 'vested in

8. OM, doc. 577; E. Keel, ed., *A Book of Texts for the Study of Marist Spirituality* (Rome, 1993), doc. 443.

the compassion of Jesus Christ', who did not come to call the just, but the sinners, knows how to use zeal, patience and gentleness.[9] Pope Leo listed the justifications used for postponing absolution – that the sinners were guilty of the greatest crimes, or were absent many years from confession, or had not probed the depths of their conscience – only to dismiss them as quite insufficient. 'The mercy of the Lord is without limits,' he reminded confessors, 'the treasury of his goodness is infinite'. The confessor must come to the sinner's aid in every way. He must show 'affectionate gentleness' and 'tender compassion', 'pour balm on the sinner's soul', console him and give him hope. He will help him, too, the pope added, citing St Raymond of Penafort, through his own prayers, alms and good works. The encyclical was a powerful refutation of the type of rigorism Colin had learned at the seminary.

Colin would have read the pope's encyclical and we can surmise the impression it made on him. Its impact was strengthened by the action of his own bishop.[10] Devie was one of the earliest and most fervent supporters of the theology of Alphonsus of Liguori.[11] The following September, when the jubilee was about to commence in Belley, Devie published his own pastoral letter directing attention to the pope's words:

> The Sovereign Pontiff, in an Encyclical Letter, has felt it necessary to give most wise counsels to confessors. Principally, he asks them to show great charity and goodness to sinners. We invite you to re-read that admirable Letter, and to make it the rule of your conduct; to this invitation we join that of reading and rereading the little book called *The Practice of Confessors,* written by the Blessed Liguori, which you will find in the Seminary of Brou and in the bishop's Secretariat.[12]

This statement was the first public declaration of any bishop in France promoting the theology of Liguori.[13] Colin wrote later that 'The bishop of Belley has been of great help to me in theology, cases of conscience, ways of dealing with things in the confessional,' adding that, on account of poor human

9. The citation is from Philippians, 1:8 – *'in visceribus Jesu Christi'.*
10. All of this encyclical merits studying. The attitude that it enjoins on confessors is quite similar to the one Colin prescribed for the Society of Mary.
11. Devie had been trained in the rigoristic theology. He related, however, how already in 1792 he got to know the Liguorian theology. His experience as a priest on the run during the Revolution and his contact with the condition of the people may well have induced him, in 1802 when in Venice, to turn to the theology of Alphonsus Liguori. Later when professor at the seminary of Viviers he taught Liguorianism. Later again when vicar-general he propagated it.
12. *Circulaire de Mgr l'évêque de Belley à l'occasion du Jubilé* (Brou), 26 Sept. 1826, cited in Boutry, *Prêtres et Paroisses,* pp 414-15. The jubilee was celebrated in each diocese for six months from the publication of the papal bull; in Belley the jubilee ran from 1 Nov 1826 to 1 May 1827. Belley's major seminary was in Brou, a suburb of Bourg-en-Bresse, the capital of the department.
13. Boutry, *Prêtres et Paroisses,* p. 414.

nature, the Society of Mary shall profess 'all those opinions which leave most scope to God's mercy'.[14] It is not unreasonable to infer that it was during this year of jubilee that Colin began to free himself from the straight-jacket of rigorism. His sermons, as retained in written form, still show rigorist tendencies, though this may be due to the influence of the great pre-Revolutionary preachers – Bourdaloue, Le Jeune and others – from whom, as was the common practice, he borrowed deeply, often literally copying word for word. The importance of the change in confessional approach cannot be overstated and it came when, for fear of a too lax approach in confession, the Liguorian theology was facing strong criticism in France. As late as the 1840s, Devie had still to defend his own endorsement of it.

The jubilee began in Belley on 1 November of that year, 1826, and, in that same month, Colin, Déclas and Jallon set out to preach the mission and proclaim the jubilee in three parishes. The first was to Innimont, high up in the Mollard de Don mountain, in the south part of the Haut Bugey, not far from Belley. The parish had grave difficulties if one is to credit the official report of Charles-Étienne Vibert, parish priest, in February 1826. 'The parish of Innimont,' he told Devie, 'is very poor, and poverty pushes people to serious crimes, to great abuses for which it is impossible to find a remedy. This is the case at Innimont.'[15] Devie came there to see for himself in July 1826 and his visit may have triggered his decision to send Colin and his companions on mission there. The church in Innimont was a fine one, dating in part from the 12th century. It was situated on a plateau which gave a panoramic view of the countryside as far as the Rhone to the west and as far as the Alps to the east, with Mont Blanc clearly visible on a fine day. The presbytery had not been lived in for some time and the missioners stuffed straw in the broken window-panes to keep out the icy air, for the village was 922 metres above sea-level. Colin's fond recollection of the mission, as relayed by Mayet twenty years later, is touching:

> Once, we arrived in a parish where there had been no priests since the Revolution. Nobody was living in the presbytery. We were laughing as we went about sweeping as best we could.[16]

It may have been here that, in the absence of any blankets, the village women gave them skirts to cover the bed.[17] The mission went well and the people were happy as a moving if amusing incident, which Colin remembered with embarrassment, revealed:

> As he was in the middle of a group of men to whom he was giving many

14. FS, doc. 37.
15. Father Vibert to Devie, 8 Feb. 1826, cited in OM 4, p. 393.
16. Keel ed., *Texts*, doc. 429, 1.
17. OM, doc. 662, 2. Colin does not specify which mission this took place at, but as likely as not it is Innimont.

signs of affection, Father Colin was surprised by a good peasant woman who, not knowing how to show her thanks, threw herself around his neck and embraced him. Another approached to do likewise but he withdrew.[18]

The warm gratitude of the people more than recompensed all the hardship they suffered in the presbytery. When they were leaving, the people accompanied them crying out: 'Long live the missioners.' For long the mountains re-echoed this acclamation as the three embarrassed missioners hurried down the slope, each carrying his little black bag. Perhaps it was at Innimont that Colin first adopted the more compassionate approach towards penitents? One cannot but be struck by the warm appreciation of the people to whom they brought the consolation of reconciliation with their God. The joy which the little group at Innimont experienced together, despite the harsh material conditions, was a memory that Colin cherished years afterwards. Later, Colin explained how he dealt with grievous sin in confession:

> When I used to hear confessions and I was perplexed, I used to say, 'O, my Saviour, what would you do if you were in my place?' Then I would feel the scales of mercy shift … 'O my God,' I would pray, 'I can feel it, you would change this heart. Well, change it in that same way, this very moment.' And I would finish up by giving absolution. If the Lord reproached me for it, I would reply, 'My God, this is the reign of mercy.'[19]

Three or four other missions followed during the winter months of November, December and January, each lasting from three to four weeks. Only the name of one of them is known: Saint-Germain-les-Paroisses, a parish with 1,000 or so inhabitants, a mere eight kilometres from Belley. A few years before, when the bishop sent out his questionnaire, the parish priest replied that 'there had been no mission there since before the revolution, I do not think that people are looking for it, and there are no funds for one.'[20] Nevertheless, Devie sent the Marist missioners at the beginning of December 1826 and they remained there until well into January. Superstition was not uncommon in many areas and in Saint-Germain there was a belief in witchcraft. Little is known of the mission which the three Marists gave but the parish register indicates that many marriages were revalidated. Again at Contrevoz, where Colin and Jallon preached together in February and March 1827, a number of marriages were revalidated.

Most of March was taken up with a mission at Tenay. The parish priest, too, had replied to Devie that the parish had never been fortunate to have a mission but, unlike his confrère in Saint-Germain, he added: 'Everything leads me to

18. OM, doc. 662, 1.
19. FA, doc. 385, 1. Colin said this in 1851 and not in direct reference to Innimont.
20. OM 4, p. 420.

believe that the parish would like one and that it would produce abundant fruit. But the parish has not the resources. It could, nevertheless, make that up by a collection and by the very willing sacrifices of the present pastor.' The people of Tenay were better off than the people of Innimont for Tenay, a sizeable town on the main route between Lyon and Belley, had cloth factories. This, however, posed a problem, for the factory chief refused to give the workers time off to attend. Colin would have no recriminations. Instead he expressed understanding of the difficulties:

> A little patience and, gentlemen, no abuse, excusing a great deal, regretting that the business of the chiefs does not permit … providing times suitable to the men and women working in the factory. If some come, congratulate them warmly, speak to them with kindness, be grateful to the employers … Little by little everybody comes. The factory chiefs are ashamed of their behaviour … Everyone did the mission.[21]

All three missioners came together for the mission to Arandas which closed the jubilee and the winter session. Habitually, they did not give missions during the summer because they needed that time to study and prepare and also because the farming people were not free to attend. That year they went out again in June to preach a mission in the little hamlet of Prémillieu.

If one is to credit that hard-working, zealous Bishop Devie, the jubilee was successful in bringing many back to the faith. Delighted with its success, Devie, in his Lenten pastoral of 1827, proclaimed his joy and consolation that, as the walls of Jericho tumbled at the blast of the trumpet, so too, when the trumpet of the evangelisers rang out, the most hardened hearts opened to the word of God.[22]

The winter of 1827-8 saw another five missions and two retreats at the seminaries. The first mission was in November at Lompnaz where they validated an irregular marriage. The parish had no priest. Next they gave retreats to the students at Meximieux and at the college in Belley. Belley was the greater challenge for they had suffered at the hands of the staff and students of the college. The invitation was also an indication of the esteem in which the new superior, Pichat, and, no doubt Bishop Devie, held them. The next was a mission at Briord, a fair-sized village of 800 people on the banks of the Rhone. At the time of the Concordat, the parish priest, Claude Duriel, sent vicar general Bochard a remarkable account of the religious state of Briord:

> The inhabitants … are great partisans of the Revolution … unreliable … ungrateful to the Church and the ministers of religion … without religious principles … They are all in an unbelievable indifference towards religion

21. OM, doc. 661, 2.
22. Cognat, *Vie de Devie*, vol. 1, pp 313-14.

… They laugh at the Jubilee … they would not be unhappy to see the churches closed again … Many refuse to have their marriages blessed. There are twenty civil marriages … Briord should be seen as another Japan in St Xavier's time.'[23]

If Briord was as pagan as Japan when Francis Xavier came, the picture was dismal and perhaps other neighbouring parishes were not unlike Briord. It would require much devoted pastoral work to evangelise the people. No details of the Marist mission there in December and January remain, but some progress appears to have taken place for, a few months after the mission, the parish Holy Rosary congregation, which was dying out, took on new life. There followed missions at Bénonce high up in the mountain, at Serrières-de-Briord and at Montagnieu. This brought them up to April 1828.

On 22 May 1828 they received a welcome recruit, Jean-Marie Humbert.[24] Humbert was a native of Belleydoux, a tiny village in the department of Ain, not far from the town of Nantua. All three of his brothers became priests and two of his three sisters, nuns. He had studied theology at Saint-Irénée but arrived there in the autumn of 1816, when Colin had already left. He had been ordained in 1819 and so had some ten years experience in the parishes. For some months in 1827 he had been part of a group of three missioners which broke up when the other two were appointed to parishes. Possibly because he had acquired a taste for the missionary work, he then applied to join the Marist group. His arrival meant that for the season 1828-9 the missioners were able to work in two groups.

After preaching the jubilee at Vaux in December and January, where all four worked together, Humbert worked alone with Colin for the rest of the season. First they went to preach a retreat at the college in Nantua, a large town on the route from Lyon to Geneva, to the north of the Bugey country. Then they went to Cuzieu, a parish neglected by the curé, who had earlier expressed his reluctance to have a retreat since his congregation was too small. The bishop came for the closing stages of the retreat and the erection of a mission cross. From there they went to Ruffieu. This mission proved physically demanding, for great crowds attended and the bishop came to confirm 600 people. Father Nicolas de la Croix d'Azolette, who had taken such care for Colin's health in both the minor seminary of Alix and in Saint-Irénée, now vicar general to

23. Cited in P. Jacolin, 'Jésus appelle les pécheurs', *Retraite Pèlerinage en Bugey, Juillet 1999*, p. 19 (Document SM 52, Paris, 1999).

24. Jean-Marie Humbert (1795-1857); ordained 1819; bursar of Belley minor seminary, 1831; bursar at Capucinière, 1834; bursar-general, 1839; procurator-general, 1854; superior at Chaintré, 1861-4; missioner. OM 4, pp 297-300; B. Hayes, 'Quasi Occulti; some of the first twenty Marists' (polycopy, Mount Saint Mary's, Milltown, Dublin 1969), pp 9-14. He took part in the building work himself. He never wasted anything and the scholastics at Belley thought him parsimonious.

Devie, complained that four missioners, not two, would have been needed.[25] This was the last mission on which Humbert worked together with Colin and perhaps because he brought a fresh eye to the scene, it is he who best described Colin in action on the last day of the mission:

> So many people came from the neighbouring villages that, with the church full, there were still more people outside than inside. How would all these people be able to hear? At the time of the sermon, Reverend Father Colin said to me, 'Go up to the choir-loft and put yourself by that little window and repeat to the crowd who can't hear me some of the words that I am going to say from the pulpit.' I did as best I could, and those who were outside were as moved as those who were inside ...[26]

Humbert leaned out through the little window in the loft and shouted Colin's sermon, sentence by sentence, down to the crowd gathered outside in the chill March weather. Favre, who was then seventeen and lived near Ruffieu, noted:

> He [Colin] was worn out in that mission and he was at bay. But he had himself carried to the pulpit, like a Francis Régis; he always came down feeling better. People were sorry for him; he was called the poor old man, and he was scarcely forty-two years old.'[27]

Coste makes the point that in reality he was only thirty-nine! Although he was clearly suffering from exhaustion, Colin's words, even as relayed by Humbert from the little window, were able to move hearts.

To discover what Colin said that so touched people's hearts it may be of use to look at his sermons. Some 141 of these sermons are still preserved written in his small precise hand.[28] Sixteen of them are on doctrinal questions, a further thirty-five on Mary, but the bulk of them, almost sixty, are on moral and confessional matter. The principal aim of the sermons was to form people's conscience and so prepare them for the sacrament of reconciliation. 'This is the work of the missioner,' Colin said, 'the conversion of sinners.'[29]

Most missioners beginning their mission work would have looked up sermons of the great missioners. Colin, conscious of the insufficiency of his training, read the classic works of missioners like Louis Bourdaloue and Le Jeune, two 17th century preachers of high renown, and many others. He used those sermons and 'Instructions' as the base of his preaching. Sometimes he transcribed them literally and even when he made his own adjustments, he followed the scheme and the reasoning of these great masters. The content, both

---

25. OM, doc. 189.
26. OM, doc. 879, 1; Keel ed., *Texts,* doc. 409.
27. OM, doc. 724.
28. Bouchard, 'Prédication morale'.
29. FS, doc. 59, 10.

the theology and the psychology, no less than the style, was that of the 17th and 18th centuries and so less suited to the world of post-Revolutionary France. Yet Colin was able to use those sermons to good effect and in them some of his own favourite themes come to the surface. When, for instance, he comes to speak of Mary, he departs from those sermons and speaks with a fervour all his own.

It is not possible to cite his sermons, but a few extracts give some of the flavour of his approach. The missioner's opening sermon 'should gain the people's trust and should be simple, noble, maternal and full of charity and … short.'[30] Colin's own opening sermon began with these words:

> May the grace and peace of Jesus Christ be with you! … It is to help you, to encourage you to keep, to increase these precious treasures, grace and peace, or to recover them if … you have lost them, that God's providence sends us as the instruments of his mercies for you … That is the object for which God's providence sends us into your midst as most unworthy instruments of his mercy for you.[31]

When he re-wrote this sermon later he was careful to keep the phrase 'instruments of God's mercies'. He went on to say that the missioners have come, he says again, 'to be eyewitnesses of your devotion and to seek, in the exercise of this one faith which unites us, fresh causes for rejoicing.' They have come, he repeated, especially for sinners, for Our Saviour came not for the just but for sinners. To allay the sinners' fears of confession, Colin insisted on the missioners' own fragile humanity:

> We are human beings like you, moulded from the same clay … subject to the same weaknesses, knowing how far man's fragility can go; nothing, then, can inspire fear or mistrust or make you apprehensive of uncovering the wounds of your soul in the sacred tribunal of penance.[32]

The importance of welcoming and being gentle with sinners was a theme that became more and more important for him. Later in life he made this appeal to his followers:

> Show great kindness to sinners who come to you in the confessional. Do not rebuff them, or appear surprised by their crimes, however great they are … Our Lord Jesus Christ knew the profound depths of the human heart, he welcomed all sinners with gentleness.[33]

His sermon on the cross of Christ was moving. At the end of a mission, when the parishioners erected a mission cross, he said:

30. FS, doc. 102, 22.
31. Manuscript sermons, fascicle 36, pp 1-2.
32. Ibid., pp 2-4.
33. Keel ed., *Texts,* doc. 492.

This cross is a monument which you raise in your midst … the seal of the covenant you have renewed with God … the trophy raised up as your triumph over demons … As long as you attach yourself to this cross you will be victorious … if you return to your sin … this cross which you raise up today will be your accuser … as you pass this way, it will reproach … your ingratitude … O cross, I embrace you; receive me in your arms. May you be engraved on my forehead, on my heart … With transport of joy we cry out and always will cry out: long live the cross![34]

Then he added, as so often, a Marian touch. 'Remember,' he said, 'that it was the blood of Mary that flowed on the cross through the blood of Jesus Christ … Vive Marie!' Bishop Devie, who was present when Colin preached during the mission at Cuzieu on 25 February 1829, was enraptured by his sermon on the cross.[35]

Colin's sermons touched many. Later, when reminding his confrères that they must win a man's heart, he recounted a moving little scene that took place during a mission he was on. After listening to a sermon, a man who had lost all religion turned to his wife and said: 'Wife, give me a rosary … Today, I wept; tomorrow I am going to confession.'[36] For some reason, Colin's sermons on moral issues, as preserved in written form, retain much of the rigorist approach from which he was distancing himself in the confessional. Their dating is uncertain, however, and there is no evidence that he preached them as they are written. If he did, perhaps for him as for many missioners, the practice was 'to preach like a lion but to confess like a lamb'.

The style of life Colin and his companions lived was another sermon. The mountainous country of the Bugey is trying in winter – the only time when missions could be given – with temperatures often below freezing. Little or no preparation had been made for Colin and his companions. Sometimes the parish where they preached had no priest. Sometimes the presbytery where they lodged was so cold and damp that they spent sleepless and shivering nights. The food was inadequate. He recorded later that after spending the whole day in the confessional and in the pulpit, when they returned they had to make their own soup or else do without. In some places, they were so badly nourished that they could not keep going.[37] Cold or hungry, they laughed through it all.[38] They took it in their stride and they were at their happiest.[39]

In moving the hearts of the people of the Bugey, something else was at work

34. Manuscript sermons, fascicle 13, pp 5-7.
35. OM, doc. 723 and footnotes, 1, 2.
36. OM, doc. 590; Keel ed., *Texts*, doc. 400.
37. OM, doc. 605, 1.
38. OM, doc. 639, 1.
39. Keel ed., *Texts*, doc. 429, 1

in Colin. After a thorough examination of his sermons, Gérard Bouchard recognised in them 'the spiritual energy of a saintly priest and the energy of a zealous preacher who vigorously proclaimed the word of God.'[40] Colin used to say that in the pulpit it is most necessary to speak from the heart. When he spoke there, he spoke from the depths of a heart that had been steeped in long hours of prayer from his youth. For the young Colin had been a man of prayer and remained so to the close of his life, as the eloquent testimony of those who came into contact with him paid tribute. 'The missioner who is not a man of prayer,' he told his confrères, 'is not a good missioner.'[41] No wonder that Humbert, witnessing in admiration the impact of his sermon on the people standing in the cold outside the church, to whom it was relayed through a window in the loft, concluded: 'So true is it that when God is with a man he needs very little to move hearts!'[42]

Colin's missions took place in the context of the heady days of the great Restoration missions. It is not easy to assess those tremendous efforts to restore the faith in France. Because of those missions, many people were reconciled to religion and changed their way of life. Some conversions, as in most revival movements, proved only temporary but others were permanent. Against those successes must be set the antagonism that the missioners' exuberance for the regime aroused. Religion did not always benefit and a backlash was on the cards. Particularly from 1821 on, this antagonism led to sharp conflicts. The triumphal procession with the mission crosses, the expense of the missions, the theme of throne and altar, called forth severe criticism. When the mayor of Loches nears Tour signed a public notice approving of the procession to plant a cross at the end of the mission, the liberal paper, *Le Constitutionnel,* angrily demanded: 'Is the State just a part of the Church? Have we fallen again under the yoke of theocracy?' Another paper, *Le Courrier Français,* denounced the expenses which, it alleged, the mission at Brest involved.[43]

The Marist missions, located in the backward and mountainous areas of the Bugey, did not stir up the confrontations that took place in many towns. The procession to plant a mission cross did not figure large in their mission. Some credit must go to Colin's good sense and moderation. Royalist though he was and loyal to the state, Colin did not mention politics and his little group recorded no real opposition to their work. An indication of his attitude may be found in his reaction ten years later to the refusal of a bishop to grant Christian burial to Count de Montlosier, whose fiercely anti-Jesuit *Mémoire,* published in 1826, had provided much ammunition for the strident anti-clerical party.

40. Bouchard, 'Prédication morale', p. 154.
41. FS, doc. 187.
42. OM, doc. 879, 1; Keel ed., *Texts,* doc. 409.
43. *L'Ami de la Religion et du Roi,* 50 (2 Dec 1826), 88-91.

Colin, however, although keenly aware of the damage the *Mémoire* had inflicted, spoke in favour of treating the Count more gently.[44] Many sermons preached during the missions of the Restoration were on 'apologetic' lines – attacking the ideas of the Enlightenment and post-revolutionary Liberalism and fierce denunciations were not uncommon. Colin, however, realising that for the people of the Bugey mountains, such sermons would be neither of interest nor of benefit, concentrated on converting sinners. He and his fellow-missioners steered clear of political comment, avoided running up expenses and abstained from denouncing people. God alone, as Jean Coste observes, is the judge of the good done by the Bugey missions. All that can humanly be said about them is that many heard the word of God preached sincerely and witnessed the simple, edifying life of the missioners. As a result, many confessed their sins, returned to the sacraments and had their marriages validated.

Those five years on the missions were more than a marking moment in Colin's development. When he was beginning, he had to overcome what he described as that 'most violent possible' crisis – launching himself into a very public apostolate, despite his desire to be alone with God. For the sake of the work of Mary he had gone ahead. To his surprise, he discovered what happiness and enrichment this ministry could bring. Even more than when in Cerdon, he had met the ordinary people who made up the Church. For a month at a time across the length and breadth of the Bugey mountains, he lived among those peasants. He would see those poorly-dressed, weather-beaten peasants and their wives, working on their little farms, or descending the mountain tracks on their way to the mission. He met and talked with them, and as he listened to their daily difficulties he began to understand better their daily lives. These were no longer the 'cases' he had met in the seminary textbooks but the flesh-and-blood people of God. He had learned much from these peasant people and advanced far in his understanding of human nature. He exclaimed one day: 'I experienced an unspeakable pleasure in relieving those poor souls; I would have done anything for their sake.'[45] Working with them, he found a fulfilment that more than compensated for his dream of a contemplative life. In the most enthusiastic words he could muster, he recorded his joy:

> I know of no greater pleasure, of nothing on earth which can be compared to the happiness of a priest who sees souls, burdened with sins, coming to cast themselves at his feet, weeping, their hearts full of contrition and then rising again intoxicated, wild with joy to the point of waiting for their confessor in the street and even kissing his feet in the mud as happened to me once during a mission.[46]

44. FS, doc. 14.
45. OM, doc. 819, 65.
46. FS, doc. 171, 1. Gaston Lessard in his lecture, 'L'ultima fatica di Coste', p. 6, brings out well Colin's evolution.

These words were uttered twenty years later. His unforgettable experiences in the Bugey missions strengthened his belief that one's spiritual attitude should be unassuming – his intuition on being hidden and unknown. When earlier he had absorbed what *The Mystical City* had said of Mary's quiet role in the early Church, it had given a more spiritual meaning to his youthful pining to be alone with God. Then as he learned more of the world, whether at Saint-Irénée or in Cerdon, he had begun to understand the sensitivities of people who feared a clergy that would dominate their lives. He commented:

> We are in an age when it is necessary to proceed quietly. The more unobtrusive we are, the more we will do God's work. Every era has its pride and ours has a good share of it. This pride leads to unbelief. Today we can succeed only if we are unassuming.

Now his experience on the missions confirmed his belief in the efficacy of an apostolate that, like the Virgin's work in the early Church, would be unassuming, would remain as it were 'hidden and unknown'.

Towards the end of the mission at Ruffieu, on 28 March 1829, Devie came to confer the sacrament of confirmation. He brought bad news. Three days before, on 25 March, Pichat, the superior of the college at Belley, had died. Pichat, an intelligent and fervent priest, was devoted to the Marist project. He was so well disposed towards Colin that he bequeathed to him all his belongings, including his house at Belley. In turn, Colin thought highly of him and may even have hoped that Pichat would be superior general now that Cholleton had become vicar general in Lyon. The death of so able and wholehearted an adherent was a great loss to the little company of five.

If Pichat's death was a shock for Colin, a further shock awaited him. Devie told Colin to return to Belley straight away to help the children make their Easter duty. Colin obeyed. Then, on Easter Sunday, 19th April, Devie told him that he was appointing him to take Pichat's place as superior of the college. Colin was quite put out and tried to refuse. He had come to like the mission work. Although he had stood in earlier for a teacher who was indisposed, he knew nothing of running a college and was now again being forced into a work he dreaded. His protests were in vain. Devie insisted. He had his reasons. He told the reluctant Colin:

> You have suffered enough in this house, you and your confrères; now you are the masters. Also, to found a society, you have to have experience; in this post, you will learn how to govern. And, finally, your health requires that you go no more on the missions.[47]

Although Devie's main reason was to find a suitable substitute for Pichat, the final reason he gave was not without foundation. As Colin admitted later,

47. OM, docs 819, 72-4; 820, 55-7; 821, 42; 723.

the cold and damp on the missions were undermining his health and already one of the missioners had asked the bishop to do something about it. Devie valued Colin too much to allow him to ruin his health and, as even Colin acknowledged later, removing him from the mission band went some way to avoid that. As he had done earlier to the seminary professors, Colin came back again and again hoping to wear Devie down. Eleven times he came to plead until finally the bishop forbade him to return. As a final ploy Colin asked for just two or three days 'to pray and to recommend this serious matter to the good and saintly Father Pichat.' The bishop was a match for him: 'You're wasting your time,' he replied, 'I am totally inspired. It is Father Pichat himself who inspires me to name you in his place. So then, you will take possession tomorrow.' He would brook no delay.

There was no rest for Colin that Easter Sunday. During the night a fire broke out near the convent of Bon-Repos. Alarmed, he ran all the way from the college to see if the convent was on fire. No damage was reported. Then, the very next day Colin was forced to take over the running of the college and to begin by preaching a panegyric on his predecessor. He knew, too, that his sermon would also be listened to with rapt attention to see what indication he would give of his own intentions as regards the college. Worn out by fatigue, he was pushed into the chapel by the priests. He recounted later: 'I was more dead than alive; I said a few words to the boys; I did not know where I was.'[48] Despite his total exhaustion, his sermon, as the text that has survived shows, is careful and well-balanced.[49] The date was Easter Monday, 20 April 1829. At the bishop's insistence Colin was to hold the title of superior for sixteen years.

48. OM, doc. 466, 8.
49. OM, doc. 190.

CHAPTER 14

Crises at Belley College

'To educate a person, to form him, what a sublime task! But to educate him in a Christian way, what a heavenly work!' Colin, *Instructions to the Professors of Belley*, 1829.

Colin took over the running of the college at Belley on Easter Monday 1829, but legally he was not in charge until the government authorised it. This authorisation was no mere formality for a crisis involving the Bourbon monarchy was developing and, because of the close link of throne and altar, it implicated the Church. At the root of the crisis was the continued opposition of the Liberals to the ultra-royalist government whom they accused of collusion with the Church. Their main complaints were the alleged secret influence of the Jesuits, the suspect activity of 'the Congregation', and the excesses of the missions. At the elections of 1827 the Liberals made substantial gains and the king appointed the moderate Martignac as prime minister. Knowing that he had to make concessions to Liberal opinion, Martignac abolished some rigorous laws and accorded more freedom of expression to the press and the Université. He also issued ordinances or regulations on education. The educational system in France, including the seminaries, had been re-organised by Napoleon under the umbrella of the Université. When the monarchy was restored in 1815, it retained the Université but placed it under the supervision of the clergy. The Sulpician, Bishop Frayssinous, whom Colin had visited in Paris, had become the grand master of the Université and the minister in charge of both education and ecclesiastical affairs. In 1828, however, Martignac's new government divided the two responsibilities, placed a layman, Vatimesnil, in charge of education and replaced Frayssinous by Bishop Feutrier of Beauvais as Minister for Ecclesiastical Affairs. Vatimesnil instituted an inquiry into Church secondary schools but many of the bishops refused to cooperate. The government issued an ordinance on 21 April 1828 removing elementary schools from the control of the bishops. On 16 June 1828, the government issued two more ordinances. One, aimed at curbing the influence of the Church in education, limited the number of pupils in Church schools to 20,000, and obliged the students, after two years, to wear clerical dress in order to emphasise their character as minor seminaries. The other ordinance obliged all teachers to sign a document declaring that they did not belong to any unauthorised religious congregation. This was aimed mainly at the Jesuits. The bishops reacted angrily and, headed by Hyacinthe de Quelen, archbishop of Paris, seventy of them issued a statement rejecting the new ordinances. Bishop Feutrier was denounced as a traitor and when he arranged a dinner for his fellow-bishops, they boycotted it. King Charles x was forced to turn to the pope, Leo xii, to persuade the bishops to accept. Leo, aware of the difficult political situation of the king and not anxious to rock the boat, urged the bishops to take a more moderate line on the ordinances. The papal action helped calm the situation, though some bishops complained of the pope's intervention as an infringement of the rights of the French or Gallican Church.

The new ordinances affected Colin on his appointment as superior of the Belley College, for by law he was now required to sign the document declaring he did not belong to any unauthorised religious congregation. What he would have done is not known, for the action of his bishop spared him a decision. Bishop Devie, a moderate in politics, but who opposed the ordinances, wrote an unusual letter to Bishop Feutrier, the Minister for Ecclesiastical Affairs. He had not asked, he said, 'M. l'abbé Collin [sic]... a most pious and intelligent man' to sign the declaration stating that he did not belong to any unauthorised religious congregation lest he receive a refusal. 'Certainly Mr Pichat, one of the finest superiors in France,' went on Devie, 'would never make that declaration, regarding it as contrary to freedom of conscience and the good of the Church.' Instead Devie asked Bishop Feutrier to accept his own declaration that 'Abbé Collin does not belong to any of those congregations destroyed by the revolutionary laws, although in declaring so, I do not disapprove of any of those congregations, for I regard as prejudicial to religion the rigorous and unjust measures which irreligion has provoked against them.' This complex statement, besides its high praise of Colin, reveals how deeply some clergy felt about the politico-religious debate raging in France. The Ministry accepted Devie's assurance. On 3 May 1829 the king signed an ordinance appointing Colin superior of the college.[1]

Colin would have been very much aware of this tense political background when he took over the college. More immediate for him was the equally tense atmosphere inside the college itself. Devie's decision to put him in charge would be regarded with some dismay by those students and the staff who up till lately had made him and his colleagues the butt of their crude irony. On that Easter Monday when he first spoke to the college, Colin was careful to eliminate from his talk any indication that might antagonise or wound his hearers, as the corrections to his first draft indicate.[2] Yet he made it clear that he was going to be in charge. He spent the rest of that school year observing

1. OM, docs 192-3.
2. OM, doc. 190.

the situation, reading classics on education, and reflecting on what he could offer this rather unusual college – half-seminary, half-secular school.

The college of Belley, closed during the revolution, had opened again in 1803. Since 1808 it had been run by the municipality primarily for lay students and had been in a languishing condition. In 1823 the authorities offered it to Devie who accepted it but wanted it to be a minor seminary. The Université protested, pointing out that the law permitted only one minor seminary for each diocese. Devie insisted and finally won out on condition, however, that lay students could attend the college and that the education be not geared uniquely to students for the priesthood. The result was a mixed college which catered to seminarians as well as to day boys from the town and the sons of wealthy families from different parts of the department of the Ain.

A report Devie sent to the ministry for Ecclesiastical Affairs in February 1828 describes the composition and activities of the college.[3] In that year, it had 200 boys, thirty of whom were day boys. The majority of them paid between 10 and 20 francs a month but twenty of them paid no fees at all. The classes ranged from elementary to pre-major seminary or pre-university; the subjects taught were French, Greek, Latin, Rhetoric, Philosophy, Mathematics. There was no strict age-limit for entrance. To the question concerning the age of admission, the bishop replied: 'When they can read and write.' The seniors were in their later teens and some would wear the soutane on Sundays and feastdays. Since the college was mainly a seminary, many of the boys went on from there to the diocese's major seminary of Brou in Bourg, the capital of the department. Forty had gone in 1826 and forty-three in 1827.

There were twelve teachers, all of whom were diocesan priests or seminarians. The turnover of staff was high for the seminarian-teachers either moved on to Bourg to finish their studies or were called to ordination. The year Colin came, five of the eleven other members left the first summer – some perhaps because of incompatibility with the new regime – and they were replaced by six new members. The ages of the staff varied from eighteen to twenty-nine. They were, then, considerably younger than Colin, who was thirty-nine.

As in his approach to the mission work, Colin's approach to his new role was practical and methodical. He had a job to do and he intended to master it, so, having first sized up the situation in the college, he sat down during the summer of 1829 and wrote out the broad lines of action. The result was *Instructions to the Professors, Prefects, Directors and Superior of the Minor Seminary of Belley.* This document of nineteen pages, one of the earliest of

3. OM, doc. 180; F. Drouilly, *Les Avis de Jean-Claude Colin au personnel du petit séminaire de Belley; Jean-Claude Colin's Instructions to the Staff of the Minor Seminary of Belley* (Rome, 1990), pp 8-10. This volume includes a presentation of the *Instructions* by Anthony Ward, a critical edition by Gaston Lessard and an English translation by William J. Stuart.

Colin's 'rules' to survive, shows Colin's vision of Catholic education, suggests the spirit that should govern the staff and provides clear rules of action for the staff. During the months before he issued it, Colin had read a number of works on education. One of those was the *Method of Learning and Teaching,* which the Jesuit, Father Joseph de Jouvancy, wrote in Latin in 1692.[4] It had become one of the basic texts for Jesuit education and was highly valued even by Voltaire. An edition was published in French in 1803 and it is probably this edition that Colin used. Another source, on which Colin drew even more was *Treatise on Studies* by Charles Rollin, rector of the University of Paris at the beginning of the 18th century.[5]

The *Instructions* Colin drew up and presented to the staff that autumn show a firm grasp of the principles of Christian education. Yet, they are no theoretical exposition of principles but are remarkably well adapted to the circumstances and needs of the college he was charged with. At the beginning of his treatise he stated that Christian educators have three basic duties to their pupils: they must form them as Christians, upright gentlemen and men of learning. In placing Christian formation first, Colin reversed the order of Rollin. Throughout these *Instructions* this priority always surfaces and the expression 'for the greater glory of God' crops up again and again. Professors, Prefects, Directors and Superior should work for the boys and give them the best example. Having established the principles, he goes into detail of how they should be put into practice. The teachers and prefects must be vigilant but also respectful, fair, and encouraging. Following the line taken by Rollin in his *Treatise,* he reminded them that while they must claim 'authority over the children', it is not 'age, nor height, nor tone of voice, nor threats, that give this authority, but an even-tempered, firm, impartial stamp of mind, that is always in control of itself, that is simply guided by reason.' Punishment should be rare and not too severe. Firmness and humanity are blended well together. Young people are immature and cannot be expected to have the conduct and seriousness of mature people.

He drew up rules on how the staff, including himself, should act towards the boys. They show remarkable understanding and respect for the boys:

We shall treat our pupils with kindness, gentleness, courtesy and firmness.

We shall sedulously rid ourselves of the spirit of favouritism.

We shall never have pupils at our beck and call.

We shall not allow pupils to come and light our fires.

We shall not allow pupils to make us presents on our feastday.

4. *Christianis Litterarum Magistris de Ratione Discendi et Docendi* (Paris, 1692). Joseph de Jouvancy (1643-1719). Jouvancy completely revised his text in 1703.
5. Charles Rollin (1661-1741). *De la Manière d'Enseigner et d'Étudier les Belles Lettres…,* 4 vols (Paris, 1726-28).

The Professors, Prefects, Directors and Superior, he envisaged as forming one teaching community, working for the good of the boys and respecting and supporting each another. He expected all the staff, for they were either priests or students for the priesthood, to come together for spiritual exercises, the Mass, the office, and other prayers. At all times they should give good example.

This document, with its mastery of both the broad outlines of education and the practical details relating to the Belley College and the type of boy it was educating, shows Colin's intellectual grasp. This is all the more surprising in that he had no training whatsoever for this difficult apostolate. The *Instructions* cannot be separated from the way in which Colin put them into practice. From the many comments Mayet noted down, it is clear that he ruled the college according to their spirit. He was extraordinarily kind to the boys. He over-looked many faults – drinking beer in the workshop, stealing luxuries from the cupboards. His manner of acting was generous and broad and at all times governed by what he saw was the welfare of the boys. A modern educator, after a comprehensive study of the *Instructions,* concluded that the Colin that emerges from them 'shows that he possesses the qualities of all great educators: knowledge and understanding of children, patience, and love of the pupils.'[6] At the same time, he asserted his authority over boys and staff:

> For offences of indiscipline, for obstinacy and, in general for anything that could be harmful to the good spirit of a house, he was formidable, immovable. He ordered expulsion for things which taken individually appeared to be unimportant but which taken together could greatly harm the spirit of the house, compromise the good understanding between masters and pupils, sow discontent.[7]

What marked Colin's attitude towards the boys was the importance he attached to the fight against sin. He had come to the college not from an academic training but directly from mission work in the Bugey where the struggle against sin had been the first concern and he brought this priority with him when he took charge of the boys.[8] Aware that many of the boys were reaching the disturbing years of puberty and, concerned to save them from sexual sin, he encouraged the teachers to go out of their way to help them, and to be especially vigilant at certain times and in certain places. He urged the boys, whenever they felt themselves driven towards wrongdoing, to come and see him. Several of them would come to him saying, 'Monsieur, I am at the end of my tether.' He would then chat with them and this would help them overcome their difficulties for a while:

> There were some who came to him immediately after they had fallen.

6. Drouilly, *Instructions,* p. 86.
7. FA, doc. 207, 3-4.
8. Coste, *Lectures,* p. 89.

Sometimes they would even stop him in the middle of the corridor to say, 'Monsieur, things are not going well.' This was how the good Father taught them to fight or to pull themselves together. He ... used to say that these open-hearted admissions were the saving of young men.[9]

He himself went around the dormitories at night and discreetly checked to see that every boy was in bed. Although this task was tiring and made him unpopular with the boys, that did not deter him. He said on one occasion: 'Messieurs, God has put me here to fight against sin, and I shall continue to do so as long as there is a drop of blood in my veins.' He learned later that some of the boys had formed a plot to strangle him.[10]

When necessary he took a firm stand. During his first year he expelled six or seven boys. Then at the end of the term he warned any pupils who were not prepared to follow the rule, to leave during the vacation. Nearly forty of the two hundred did not return. Nor was he less vigorous with the staff. Those who would not accept his authority, he had no hesitation in asking to leave. That summer of 1830 which saw so many students depart, saw five of the staff also leave, a number at his request.[11] He said to one at the beginning of the vacation: 'You did what you liked during the year. To everyone his turn, Monsieur. Please do not return here.' Another who had asserted that the superior was only the first among equals he also dismissed. A third was asked not to return for, as Colin told him, he stuck too much to his own judgement. By the beginning of the school-year 1830-1, there was no doubt as to who was in charge. Later on, he would make even more sweeping dismissals.

If the *Instructions,* written so early in his career as headmaster, show a comprehensive grasp of the principles, his action over the following years reveals other traits – a wide understanding, a firmness of purpose and a decisiveness in action. The combination of single-minded concern for the college and the authority with which he carried it gave him a complete ascendancy over teachers and pupils. They reveal him as a man who could both inspire and govern. There were other battles, however, in which he was engaged at the same time, and for these he needed talents of a different order.

In June 1830, the differences between Bishop Devie and Colin came to a head. The bishop was fully determined to transform the Marist group into his own diocesan religious group and used all the means in his power, fair and unfair, to bring this about. One questionable method he used was to call each of the Marists apart separately and try to win them to his way of thinking, while, at the same time, forbidding them to mention a word to Colin or to each other. Another time, he appears to have used the occasion when Colin

9. FA, doc. 331, 6-8.
10. OM, doc. 476, 2.
11. OM, doc. 507.

came to him for confession to bend him to his will. Colin vowed never to take him again as confessor! Devie formed the plan of starting a diocesan mission group aggregated to Bochard's Congregation of Missioners of Lyon, often called Missioners of Chartreux. To persuade Colin to take part, he brought two of these missioners to Belley to twist Colin's arm. One was Mioland, whom Colin had as liturgy professor in Saint-Irénée and who was now the general superior of the congregation. The other was Father Jean-Marie Ballet, a likeable priest, who entered the seminary one year after Colin. The Missioners had agreed to give Ballet to Devie to start the Belley branch. Colin refused to join. The bishop insisted. It came to a show-down and Colin and his companions stood their ground. Colin stated his position firmly:

'I shall never agree to join these men; I cannot share your views. If I was stupid, if I made a mistake in thinking of the Society of the Blessed Virgin, I do not wish to be stupid again, and make a second mistake. If you will have the kindness to place me somewhere as a curate, I shall be only too honoured, wherever you place me.' This reply upset the bishop. Father Déclat and Father Jallon also made a reply which I always admired and gave me a good laugh. Tormented by Bishop Devie, they ended up saying: 'Well, bishop, we shall consent to become Missioners of Lyon but on condition that Father Colin will be the superior.' In truth, only God could have inspired them to make that reply. It pulled the bishop up sharply, and the plan was derailed.[12]

When persuasion failed, the bishop was not above pulling rank and appealing to his authority. The dialogue between these two strong-willed men became riveting:

'After all,' [Devie said to Colin] 'who is your superior?' 'You, my Lord.' 'Well then,' [said Devie]. 'Well then,' [replied Colin] 'the worst position in your diocese is more than I deserve; give the order and I'll go there right away.' 'We're not talking about the worst position, we're talking about a diocesan congregation.' 'The evangelical counsels are not obligatory.' 'But you have already decided on the evangelical counsels.' 'I did intend to begin a work of that kind, it is true. If I have fooled myself once, I have no wish to be foolish again and fool myself a second time; either this work or none at all.' 'And what convinces you that this work is the will of God?' 'Your Lordship, I have vowed three thousand Masses to that purpose.'[13]

At these words, Colin relates, the bishop trembled all over. The unwavering stand of Colin, his strength of character, his total conviction, which he also imparted to his two colleagues, are impressive. His resolve he sealed by the

12. OM, doc. 547, 11.
13. OM, doc. 725, 4-5.

most solemn manner he could envisage – the offering of thousands of Masses! Devie, committed to the welfare of his diocese and implacable in working for it, was a person of deep religious faith, and drew back at least for the moment. Yet if Colin did not yield, he certainly suffered in the struggle with the bishop. To Julian Eymard and Mayet, in 1842, gesticulating with his right hand as he used to do when he spoke of something which he felt very deeply, he said:

> Fathers, the greatest cross of the Society, yes, the greatest, I have no hesitation in saying, my greatest cross and that which will be my greatest crown in heaven if I made use of it, are the contradictions and sufferings which Bishop Devie inflicted on us. I would have preferred an open and declared warfare, a striking persecution. But no; we found ourselves constantly back where we started. He went against us always and everywhere. He harassed us unceasingly; all that was done surreptitiously.[14]

Jeanne-Marie Chavoin confirmed that Devie was a terrible cross for Colin. He had no let-up, no where to turn except to her whose work he was convinced he was called to do. In anguish, he prayed to Mary with a cry from the heart:

> O great Queen, let our prayers rise up to you and do not despise the sighs of your humble servant. Why do you forsake us …? Why do you not assist us in our affliction, especially when it is caused by our desire to make you known and loved by all? You see how the enemy has drawn his bow and stiffened his arm against us, and we have no one to defend and reassure us … O Holy Lady, break the bonds his malice has forged and set us free so that … we can faithfully fulfil the promises which we have made to you.[15]

His distress is palpable. In the conflict in which he was engaged, he had not lost but neither had he won, and the struggle was an unequal one. The bishop was in a position of authority and was quite as determined as Colin and, since they lived so close to one another, the pressure was constant. For the moment at least the battle had ceased, suspended rather than over.

Perhaps the main reason why Devie ceased to harass Colin was the storm that broke over the Church in France in July 1830. The political scene had grown sombre over the previous few years. The king, blind to the dangers threatening his throne, had replaced the moderate ministry of Martignac with the more reactionary one of Polignac who was well-disposed towards Church schools. It looked certain that Champagnat would receive the state recognition he sought for his foundations. Polignac, however, lost badly at the elections of June and July 1830. In a desperate act to maintain power, he abolished the freedom of the press, dissolved the new parliament and limited the vote to the rich. The Liberals roused the populace and after a revolution during 'the three glorious'

14. OM, doc. 547, 10.
15. OM, doc. 219.

days of 27-29 July, which cost a thousand lives, seized power. Charles x was forced to flee. The collapse of the throne made the altar tremble and the Church now paid for its close association with the regime. In Paris, the archbishop's palace, the Jesuit noviciate and the house of the Missions of France were sacked. Crosses on churches were torn down and in Paris all the churches had to close. Only on Sunday did the clergy dare open the churches. To go out in clerical dress was to risk being attacked or insulted. Diocesan retreats were cancelled. Several bishops, including the cardinal archbishop of Rheims, had to flee to England. In Paris, Archbishop de Quelen went into hiding. Trouble flared up from time to time and seven months later the mob sacked the church of Saint-Germain-l'Auxerrois in Paris on the occasion of a Mass for a member of the Bourbon royal family.[16] Champagnat had trouble at the Hermitage. A Crown Prosecutor brought a detachment of soldiers to search for a marquis whom he alleged was hiding there. The intrepid Champagnat opened every room for him and the affair ended well. For well over a year an uneasy atmosphere prevailed throughout the country. Many crosses erected during the missions were torn down. The new king, Louis-Philippe of the house of Orleans, was Voltairian in outlook though not disposed to get involved in Church affairs. His government, however, was anti-clerical and defended the sacking of the church of Saint-Germain in Paris and pursued an unfriendly policy towards the Church.

It was against this unpromising background that the group of Marists now took a significant step forward. Champagnat was the main influence in bringing this new move to a successful conclusion. He had passed through some difficult years after Courveille and Terraillon left in 1826. He was now the only priest at the Hermitage and was responsible for the training of the great number of brothers his work was attracting, most of whom were very young. He approached the diocesan authorities and persuaded them to give him Étienne Séon. Séon, who was ordained priest in June 1827 at the age of twenty-four, had long been interested in the Marists and, in May of that year, had proposed to Champagnat that he join him. The prospects for the priests' branch of the project, however, looked so bleak that, according to the account Séon gave Mayet twenty years later, Champagnat had begun to lose hope of it ever succeeding.[17] His hesitancy soon passed. In 1828, he assured Cattet that 'I never doubted but that God wanted this work' of Mary and by that he intended especially the priests' branch.[18] Ably seconded by Séon, a determined searcher for recruits, Champagnat began to promote the Lyon branch for all his worth. 'Whatever happens,' Champagnat told Brother John-Baptist, 'I am resolved to work to

16. P. Thureau-Dangin, *Histoire de la Monarchie de Juillet,* vol. 1, (Paris, 1888), pp 246-59.
17. OM, doc. 625, 11.
18. OM, doc. 185, 2.

make it [the priests' branch] succeed, with all my strength and to my last breath.' Determinedly, he approached the Lyon diocesan administration again and again, to give priests for the work. Well-esteemed by many of the vicars general, he succeeded in getting good recruits. Séon was mainly responsible for seeking out Jean-Antoine Bourdin, whom Champagnat received into the Hermitage in the summer of 1828. Jean-Baptiste Pompallier was recruited in 1829 and Jacques Fontbonne in 1830.[19] At a retreat in Belley in which he, with Bourdin and Pompallier, participated, the Lyon and Belley groups agreed that more unity was needed between them. Neither of the diocesan authorities was agreeable. This did not deter Champagnat for whom the unity of the Society was always of central importance. Fearing that if some definite organisation was not soon developed, the two small groups would remain weak and their project a mere dream, he urged them to go ahead without informing the bishop and give themselves a recognisable centre and head. Although the cautious Colin was opposed to this course, he came round to Champagnat's point of view. An election meeting was planned for Lyon but the venue was changed to Belley. Two circumstances dictated the change. Since it was decided not to notify the bishops, it would be easier for a group to slip out of Lyon than out of the little town of Belley where they were right under the nose of the bishop. Moreover, since the wave of anti-clericalism was still sweeping the country after the July revolution, priests could not visit one another without being suspected of a conspiracy and constantly ran the risk of being arrested.[20] A large group of eight priests travelling into Lyon might arouse suspicion whereas a small group leaving Lyon for the countryside would arouse less suspicion.

So it was that late in the autumn of that eventful year of 1830, Marcellin Champagnat and the Lyon group, dressed probably in lay clothes, set out on the 100 km journey to Belley for the meeting.[21] Arriving there they were met by the group of eight other Marists. This dozen or so men felt that the time had come to give the project cohesion and substance. Of the original twelve at Fourvière fourteen years before, only three were present. These were: Colin, Champagnat, Déclas. Also present was Pierre Colin who had come in 1817. All the others – Jallon, Humbert, Convers, Séon, Bourdin and Pompallier – had joined the group over the previous five years. Terraillon was not present for, since he had abandoned Champagnat and taken up work in the diocese, his position was less clear. Colin, however, always included him among the Marists. The Marist group, including sisters and brothers, now numbered about a hundred.

19. Étienne Séon (1803-56), b. Tarentaise, (Loire) ordained June 1827; Jean-Antoine Bourdin (1803-83), b. Vernaison, (Rhone) ordained December 1828; Jean-Baptiste Pompallier (1801-71), b. Lyon, ordained June 1829.
20. Thureau-Dangin, *Monarchie de Juillet,* vol. 1, pp 248-9.
21. It is not certain how many of the Lyon group came to Belley for the meeting.

After a short retreat and much reflection and prayer over the next few days, they solemnly chose a Central Superior. Unofficial, indeed secret, though both meeting and election were, the tiny group of priests had taken a major step towards providing the Society of Mary with an organisation and a leadership. It would be a morale booster for them all. The man these zealous young priests elected, and into whose hands they were unhesitatingly confiding their hopes and lives and the future of a religious venture dear to them, was Jean-Claude Colin. He had just turned forty. His total commitment to the project over the previous fourteen years and patient negotiations to secure its success, his unremitting work on the rule, his tireless commitment to the Bugey missions, his firm government of the Belley College, and his prayerfulness and devotion to Mary, were overwhelming reasons for the unanimous choice. The group gathered round to congratulate him and impress on him their great joy. It remained to be seen if he would realise their dream of a Society of Mary which he had played such a part in keeping alive.

A meeting of the Lyon priests, on the 8 December 1830, to elect a provincial superior followed the election of the central superior. They chose Champagnat. Archbishop de Pins, informed of this election but without making the slightest reference to it, then accorded Champagnat the title of superior of the Society of Mary, praising him and the society's work highly.[22] The election of a provincial superior was a necessary move to preserve unity in the Lyon branch, for the group was about to take over a new house. This was the medieval Cistercian monastery of Valbenoîte, near Saint-Étienne, where the curé, Jean-Baptiste Rouchon, had invited them. A small Marist community, consisting of Étienne Séon and Jacques Fontbonne, set up there in 1831. A year later, because of the new situation that the Valbenoîte house had created, Colin made a move that caused disquiet among the Lyon Marists.

After his election as central superior, Colin had shown himself keenly aware of his responsibility for governing the two little groups. His letters show an anxiety to keep the Marists united.[23] In writing to the group in Lyon, which was not under his immediate control, he attempted to keep them as close as possible to the way of living of the Belley group. Gently, he played down the too detailed rule, which probably Pompallier had drawn up. Then, in December 1831, he thought to clarify the situation in Lyon as regards the priests and brothers, by requesting that Champagnat, while remaining in charge of the brothers, step down as superior of the priests and allow a new superior to be elected. He went so far as to specify how the election should take place, what prayers and hymns should be recited or sung and to make it clear that Terraillon, who had deserted Champagnat, must be regarded as a member of

22. OM, docs 224, 226.
23. OM, doc. 221.

the Society and would have a vote. His suggestions were not at all well received by the Marists in Lyon. Champagnat was popular. Besides, he needed to have some priests to help him in the Hermitage and was unhappy to see all of them engaged in other apostolates. The reply of the Lyon group has not been preserved but Colin wrote again on 3 February 1832, to explain his position. While pointing out the advantage of having a distinct superior for the priests, he nevertheless withdrew his suggestion.[24] Later in the year, however, it was decided that his plan was the right one and Étienne Séon was elected superior of the priests in the diocese of Lyon. The problem had been resolved to the satisfaction of all.

In the same letter of 3 February, Colin raised another matter that was to cause a more lasting difficulty. He suggested that there be two groups of brothers – Marist brothers who would teach and 'Joseph' brothers or coadjutor brothers who would assist the priests in their work. Coadjutor brothers formed part of his plan for the Society and in the text of the rule, which he presented to Macchi in 1822, he had devoted a number of articles to them. The Fourvière group probably intended coadjutor brothers from the beginning, for they would have thought of the society along the model of earlier congregations, all of which had coadjutor brothers. Since there was now a body of priests in Belley, Colin felt the time had come to set up the coadjutor brothers. One of his suggestions was that they should wear different attire from the brothers engaged in teaching. A Joseph brother could never become a Marist brother but a Marist brother could become a Joseph brother. This was far from Champagnat's idea. From the beginning he had asked and been entrusted with the establishing of brothers who would teach religion. He had no intention of assimilating them into Colin's coadjutor brothers. According to a tradition in the Hermitage, the brothers felt that Colin's idea was an odd one and that he wanted to take brothers from the Hermitage to serve the priests.[25] Colin, again recognising opposition to his views, did not press his point but the problem was to recur more sharply later. What is remarkable in those letters is, on the one hand, the authoritative attitude Colin assumed immediately after becoming central superior and, on the other, his and Champagnat's willingness to listen to one another and arrive at an agreement.

Colin could not devote all his time to the affairs of the Marists, for a major crisis was looming in the college. This time it involved both staff and boys and was part of a general unease troubling the post-revolutionary Church. Not all Catholics maintained a negative reaction to the ideas of the French Revolution.

24. OM, docs 241, 243.
25. F. Avit [Henri Bilon], *Annales de l'Institut: divisées en neuf étapes; rédaction commencée en 1884; La Rude Montée*, vol. 1, (Rome, 1993), pp 88-9. Henri Bilon (1819-92); took the habit, 1838; visitator, 1848; assistant general, 1876.

While horrified by its excesses, many viewed with concern attempts to return to the pre-revolutionary Church of privilege and close connection with the state. They favoured political democracy and freedom of the press. During the 1820s, Daniel O'Connell led a successful democratic movement of Irish Catholics, which finally succeeded in achieving Catholic Emancipation for the whole of the British Empire. O'Connell's Liberal Catholicism, fuelled by national sentiments, was pragmatic but on the continent, where his movement roused the interest of many Catholics, the Liberal Catholic movement that emerged had the consistency of a system. It flourished in many countries, Belgium, Italy, and Rhineland Germany, but it was in France that the leaders and thinkers associated with the movement emerged. The acknowledged head was Félicité de La Mennais, a Breton priest. La Mennais had lost the faith after reading Rousseau but had been converted by his brother and went on for the priesthood. A warm-hearted man, he set out to put his talents as a thinker and writer at the service of the Church. Already in 1802, François-René de Chateaubriand had written *The Genius of Christianity*, an enthusiastic and influential apologetic for the Church and in 1819 Joseph de Maistre, with his powerful advocacy of the papacy in his epoch-making book, *Du Pape,* had launched Ultramontanism. La Mennais took a similar line. The papacy, he wrote, was vital for the Church and for civilisation. At first he also supported royal authority and his motto was 'the pope and the king'. Soon, however, he lost faith in the monarchy and championed 'the pope and the people'. He argued passionately that the Church should not identify itself with the absolutism of kings but with the freedom of peoples.

La Mennais and his group launched a newspaper, with the bold title *L'Avenir* (The Future) whose motto was 'God and Liberty'. It was a brilliant paper. 'Never had the Catholic faith been expressed in prouder and more vibrant language.' Every number was like a manifesto. The first number reminded Catholics to claim their rights like everyone else and warned anyone who would fetter them that they would break their chains on his head. The third number took up the thorny question of the separation of Church and State. La Mennais' editorial was electric. Since he who pays the piper calls the tune, the clergy would never be free as long as they accepted to be paid by the government:

> This is what Irish Catholics had rightly felt, who have many times rebuffed the efforts of the English government to impose it. As long as we do not follow their example, Catholicism will have a precarious and feeble existence among us.

The only solution was to abandon their dependence on the government and refuse their pensions. 'The scraps of bread thrown to the clergy,' he went on, 'are the title deeds of her subjection … It was not with a cheque drawn on

Caesar's bank that Jesus sent his apostles out into the world.'[26] The union of throne and altar, the hankering after a Bourbon restoration, came in for his bitterest attacks. 'Did the Son of man die on a gibbet 1800 years ago in order to re-establish the Bourbons on the throne?' he thundered. His urgent plea to the Church was to 'Break irrevocably with these men whose incurable blindness endangers religion, who sacrifice their God to their king, and who would profit by their victory to degrade your altars to the level of a throne.'

La Mennais was soon joined by a host of able collaborators among whom were Henri Lacordaire and Charles Count de Montalembert. Lacordaire, too, had lost the faith from reading Rousseau. He had reconverted, however, and became a fervent and brilliant preacher and was later to re-introduce the Dominicans into France. Montalembert, the youngest of the three, intrigued at the success of Daniel O'Connell in combining Catholicism and freedom, had gone to Ireland, 'that island where the sacred cause for help in France had been for centuries incarnate in the lives of the clergy and their people'. Having read the first numbers of *L'Avenir* he wrote to promise his support for La Mennais and hurried back to join up with him.

In July 1830, immediately after the revolution, *L'Avenir* became the voice of a new type of Catholicism that was far removed from the royalist and conservative Catholicism of the Restoration. It supported liberal or 'revolutionary' Catholicism everywhere – Belgium, throwing off the yoke of the Dutch king, Poland, attempting in sympathy with Belgium, to rebel against the Tsar, and Ireland struggling for equality in religion from its Protestant government. La Mennais' cry was a clarion call: 'Where the people are, there is Christ! Their struggle is Christ's struggle!' *L'Avenir* advocated four freedoms: freedom of the press; freedom of education (that is not to be subject to the Université); freedom of the Church from the State; freedom of conscience. Freedom of the press had not been dear to either governments or Catholic authorities. Freedom of conscience would not be popular in many religious circles or in Rome, where the old maxim of 'outside the Church there is no salvation' was often interpreted strictly. Freedom of education was not popular either with the new government of Louis Philippe. Yet, the young leaders of the movement were not content to preach this for Montalembert, with Lacordaire's help, defied the government and the Université by opening his own school. Though they argued their case for educational freedom brilliantly and won the admiration of many Catholics, Montalembert and Lacordaire were jailed.

When these liberal sentiments appeared in *L'Avenir,* a chorus of opposition arose on every side. The anti-clericals and atheists denounced La Mennais and his associates as 'humbugs in disguise'. King Louis Philippe and his ministers

26. *L'Avenir,* 18 Oct. 1830, cited in C. de Montalembert, *Journal Intime Inédit,* ed. L. Le Guillou and N. Roger-Taillade, vol. 2, (Paris, 1990), p. 110.

were outraged that they prophesied a republic. The bishops were furious because *L'Avenir* wanted a separation of Church and State. For them this was an attempt to laicise society, for they believed that Church and State should cooperate for the common good. Furthermore they were unwilling to abandon state subventions and salaries. Bishops banned *L'Avenir* in their dioceses. Seminarians were forbidden to read it under threat of being denied holy orders.

For many lay Catholics and the younger clergy, this was new and heady wine and many rallied to La Mennais instantly. For too long they had seen the Church associated with the monarchy and blind conservatism. Many of them had valued the best ideas of the Revolution – liberty, equality and the abolition of privilege. They wanted a Church no longer burdened with a feudal past, but freed to pursue its mission as it wished. They dreamt that the rejuvenation of the Church was at hand. In Belley College, the young priests and seminarians were no exception. *L'Avenir* and its programme for a new liberal and democratic face to Catholicism carried them away. The priest professors came together and wrote a joint letter of support to *L'Avenir* in praise of La Mennais and took out a subscription to the paper:

> Please put the following in your next issue: God and Liberty. Such is the Catholic and French cry. It remained buried in our hearts until *L'Avenir* appeared and it has come out now with the most lively enthusiasm since M. de La Mennais has given us his courageous example. May his generous efforts be crowned with speedy success.[27]

All the teachers – priests and seminarians – signed, with three exceptions. The German-born prefect of studies, Father Richter and the two Colins did not. According to Mayet the staff tried to persuade Colin to sign too and wanted to put his name to the document. His retort was that if they did, he would issue a formal and public denial. 'When my bishop gives the word, I will follow him.'[28] At this time, however, Bishop Devie was in no position to give a strong lead. He was still recovering from an operation for cataract.[29] Devie was Gallican and royalist, whereas La Mennais was Ultramontane and scornful of kings and princes. Devie was not a man of extreme views and his judgment on the paper was a cautious one:

> *L'Avenir*'s style ... was admirable. The intentions of its editors are good. They want to liberalise Catholicism in order to catholicise the Liberals: with some this objective has been achieved. Only time will tell whether this project will achieve more good than evil. There are in the manner, the princi-

27. OM, doc. 612 and footnote 1.
28. OM, doc. 612, 2-3.
29. OM, doc. 853, 25 and footnote 4. Cognat, *Devie,* vol. 2, p. 27.

ples … of this journal many things that afflict and frighten me. Many of my fellow-bishops judge it far more severely.[30]

Given his reticence about the paper and the feelings among his fellow-bishops, he was not pleased that the priests in his seminary, a few hundred yards away, were going all-out to support a paper that ridiculed the position of the hierarchy and so he forbade the priests in the college to take the journal. They poured scorn on his prohibition and ordered four copies instead of the one they had been taking. The burden of what action to take fell on the superior of the college. The situation was a tricky one for Colin. He was out of sympathy with the ideas of La Mennais. Like most clergy who remembered the Revolution and its horrors, he was still a royalist and having seen how many crimes were committed in the name of Liberty, he relied on order as the best way for a Christian society. His judgment on *L'Avenir* was more severe than Devie's:[31]

When I saw that the journal *L'Avenir* made so much noise, stirred up such divisions – and the programme it advocated did the same – I said right away: the work of God does not make all this noise; when the Good Lord speaks, he produces peace and acceptance.

The vibrancy of *L'Avenir*, its unmeasured language and violent denunciations were offensive to the man whose motto was 'hidden and unknown'. In the college, however, the priest-teachers and many of the students thought differently. Discipline vanished as the teachers colluded with the boys and hailed the ideas of *L'Avenir* as the breaking of a new dawn. Julien Favre, who succeeded Colin as general, was at the college that year and remembered well the rebellious atmosphere:

Everyone wanted to be free. *L'Avenir* inflamed the young clerics. One walk day, the boys took off their uniforms, and carrying wooden hatchets and marching like a battalion began to sing the Marseillaise or the Parisienne in a frenzy like intoxication. In that fine choir, there was, I think, one of the teachers who played his part. They wore a wild look. When they came to the wood, they uttered such yells and took on such an arrogant air that the older M. Colin, … who accompanied them, took alarm and believed that they were going to kill him.[32]

Colin's opposition to *L'Avenir* aroused intense antagonism in the college. People in the town woke up each morning to ask if he were still alive.[33] So trying was that year of 1831, he said, that his hair turned white.[34] Unable to make

30. Devie to a friend, 2 Feb. 1831, cited in Cognat, *Devie*, vol. 2, p. 24.
31. OM, doc. 522.
32. OM, doc. 476, c.
33. OM, doc. 699.
34. OM, doc. 476, c.

much progress against such a strong current, he bided his time. When the end of the school year came at last, he acted decisively. Sure of the support of Devie who had given him complete freedom, he had all the professors who had signed the subscription to the paper moved elsewhere in the diocese. He broke the school up into three divisions after the manner of Jesuit schools. In a painful operation, he managed to neutralise the influence of the vicar general in charge of seminaries, Ruivet. Then he brought in his own Marists. Deschamps, Antoine Séon and Bourdin came in as prefects of discipline and four or six others as teachers. Pierre Convers became vice-superior. *L'Avenir* was totally banned from the school. Colin had shown the tougher side of his nature and demonstrated that he could take determined action and command respect. For the remaining years that Colin stayed as an active superior, there was no further trouble. Later in life he twice referred to his actions to restore discipline as his master achievement.[35] The incident reveals a certain resoluteness.

As for the Liberal Catholics that year proved a decisive one. La Mennais announced in his journal that they would appeal directly to the Pope above the heads of the bishops and, towards the end of 1831, with Lacordaire and Montalembert, he set off for Rome. Styling themselves 'pilgrims of God and Liberty' they hoped to persuade Gregory XVI to accept their programme of reform for the Church. Montalembert passed through Lyon where he converted priests and others to his views. He also admired the 'canuts' or weavers who rose in revolt at the end of November.[36] In Rome, although the three finally had a papal audience, the pope made no comment on their mission and they returned to France empty-handed. It was only months later, on 15 August 1832, that a reluctant pope, under continuous pressure from the French bishops and Metternich, the Austrian chancellor, whose army was the sole guarantor of the Papal State, issued the encyclical *Mirari Vos* which condemned many of the ideas put forward in *L'Avenir.* Gregory refused to censure La Mennais and his companions but the condemnation, repeated later in the encyclical *Singulari Nos,* appeared to justify those who like Colin, opposed the movement.

The sweeping changes Colin made meant that the following school year, 1831-32, began and ended on a better note. Before that year began, Colin, taking seriously his role of central superior, decided to use the college for a retreat for the Marists at Belley and the five who could come from Lyon. This retreat was another milestone. It was the first retreat ever in which almost all of the Marist aspirants participated. It took place from 1-8 September 1831 and Colin had invited as preacher Joseph-Marie Favre, a well-known missioner and author of pastoral works including one on penance and on frequent communion. He

---

35. OM, doc. 476, 1-2.
36. C. de Montalembert, *Journal Intime Inédit,* ed. L. Le Guillou and N. Roger-Taillade, vol. 2, (Paris, 1990), pp x-xi, 249-50. Montalembert also met Cholleton.

proved an admirable choice. One day, during the retreat, Colin confided his difficulties to him, relating the obstacles the authorities were making for him. Favre said nothing and left. Early the next day he came into the room and said to Colin: 'Forward! Courage! Your work will succeed'.[37] Colin saw it as a sign. Favre gave new heart and encouragement to Colin and to the Marist aspirants. At the end of this retreat, they drew up an act of consecration to the Blessed Virgin:

> Holy Virgin, behold the children which your divine Son has given you, and whom you have chosen to work at the project of your Society. They recognise that they are quite unworthy of this favour and, prostrate at your feet, they ask you to accept the rightful tribute of their gratitude. We promise to cooperate by all the means at our disposal for the success and extension of your Society, and throughout our lives to work for the glory of your divine Son, and your own … Be for us always, Holy Virgin, a Mother full of tenderness and mercy … Obtain for us to be faithful to our last breath to the grace of our vocation, and to see all of us united one day in heaven around the throne of your glory, as we now are at the foot of your image.[38]

Eighteen aspirants signed this declaration. Their names are like the roll-call of the first generation of Marists: Terraillon, Champagnat, Chanel, Grandclément, Pompallier, Jallon, Maîtrepierre, Déclas, Deschamps, Convers, Humbert, Debelay, Bourdin, Bret, Rouchon, Cellier and of course the two Colins. Absent were Étienne Séon and Fontbonne who stayed behind to look after the Hermitage and Valbenoîte. Absent, too, was the latest recruit, Chanut. Apart from Cellier who died in 1832, Debelay and Grandclément who abandoned the project, and the elderly Rouchon, whom Colin advised not to join, those were the men who formed the early society. The act of consecration recalls the Fourvière promise fourteen years before. The sheet of paper containing it together with the eighteen signatures, was carefully preserved and signed again and again after subsequent retreats in 1834, 1837, 1838 and 1839, until three pages of its four pages could take no more signatures. This act of consecration was to remain the model act of closure for future Marist retreats.

The retreat of the following year, 1832, was remarkable for another very different reason. Colin and the five Marist aspirants from Belley went to the seminary of Saint-Irénée to make the pastoral retreat in September. Like a ghost from the past returning to his old haunts, Courveille turned up too. Jeantin recounted what Colin told him many years later in 1869-70:

> Courveille began again to assume mysterious airs and threatened them that they would incur God's curse if they continued not listening to him. Then

---

37. OM, doc. 819, 82, a.
38. OM, doc. 236.

Father Colin, moved by a noble zeal, said to him: 'Do you think we don't know about your conduct?' At these words he kept an embarrassed silence. It was all over.[39]

A short while later, the researcher, Father Detours, described the encounter in sharper terms:

He [Courveille] reproached Father Colin for taking on himself and exercising the role of head of the Society and threatened him because of such usurpation, with the wrath of heaven. Father Colin replied to him: Don't put on such airs and don't speak like that, you are no more than an unworthy priest. He then revealed his offence.[40]

Since, apparently, Detours is dependent upon the account Colin gave Jeantin, it is probable that what he adds is an elaboration and he may be putting words into Colin's mouth. In both accounts Colin shows a steely resolve. Although very merciful in the confessional, when it came to the good of the Society to which he had committed himself, he was unyielding. By his conduct, Courveille had jeopardised the fledgling Society and Colin feared that, if he recovered any influence, he would remain a threat to the project. His reaction, too, like that of Courveille's uncle at Apinac when Courveille's problems returned, reflects also horror at what he saw as the disgrace Courveille had brought on the priesthood.[41] Like his contemporaries, Colin would have applied to Courveille's sin the words of Jesus: 'He who scandalises one of these little ones, it were better if a millstone were tied around his neck and he were cast into the depths of the sea.' Apart from mentioning him in some letters to Champagnat, Courveille's name never passed Colin's lips for thirty years until, finally, the great controversy on the origins of the Society in the 1860s forced him to speak of him again. Although anger at Courveille may have played a part, Colin's long silence is more an indication of the veil of charity he wanted to draw over the incident and the shame it caused. It is probable that correspondence concerning Courveille perished in the fire Colin made of his papers in 1841. For Courveille, his rejection by his fellow-Marists was a fearful humiliation at a time when he felt, possibly, that he was being accepted again in the diocese. The editors of *Origines Maristes* suggest that the upset he suffered may have brought on more quickly the grave offences he committed at Apinac.

In the autumn of that year 1832, Devie returned to the attack. With thirteen Marists in Belley all living at the college, Colin wanted to acquire a house

39. OM, docs 819, 78, a; 820, 30.
40. OM, doc. 872, 44.
41. OM 3, p. 275, footnote 1. At Apinac, according to Lagniet, Courveille was accused of the same crime with boys. When his uncle, who was curé there, learned of it, he locked the sacristy door, saying: 'Miserable man, for too long you have said Mass; you will never again say it here.' OM, doc. 819, 28-9.

of their own. Devie promised to give the Marists the old friary of the Capuchins, the 'Capucinière', in exchange for the house Pichat had left to Colin. Devie was slow to fulfil his promise and finally he changed his mind altogether. Fearing that Colin would begin a novitiate there, he again demanded that they accept to be diocesan missioners. Colin pleaded to be allowed to put his project to the pope, but Devie would not hear of it. On one occasion he treated Colin very roughly indeed and, calling the other Marists into his presence, he threatened to scatter them across the parishes in the diocese. As Colin avowed, the Society of Mary appeared to be within inches of disappearing altogether.[42] Before the Marists were able to take possession of the Capucinière, another outburst took place. This time it came from Colin:

> I felt an incredible revulsion against His Lordship, the Bishop of Belley. It was at the time when we had just bought the house of the Capuchins. His Lordship created many difficulties when a certain decision had to be made. Immediately, without giving myself the time to reflect, I ran to the palace; had I reflected, I would have stopped. Swiftly I passed through the streets; I entered the palace, knocked, quickly pushed open the door and threw myself at the bishop's feet, confessing my hurt, my revulsion and asked pardon. The good bishop received me like a good father, embraced me and consoled me. That was the end of it.[43]

If Colin's tempestuous temper comes out in this outburst so also does his openness. It won over the bishop whose temperament was just as strong. Colin had set his heart on getting the Capucinière and nothing would change him. Not content to make the most emotional of pleas to the bishop to follow through with his promise, he called on the help of the Blessed Virgin to finalise the deal. He received Devie's permission to bless the house and the chapel and he and a number of Marists assembled there. Present were Fathers Pierre Colin, Convers, Deschamps, Brothers Jean-Baptiste Cartier, François-Xavier Girod and Théodore Millot and a student from the seminary, Jean-Marie Millot. Colin turned it into a solemn ceremony and wrote an official record of the occasion:

> On 7 October 1832, Holy Rosary Sunday, seven years, four months, and fifteen days after our arrival in Belley, after requests often repeated in vain, we, the undersigned, priest, superior of the minor seminary of Belley, authorised by My Lord the Bishop of Belley, have blessed a temporary chapel and the house called after the Capuchins as destined to become the cradle of the Society of Mary.[44]

Besides the not too veiled criticism of Devie's delaying tactics, what is inter-

---

42. OM, doc. 746, 20.
43. OM, doc. 515, 2.
44. OM, doc. 251. Colin later called other locations the cradle of the Society.

esting in this somewhat solemn statement is the meticulous measuring of the time – an indication of how important the move was for him. Devie had allowed them to bless the house but not to move in. The Marists promised Masses and rosaries for the intentions of the Blessed Virgin but on condition that 'she obtain for us the entry to this house before Christmas'. Their prayers were answered. In November of 1832 de Pins authorised the Marist priests in Lyon to group together in the priory of Valbenoîte. Devie, realising he was not overcoming the resistance of the Marists and not wanting to be outdone in generosity by de Pins, finally let them have the Capucinière and Pierre Colin, Déclas, Jallon and five brothers went to live there. It was a further step because now for the first time the Marists had a house of their own. To his chagrin, however, he was not allowed to live in the Capucinière, for Devie wanted him in the college. Still, as he happily explained to Champagnat, 'the two houses [Belley College and the Capucinière] are as one'.[45] He was overjoyed. In these exasperatingly tedious negotiations Colin had shown his colours – confidence in Mary's support, a clear vision of what he wanted and the perseverance to keep at it until he got it.

The three and a half years from the time he became superior of the college in Belley brought to light many characteristics of Colin. The *Instructions* to the staff showed a perceptive intellect capable of observing and analysing the educational scene and devise rules that were both theoretically sound and eminently practical. Determinedly, he swept aside opposition to his control of the school – rebellious boys, refractory teachers, 'radical' clerics. Yet he was kind and considerate of the weakness of the young and anxious to help them in the crisis of adolescence. If he was determined in his conduct of the college, he was more determined still in the pursuit of his great project of the work of Mary. He had dealt resolutely with Courveille, fearing that he was an obstacle who could destroy it. In his great battles of 1832 with Devie, he complained of the stubborn opposition of the bishop, but he was equally stubborn and strong-willed. His desire to organise others along the way he passionately believed the Society should go became evident as soon as he was made central superior for he attempted to impose his vision of what the Society should be on such matters as the rule, the separate superior for the priests and the setting up of the brothers. Although on some matters he was prepared to listen to opposing opinions and to compromise, he would allow nothing to stand in his way on anything he believed essential to his vision of the Society of Mary. Only the clear decision of the head of the Church would turn him from his purpose of establishing a society which he believed the Blessed Virgin wanted. He was soon to engage in this decisive test.

45. OM, doc. 255, 2.

Two years earlier, in a letter to Champagnat of 24 November 1830, Colin had written: 'I forgot to say that I am thinking of renewing our correspondence with the nuncio in Paris, who is now a cardinal.'[46] These almost throwaway few words were to mark the beginning of a new chapter in the story of the Marists and of Colin.

46. Colin to Champagnat, 24 Nov. 1830, OM, doc. 222, 8.

CHAPTER 15

'Rome, Rome, Rome!'

'When as a young priest he thought about the Society, Father Colin used to say: "Rome, Rome, Rome!" That sole word made his heart race and electrified him. Like his country's name for an exile, or a harbour's name for a lost ship, or the cry of deliverance for a prisoner, so was it for him.' Mayet, 'Mémoires', December 1845.

As he had indicated to Champagnat, Colin contacted Cardinal Macchi whom he had seen twice in Paris ten years before, now a curial Cardinal in Rome. Macchi was sympathetic and, in his reply of 25 July 1831, advised Colin to come to Rome to treat of the project in person. When Colin asked his bishop's permission, however, Devie replied that because of 'the troubles in Italy' the time was unfavourable and that, given the state of affairs in France, the Curia would not be able to give proper consideration to the affair. Colin may have felt that the bishop was merely seeking an excuse to fob him off but the unrest in the Papal State did give legitimate cause for concern right through the year 1831. There was a new pope, Gregory XVI. On 6 February 1831, the very day he was crowned, he learned that a revolt had broken out in the northern sections of the Papal State. The 'Legations', as this part of the papal territory was called, were economically and politically different from the more traditional area around Rome and the insurgents, many of whom were members of the secret revolutionary society of 'Carbonari' and Freemasons, opposed clerical rule and declared that their goal was the unification of all Italy. Encouraged by revolutions in France and Belgium, they had taken over the second city of the Papal State, Bologna, and other major centres. Rome itself was under threat. When the Papal Legate sent to restore the situation was imprisoned, Gregory called in the Austrians, who re-established order. Within a few months, however, the revolt broke out again but in January 1832 the Austrians and the papal army crushed it. This time the Austrians remained in Bologna and the French, to spite the Austrians, occupied the important papal port and citadel of Ancona. This fighting was in itself more of a police operation than a campaign but the calling in of foreign armies was heavy in consequences. 'Formerly the pope could not defend his State from Austria without French help, or from France without Austrian help. Now he could not defend himself from his own subjects without

Austrian or French help.'[1] Among middle class Italians, angered by the presence of foreign armies in Milan, Venice and now in the Papal State, the idea of 'Italy for the Italians' slowly gained support. Right throughout the rest of Colin's life the problem of the relationship of the pope and the Papal State with Italian nationalist aspirations, usually referred to as 'The Roman Question', was to become more divisive and to involve Catholics throughout Europe.

In the short term, however, peace was restored in Rome by February 1832 and in 1833 Colin decided on a fresh attempt to go there. Apart from Macchi's advice there was another reason underlying his determination to go to Rome. He wanted to fulfil the vow he had made at Cerdon some thirteen years earlier to work for the establishment of the society until it had been submitted to the pope in Rome. At first Devie renewed all the obstacles, still hoping to form a group of missioners attached to his own diocese. Colin was persistent and his letter to Macchi proved decisive. Macchi did not reply directly but wrote instead to Devie urging him to let Colin come to Rome. After receiving Macchi's letter, Devie saw Colin and the following dialogue took place between them:

> If you refuse me permission to go to Rome, I will not go; but please, for God's sake, do not refuse me. – Go, since you want to, but you will obtain nothing. – I am not going to obtain anything. I go to satisfy an obligation of conscience, a promise I made to God and, if I get nothing, to be free afterwards and be able to do what I want.

Taken aback when he learned that Colin had written to Rome, Devie was further shaken when he heard about the oath and gave a reluctant consent:

> So you wrote to Rome. Father answered, My Lord I vowed that I would labour for this work until the Holy See had manifested what it thought of it. The bishop said, Oh! You had made this vow. I did not know. Then, go to Rome.[2]

That youthful vow, then, had proved quite significant. It constituted the thread running through all Colin's efforts from 1819 until 1833, the link that joined together his spiritual experiences in Cerdon with his pilgrimage to the eternal city in 1833. Mayet's account in 1845 caught the magic that the word held for Colin: '"Rome, Rome, Rome!" That sole word made his heart race and electrified him. Like his country's name for an exile, or a harbour's name for a lost ship, or the cry of deliverance for a prisoner, so was it for him.'[3] During the darker moments of frustration when progress was nil and the dream further away than ever, the thought of Roman approval sustained him. In

1. O. Chadwick, *A History of the Popes 1830-1914* (Oxford, 1998), pp 6-12.
2. OM, doc. 819, 85.
3. OM, doc. 622.

another tangible way, the vow was to sustain the other aspirants. Intuitively they realised that Colin had made an unbreakable commitment to work for approval of the project. It may well have been decisive in influencing them to choose him as their central superior in 1830.[4] Earlier that year, the clear-sighted vicar general of Lyon, Cattet, told Champagnat straight out that the only way the Marist groups could unite and expand would be for the bishops to agree or the pope to intervene.[5] Colin, despairing of the bishops who merely placed obstacles in the way, was determined, now that he was in charge as superior, to travel the Roman road.

By 1833, the time seemed ripe. In France, the political climate had improved. François Guizot, Minister for Public Instruction, told an assenting chamber of deputies: 'Primary education must necessarily include moral and religious teaching.' Guizot's law of 28 June 1833 was a sign that the regime was well-disposed to religion for it guaranteed its central place in education. Although by insisting that teachers possess certificates, the law created diffi-culties for Champagnat, the brothers' group was still progressing rapidly. The rest of the Society was also growing. With thirty-eight sisters, the convent of Bon-Repos at Belley was bursting at the seams and Jeanne-Marie Chavoin had to refuse or delay would-be postulants. With the support of Colin, Champagnat and Pompallier, she was searching hard for a new foundation and finally opened a house at Meximieux where Maîtrepierre was superior of the minor seminary. As for the priests' branch it had acquired two houses: the Capucinière in the diocese of Belley and Valbenoîte in the diocese of Lyon. Their number had increased to seventeen. The Society, then, had a respectable presence in no less than three dioceses: Belley, Lyon and Grenoble, where Champagnat had established the brothers. All this meant that by now, Colin had something tangible to put before Rome. The Society had a central superior and many members, brothers, sisters and priests.

Marist priests at Belley signed an appeal to the pope, explaining their origin and purpose and giving some details on their progress in the dioceses of Belley and Lyon.[6] It differed little from the letter that the Colins and Courveille had sent in 1822. Devie had given his consent and de Pins' soon followed. Colin claimed later that he was able to use the rivalry between the two bishops, Devie and de Pins, for each wanted to be able to claim the soci-ety as originating in his diocese. Colin recounted that when de Pins agreed to let the Marists have Valbenoîte, Devie countered by letting them have the Capucinière. 'I push one by the other,' he added, 'and God's work gets done.'[7]

4. OM, doc. 625, 19.
5. OM, doc. 213, 3.
6. OM, doc. 269.
7. OM, doc. 752, 29.

So it turned out as regards permission to go to Rome. Philibert de Bruillard, Bishop of Grenoble, also wrote a letter of recommendation. Bruillard's letter has not survived, de Pins' was formal but Devie's was a remarkably warm one. He praised the pilgrims for their exemplary piety, sincere humility and their edifying and proven devotion to the Church. He concluded by affirming that the project they had in mind was a most holy one.

Colin travelled first to Lyon, bringing with him a declaration to the pope which was to accompany the rule. This declaration, dated 23 August 1833, signed by the seventeen priests, set out the four branches of the Society: priests; brothers – both Joseph or coadjutor brothers and teaching brothers; sisters, and lay people.[8] A large group of Marists then climbed up to the sanctuary of Our Lady of Fourvière where the promise of 1816 had been made. This time it was Colin who celebrated Mass for the group and they all renewed their commitment. Then, on 29 August 1833, Colin and Peter Chanel from the Belley group and Antoine Bourdin from the Lyon group, sailed down the Rhone to Marseille on the first leg of their pilgrimage to Rome. They arrived at Marseille on the morning of the 31 August but had just missed the steamboat. It was not until 4 September that they could embark on a sailing boat, *Our Lady of Good Help,* a name which seemed auspicious for their venture. Colin and Chanel, particularly, had bouts of sea sickness. The boat sprang a leak and had to put in at the port of Ciotat, not far from Marseille. It was five days before they could put to sea again. A storm arose and they had to seek shelter off the coast of the island of Elba. The storm abated but when they headed out to sea it grew worse and they had to put in at the port of Santo Stefano on the coast of Tuscany. Becalmed there for a day they set sail again and slowly gained the port of Rome – Civitavecchia. There they had to remain on board over night. A new hazard arose. Cholera was raging in much of western Europe and had made deep inroads in France and at first it seemed likely that the three would have to spend time in quarantine. To their relief, the Cardinal Governor sent word that they might proceed to Rome. Before daybreak, on the 15 September 1833, they eventually arrived at the Porta San Pancrazio and entered the eternal city. The journey had taken seventeen days. They took up lodgings near the French church, San Luigi dei Francesi, possibly on Via della Scrofa or the Street of the Sow, which probably took its name from an inn called 'La Scrofa'.

They wasted no time. On the day after they arrived they presented themselves to Cardinal Macchi to whom they confided their documents. He passed them on to the pope who sent them to Carlo Odescalchi, Cardinal

8. OM, docs 282, 283.

Prefect of the Congregation of Bishops and Regulars. To their dismay, the pilgrims discovered that they had arrived just as the vacation was beginning and everywhere they were told to come back after Saint Martin's Day – 11 November. Their request for an audience with the Holy Father was refused, for Gregory was on his way to Castel Gandolfo. Macchi kindly took a hand and arranged an audience for 28 September at eleven o'clock. The morning of the audience they learned that it would take place two hours earlier and they had only three-quarters of an hour to get there. It was quite a rush and when they arrived they were reprimanded for not having the proper outfit. They were then ushered into the presence of Pope Gregory XVI. It was to this moment that Colin, for over a decade, had been looking forward. He would pour out his heart to the Holy Father. He had a secret to tell him – the origin of the rule – and he hoped to get the pope's blessing for the new Society of Mary. It was not quite how things worked out.

The man into whose presence the three pilgrims came was Mauro Cappellari, a Camaldolese monk, who from 1826 to 1831 had been Cardinal Prefect of the Congregation of the Propagation of the Faith, commonly called Propaganda Fide, or simply Propaganda.[9] In February 1831, he had been elected pope. He had been abbot of the monastery of St Gregory the Great on the Coelian hill and he admired Gregory VII, the champion of the papacy against the secular power.[10] Like most clerics and most public figures of his time, he had recoiled in horror from the excesses of the French Revolution. In 1799, at the darkest hour for the Church of Rome in modern times, when the sick and elderly Pope Pius VI had been abducted and cruelly dragged across the Alps to die of exhaustion at Valence, Cappellari had not lost hope. He had published a vindication of the Papacy, entitled *The Triumph of the Holy See and the Church*. It was a courageous act of hope and trust. He remarked later with characteristic humour that no one had heard of the book until he became pope. In 1808, when the French took over Rome, he was forced to leave. He was a kindly and ascetic man who still lived according to his monastic rule. He slept on a mattress of straw, rose to pray at four a.m. and was sparing in diet. His personal appearance was not prepossessing. According to one description, Gregory 'was ugly and coarse in

9. The Congregation, renamed the *Congregation for the Evangelisation of Nations* in 1967, had been given definitive shape in 1622. Besides the foreign missions it looked after Catholics in countries which had not a Catholic government. Roman Congregations are the executive departments of the Roman Curia. They consisted of cardinals under a cardinal-prefect, with a secretary and other officials.
10. On Gregory, *Gregorio XVI, Miscellanea Commemorativa*, 2 vols (Rome, 1948); R. Aubert, 'Grégoire XVI', *Dictionnaire d'Histoire et de Géographie Ecclésiastiques*, vol. 21, cols 1445-52; P. Boutry, 'Grégoire XVI', *Dictionnaire Historique de la Papauté*, ed. P. Levillain (Paris, 1994), pp 767-73; Chadwick, *History of the Popes*, pp 1-60.

appearance and did not look like a pope or even a sovereign for he was short and broad and round'.[11] Montalembert, who with La Mennais and Lacordaire had come to Rome two years before, to put the Liberal Catholic case to him, had expected to find a great patriarchal Pontiff but found that he had no air of distinction about him. He noted, with disappointment, his 'excessive simplicity'. When the three were received in audience, Montalembert remarked: 'He looks very well, but does not seem very noble or religious. He had one of his hands in his pocket.'[12] That simplicity may have had a greater appeal for Colin than for the count. Gregory, however, was a man of culture and visitors normally found it interesting to talk with him. The talking did not proceed too well for the three Marists, however, for language proved a problem. Piously, Bourdin described the scene:

> Imagine our eagerness and our satisfaction, despite the rain which fell in abundance. It is true then that we arrived at the throne of the Vicar of Jesus Christ. There, humbly prostrate, we kissed not only the holy slipper, but the sacred ring also, holding in our hands that which blesses the whole world. His Holiness raised us up, and standing there conversed for quite some time with us.[13]

Chanel tried to speak in Italian but got tongue-tied. Bourdin then tried Latin but also stumbled. Then Colin spoke up in French to the pope's surprise. Finally, the audience was conducted by Colin speaking in French and the pope in Latin. Colin adds:

> I had a petition which I was holding between my fingers which were clasped and intertwined. The pope took it; he read for a long time then he said to me: The Pontiff does not approve before examination. Then he took up his pen and wrote, 'To Cardinal Odescalchi.' I had the courage to say: 'Most Holy Father, he is away'. Then he had the kindness to put, 'to Monsignor Polidori.' He was the Secretary of the Congregation of the Council.[14]

The petition he gave the pope was a request for a whole series of indulgences for the Third Order of Mary. The audience was over. Backing out of the pope's presence proved an ordeal. They almost tripped on the hem of their cassocks, and instead of going towards the door, they strayed around the hall. 'To the right,' the kindly pope called out, in vain because they were still straying, and then Gregory rang for a chamberlain to show them out. Colin,

---

11. Chadwick, *History of the Popes*, p. 3.
12. Montalembert, *Journal*, vol. 2, p. 299. Earlier, when he first saw Gregory, Montalembert recorded a similar impression: 'Unfortunately the present Pope has no air of distinction about him and is as if overcome by his very office.' Ibid., p. 271.
13. OM, doc. 289, 1.
14. OM, doc. 466, 12.

perceiving that the comedy was to become public, turned quickly towards the door and the three of them shot out before the chamberlain could catch a glimpse of them.[15] So ended in comedy the audience he had looked forward to with so much anticipation.

One lesson Colin was learning was that in Rome people were not in a hurry. Early on he commented: 'I shall find plenty in Rome to try my little patience; for, we French want to do everything in a day; this is what the Italians tell us, who repeat incessantly: Patience, Patience.'[16] The three pilgrims had plenty of time to visit the city. From their lodgings they could easily walk to all places of interest, for Rome, with its 150,000 inhabitants, was, at that time, a small city enclosed within the ancient walls. Bourdin tells us how the three pilgrims occupied themselves:

> Every day we make little pilgrimages of piety. We change altars every morning. Lately, I celebrated in the room of St Louis Gonzaga, where his body lies. Today, it is on the tomb of St Ignatius ... after my thanksgiving I had the benefit of paying a visit to the Father General of the Society of Jesus. Father Colin and Father Chanel were at the Carmelite house.[17]

Like Bourdin, Colin celebrated Mass on the altar of St Louis Gonzaga and also on the altar of St Stanislaus Kostka, Jesuits who both died quite young, and prayed for the boys at the college in Belley.[18] Since they stayed right next door to the French national church, San Luigi dei Francesi, they would have often prayed in that beautiful church where some of the finest of Caravaggio paintings – the story of St Matthew – decorate a chapel. Many famous Frenchmen are buried in the church. They visited three of the four basilicas: St Peter's, St Mary Major's and St John Lateran's. St Paul-outside-the-walls had been totally destroyed by fire in 1823 and had become one vast construction site. They visited the Mamertine prison where St Peter was thought to have been imprisoned; the Scala Santa, supposedly from Pilate's residence, which Jesus climbed before his crucifixion; and many other sacred places.

With the Curia on vacation it was evident that it would be many months before their case was considered, so it was decided that Chanel and Bourdin should return to Belley where they would be needed for the opening of the college. They all three went together to Loreto to see the house reputed to be the house of the Blessed Virgin.[19] Bourdin and Chanel then went to France. Colin stayed for a week longer in Loreto. While there he said Mass six times in the holy house. The bishop received him very well and invited Colin to

15. OM, doc. 752, 37.
16. OM, doc. 295, 3.
17. OM, doc. 287, 2.
18. OM, doc. 295, 7.
19. OM, docs 564, 624.

dine with him two days in a row. When he invited him to return the next day, Colin, from shyness or modesty, took flight. Colin was captivated by the holy house and was reluctant to leave it. Loreto, at that time, was one of the foremost shrines in Italy if not in Europe and Colin, with his devotion to the Blessed Virgin, would scarcely have left Italy without visiting it. He returned to Rome on 16 October. This time he lodged at the Franciscan house attached to the church of the Holy Apostles, opposite the Odescalchi Palace, where Cardinal Odescalchi lived and had his offices. Colin liked praying in the gallery of the church of the Holy Apostles. Near the church is a delight-ful little shrine called Madonna dell'Archetto, Our Lady of the Little Arch. Here, too, he often went to pray to the Blessed Virgin. He went to the Coliseum, the scene of so many cruelties in Roman times and where so many people, including Christians, had been thrown to the wild beasts who were also slaughtered in their thousands. Its haunting memories and stillness made a deep impression on Colin. There he used say the office and make the stations of the cross. Writing to Champagnat of the beauty of the churches, he added:

> Here at every step one finds something to nourish and excite piety; we have venerated the table on which the Last Supper took place; we have visited the catacombs of St Sebastian where thousands of holy martyrs rest, the prison of St Peter.[20]

A French priest from Chartres, Father Paul Trinchant, with whom he became very friendly, took him to see many 'pious curiosities' and 'monu-ments of devotion'. He was thrilled by the Romans' devotion to Our Lady, even if he did not care for the manner in which it was manifested:

> One cannot describe the devotion of the Romans for the Blessed Virgin. You would have to be here to get an idea of it. From the beginning of Advent, novenas are made publicly before the Madonnas which are found in every street; however, these novenas are accompanied by folk music which I do not find beautiful and which deafen one the whole day long.[21]

For all that, the sights of Rome were secondary to him and he recounted that he did not go much to see the strange and remarkable buildings nor did he pay any attention to some of their artistic beauty. Rome was in the grip of the flu, Colin told Jeanne-Marie Chavoin, but he remained healthy enough and had a good appetite although he did suffer from colic.[22] This he blamed on the way the Romans cooked the food:

> The only thing that often upsets me is the way they prepare food here, almost always in oil and highly seasoned. Two nights ago I was up seven

20. OM, doc. 288, 5.
21. OM, doc. 295, 6.
22. OM, doc. 296, 1.

or eight times; and it has been ten days since I have able to celebrate Mass because this indisposition doesn't allow me time. This discomfort has been with me for a fortnight which nevertheless does not prevent me from attending to business, making small trips, etc.[23]

He used his time, too, to speak on 'moral matters with the various priests and theologians I could consult, to see what was the Roman way of doing things.'[24] He discovered that there were other priests on missions similar to his in Rome. He dined with the Missioners of France who had just been assured of Roman approbation.[25] The question of uniting the Marists with them came up but nothing came of it.

More pressing for him was the need to get advice on the Marist project. The rule was a constant concern of Colin, and over the years, in the midst of all his other work, he never ceased to reflect on what it should contain. In his letter to Cardinal Macchi on 15 April, 1833, announcing his forthcoming trip to Rome, he wrote: 'We shall then have the honour of presenting the almost completely revised constitutions of the Society of the Priests of Mary to Your Eminence', an obvious indication that he had been working hard at a revision over the previous few years, probably since his election as central superior in 1830. From the moment he had arrived in Rome he had consulted experts who examined the project and commented that 'the style was fairly good'.[26] Colin had not brought the full text of his rule to Rome for he had come to seek general approval of the project rather than specific approval of the rule, as yet unfinished. He had, however, brought an abridgment. When he showed it to those whose advice he was seeking, they expressed surprise that it dealt only with the priests' branch while he was seeking approval for all four branches – priests, brothers, sisters and laity. He set to work during October and November to fill that gap. The result was the *Summarium,* or summary. It is the earliest substantial version of the rule that has survived and has an important place in its history. In it one can see how Colin's thought developed and, for the first time, glimpse his overall view of what the society should be.

The aims of the Society are briefly stated: they are the classic ones of the salvation of one's own soul and that of others. Mary is often invoked for the Society undertakes its work under the auspices of the Virgin and she is the *Domina,* the head of each house. There are chapters on the four branches, a

23. OM, doc. 295, 2.
24. OM, doc. 517, 1.
25. The Society of the Missioners of France were founded in 1815 by Jean-Baptiste Rauzan (1757-1847) perhaps the greatest of the missioners of the Restoration period, 1815 to 1830. Rauzan was in Rome up to September 1833. OM, doc. 295, 2.
26. OM, doc. 289, 6.

chapter on administration and another on finances. Only the chapter on the priests, which takes up 85 of the 127 articles, is well developed. Bodily penances are no longer prescribed but left voluntary. The section on missioners bears the mark of Colin's experience in the Bugey missions, for the themes dear to him recur here: missioners are instruments of mercy; they must commend themselves and their listeners to Mary; their conduct towards the local clergy must be unassuming; they must avoid expense; they must be men of prayer.

The *Summarium* casts light on the question of Colin's conversion to the moral theology of St Alphonsus of Liguori. Article 49 of the *Summarium* lays down that the missioners 'should read the works of St Alphonsus of Liguori with special attention and follow his practice in the direction of souls.'[27] This article is part of the chapter on the priests which Colin, almost certainly, had drawn up before he came to Rome and indicate that his conversion to Liguorianism was completed before he came to Rome. That conversion probably began at the time of the pope's exhortation to confessors during the jubilee year of 1826 and its endorsement by Colin's bishop Devie. In 1830 Devie published his important *Ritual of Belley,* in which he again urged his priests to follow the theology of Liguori. A further influence on Colin may have been Joseph-Marie Favre, a convinced Liguorian and one of the most esteemed missioners of the day. Colin had the highest respect for Favre and believed that, during the retreat of 1831, God had sent him to support and encourage him. Favre, he related later, often gave him support in the difficult early years. Colin's reflections on his own mission experience probably sealed his conversion to Liguorianism.

Since coming to Rome, he also had been able to read the Jesuit rule in the great Casanate library, a public library founded by Cardinal Casanate, adjoining the Dominican Convent of the Minerva. He borrowed very little from that rule at first but after his return he was to make extensive use of it, especially when he was penning the chapters on government.[28] At the end of the *Summarium,* Colin added a supplication which set forth what he hoped to obtain from the Holy See. The few months in Rome had made him more realistic and all he now sought was that the Marists be allowed to receive recruits, elect a superior general and take the three vows. In addition, he requested that indulgences be granted which would entice people into the Third Order of Mary.

On 9 December he was able to give the *Summarium* to Cardinal Odescalchi and four days later he had a meeting with the cardinal.[29] Carlo

---

27. *Summarium,* numbers 49, 77. *Antiquiores Textus,* fascicle 1.
28. J. Coste, *Studies on the Early Ideas of Jean-Claude Colin - 1* (Rome, 1989), pp 26, 190-2.
29. Carlo Odescalchi (1786-1841) b. Rome, ord. 1808; cardinal and archbishop of Ferrara, 1823;

Odescalchi, of an illustrious family which had given several cardinals and one pope to the Church, was a pious priest who had a reputation as a preacher. In addition to being prefect of Bishops and Regulars, he was arch-chancellor of Rome and soon to be vicar-general. Well-disposed to religious orders, he had helped the Brothers of Christian Doctrine, the Dames of the Sacred Heart, and Vincenzo Pallotti's Pious Society of the Missions. He had already petitioned Pope Gregory to be allowed to abandon his cardinalate in order to join a religious order, in vain at first, but successfully in 1838. He became a Jesuit and lived a life of exemplary poverty and devotion. It is not surprising that Colin found the meeting with this admirable cardinal satisfying.[30] It was the substitute for the meeting he had for so long wished for with the pope, and Colin was able to pour out his heart to the sympathetic cardinal. Odescalchi told him that the project was good and, as Colin reported happily to Convers, held out good hopes. Yet he warned Colin that the project was somewhat 'vast'. Encouraged by the warmth of Odescalchi's reception, or caught up in his own passionate enthusiasm, Colin did not appreciate the significance of the cardinal's reservations on the vastness of a society with four branches. Odescalchi added that his project would go before the Congregation for Bishops and Regulars after an examination and report from Cardinal Castracane.

Cardinal Castruccio Castracane degli Antelminelli, a man with a reputation for learning and piety, came of a noble family from Urbino.[31] Attached to his native city, he bequeathed his wealth to a boys' orphanage there. He had been secretary of the Congregation of Propaganda from 1828 at a time when Mauro Cappellari was prefect. A few months before he met Colin, he had been promoted cardinal and became a member of the Congregation of Bishops and Regulars. It was in that capacity that he met with Colin and reported on the project. Over the next months, the two men saw one another often and established a good personal relationship. Yet Castracane was exacting when it came to Roman policy and put pressure on Colin to conform to it. He was new to the Congregation and it would appear that this was his first case. Although fair in his judgement, he was not very familiar with religious life, as some of his comments appear to indicate.

When he read the *Summarium,* Castracane professed not to be clear

prefect of Congregation of Bishops and Regulars, 1826; vicar-general of Rome, 1834; entered Jesuits, 1838; Liguorian in moral theology. A. Angelini, *Storia della vita del P. Carlo Odescalchi* (Naples, 1855), pp 190-290.

30. OM, doc. 296, 2.

31. Castruccio Castracane degli Antelminelli (1779-1852), secretary of Propaganda, 1828; cardinal, 1833; prefect of Congregation of Indulgences, 1834; cardinal-bishop of Palestrina, 1843; president of administrative commission for Papal State, 1848.

about its meaning. As a result, Colin spent the end of December on drawing up first one summary but then, since that had not sufficient detail on the vows the Marists were to take, a more complete summary. Two days before Christmas 1833, he wrote to Cholleton: 'I tell you almost nothing about Rome. Staying at the convent of the Holy Apostles, I live almost as a hermit and hardly ever go out except for my business.'[32] Most of the meetings with Castracane took place in January 1834. It was during one of those meetings that there occurred the scene when Castracane, astonished at the extent of Colin's proposed society, began to laugh and jested: 'But, then, the whole world is going to become Marist?' 'Yes, Your Eminence,' Colin replied, 'the pope, too; he is the one we want as head.'[33] Castracane may have jested but Colin was deadly serious. For him, the Society of Mary would be open to everyone; it was, after all, 'the city descended from heaven', of which Maria of Ágreda wrote so eloquently, whose twelve gates would be open to all at all times; the Church renewed in the last days.[34]

Apart from fascinating episodes like this, Colin has left little account of the discussions, but Castracane gave his own version when reporting to the Congregation. According to this, Castracane told Colin that the idea of a society with four branches was 'monstrous' and Colin eventually agreed. Under continuous pressure from Castracane, Colin finally reduced his request to a plea that the priests' branch in Lyon and Belley be allowed to elect a superior and that indulgences be granted to the priests, brothers and sisters.

Colin now realised that he was not going to succeed. He asked that the Congregation's reply be addressed to Bishop Devie. 'I foresee,' he told Convers, 'that that reply will be quite simple, and that all it will do is to give some advice on the plan of the Society, which, in general, they find too vast.' A little wistfully he added that if the Marists had presented the plan for the priests on its own and with completed rules, they would be well on the way to approval.[35]

Little did he realise what was to take place at the meeting of the Congregation of Bishops and Regulars on 31 January 1834. Castracane's report was devastating. In it he had examined Colin's scheme under three headings – was it advisable to have another religious institute; was the structure Colin proposed for it appropriate, and what of the rule for the four branches? On each section he made the severest of criticisms.

On the first point he declared that it was unwise to multiply institutions.

32. OM, doc. 298, 3.
33. OM, docs 427, 2; 752, 36.
34. FS, doc. 1; Coste, *Marian Vision*, pp 316-24.
35. OM, doc. 303, 3.

The Marist brothers would only duplicate the work of the brothers of the Christian schools. As for institutes of sisters in France which were dedicated to the education of young people, it was impossible to count them. On the second point – Colin's plan that all four branches should depend on the one superior general – he rejected it as neither necessary nor advisable. As it was, the superior general of every order knew how difficult it was to deal with the affairs of his own order, not to mind attempting to deal with three. Furthermore, the idea that the superior would preside over the confraternity of men and women of every state of life and in every country was both highly extravagant and irregular and would subtract the laity from the authority of their bishops. Such a worldwide confraternity under one superior could arouse the suspicion of governments. On the third point Castracane was equally critical. Colin envisaged that the priests would take simple and perpetual vows when they reached twenty-four and again when they reached thirty and that the superior general would be able to dispense them from the first profession, whereas only the Holy See could dispense them from the second. All of these provisions, Castracane wrote, were in violation of religious life, for they ran counter to the perpetual nature of religious profession.

Castracane's criticisms need examining. His assertion that the need of the poor for education, which the Marist sisters and brothers were undertaking to meet, was already adequately dealt with by existing orders scarcely accords with the enormous expansion of teaching brothers and sisters during the rest of the 19th century. His criticism of the type of vow did not take into account developments in recent times which had begun to offer modes of religious life other than the solemn vows of the older orders. His criticism of Colin's proposal to allow his religious to keep the ownership of their property while leaving the use of it to the religious institute, could indeed be seen as a violation of the vow of poverty. In fact, however, given the precarious situation of religious orders in many countries, including France, the distinction between ownership and use was a practical one for religious orders. Later it would be incorporated into the law of the Church. More substantive was his criticism of the vastness of this four-branched Society. It was not quite unheard of as Castracane alleged, for in some orders the superior general was the head of different branches. Yet Colin's views on the branches were not fully worked out and the unwieldiness which Castracane mentioned was there. His fear that governments might be alarmed was not as unreasonable as might first appear. Many Liberals and governments were paranoid as regards religious orders and feared the existence of a vast Jesuit conspiracy.

After these harsh criticisms, Castracane came to Colin's final, whittled down, requests: permission for the priests to elect a superior and the indulgences. Here he was compassionate. He pointed out that both the bishops of Belley and

Lyon had commended the zeal of the Marists. He also felt that the Congregation should have pity for Father Colin, who had travelled to Rome and remained there for a considerable time. It would be wrong to send him away empty-handed. He proposed that as a consolation they allow the priests of the two dioceses to elect a superior, with the consent of their bishops, on the understanding that this did not imply any canonical approval by the Holy See. As for the indulgences, he advised that they be granted but only to the priests' branch.

The members of the Congregation of Bishops and Regulars met on 31 January 1834 and approved in full Castracane's report. The question of communicating the decision became of crucial importance. Colin had asked the reply of the Congregation be sent to Devie without realising how devastating it would be. The Congregation decided that letters be sent both to Devie and de Pins and that they would spell out the reasons why it rejected Colin's plan. Castracane drafted a minute for letters which were signed by Odescalchi. This minute was more critical than the report. The very first phrase was damning: 'After a thorough examination [of the project] it is apparent that on no account can it be approved.' Then, leaving aside the objections in the report concerning the multiplication of institutes and the vows, the draft letter went on to dwell on the structural faults and on the third order.

> The most Eminent Fathers have judged that it errs in many ways and contains many things foreign to an institute of the Church. For what could be more extraordinary than the proposal to set up a society which has three kinds of persons ... and one Superior general to whom all submit and obey.

The congregation of the laity came in for particularly harsh criticism:

> How extraordinary, how alien to the custom of the Church seems this idea of a universal confraternity ... What certainly cannot be passed over is that particularly extraordinary idea that whereas other sodalities are erected and brought together under the auspices and authority of the bishop, this kind of confraternity, downgrading the authority of the bishop, owes submission and obedience to the person who is at the helm of the whole Marian society.[36]

At one blow, these letters were calculated to destroy the whole project of the Society of Mary which Colin had dreamt and worked for since 1816. Devie and de Pins would undoubtedly have used them to force Colin either to abandon the idea altogether or to work within the diocesan framework. News of Rome's condemnation would have spread like wildfire throughout the dioceses. Marists would have lost heart. New recruits would have drawn

36. OM, doc. 309.

back from joining a society which Rome had categorically declared could on no account be approved. Even Colin might have given up. He had fulfilled his vow of continuing to work on the project until he had submitted it to Rome. He had now done just that and 'Rome had spoken, the case is over'.

For the moment, however, he was spared all that. Blithely unaware of what these letters contained, Colin began to wind up his business and to prepare to go home. Although he realised he had not gained what he wanted, he was more sanguine than the facts merited. Furthermore, he felt that he had learned much. He told Convers how he had asked that the reply be sent to Devie and added:

Our little manuscript has passed through all the stages of the most thorough examination ... I have already received counsels which will be of the greatest use to me for the rest of my life. This trip is one of the great graces the good Lord has given me since I began to work on the project of the Society. From now on, it will help me to be more at peace and walk on safer ground in my efforts for the project.[37]

He was beginning to enjoy himself in this religious world which was Rome and was learning, too, something of Roman wisdom:

The stay in Rome becomes more and more pleasant for me. Here the air is, in a way, pure and sanctified. All things lead to religion, speak of religion. You cannot take a step in the streets without finding an object that leads you to God. It is here that one enjoys the true liberty of the children of God. Here religious principles are not severe; both in their decisions and their practices, the way to heaven is gentle and easy. They are much less severe, much less punctilious than we in France.[38]

He had formed a close friendship with Trinchant with whom he often dined and walked. This contact proved the most important one Colin made in Rome, for Trinchant became a devoted friend of Colin and the Marists. Colin wrote of him later:

He knew the places, the persons; he brought me everywhere, and right up to those people who could get me what I wanted, and, by his help, I obtained all. I placed my trust in him and told him quite simply all our affair. I made him *au courant* of everything. He was enraptured, amazed and he took our affair more to heart that any of us could have done![39]

Before he left Rome on 7 February 1834, Colin took the important decision

37. OM, doc. 303, 3.
38. OM, doc. 303, 4.
39. OM, doc. 427, 14. Paul Trinchant (1800-35) honorary canon of the diocese of Chartres and secretary to the bishop; postulator for the cause of St Jeanne de Lestonnac. He came to Rome because of bad health.

of asking Trinchant to look after the Society's interests. He could not have made a better choice. Perhaps the knowledge that the affairs of the Society were in the hands of such an able and devoted friend to the project gave Colin courage, for, despite what Castracane had said, he returned to France optimistically enough. He arrived at the Capucinière on 21 February 1834 to a warm welcome. Peter Chanel described how delighted the boys in the college were to see him. In the refectory there was a joyful uproar: 'Music, cakes, wine, our youngsters lacked for nothing.'[40]

It was generally believed that approbation would come sooner or later. The very fact of having treated with Rome and having discussed the Marist project with the cardinals and that the dossier was under active consideration by the Congregation gave Colin a certain standing. About this time, he left the college and moved to where he had wanted to go the year before – the Marists' own house, the Capucinière, which Colin called affectionately 'the cradle of the Society'. Colin was happy enough as he told Champagnat:

> The Society of Mary has been seriously examined, and brought to the Congregation of Regulars ... The aim of my journey was solely to consult about our enterprise and to fulfil a vow which I had made long ago to work at the project until it had been submitted to the Sovereign Pontiff; so, from the outset, I stated clearly that it was in no way a matter of seeking the approbation of the Society, for which we would later present more complete rules, but for the moment we sought only advice and the Holy See's consent to continue the enterprise.[41]

The importance for Colin of the vow he had taken is evident. At an earlier stage in his life he felt compelled to take on the burden of seeing the project through, at least until the Holy Father had pronounced on it. The responsibility he had reluctantly assumed when he feared that the project was foundering, he had now discharged. His categorical claim, however, that he was in no way seeking the approbation of the Society, is surprising, for the obvious understanding of his appeal to Rome was to obtain approbation. This, moreover, would appear to be the thrust of the Marists' supplication to Pope Gregory on 23 August 1833 when Colin was setting out for Rome. Both, however, can be understood as seeking encouragement to go further with the project or asking for more than they dared hope for. It may also be that early on, during his stay in Rome, Colin realised that more work had to be done and that, in his discussions with the Curia, he already had lowered his sights accordingly. For the moment he was putting the best gloss he could on the results of his trip.

40. OM, doc. 306.
41. OM, doc. 307.

Colin still had to face down major obstacles in Belley. Devie remained hostile to the project and was not above telling him that he had come back empty-handed. The bishop had not yet abandoned his attempt to hold on to this talented priest and his companions. It was at this time that the incident of the camail occurred.[42] The camail or mozzetta, the short cape which canons wore, was a stylish little vestment, in blue or purple with red or scarlet trimmings complete with rabbit-fur. Several times Devie offered it to Colin, who always found a way to evade the question. Then one day Devie said to him: 'Father Pichat left you some camails.' 'Yes, your Lordship,' replied Father [Colin]. 'Would you please bring them here?' requested the bishop. Colin, guessing what was in Devie's mind, obediently brought the camails but left them with the porter at the bishop's palace. Finally he could dodge no longer. On 15 June, Devie made him a canon of the cathedral and chief vicar general of the diocese.

Despite the pressure in Belley, Colin, apparently encouraged by reports from Trinchant, still had hopes of Roman approval and waited anxiously for the decision of the Congregation. Finally, on 21 March, he wrote to Odescalchi informing him that Trinchant was now his agent, renewing his request for approval and promising to use the Cardinal's instructions as the very first rules of the society.[43] It is clear from this letter that, despite what he had conceded to Castracane earlier, he still cherished hopes for a broader approval for his plan. His request set off a whole train of events. The sequence of these events proved important.

The immediate effect of his letter was to stir the Congregation into activity, though with consequences Colin would not have wished. The Prefect, Odescalchi and the Secretary, Archbishop Canali, signed Castracane's letters to Devie and de Pins, dating them 8 April. Before they could be sent, however, the decision of the Congregation, like all such Curial decisions, had to be sanctioned by the pope in an official audience. For some reason the audience to sanction the Congregation's decisions of 21 January was delayed until 20 June. On that date Pope Gregory approved the decisions to reject Colin's project and granted the indulgences, but to the priests' branch alone.

Three days after the audience, important changes took place in the staff of the Congregation for Bishops and Regulars. Giovanni Soglia replaced Canali as the Congregation's Secretary. Soglia was unfamiliar with the Marist case but, following correct procedure, he sent the papal decision to the Congregation of Indulgences whose task it was to prepare the Briefs announcing the indulgences. Normally, the Briefs would then be sent to de Pins and Devie and that would also be the appropriate time to send the

42. OM, doc. 523, e.
43. OM, doc. 308.

letters explaining why Colin's project had been rejected. The information that the Congregation of Bishops and Regulars sent to the Congregation of Indulgences, however, was inadequate. As a result, the Congregation of Indulgences thought that the Society of Mary and the lay Marian Confraternity mentioned in the correspondence were one and the same, and it granted the indulgences to this lay Confraternity. The three briefs announcing this grant to the 'Marian confraternity' of Belley, signed by Gregory XVI, were sent to Colin on 12 and 14 August 1834.[44] The action of the Congregation of Indulgences ran counter to the decision of the Congregation of Bishops and Regulars which, at its meeting of January, on Castracane's advice, had explicitly confined the grant to the priests' branch alone. The issuing of those briefs meant that the lay confraternity had received the approbation of the Holy See.

Profiting from this unintentional approval, Colin's agent, Trinchant, withdrew Colin's original application for approbation for the whole Society and sent in a fresh request, omitting all mention of the lay confraternity.[45] He knew that the lay confraternity had proved a major stumbling block and, when he saw that it had been approved, he astutely seized the opportunity to resubmit Colin's project unhampered by that obstacle. His action prevented the Congregation from taking any immediate decision, for it would have to examine the revised application before the letters to the bishops could be sent. Castracane again examined the request but, though he noted that the request concerning the confraternity had been dropped, he was as opposed as ever. Even Colin, he said, considered this society with four branches nothing less than a delirium. Then, surprisingly after such scathing criticism, he added, with typically Roman prudence:

> It is not expedient, I believe, to give a reply that would express disapproval because I note, that, in fact, the three branches of the proposed Marian Society exist, and, as appears from the testimony of the bishops, not without advantage to these dioceses. To let them continue … is no proof of the Holy See's consent, benefits these dioceses, and hands the decision … back to the most prudent of all counsellors – Time – which will reveal the advisability or inadvisability of three Institutes under one sole Superior.[46]

After this cautious assessment, Castracane went on to renew his earlier advice that the priests be allowed to elect a superior, though on condition that they realise that this did in no way entail canonical approval. In conclusion, he advised that the letters to the bishops be now dispatched for that

44. OM, docs 312-16.
45. OM, docs 326-7.
46. OM, doc. 335, 8.

might stop the Marists from coming back to bother the Congregation again. He adjusted the letters to the bishops to allow for the omission of the confraternity in the revised request Trinchant had made. The threat of extinction, which the letters posed, once more hung over the society. For some unaccountable reason, however, the letters remained in the office of the Congregation and were never sent. What happened to Castracane's new report is not known. Perhaps Castracane himself decided to give that prudent counsellor 'Time' a chance. Perhaps it was bureaucratic inefficiency compounded by changes in personnel. More likely, it was deliberate interference by Paul Trinchant, Colin's friend and agent. According to Colin, he had stopped the letter that the Congregation was to send to Devie and de Pins.[47] His ability in dealing with the Congregation was demonstrated in August 1834 when his new draft forced a complete reconsideration of the case.[48] It is not improbable that, knowing Castracane's unfavourable report and his request that the letters be sent, Trinchant managed to persuade someone in the Congregation to wait till things developed further or until he prepared a new petition. One of the *minutanti* or clerks, at the Congregation for Bishops and Regulars, Canon Giovanni Crociani, was involved in Marist affairs from 1833 to 1853 and was well-disposed towards Colin.[49] Father Victor Poupinel, a reliable observer, who accompanied Colin on his second trip to Rome in 1842, related that Crociani was 'enchanted by the Father's [Colin's] modesty, by the prudence he noticed in him and even by his patience'.[50] Crociani, at Trinchant's request, may well have played a part in shielding Colin's project. Some action by Trinchant seems the most satisfactory explanation of what happened. Colin said later that 'during the efforts to obtain approbation, he wrote to me many times, and I kept all his letters; they could be of use some day.' Sadly, that correspondence has been lost, destroyed, no doubt, when Colin burned his papers.

On 24 August 1835, a year after he submitted the revised Marist project to the Congregation, Trinchant died at the age of 35. Colin said later of him: 'Ah!, yes, we owe him great gratitude.' Mayet went to some pains to find out more about Trinchant. He was impressed by what he heard and, remarking that the last act of his life was his representation on behalf of the Society, declared: 'May he always be inscribed in our hearts and in our annals as Marist and in the heart of the Blessed Virgin.' In Chartres, Mayet was told that Trinchant was admirable both for his zeal and charity, one old man

47. OM, docs 317, 8; 427, 15-16 and footnote 3; 535, 37-8.
48. OM, doc. 308.
49. Little is known about Giovanni Crociani except that he was a canon and a *minutante* or minute writer of the Congregation of Bishop and Regulars.
50. OM, doc. 544, 6.

going so far as to say that he had never met a confessor to compare with him. After praising Trinchant as a zealous, charitable man, Mayet added: 'Mary, you sent him to Rome for the sake of your little Society.'[51] To this kindly, efficient priest, Colin and the Marists owe very much.

For whatever cause, then, the Marist file appears to have been put aside and forgotten. Nothing was to be heard about it until a year later when the needs of the universal Church caused it to be brought out again.

51. OM, doc. 427, 14-17, k.

CHAPTER 16

Approbation and Mission

'I would like you ... to understand that the Sacred Congregation was primarily led to approve your Society so as to make you more eager to take on the difficult task of the mission, so that devoting to it your splendid energies, you plant the Catholic faith in southern Polynesia.' Cardinal Castracane to Colin, 12 March 1836.

On a July day in 1835, Jean Cholleton, vicar general of Lyon and close friend of the Marists, had just finished Mass in the cathedral of Saint-Jean in Lyon when a worried canon came up to speak to him.[1] He was Jean-Louis Pastre, a retired missioner.[2] 'Cardinal Fransoni, the Prefect of Propaganda, wrote to me from Rome,' Pastre told Cholleton, 'to offer me the mission of Western Oceania.' Why the head of a Roman Congregation should disturb a retired priest with the fantastic offer of a mission constituting such an enormous area of the globe, is an absorbing story.[3]

Giacomo Fransoni was the Cardinal in charge of the Congregation of Propaganda Fide which co-ordinated Catholic mission policy.[4] One new area that had opened up for mission work was the vast area of the Pacific which was coming to be called Oceania. Protestant missioners had begun to evangelise, but there remained many lands where the gospel had not yet been preached and, moreover, Catholic and Protestant regarded each other's mission as flawed or worse. In 1825, Propaganda had entrusted the mission in Hawaii to the Fathers of the Sacred Hearts of Jesus and Mary or Picpus Fathers, founded in 1800 by Father Marie-Joseph-Pierre Coudrin.

1. OM, doc. 657, 1.
2. Jean-Louis Pastre (1779-1839) b. Fenestrella in Piedmont; ordained for diocese of Lyon, 1808; missioner in Bourbon Island, 1817-28; apostolic prefect, 1822; returned to France, 1828; titular canon of Saint-Jean's Cathedral, Lyon, 1829.
3. Valuable studies of this section are Reiner Jaspers, *Die Missionarische Erschliessung Ozeaniens* (Münster, 1972), pp 186-95; Ralph M. Wiltgen, *The Founding of the Roman Catholic Church in Oceania, 1825-1850* (Canberra, 1979), pp 101-21; Mauro Filippucci, 'La ripresa dell'attività missionaria nel primo ottocento: la Società di Maria e l'Oceania' (Tesi di Laurea, Università degli Studi di Bari, 1984-5). This thesis is a thorough account of the beginnings of the Marists and of the Oceania mission.
4. Giacomo Fransoni (1775-1856), b. Genoa; nuncio to Portugal, 1823; cardinal 1826; prefect of Propaganda, 1834-56.

At much the same time, Peter Dillon, a red-haired Irish sea-captain, who had sailed the Pacific for many years, came on the scene.[5] Dillon had achieved fame, when, in 1826, sailing north of the New Hebrides in his small ship, the *Saint Patrick,* he had located, in the Santa Cruz archipelago, the long-lost wreck of the celebrated expedition of La Pérouse that had sailed from Botany Bay in February 1778. For this discovery King Charles x had knighted Dillon, awarding him an annual pension and making him a Chevalier of the Légion d'Honneur, a title in which he took pride. In 1829, Dillon told the rector of the Irish College in Paris, Father Patrick McSweeny, of his plan to bring Catholic missioners to the Pacific islands and McSweeny had put him in contact with Father Henri de Solages, vicar general of the diocese of Pamiers, near Toulouse, in southern France.[6] De Solages' great ambition in life was to work for the people of 'the South Sea Islands'. In 1829 he had accepted being appointed prefect apostolic to Bourbon or Reunion Island, some 700 kilometres east of Madagascar, in order to use it as a launching pad for the evangelisation of Oceania.[7] He met Dillon and together they had matured their plans. De Solages so impressed Propaganda that in January 1830, it had entrusted the whole of the South Sea Islands to him. In 1832, however, it removed the eastern section from his jurisdiction and confided it to the Picpus Fathers. De Solages had died shortly before this decision was made and Propaganda, unwilling to entrust the whole area of the Pacific Islands to the Picpus Fathers lest they be overstretched, decided to look for someone to replace him. This was why Fransoni wrote to the mission-minded and experienced Canon Pastre in Lyon. This Piedmontese priest had been a missionary on the Bourbon Island and had become its prefect apostolic. In 1828, however, he had returned to France to seek more help for his mission. While he was there, he found that his health was not good and he did not return to the missions. A priest of the diocese of Lyon and an honorary canon of the Cathedral of Saint-Jean, he had settled down to a quiet life of retirement. Fransoni's letter disturbed this peaceful existence. He replied to Fransoni on 17 July giving his reasons for not accepting the offer:

> What use could a priest be who has none of the necessary knowledge of what is suitable for a vicar apostolic? Especially, how, at the age of fifty-five, could he learn new languages, go round Cape Horn, Tierra del Fuego, or force himself to traverse the immense forests of southern America?[8]

5. Peter Dillon (1788-1847). A colourful person and, in ways, a character of contradictions. J. W. Davidson, *Peter Dillon of Vanikoro: Chevalier of the South Seas,* ed. O.H.K. Spate (Melbourne, Oxford, 1975), L. Jore, *L'Océan Pacifique au temps de la Restauration et de la Monarchie de Juillet (1815-1848),* vol. I, (Paris, 1959), pp 161-76.
6. Gabriel-Henri-Jérôme de Solages (1786-32); for a good account of the work of de Solages and Dillon, see, Wiltgen, *Church in Oceania,* pp 23-88.
7. Cited in Wiltgen, *Church in Oceania,* p. 24.
8. OM, doc. 338.

His poor health, too, made it impossible for him to return to the missions. Although he was unable to go himself, Pastre, anxious to help the mission in any way he could, began to cast around for someone else. This was why he had approached Cholleton that morning after Mass: 'It costs me a lot to refuse,' he told Cholleton. 'If only I had someone to offer to His Eminence. Would you know a priest who might be suitable?'[9] To his delight, Cholleton replied that he knew the very man, a young priest named Jean-Baptiste Pompallier. Pompallier was a bright, energetic, up-and-coming young priest, who had joined the Marists at the Hermitage in September 1829, shortly after his ordination. He had taken part in the election of Colin as central superior a year later. He often represented the Marists with the diocesan authorities in Lyon by whom he was well regarded. After 1832, however, while preaching retreats like the other Marists, he lived alone at Fourvière where he was chaplain to a group of laymen who had formed a Third Order of Mary. Pastre went to see him and was impressed. Pompallier willingly accepted his invitation but needed to consult his colleagues. He wrote to Colin who strongly encouraged him to take the mission: 'It is with the greatest pleasure that I shall see you set out for this foreign mission,' he wrote, 'Do not refuse what the Lord himself offers to you. The same Providence will find you associates. Be full of courage, then.'[10] Only then did Colin mention the possible role of the Marists:

You will usefully serve the Society of Mary in devoting yourself to the salvation of these poor infidels. It seems to me that God requests from the Society that devotion ... So, the offer which Father Pastre will make to the Prefect of Propaganda of members of the Society to replace him in this mission could only be very welcome and advantageous to the Society.

It is possible that it was Pompallier who suggested to Colin the opportunity which Fransoni's request offered, for a few months later he told Champagnat that 'the mission in itself is subordinate in my mind; and the obtaining of a brief of authorisation or at least of centralisation for the recently founded Society of Mary, is uppermost. If that takes place, I shall be quite content to go to the ends of the world, to the islands of the Pacific Ocean'[11] Whether or not Pompallier first suggested the link between acceptance of the mission and approbation of the Society, Colin, on whom the ultimate responsibility for the group rested, showed himself both generous and perceptive. While encouraging Pompallier to work for 'poor infidels', he saw the opening for the Society and seized it. He was taking a major decision. Yet it was not mere opportunism. Already in his letter to Pius VII in 1822, Colin had made clear this readiness to engage in foreign missions 'in whatever part of the world to which the

9. OM, doc. 657.
10. OM, doc. 340, 1.
11. OM, doc. 347, 5

Apostolic See would wish to send us.' The same phrase 'in whatever part of the world' recurs in the Appeal of the Marists aspirants of August 1833 and in the *Summarium* of the rule which he presented to Rome later that year.

Colin, who had by no means abandoned the hope of obtaining approval for the brothers' branch, went on to say: 'But in his letter Father Pastre must … mention the branch of the priests and the branch of the brothers who could both devote themselves to this mission.'[12] He did not, however, mention the sisters.

When Pompallier, armed with this letter, confirmed to Pastre his readiness to accept the mission, the canon was delighted. On 7 August he wrote to Fransoni to report his success:

> As regards the apostolic vicariate of the Friendly Islands, Fiji etc. etc. and New Zealand, I have spoken confidentially to a priest of the Society called Marists. This Society, which up to this has the sanction of only the bishops of Lyon and Belley but which is very soon to be approved by Apostolic authority, differs only slightly from the Society of Jesuits in respect of its function and rules.[13]

This Marist priest, Pastre said, had received an encouraging letter from his superior which Pastre now enclosed, although Colin had never intended that his frank letter to Pompallier would find its way to the Congregation of Propaganda in Rome. Pastre did not mention Pompallier's name. This was written on the outside of Colin's letter which, however, was detached before it reached the cardinals of Propaganda. As a result, it was months later before they learned the name of the priest he recommended.

Pastre wrote again to Fransoni on 2 September in reply to his further query about the extent of government support and the availability of missioners. He told Fransoni that five would suffice to begin the mission and he was sure he could get that number without going outside the diocese of Lyon. Then, in confidence, he disclosed to Fransoni that Archbishop de Pins, 'the ordinary of this diocese, which provides so many subjects for different congregations and missions, would welcome a recommendation which the Sacred Congregation might make to him for this or that mission'. After his letter, Pastre added an important postscript stating that de Pins 'approves the offer of the Marists for the mission in question.'[14]

Meanwhile, on 12 September, into this involved story of Propaganda's search for missioners for Oceania, there now entered a new name – Father Marin Ducrey. Fransoni had not replied to Pastre's letter of 7 August but on 12 September had written to Ducrey, the founder of a clerical school and later a

12. OM, doc. 340, 1.
13. OM, doc. 341.
14. OM, doc. 343.

minor seminary at Mélan, Tenninges, near Annecy in Savoy.[15] Like Pastre and many French clergy of the time, Ducrey had a special interest in the missions and was enthusiastic in spreading the Lyon-based Association for the Propagation of the Faith. He encouraged the students in his minor seminary to think about a missionary vocation. To ensure the continuation of his minor seminary, he had sought unsuccessfully to persuade various religious orders to staff it. He also approached Propaganda, and Castracane, the secretary, came to Savoy to meet him and visited the seminary in October 1832. A transfer of the minor seminary to Propaganda involved many difficulties from the civil authorities and nothing came of the venture. Finally, with Propaganda's consent, Ducrey handed over the minor seminary to the French Jesuits in October 1833. Fransoni, who was in contact with him and knew he no longer ran the minor seminary, wrote to him in December 1833 to tell him about a mission he was preparing and to ask could he send the names and addresses of two suitable priests. Ducrey never replied. Now, nearly two years later, in September 1835, Fransoni wrote again reminding him of his previous request and telling him about a new mission:

> In December of 1833, I informed you that, as a result of your communication, the Congregation would count on you for two priests, students of your seminary in Mélan, to send as missioners … and asked you to give their names, surnames, qualities, and addresses … Since I am now thinking of opening another most interesting mission in Southern Oceania, I am letting you know about it, so that if you should have some suitable and zealous priests to propose for it from among those educated for the missions in the … seminary, you would be so kind as to give me the relevant details.[16]

15. Marin Ducrey (1766-1834), b. Savoy; ord. 1792; refused the oath to the Civil Constitution; founded minor seminary, 1809; zealous promoter of Society for the Propagation of the Faith in Savoy and Italy. F. Marullaz, 'Histoire de Mélan; Rev Marin Ducrey et le collège de Mélan (1804-1834)', *Mémoires et documents de l'Académie salésienne* 42 (1922), 1-191; C. Sorrel, 'Marin Ducrey - Prêtre séculier, enseignant', *La Savoie, Dictionnaire du Monde Religieux dans la France Contemporaine,* vol. 8, (Paris, 1996), pp 172-3.

16. Fransoni to Ducrey, 14 Dec 1833, Lettere, decreti della Sacra Congregazione e Biglietti di Monsignore Segretario, 1833, vol. 314 ff. 843; Fransoni to Ducrey, 12 Sept 1835; 1835, vol. 316 ff. 672-3, Propaganda Fide Archives. Ralph Wiltgen on P.107 of his authoritative work on the Church in Oceania suggests that Fransoni, put on his guard by Colin's letter which Pastre enclosed with his own reply, was now offering the mission to Ducrey. In his letters of December 1833 and September 1835, however, Fransoni asked only for the names, addresses and qualities of suitable priests. There is no mention of offering the mission to Ducrey. Fransoni knew for two years that Ducrey had given his college to the Jesuits in 1833, and so had no college from which to furnish a body of missionaries. Moreover, Colin's letter does not appear to have upset Propaganda for when Propaganda examined the case for setting up the vicariate of Western Oceania, it was cited favourably. Fransoni, who had contacts with Ducrey through his brother, Luigi Fransoni, Archbishop of Turin, casting around for possible missionaries and knowing how keen Ducrey was on promoting missionary vocations, was hoping he could find some suitable priests.

Nothing came of this approach, however, for the good reason that Ducrey had died a year and a half before. Ten days after writing to Ducrey and before he could have expected a reply, Fransoni turned to Archbishop de Pins in Lyon. Taking advantage of Pastre's welcome, if confidential, assurance that the archbishop would support any demand for priests for the new mission, Fransoni warmly complimented de Pins and assured him that he would put the matter before the Congregation. In a sense, he was presenting de Pins with a fait accompli.[17] The letter, which was quite brief, confined itself to this one matter. De Pins did not reply until 20 November, some two months later! The well-informed Pompallier told Champagnat what had happened: Fransoni's letter had lain forgotten among the papers of de Pins' secretary for over a month. Cholleton, Pompallier's informant, told him of the contents which he in turn conveyed to Colin, Champagnat and the others. The news was good, Pompallier commented. A week later, on 20 November 1835, de Pins replied to Fransoni. He first reassured Fransoni that he intended to find the best workers for the new mission and went on to say:

> Already the Society of the priests of Mary, which works with success in the dioceses of Lyon and Belley and, at this moment, is seeking approbation from the Holy See, could provide five or six good subjects to begin with and will take on the task of maintaining the necessary number of missionaries. For its part, the Association of the Propagation of the Faith will do all in its power to include this mission in the grants it distributes.[18]

De Pins' reply to Fransoni shows that the Marists had his full support and that it was they, and no others, that he had in mind for the mission. This letter is important because it brought the Roman Curia to reconsider the Marist project. Although de Pins does not mention Colin, the specific promise that the Society of Mary would supply five or six missionaries right away and would maintain a supply in the future could only have come from an engagement given by the central superior of Marists. It is clear that Colin had been in contact with de Pins, moving quickly and decisively in the hope of clinching a deal on approval. Colin had committed the Marists to a challenging enterprise. It remained to be seen how Propaganda would react.

This letter was welcome news for Propaganda and it scheduled a general meeting for 20 December to decide on the question. As was customary, a reporter was appointed to examine all aspects of the question and to report to the Congregation and put before it the questions that had to be decided. Although the seventy-two year old Cardinal Fesch was originally designated for the task, it was Castracane who presented it, and an expert in the Congregation

---

17. OM, doc. 344. Filippucci, 'Ripresa dell'attività missionaria', p. 156.
18. OM, doc. 349.

probably drew it up. The report contained twenty-one points or paragraphs. Nineteen of these dealt with the history and advisability of setting up this new vicariate of Western Oceania, concluding with a section on the inadvisability of confiding it to the over-stretched Picpus Fathers. The last two points focused on whether or not it should be confided to the Marists.[19] Colin's letter to Pompallier and de Pins' letter to Fransoni were singled out for attention. The report went over the recent history, how Pastre had communicated the project to a priest of the Lyon diocese whose name it did not know. This priest was also a member of the Society of Mary, existing in the dioceses of Lyon and Belley though it had not yet been approved by the Holy See, from which it had received only a Brief of Praise. This was not quite accurate for the Society had not received a Brief of Praise but only a letter from Pius VII praising the work. The report went on to say that the unnamed priest had consulted with his colleagues and his superior and summarised Colin's letter declaring that the mission was in keeping with the work of the Institute, but asking that the Marists should first be organised into a group and await a bull of approval from the Holy See. Turning to de Pins' letter, the report referred to his praise for the society and its readiness to provide the missionaries. It mentioned, too, his assurance that the Society for the Propagation of the Faith in Lyon would help financially. The report concluded with the customary questions to be decided: (1) Should a new apostolic vicariate be established in western Polynesia? (2) If the answer were affirmative, to whom should this new mission be confided?

The Congregation of Propaganda met on 23 December. Among the cardinals present were two who knew well the complicated negotiations for the approval of the society: Cardinals Castracane and Giuseppe-Antonio Sala.[20] Sala, the new prefect of the Congregation of Bishops and Regulars, had early knowledge of the Marists, for it was he who replied to their letter to Pius VII in 1822. Although not long prefect of the Congregation, he was in a position to be informed about the previous year's meeting on the Marist project. On the first point as to whether a new apostolic vicariate be established in western Polynesia, the cardinals present decided in the affirmative. They then debated the second point – to whom should the mission be confided. Sala urged that Father Colin should be encouraged to take on the mission by holding out the hope of Roman approval for his Marist society. Castracane, however, asked that such approval be limited to the priests' branch. The Congregation finally took two decisions. The first was to set up the vicariate in Oceania. The second was to entrust the vicariate:

> to the Priests of the Marian Congregation of Lyon and Belley; that, through both the Archbishop Administrator and Father Pastre, every effort be made

19. OM, doc. 351, 20-1.
20. Most curial cardinals were members of more than one Roman Congregation.

to ensure that the Marists' superior not withdraw from the task of the mission, by holding out to him the hope of receiving the approval of the priests' branch of his congregation.[21]

The decisions were taken on the basis of these interventions of Sala and Castracane. They were to shape the future history of the Marists. A society composed of four branches would not materialise. On the other hand, the approval of the Society was irrevocably linked with the mission to Oceania. Had it not accepted the mission, Colin's project might have languished for years. As we have seen, however, even from the years at Cerdon, Colin had stated the Marists' willingness to work for the salvation of souls, 'in whatever part of the world'. The link then between mission and approval which Castracane was affirming was a natural one, in line with the original thrust of the Society.

The next to enter this complicated process was Pope Gregory XVI, for Propaganda's decision needed the pope's confirmation in an official audience. Quite early after the Christmas holiday, Monsignor Angelo Mai, secretary to Propaganda, arranged this audience. He had drawn up a handwritten account of what took place at the meeting of Propaganda and of Castracane's report. His account introduced one major change from that report: the territory included in the new vicariate had been greatly enlarged. The boundaries now stretched from the vicariate of the Picpus Fathers in eastern Oceania to New Guinea and from the Marianas and Marshall Islands in the north to New Zealand in the south. Mai mentioned Colin's willingness to accept the mission, together with his request for prior approval of his society and Propaganda's decision that he should be given well-founded hopes for such approval. The audience with Gregory took place on 10 January 1836. It would be little more than a formality, for Gregory was devoted to the missions. When he had become Cardinal Prefect of Propaganda in 1826, he had enthusiastically re-organised and reinvigorated it. He it was who had promoted the first efforts to provide missionaries for Oceania and had signed the decree of 1830 confiding the mission to de Solages. He would have been pleased to see the efforts to provide for that mission at last on the verge of success. At the audience of 10 January Gregory gave full approval. On 23 January Fransoni wrote to de Pins and to Pastre telling them of the decision to set up the mission and to entrust it to the Marists. He asked both of them to do all in their power to persuade Colin not to refuse the mission, by holding out to him the hope of approval of the priests' branch of the Marists.[22] Two needs had converged – the Marists' desire for approbation and the Church's desire to evangelise Oceania.

Fransoni's letters came not a moment too soon. Strains were beginning to tell within Marist ranks. Perhaps the tension of waiting for approval was

21. OM, doc. 352.
22. OM, docs 359, 360.

beginning to take its toll. The separation into two very different dioceses was making unity of purpose difficult. The problem arose particularly as regards the community at Valbenoîte. The curé, Jean-Baptiste Rouchon, who had thoughts of becoming a Marist himself until dissuaded by Colin, had invited them there on the understanding that they help him in the parish, but be free to give missions. The priests had come there in November 1832 and one of them, Étienne Séon, had been elected superior of the priests' branch in Lyon, in an effort to give it its own structure and identity. Things did not work out well. Champagnat complained to Cholleton and to Colin that the priests were too involved in the parish work and had time neither for recollection nor for preparing their mission work. It was no training for religious life. Generously, Champagnat offered to give the priests' branch a fine property at Grange-Payre, near the Hermitage, which he had inherited. His plan, as he explained to the vicar general, Cholleton, was to bring all the priests from Valbenoîte there except Séon who would help out Rouchon.[23] He asked Colin to send Pierre Colin from Belley to the new house to direct the Marist aspirants there. Colin was very touched by Champagnat's generosity and concern for the Society but disappointed at the reaction of some of the Lyon priests. He encouraged Champagnat to try to reawaken a spirit of faith among them, remarking: 'Ho! How very far all of us are still from the attitudes which the first Jesuits, the first Franciscans etc. had.'[24] Colin was prepared to send his brother Pierre there, but wanted to wait until Cholleton would reply in the name of the diocese. When some time later Champagnat again approached Cholleton expressing his fears that the priests' branch at Valbenoîte would founder and renewed his offer of Grange-Payre, Colin, while praising his generosity and commitment, advised him to proceed cautiously:

> I must, nevertheless, tell you some little fears I have in relation to your excellent proposal of transferring the cradle of the Society of Mary in Lyon to your house near Saint-Chamond. I fear that Father Séon is tiring of it and would use this as an opportunity to withdraw, which would be very inconvenient. Arrange everything with peace and gentleness. Your views are good but, if you cannot execute them without disturbing the peace and the union of hearts, one must temporise and take the time needed to know better and better the most holy will of Jesus and Mary.[25]

Although Colin, always ready to put the success of the project first, advised patience, difficulties persisted with the Lyon group and a year later he was still grappling with some problems there, though what they were is not clear. Some of the Lyon priests, it appears, did not like all the decisions taken in the remote

23. OM, doc. 321, 3-4.
24. OM, doc. 322, 1.
25. OM, doc. 324, 2.

diocese of Belley. By the end of 1835, Colin was losing patience. He thought it might be necessary to concentrate all the Marists in Belley but Cholleton advised him against this drastic solution. On 19 January 1836, a frustrated Colin told Champagnat that his wish, 'the most ardent of my heart', was to be rid of the thankless job of central superior. Cholleton should be in that place. Until that change was made, however, he, Colin, as central superior should be in charge of all negotiations with the bishops and of all new enterprises. Otherwise the Marists would get nowhere. What should we do, he asked rhetorically, if we really want the work to succeed?

> We should agree more than ever among ourselves; we should enter no nego-
> tiations with the administrations of Belley or Lyon without having first
> come to an agreement among ourselves. The certainty that I never do any-
> thing without Father Cholleton, should remove from you all disquiet, all
> fear that I put the interests of Belley before those of Lyon. Moreover, all I
> want to see is the general good of the Society, whose principal aim is to be
> united and to work together with the bishops.

Colin's rejection of any intention of favouring the Belley branch is con-vincing. The general good of the Society, as always, is what Colin claims to be his guiding principle and he believes in the importance of his own role as super-ior. While his plaintive letter revealed his frustration, it also showed his determination that the Society should be run on the lines he was sure were right. He was disappointed at the disunity of purpose that had crept into the members of the Society. From this he exempted Champagnat and Pompallier:

> It is in you and Father Pompallier that I have most trust; it is in you two
> that I find most that religious spirit so necessary for the success of such a
> work. I am not far from thinking that it will be by you also that the Society
> will consolidate itself in the diocese of Lyon.[26]

Roman approval could not have come at a more opportune time. That news was enough to silence all dissension. Pope Gregory had approved Propaganda's decision to offer the Oceanian mission to the Marists and to hold out to them the prospect of approbation. By early February, Fransoni's letters of 23 January to de Pins and Pastre had been communicated to the Marists. All now changed. The euphoria that the impending approval of the Society of Mary created swept away whatever minor crisis the Society was experiencing. Colin's persev-erance and leadership had been vindicated; his vision realised. Dissension van-ished. A delighted Colin wrote to both Castracane and Fransoni on 10 February 1836 telling them of the joy the news had brought:

> The priests of the Society, to whom the Archbishop of Amasea [de Pins]
> communicated the letter, joyfully seize this favourable opportunity to fulfil

26. OM, doc. 358, 4.

one of the goals of their Society and full of confidence in the help of Jesus and Mary accept with gratitude the proposed mission.[27]

Since, however, the Oceanian mission would disperse the members of the Society, Colin made the not unreasonable request that the Holy See help them bond together beforehand by allowing them to take the vows of religion. This, he pleaded, should be accorded at least to the priests of the Society. It is note-worthy that he says 'the priests of the Society' not 'the Society of Priests'! Although he realised that if approbation came now it would only be for the priests, it is clear from this choice of words that he still regarded all Marists as forming only one society. Approval of the priests' branch would be a beginning, however, and Colin redoubled his appeals, turning to Pastre and to de Pins ask-ing them to second his efforts. Two other matters concerned him. He wanted permission for Marists to take simple vows from which the superior could dis-pense. He also wanted to revise the rule for he believed that he would need to have it sanctioned before the society was approved.

Colin's worries were groundless. What he did not know was that the Congregation of Bishops and Regulars had already taken in hand the request for approbation. After the audience with the pope on 10 January, Sala, the card-inal prefect of that Congregation, drew up a letter to send to de Pins in Lyon. Since he was not long in his job and was unfamiliar with the difficulties that had blocked the Marist project in 1834, Sala consulted Castracane. Castracane, after explaining what the difficulties were, wrote a new paragraph for insertion in the letter, which stated bluntly that Colin's project had failed because it pro-posed a four-branched society under one superior which he condemned as 'quite abnormal and unheard of'. Once again, the Marist project faced major embarrassment, if this were part of the official document arriving in Lyon. Sala, however, although he duly included Castracane's paragraph in his letter to de Pins on 28 January 1836, struck out the harsh comment 'quite abnormal and unheard of', merely saying that 'it did not seem at all advisable to group together under one superior four different groups destined for different works'. He made the Curia's position as regards approval clear. 'If the society is presented for approval by the Apostolic See on behalf of the priests only,' he wrote, 'I have no doubt that the decision of the Sacred Congregation would be in favour of their request.'[28] This compromise was Sala's own suggestion at Propaganda's meeting, as modified by Castracane, where it had provided a solution to the problem.

The Congregation of Bishops and Regulars met on 11 March 1836, to decide on the question and again Castracane reported. Since Colin no longer held out

27. OM, docs 367, 1; 368.
28. OM, doc. 365, 1.

for the approval of the four branches of the society, there was no further problem. Furthermore, as Castracane noted, another factor had emerged: 'the new mission in Polynesia'. It would be advantageous to have the Marists because 'a congregation will be there which, as the number of missionaries diminishes, will always provide new ones.'[29] Castracane, who appeared a stumbling-block for Colin's endeavours, had been secretary to Propaganda when Pope Gregory was Cardinal Prefect and was genuinely interested in the mission for Oceania as other letters of his show. He did his best, too, to expedite matters. As for the question of simple vows and the superior's power to dispense from them, Castracane, despite his grave reservations the previous year, now raised no problem. The Sacred Congregation accepted his recommendations and decided to formally petition the pope for a brief of approval of 'the congregation of Priests of the Marian Society', with a faculty to the priests of the society to take 'the three simple vows from which the superior of the society can dispense.' On that same day, the Congregation's decision was brought to Gregory XVI who approved it and ordered an official Brief of Approval to be drawn up. The following day, the 12 March 1836, Castracane wrote to Colin, telling him that once he had dropped the idea of four branches there would be no difficulty about approval. He added:

> I would like you to understand, however, that the Sacred Congregation was led to approve your Society principally in order to make you more eager to take on the difficult task of the mission, so that devoting to it your splendid energies, you might plant the Catholic faith in southern Polynesia and with the help of God, who gives the increase, you will continue vigorously the work once begun. Commending myself to your prayers and to those of your priest colleagues, I remain at your service.[30]

The link between the approbation of the society and the mission of Oceania could not be more clearly stated.

In Rome, matters were rapidly approaching a finale. A copy of the decisions of the Congregation of Bishops and Regulars was sent to the Secretariat of Briefs. The Secretariat drafted a Brief and a summary of it was submitted to the pope. On 29 April 1836, Gregory XVI placed 'placet M', M standing for his name in religion 'Mauro', at the foot of the document. This placet or approval was the official act of approbation. The Brief was then properly prepared on parchment and sent to Colin. Towards the third week in May of that eventful year of 1836, the sealed Brief arrived in Belley. Jeantin who had apparently had an account from eyewitnesses described the scene:

> Unopened, it [the packet] was placed reverently on the table. All present approached it one by one, knelt and kissed it respectfully, as a sign of their

full and entire submission to what it contained. Then, having opened it, they saw what it was with a joy mingled with surprise and confusion.[31]

It was, indeed, what they had longed for – the official approval of the pope for the society – the Brief *Omnium Gentium.* It was dated 29 April 1836, the day Gregory had placed his placet on it. It was an important document, the most important the Marists had received to date, for it brought their society into official existence.[32] It ended years of struggle for Colin. His vow had been fulfilled for he had placed the project of a Society before the supreme authority in the Church. The head of the Church, after mature consideration, was convinced that the society, devoted to the glory of God and the honour of Mary, had a role to play in the salvation of the world. Colin's first great objective had been achieved – the Society of Mary had been approved. True, only the priests' branch had been approved, but it was a glorious beginning and everyone was overjoyed. Champagnat was quite overcome:

> To describe the joy, the happiness, the consolation Father Champagnat experienced when he got the news is quite impossible. After giving humble thanks to God for that marvellous favour, he wrote to Reverend Father asking to be allowed to take his religious vows.[33]

Champagnat must have felt a little sadness that the brothers had not been approved, but he knew from Colin the strength of the opposition at Rome, and he could hope that that approval might follow. Overjoyed, too, were Pierre Colin, Déclas, Terraillon – for whom it was the culmination of twenty years of praying, working and waiting – and the other Marists. Up the road in Belley, in the convent of Bon-Repos, Mother Saint Joseph, and her sisters, many of whom were relations of the priests, were among the first to know and to rejoice. From the time she had arrived at the presbytery of Cerdon, nearly twenty years before, she had made a powerful and sustained contribution to the project, undertaking missions to different diocesan authorities, sustaining Colin in doubt and difficulty, and always praying with total confidence in its success. Her joy now was great and, if the sisters were not yet approved, she, like Champagnat, felt a great beginning had been made. Even if all they sought had not been granted, the Marists had every right to be happy at Rome's decision. The Society of Mary would be approved and, at the same time, it would become an integral and important part of the Church's mission. It would attempt to realise the presence of Mary in the Church and would break new ground by bringing the gospel of Christ to places where it had not yet been

31. Jeantin, *Colin,* vol. 1, p. 289.
32. J. Coste, 'The Brief "Omnium Gentium"; two readings of a basic text', *Forum Novum,* 2 (1992), 29-49.
33. Furet, *Life of Champagnat,* pp 206-7.

proclaimed. The next few months would see how these twin decisions of approbation and mission would be put into practice.

CHAPTER 17

Professions and Partings

'In the year 1836, Saturday the 24 September, feast of Our Lady of Mercy, Jean Claude Colin … made the three simple and perpetual vows which he promised to observe according to the rules of the Society of Mary and the tenor of the Brief of the Sovereign Pontiff Gregory XVI.' Act of profession.

'on whatever distant shore'. *Summarium,* no. 42.[1]

Preparations to carry out the twin Roman decisions made that summer of 1836 a busy one, as Colin and the Marists prepared for the ceremony of the election of a superior general and of profession and for the departure for the mission. The two events, seen as complementary, were timed to take place as close as possible to each other: the ceremony on 24 September, the departure for Oceania on 25 October. In an area, such as Oceania, that had not been constituted into a diocese, it was normal to entrust its administration to a vicar apostolic, who would have all the powers of a bishop but would govern in the name of the pope. Who should be appointed to that office had now to be decided. Cholleton had recommended Pompallier. Colin, too, whatever he may have written later, had told Pompallier that 'At the present moment, I can scarcely see anyone but you who could fill the position'.[2] De Pins recommended him to Propaganda who nominated him as vicar apostolic. On 17 April, this nomination was approved by Pope Gregory and confirmed in a Brief of 13 May. Pompallier went to Rome to receive his appointment where he found the cardinals loud in their praise for Colin and for the generosity of the Society of Mary. On 30 June, he was ordained titular bishop of Maronea and vicar apostolic of the immense expanse of Western Oceania.[3] On his return to Lyon, Pompallier, who even before he went to Rome was already seeking both men and material for the mission, redoubled his preparations.

Before the departure for the mission, however, other momentous events would take place – the first profession of Marists and the election of a superior general. The preparation for this long-awaited event posed preliminary prob-

---

1. The literal translation of that key phrase *in quavis mundi plaga* which Colin included in the letter to Pius VII in 1822, in the *Summarium* and later in his constitutions is 'on whatever shore of the world'.
2. OM, doc. 340, 3.
3. OM, docs 387-90.

lems for Colin. It had to be decided not only where they should meet but who should be invited to take vows and elect the superior general. Since both de Pins and Devie wanted to claim the Marists, the first question was trickier than it appeared and later Colin said it placed the Society in 'great danger'! As he had done so often before, Colin went to Bon-Repos to seek the prayers of Jeanne-Marie Chavoin and the sisters. Later he related what happened:

> While I was waiting for a sister to present my request, I saw a painting of the Blessed Virgin represented as opening her arms. I knelt down and said to her: 'This is not my affair; it concerns you'. At that very moment the Blessed Virgin suggested to me the plan I should follow and I saw clearly what I should do.[4]

This simple, some might call it naïve, confidence in the Blessed Virgin was typical of Colin. The solution he believed the Virgin suggested to him was to announce that the Marists would meet in Belley to establish the Society, but that they would set up their motherhouse in Lyon. The compromise worked. It is worth remarking how naturally it occurred to Colin to go to the sisters at Bon-Repos. Not merely had the sisters a Marist priest as chaplain or superior but they saw themselves, and were so regarded, as an integral part of the society. The sisters still looked to Colin as the one singled out by God to lead them to full approbation and to give them the rule. Peter Chanel expressed the hope that the sisters could soon join them in Oceania, and others, though probably not Colin, would be of the same mind.[5] Neither the sisters nor the brothers could be present at the professions but they supported the priests in their deliberations with their constant prayer and eagerly awaited the outcome.

Who would be invited to that historic meeting and by what criterion they would be chosen is not clear. Including Pompallier, twenty-one arrived at Belley – one arriving late – to make the retreat to prepare them for the election and the profession. One or two more may have been invited but did not come. Of the original group who signed the promise of Fourvière, only four remained – Colin himself, Marcellin Champagnat, who had done so much for the project and had now 200 brothers in his care, Étienne Terraillon, curé at Saint-Chamond, and Étienne Déclas, still preaching missions. Pierre Colin, the earliest recruit, had come in 1817. He had been Colin's right-hand man and since the failure of Champagnat's scheme to put him in charge of a new house near the Hermitage, he was residing at Valbenoîte. The other sixteen had all joined after 1825 and mostly in the 1830s. Étienne Séon was superior of the Lyon priests, lived at Valbenoîte and conducted missions. Claude-Marie Chavas was also an assistant priest at Valbenoîte and was director to Claude Bret. Jean-Baptiste

---

4. OM, doc. 677.
5. C. Rozier, ed., *Écrits de Pierre Chanel* (Rome, 1960), doc. 31; RMJ, doc. 169.

Pompallier must also be counted, for he played an important role at the meeting and voted for the superior general. Now bishop and prefect-apostolic and actively preparing for the mission, he had relinquished the post as chaplain to the school run by the Third Order at La Favorite, in the western suburb of Lyon. Jean Forest had replaced him and was living in the Fourvière Tower where Pompallier had resided when in that apostolate. Catherin Servant was at the Hermitage with Champagnat. He had volunteered for Oceania. Two others – Jean-Marie Humbert and Antoine Jallon – were missioners working with Déclas and living in the Capucinière in Belley. Humbert had been bursar at the College in Belley and retained that role at the Capucinière. Denis Maîtrepierre was not living in a Marist community, though in 1829 he had sold his possessions and given the proceeds to the Marists. He had an important position as superior of another minor seminary in the diocese, Meximieux, a hamlet halfway between Cerdon and Lyon. Chanel, Colin's companion in Rome, was a gentle soul, not tough enough for his post as vice-superior in the College at Belley. Bret had come from Valbenoîte for the meeting. He had been one of the first to volunteer for the mission and to cling to his decision despite the pleas of his family. He was the first of the group to die, barely six months later. Chanel, Maîtrepierre and Bret had been friends since they studied together at the seminary of Meximieux.[6] They had intended to go on the American mission with the then superior, Pierre Loras, the future bishop of Dubuque. Apparently, Devie would not permit it and may have pushed them towards the Marists whom he still had in mind to become his diocesan missioners. Jean-Antoine Bourdin, Colin's other companion in Rome, was teaching the humanities and rhetoric in the minor seminary of Belley. The thirty-year-old Pierre Convers had been vice-superior of the College, but from 1834 he was in charge of the Capucinière. Then there was the twenty-nine-year-old Antoine Séon, who had been four years at the College at Belley, first as prefect and then as both director of the students and bursar. Jean-Baptiste Chanut, who arrived at the meeting in Belley two days late, was also twenty-nine and had been teaching theology in the Capucinière. Pierre Bataillon, the latest recruit, was but twenty-six. He had joined the Marists with the foreign missions firmly in view. Even younger was another of the most recent recruits – the twenty-five-year-old Claude-André Baty – who was also resident at the Capucinière, probably giving some classes there. If Baty was the youngest, Déclas, at 53, was the oldest. The average age of the twenty priests was 36. Only one left subsequently – Jean-Baptiste Chanut.

The background of the group is of interest. All of them came from the area bounded by the three departments of the Rhone, the Loire and the Ain. Five were from the department of the Ain, eight from the Loire and a further eight .

6. Humbert, Mayet, Théodore Millot, Pastre, Pichat also studied at Meximieux.

from the Rhone, including three from the city of Lyon. The majority – 14 of the 21 – came from the country. The fathers of ten of them – the two Colins, Déclas, Étienne Séon, Forest, Servant, Humbert, Maîtrepierre, Chanel, Bourdin and Bataillon – were farmers who owned their land. Three more – Terraillon, Baty and, possibly, Jallon – were farmers who rented the land they tilled. Seven were not part of farming stock but three of those (Champagnat, Chanut and Convers) came from small villages where the mentality would have been close enough to that of the farming community. Two of those were merchants: Chanut's father was an ironmonger and Champagnat's father who was also described as farmer. Convers' father was a miller. Only the remaining four came from non-rural background: Chavas from the town of Saint-Chamond where his father was a nailer, and Bret, Antoine Séon and Pompallier, from the great city of Lyon. Bret and Antoine Séon were shoemakers' sons. The third from Lyon, Pompallier, was the exception to the whole group for his people were of independent means. In general, then, the parents were from the country most of them owning land. Others were merchants and artisans, but there were no professional people among them. The group was, in its social origins, neither very wealthy nor impoverished. The social composition of the group corresponded quite closely with that of the priests entering both the diocese of Lyon and the diocese of Belley from the major seminaries.[7]

Some other aspects of the group are worth noting. They had little or no knowledge of religious life. This was not surprising, given the suppression of religious orders from the beginning of the Revolution in 1789 to the fall of Napoleon in 1815. They had all trained as diocesan priests. Before the division of the diocese, this training had taken place at Saint-Irénée in Lyon but after the division of the diocese some had trained in the seminary at Brou for the diocese of Belley. Ten came from the diocese of Lyon and eleven from the diocese of Belley. Because of recent jealousies, the first article of the rule of the retreat was: 'Not to speak of either Lyon or Belley.'

The group met in the college at Belley on 20 September 1836 and began with a retreat of four days.[8] These sessions were held in the physics laboratory of the college. Pompallier gave two conferences a day. Colin also gave two conferences a day on the rule. The text has not survived. From 1834 to 1836, and especially when approbation seemed imminent, he had reworked the text which he had presented to Castracane in Rome and though it was not complete, he was anxious to share it with the first Marists. Surprisingly, he had difficulty in explaining himself, as Maîtrepierre, who was present, related:

7. Grange, 'Recrutement', pp 82-8. Boutry, *Prêtres et Paroisses,* p. 191. Courveille's origins were not dissimilar from those of the twenty. His parents were lace-merchants from the town of Usson, in the Loire.
8. OM, docs 402-6. A. Forissier, 'Les deux premiers mois du Supérieur Général', typescript, APM.

To nourish his exemplary humility, the Lord left him with a trouble in his speech, a difficulty of expression and even an extraordinary scarcity of ideas. All of us felt, nevertheless, the spirit of God hidden under this apparent poverty and we admired in him an active courage, a solid firmness, a spirit both subtle and farseeing, a rare prudence and a charming modesty.[9]

Despite Colin's difficulty in expressing himself, it is evident from this account that this was a memorable experience. For four days they listened to the man they saw as their leader expound to them the rule, which he was convinced he was inspired to write and in which he had striven so long and so hard to express his vision of the Society of Mary. For many present, in particular those bound for the missions, it was perhaps the only exposé they ever received of that rule of life that was to guide their new life as members of a religious order. In a sense, it was their novitiate, their 'Marist' training. Their letters would show how well they had assimilated many of the key ideals.

The fifth and last day was the 24 September 1836. For all, and particularly for Colin, it was a day charged with almost unbearable emotion. It was time to elect a superior-general and time, too, to take the first vows. For this more solemn moment, they left the college and went to their own house, the Capucinière, which Colin had wrested from Devie four years earlier. Before the election they had an hour and a half of mental prayer. Then beginning with Pompallier, they placed their votes in the urn. Bourdin and Bret kept the minutes of the meeting and gave an emotional account of the atmosphere and of the reaction of Colin, as the votes were counted and his name came up again and again:

> At the solemn moment when such a heavy burden was to weigh on one head, the silence became more than imposing, a religious emotion seized the assembly; it heightened when at each vote could be heard the sighs of the one whom God, in his infinite wisdom, had chosen from all eternity … M. Jean Claude Marie Colin having received all the votes, was proclaimed superior general of the Society of Mary …[10]

Maîtrepierre, an acute observer, added some other details:

Bishop Pompallier … read out the votes in a loud voice and showed them to the two scrutineers. According as the name of Father Colin was read out his tears increased, but they poured down his face when Bishop Pompallier took his hand and led him to the chair prepared for the occasion.[11]

9. OM, doc. 752, 43.
10. OM, doc. 403, 19. It is clear from other accounts that Colin voted for Cholleton, OM, docs 435, 1; 615.
11. OM, docs 752, 47; 684, 1.

At the invitation of Humbert, the master of ceremonies, Champagnat addressed the newly-elected superior general:

He [Colin] could not refrain from sobbing when Father Champagnat came up to him and with a strong and rough accent, began his speech: Monsieur Superior, we have just given you a very bad present. What miseries wait for you in your administration! Your dignity lifts you up only to expose you to winds and tempests .... When your sons pass before the great Judge, you will be on the carpet and, if just one is condemned through your fault, you will answer for it.

This candid, if undiplomatic, speech was not untypical of the down-to-earth but warm-hearted Champagnat. It so impressed the hearers that his words and even his accent were remembered many years later. One wonders whether it frightened Colin or encouraged him. For the moment, however, despite the emotion flowing through the assembly, business had to go forward and an assistant to the superior general had to be elected. The votes went in favour of Pierre Colin. Immediately Colin, mastering his intense emotional upset at his own election, became, as always, sharply alert when a situation developed that might injure his beloved society. Its leadership must not become a family affair. Swiftly crossing the room to his brother, he ascertained that his brother did not seek to be elected, whereupon he withdrew his name. Terraillon was chosen as assistant instead.

Next came the taking of the vows. Humbert preached a sermon on the theme 'God loves a cheerful giver'. Then Colin made his profession before the altar 'in the presence of all his confrères' and promised to keep the three vows 'in accordance with the rules and constitutions of the said Society of Mary and the tenor of the Brief of the Sovereign Pontiff, Gregory XVI'. The others then made profession of the three vows 'into the hands of M. Colin.' Finally, Pompallier, who as a bishop could not take religious vows, pronounced a solemn statement of attachment to the society, affirming that he wished to remain a member of it 'until my last breath'. To end that momentous morning, Colin celebrated Mass and gave communion to the others. There followed Benediction of the Blessed Sacrament, they sang the *Salve Regina*, the *Sub Tuum* and the *Te Deum*. Afterwards, they crowded round Colin asking his blessing and he asked for theirs. There was much congratulating and embracing.[12] Colin tried to serve at table but was prevented. That afternoon it was back to business, for before they dispersed, meetings had to be held. The main task was how to replace the men going to Oceania. The number of priests left in France was now only sixteen –

12. OM, docs 403, 21-5; 752, 49-52.

five less than there had been.[13] Colin, too, would now be burdened with organising and administering the young society and he would have to be freed for that work. The meetings that afternoon of the 24 September began the necessary re-organisation. All went to see Bishop Devie to inform him of what took place. He gave them his blessing. It had been an extraordinarily busy day and an emotionally exhausting one for Colin. For Marists that day marks the formal beginning of the priests' branch of the Society of Mary.

The Society of Mary was now canonically in being, with twenty members of whom Colin was the superior general. If, for twenty years, he had dreamed and lived for the recognition of the society, never had he believed nor wished that he could be placed at its head, presumably for life. That result was no surprise to anyone except to him, for they had all voted for him. His own choice for general was Cholleton as he had earlier on confided to Devie. Certainly, he never wanted the task for himself. He repeated this disclaimer so often and with such vehemence, that one must take his words seriously:

I worked at the affairs of the society from 1816 to 1836 but always with the intimate conviction that my mission would finish when a superior general would be named. The idea never came into my head that I might be it.[14]

It almost brought him to rebel against God and to lose faith in the Blessed Virgin. He went so far as to say:

Ah, then, for the first two years, I could scarcely submit my will to God's will ... I could not forgive the Blessed Virgin for bringing me to this point. ... certainly, when I die, when my soul will separate from my body, I do not think that I shall suffer agony as great..[15]

This was no passing mood. In 1838 he said that if he had known that he would be elected, he would have become a Trappist.[16] In 1839 he repeated that had he suspected he would be made superior, he would have left the Society.[17] Yet his reaction was naïve. His position as central superior, his never-ending work on the rule, the trips to Paris, the battles with the Belley and Lyon administrations, the vow to put the project before the pope, the interviews with Odescalchi and Castracane – all had placed him, willy-nilly, at the heart of the project. Except for Champagnat, who could be seen as a co-founder, but whose great achievement was that of founding the brothers, no one else had contributed remotely as much to achieving what had now come about. The choice on 24 September was the only possible one for the first Marists. No one else

13. It was probably at this time that Jean-Claude Deschamps (1803-84), an aspirant, withdrew, possibly because of Colin's refusal to accept him for the mission.
14. OM, doc. 502.
15. OM, doc. 547, 6.
16. OM, doc. 435, 1.
17. OM, doc. 504.

was as well equipped to bring together the twenty priests from two dioceses and mould them into a religious order. No one else had shown the vision to imagine what a society the Virgin Mary would have wished. Champagnat in his homely way had spoken what for Colin was a sobering truth – he was now responsible for the twenty priests who put their trust in him and followed him. He had a responsibility, too, for the Oceanian mission he had accepted on their behalf. He shrank from such a heavy responsibility but despite his forebodings on that September afternoon, he it was who had brought the situation about, and it was now up to him to lead them forward. The days of imagining the future society were over. The days of responsible government had come. Mayet reported later:

> During the two years that followed his nomination as general, he experienced a profound sadness that overcame him. Immediately and at one glance, he told us, he saw all the difficulties of his office and all the obligations. Immediately, too, he understood how difficult it would be to unite many members coming together but who had never done a novitiate ...[18]

The next few years would reveal whether or not he would be able to weld these two groups of priests from different dioceses into a cohesive religious body, whether or not he could make practical the inspirations he had jotted down for the rule at Cerdon, and make the Society of Mary a new force for good within the Church.

With the first profession on 24 September 1836, the society had been established. Now the mission to Oceania, the other part of the Roman contract, had to be fulfilled. The departure of the missionaries was scheduled to follow, one bare month after the first professions – a very short time to prepare for such a momentous undertaking. Much had been done already, for Colin and Pompallier had been casting around for men and materials from the time the first news came through. There had been no lack of volunteers for the mission and selection had to be made. The whole Marist family felt involved. At Bon-Repos, the sisters would have liked to go. Chanel spoke of that possibility more than once to his sister, Sister Dominique, and Mayet told the missionaries a few years later that 'several of them are only longing for the day when God will call them to leave everything in order to go to the help of their poor sisters, the reverend savages of your shores.'[19] Colin, who found it difficult to understand female psychology, was unwilling to take the responsibility of sending sisters to what was such a distant and difficult mission and thought that their role was to

18. OM, doc. 592.
19. Chanel to Sister Dominique (Françoise), 21 Nov/23 Dec 1836; 23 July 1837, *Ever your poor brother, Peter Chanel: Surviving Letters and Futuna Journal,* Translated by W. J. Stuart and A. Ward (Rome, 1991), p. 109. Mayet to missionaries, Apr 1844, *Index Mother Saint Joseph,* doc 299, 3; RMJ, doc 272, 8.

pray for the work of the missionaries. At the Hermitage there was equal enthusiasm and Champagnat himself volunteered, but Colin felt that the brothers needed him more. For the brothers this was a new apostolate and a number volunteered. Pompallier, who even before his ordination as vicar apostolic was assuming a leading role, asked Champagnat to make the selection. Three brothers were finally chosen, of whom two were from Champagnat's group of teaching brothers in Lyon – Marie-Nizier Delorme and Michel Colombon. The third was Joseph-Xavier Luzy who was in Belley. The inclusion of the teaching brothers as an integral part of the mission group was paradoxical, for Rome had objected all along to a society which would include brothers, priests, sisters and third order members under the one head. Colin's plea that they be approved for work on the mission had gone unanswered. Their status was ambiguous and proved unsatisfactory for them.

The four priests selected were Claude Bret and Peter Chanel from the Belley group and Catherin Servant and Pierre Bataillon from the Lyon group. Though Bataillon was new, the others had been associated with the society for some time. In an atmosphere of joyful expectation, the seven Marist missionaries and Pompallier were in haste to fulfil their commitment.

In the midst of his other task of reorganising the group and of filling the gaps created by the departing missionaries, Colin took time to write the missionaries a letter dated 13 October – the first circular letter of a Marist superior general.[20] Colin's ideas about religious life were still somewhat theoretical, yet in this letter to those young religious, departing without the benefit of novitiate, religious life experience or even a written rule, he gave advice that was both uplifting and practical. In it he admitted to a secret envy that he, too, could not go with them to Oceania. Then he reminded them to count not on themselves but on Jesus and Mary. In a passage, lyrical in its intensity, he spoke to them from the heart:

> Never lose sight of the presence of the Saviour of the world; it is in his name that you depart; it is he who sends you: as the Father sent me, so I send you. He will be with you everywhere, as long ago he was with his Apostles; he will be with you in your trips, in your travels, on land, on sea, in the calm as in the tempest, in health as in sickness; if you are hungry or thirsty, he will be hungry or thirsty with you; it is he who shall be received in your own persons; who will be persecuted, if you are persecuted; who will be rebuffed, if you are rebuffed … See him everywhere intimately united to you, sharing your work, your sufferings, your joys, your consolations. Bring to him the glory of all your actions, forgetting yourselves, seeing yourselves as but base

20. Colin to departing missionaries, 13 Oct. 1836, G. Lessard, ed. 'Projet d'édition des lettres écrites par Jean-Claude Colin sous son généralat, 1836-1854' (Hull, 1985), fascicle 1, pp 6-9.

instruments. It is in the continuous reminder of this divine Saviour that you will find your strength, your peace and all the light you need.

After this very scriptural and Christ-centred exhortation for their apostolic work, Colin turned to their spiritual life. They were always to remain men of prayer. No day should pass without reciting at least a few decades of the rosary. In their appearance, they should always be simple, modest, poor, though clean in their dress. Isolation must be avoided – prudent and necessary advice for the sake of which Colin was prepared later to fight many battles. He appealed to them for unity. 'Remain, then,' he said, 'united in Jesus and Mary; no quarrelling, no arguing among you, obedient to Bishop Pompallier as your bishop and your superior.' Finally, he called on them to have courage and never let melancholy overcome them. Embracing them from his heart, he promised them the prayerful support of all the society. Since he had not got the complete rule, he sent them an extract from the constitutions, adding a prudently pragmatic comment: 'I know that you can observe no other rule than that which circumstances will permit.'

Writing to Pompallier a few days later, Colin told him that the letter he had sent the missionaries had not been written lightly. 'Remember,' he said, 'that these instructions are in no way from me, that they cost me many days of prayer.' To help him in his choice of future missionaries, he asked Pompallier to keep him informed of the dangers they encountered. He appealed to Pompallier to help them to be happy in their lives: 'Try with all possible means to maintain among them unity, peace and a holy gaiety.' It was not often Colin spoke of gaiety. He included in this letter an exhortation, part of which he may later have regretted. 'Have for each one of them,' he wrote, 'the heart of a mother and father. *You are their bishop and their superior; they owe you obedience and respect on both these grounds*'.[21] The emphasis was Colin's. In his carefully meditated letter to the missionaries five days earlier, he had placed the same emphasis on obedience to the bishop and had even repeated it in a postscript. In his words both to his confrères and to Pompallier, Colin had fastened tightly the bond between bishop and missionaries, not perhaps realising that this insistence on regarding Pompallier both as their bishop and their religious superior would allow no court of appeal for the Marists if relations between them soured. Shoals were lying ahead. Did an inexperienced Colin allow the euphoria of the approbation of the society to carry him away; was it his uncompromising understanding of obedience or simply his inability to judge characters? It is not clear. More likely it was an over-anxiety to promote unity – 'be of one mind and one heart' was a favourite theme – and to avoid all dissension. At the time he wrote, his advice was natural enough, for between the bishop

---

21. Colin to Pompallier, 18 Oct. 1836, Lessard, 'Lettres écrites par Colin', pp 9-11.

and the society a close unity prevailed. Pompallier had often expressed his devotion to the society. Shortly before he left, he wrote to Colin:

> Allow me to state that, from the very beginning, I accepted the mission of Oceania, in view of – and principally in view of – the good that I presumed to understand would come from it, and which indeed has come from it from the Holy See for our dear little society.[22]

If, as later history was to show, it was a mistake to confide the missionaries totally into Pompallier's hands, this assertion of his predilection for the society seemed genuine enough at the time, though it might be challenged later. Pompallier, moreover, asked Colin to be his vicar or representative in France, another indication of the unity of purpose between the two.[23] Colin gave this advice to Pompallier: 'Be happy to take the advice of your missionaries that will interest them in your enterprises and will contribute towards unity.'[24]

Besides the spiritual instructions in his letter to the missionaries, Colin was bidding them farewell, for this was the time for farewells.[25] Already before he had written the letter, some had left Lyon. The missionaries made their last will and testament, Chanel making his on 29 September. Catherin Servant was already in Paris awaiting orders to sail when he made his will, leaving all to his two sisters except what he had as a Marist. An embarrassing moment arose when it was discovered that Brother Marie-Nizier was under age. He was only twenty and had to go home to his parents to receive their permission.[26] All had visits to pay – to their parents, their parishes, their friends. Many partings were hard. Peter Chanel's friends raised so many objections that the gentle impressionable young priest wavered. Jeanne-Marie Chavoin played a decisive role. The priests used to visit the sisters who were also busy providing useful items for the missions and for the new house that was to open in Lyon. Chanel had added reasons to go to Bon-Repose, for his dearly-beloved sister, Françoise, now Sister Dominique, was there. Jeanne-Marie, who had helped him when he was superior of the College, for he was too soft, knew of his doubts and spoke encouragingly to him:

> 'Oh! Father Chanel, what great grace God has shown you!' And to keep up his courage, she added a few energetic words about priests who grow

22. Pompallier to Colin, 5 Nov. 1836, C. Girard ed., *Lettres reçues d'Océanie par l'administration générale des pères maristes pendant le généralat de Jean-Claude Colin* (Rome, 1999), doc. 3, 3.

23. Ibid., doc. 3, 7.

24. Colin to Pompallier, 18 Oct. 1836, Lessard, 'Lettres écrites par Colin', p. 10.

25. On the attitude of the missionaries and the spiritual value they attributed to their mission, see the excellent study in M. Filippucci, 'Ripresa dell'attività missionaria', pp 233-57, to which this account is indebted. Stendhal's attribution of very materialistic motives to seminarians in *The Red and the Black* becomes quite implausible when one examines the expressed motives of the Marist group departing for the missions.

26. Bataillon to Colin, 25 Oct. 1836, Girard, *Lettres reçues d'Océanie*, doc. 2, 5.

mouldy in the midst of comfort and do nothing for God's glory. He let himself be easily persuaded by her enthusiasm, and they thanked God together for the great favour he had received in being so chosen. In a few days the temptation faded away and was overcome.[27]

Jeanne-Marie told Mayet how Peter and his sister Françoise parted: 'His last goodbye was as simple, as calm as if he were only leaving her to go to the Fathers' house in Belley. "Goodbye, Sister. Goodbye, dear brother." And each quietly withdrew.'[28] Later, Françoise asked Jeanne-Marie for permission to cry! Poor Peter Chanel could not bear to partake of the last meal with his widowed mother. He left after Mass, leaving it to the curé to break the news and writing to his sister Françoise in Belley asking her to excuse him to their mother.[29]

If the devout Peter Chanel was troubled, others also found it difficult. Friends and relatives raised objections. Claude Bret's mother wept as she tried in vain to dissuade her only son from going, but he held firm. Even more touching were the first words Brother Joseph-Xavier Luzy wrote in his diary: '… I am leaving my native land amid tears and desolation, I leave my mother who swooned into the arms of two women, our neighbours.'[30] The twenty-six-year-old Pierre Bataillon wrote to Colin:

> Never were realised more than in me the Holy Spirit's words: 'God chose the weak of this world, to …' So this truth begins to appear in the hope of always having the support of my brothers' prayers which makes me undertake this so difficult career; I adjure you in the name of Our Lord Jesus Christ: at the holy altar remember often the youngest and the most pitiable of your children.[31]

'Be brave,' Colin had told them in his letter, 'do not let fear or sadness enter your hearts.' As the time came for departure, they needed such encouragement. The decision to leave their homeland for a mission on the other side of the world was a difficult, indeed heroic, one. They knew they were setting out across the great oceans to live a lonely life on some island in the Pacific. Yet all of them were from the heartland of France and few of them would have even seen the sea before. They had little or no knowledge of a missionary's work and there was no mission theology to help them. Colin knew little about the missions and had not received much help from the Congregation of Propaganda Fide.[32]

---

27. RMJ, doc. 105, 3.
28. Ibid., doc. 105, 1.
29. Chanel to Sister Dominique (Françoise), 21 Nov/23 Dec. 1836, Ward, *Ever your poor brother,* p. 109. Chanel's father had been killed in an accident the previous year.
30. *Journal of Brother Joseph-Xavier Luzy,* p. 5, APM.
31. Bataillon to Colin, 25 Oct 1836, Girard, *Lettres reçues d'Océanie,* doc. 2, 1.
32. When, a few years later, he consulted Fransoni, the reply was vague and of little help. Colin to Fransoni, July 1839, Fransoni to Colin, 27 Aug. 1839, Correspondence Colin-Fransoni, 1839, APM 412.10.

Although there were some Europeans there already, the tiny group knew little or nothing about the peoples to whom they were going, nor did they know their language or culture and could not know what to expect when they arrived. More tangible was the fact that they were parting from their families, perhaps never to return. As one of them wrote at the end of his letter of farewell to Colin on 25 October, 'A Dieu! ... au ciel!!!' ('Farewell! Until we meet in heaven!!!').[33] By a quirk of fate, the writer of this letter, Bataillon, was the only one of the Marists to return to France, though not until after he had been made bishop! None of the others ever saw home again and two of them were soon to die untimely deaths.[34]

Letters like Bataillon's must have moved Colin greatly. He knew he was sending out young men who might never return. It could appear that it was easy for him to encourage others to undertake such a daunting mission. Yet, the dangers facing the departing group weighed less heavily on him for he would have accepted the idea of martyrdom for the faith. Twenty years before, as a fervent young man, he had signed the Fourvière promise, pledging his readiness to accept suffering and 'even torture for the greater glory of God and the honour of Mary.' In his letter to Pius VII in 1822 and in his drafts of the rule, he had repeated the readiness of Marists to work for the salvation of souls 'on whatever distant shore'. He knew that devoting oneself to the foreign missions, which this willingness implied, could spell martyrdom. He would have absorbed the fervent atmosphere in Lyon where Catholics, clergy and laity, were passionately excited about the foreign missions. Zealous priests urged volunteers.[35] Every two months the *Annales* of the Association for the Propagation of the Faith came out, which, in addition to soliciting support for the missions, encouraged many men and women to become missionaries. What can be said of Colin is that he never neglected the missionaries. He wrote to them, sent out many to join them, canvassed funds for them, and fought battles with bishops to make sure they were not condemned to an isolated existence.

Whatever the dangers, it was with joy that the group set out, for they had set in their hearts the desire to bring the gospel to people in any part of the world to which they might be sent – 'on whatever distant shore' as Colin's rule read. What motivated them was stated very simply by Pompallier in a letter to de Pins in November 1836: 'How happy I am to cross the ocean to gather for

33. Bataillon to Colin, 25 Oct. 1836, Girard, *Lettres reçues d'Océanie*, doc. 2, 7.
34. The youngest, Brother Marie-Nizier, Peter Chanel's companion, came back to Europe almost forty years later but died in London before reaching France. Antoine Colombon, Brother Michel, left the society. The two who died were Bret, buried at sea in 1837, and Chanel, martyred on Futuna in 1841.
35. The superior of Saint-Irénée from 1841-70, Jean Duplay, a contemporary of Colin, strongly encouraged missionary vocations. Between 1841 and 1870, 46.5% of the diocesan priests of Lyon (about 120) left for the missions. Essertel, 'Réseaux et vocations missionnaires', p. 64.

the Good Shepherd many sheep which are not and have never been in his fold. How happy I am to be called to sacrifice my life for their salvation, as well as for the glory of Jesus Christ and of the Most Blessed Virgin.'[36] Catherin Servant expressed his willingness to drink the chalice the Lord offered and to share in his crucifixion.[37] The other missionaries re-echoed those sentiments. The possibility of suffering martyrdom was not absent from their thoughts.

Four of the missionaries – Chanel, Bataillon, Marie-Nizier Delorme and Michel Colombon – made a last pilgrimage to Our Lady of Fourvière. Around the neck of the little wooden statue of the Virgin in the sanctuary they hung a magnificent silver-gilt heart on which they wrote 'missionaries of Polynesia'. Inside the heart on a long roll of paper they placed an act of consecration to the Virgin together with the missionaries' names. They left room on the roll for the thousands of others that they hoped would follow them.[38]

Preparations moved quickly forward. In the early days of October, two weeks or so after the professions, Pompallier, Bret, Servant and Brother Joseph-Xavier Luzy had already left for Paris. A second group left in the middle of the month. Arrangements proceeded so rapidly that some important decisions as regards wills and so forth were taken rather late. Pompallier reported in early November that he had received 20,000 francs from Propaganda Fide in Rome and a further 20,000 from the Association for the Propagation of the Faith.[39] In early October, Chanel, Bataillon and Brother Marie-Nizier went on to Le Havre to buy some necessities.[40] In Paris, Servant, dressed in lay clothes, was going around picking up useful items from suppliers to smithies and textile weavers. Pompallier had bought a copying press for, as he told Colin, the Methodists had used them 'to send round their heretical doctrines' and he intended to compete with them.[41] An account sent to Colin gives an idea of what the missionaries bought – cloth for themselves, hats, clothes and cloth for the native people, furniture, leather, gardening tools, ironmongery, sacred vessels, linen and so forth.[42]

---

36. Pompallier to de Pins, 10 Nov 1836, Pompallier Papers, APM.
37. Servant to his relations, 11 Nov 1836, Servant Papers, APM.
38. Chanel to Terrier, 29 Oct.-2 Nov. 1836, Rozier, ed., *Écrits de S. Pierre Chanel,* p. 132. Bataillon to Colin, 25 Oct 1836, Girard, *Lettres reçues d'Océanie,* doc. 2, 2.
39. Pompallier to Colin, 5 Nov. 1836, ibid., doc. 3, 5. The combined sums would have amounted to 1,586 pounds sterling in 1836. The role of the Association for the Propagation of the Faith, where Pauline Jaricot was the moving spirit, was of capital importance not merely in encouraging the faithful to maintain a generous contribution to the missions but also in promoting a missionary vocation among many young men and women. Françoise Perroton, who initiated the movement that evolved into the Missionary Sisters of the Society of Mary, was one of those.
40. Claude Bret's Journal, 12 Oct 1836, Girard, *Lettres reçues d'Océanie,* doc. 1, 1; Servant to his relations, 16 Oc. 1836, Servant Papers, APM.
41. Pompallier to Colin, 28 Nov. 1839, Girard, *Lettres reçues d'Océanie,* doc. 5, 15.
42. Pompallier to Colin, 28 Nov. 1836, ibid., doc. 5, 6.

Pompallier was prepared to seek help for the mission anywhere he could get it and changed political circumstances provided the possibility of approaching members of the government. By now, six years after the July revolution, the monarchy of Louis-Philippe was firmly established and experiencing economic prosperity. It had moved steadily away from its republican, Bonapartist and socialist allies of July 1830, suppressing them as firmly as it crushed supporters of the previous legitimist regime. The most notorious of its repressions was in Lyon itself where in 1831 and again in 1834 the *canuts* or weavers had revolted, demanding a minimum wage. In April 1834 Pompallier had witnessed some of the horrors of the second revolt. Government forces shelled Fourvière which was occupied by the insurgents and after five days of fighting, relentlessly suppressed the rebellion.

Though the government was anti-clerical at the beginning and banned army chaplains and reduced the Church budget, by the mid 1830s it was gradually moving away from that position. This was a period, too, of colonial expansion, with intense rivalry between England and France in Africa and particularly in Oceania. Soon the two countries would come close to war over their competing claims in that vast area, arising from the complaints of the English missionary, George Pritchard. England was a Protestant state and supported the British Protestant missionaries in the Pacific. Would the July Monarchy in France support Catholic missionaries? The King was voltairian, the prime minister, Count Molé, who headed a centre-right government, was a Liberal and the ablest of his ministers, François Guizot, a Protestant.

Pompallier went to see Guizot, Minister of Public Instruction, on a matter of education in France. Guizot, who was soon to be prime minister, received him well and promised his support. Pleased with Guizot's warm welcome and interest, Pompallier went to see the royal family – King Louis-Philippe, Queen Amelia and Madame Adelaide of Orleans, the King's sister, a devout Catholic. They showed great interest in the Oceanian mission and promised their protection. In addition, they gave Pompallier small presents for the work, the King giving 1,000 francs, the Queen 500 francs and Madame Adelaide rolls of white calico to clothe those they would baptise in the mission.[43] Count Molé, too, who was also Minister for Foreign Affairs, promised support. It was a positive sign of the good relations now existing between Church and State. The goodwill of Louis-Philippe and the ministers towards Pompallier was an indication of the readiness of every French government, anti-clerical or not, to support French missionaries, for they would establish and strengthen 'the French presence' abroad. Pompallier reported with satisfaction that 'At Paris, from both

---

43. Pompallier to Colin, 5 Nov 1836, ibid., doc. 3, 13. Pompallier to de Pins, 10 Nov 1836, Pompallier Papers, APM.

government and court, I received all the favours due to my position.'[44] Yet if the French government was prepared to support the Marist mission, it is worth noting that it was Pope Gregory, not the French state, that had initiated the mission to Oceania. The Marist missionaries were not following the French flag and indeed many of the countries to which they were to go had no French presence.

By now the other missionaries joined the first group at Le Havre. As it turned out, there was no need for haste. Determined though the Marists were to leave for the mission within a month after the professions, the departure date of their ship – the *Delphine* – was put back time and again. At first it was the task of loading. Then it was unfavourable winds and extremely stormy weather that kept the ship in the harbour. While waiting, the missionaries and the Marists in Lyon and Belley kept contact. Pompallier wrote many long letters to the Marists, to de Pins and to his relations. Pierre Colin, Terraillon and Colin replied. As the weeks went by, the missionaries eagerly snapped up any news of the doings in Lyon and Belley. These were exciting times. The priests' branch which numbered only twenty on 24 September was attracting many valuable recruits and by the new year would have a dozen postulants or novices. To the missionaries, this meant that they would not be abandoned in Oceania but that others would soon follow. To the sixteen remaining in France it meant that they could not merely continue the work, despite the loss of the missionaries, but could develop further. To all it seemed that God was blessing the society.

In November came other news that all the Marists had been waiting for. Following the decisions at the time of profession, Colin had been looking for a house in Lyon which would serve as novitiate and in particular as mother-house or residence for the superior general. Belley was not central enough for a society which would soon have missionaries in the remotest parts of the world and which would expand in France also. The Brothers of the Christian Schools who had a property at 24 Montée Saint-Barthélemy were willing to rent part of it, consisting in a small house and garden, to the Marists. Colin, who wanted to buy a more suitable residence, decided to rent it for two years only. With Pierre Colin as superior and novice-master, it served as a novitiate for a year and a half. Then, in 1837, the Marists took possession of Puylata, 4 and 6 Montée Saint-Barthélemy, which became the novitiate for a while and the mother house of the Society until 1860. Colin was to live there and to govern the society from there for close on eighteen years. This address would become familiar to all the missionaries and to all Marists for to it they would send their many letters to Colin recounting their successes and their difficulties, for years to come.

During these months, the missionaries stayed in the house of Madame

44. Pompallier to Colin, 5 Nov. 1836, Girard, *Lettres reçues d'Océanie*, doc. 3, 13.

Dodard, a widow, who used her financial resources to provide accommodation for missionaries passing through Le Havre. The generous widow took seriously ill on 18 December and all eighteen missionaries in her house gathered round her bedside holding candles in their hands while Bishop Pompallier gave her viaticum. On 22 December, ten days before her death, he gave her extreme unction.[45] Two days later, on Christmas Eve, after two months of waiting, the Marists eventually were able to sail. Bret wrote in his journal: 'It is snowing, it is freezing' but a north-easterly wind had struck up and it was for this that 'we have been waiting for two months.'[46]

An incident occurred as they cleared the harbour. Because of the storm, which was so severe that some ships leaving Le Havre had been shipwrecked, the harbour master had strung a stout rope across the entrance to the harbour to prevent ships going out together. When the *Delphine* sailed out, this rope got caught between the rudder and the stern-post. The ship forced its way forward but the rudder, severely damaged, was almost torn from the ship. This was to have serious consequences later.[47] For the moment, however, the damage was unnoticed by everyone including the missionaries. Their mind was on other things. As the *Delphine* crossed the bar at noon on that Christmas Eve 1836, and sailed into the wide ocean, their thoughts were turned more to those distant places where they would land and begin their work on 'whatever distant shore'. The Marist mission, like the Marist society, had been launched.

45. Bret's Journal, 12 Oct; 21, 22 Dec 1836, Girard, *Lettres reçues d'Océanie*, docs 1, (and note 1); 21; 22. Madame Rose-Victoire Dodard (1757-1837), died on 1 Jan. 1837. She had always wished to die with her house full of missionaries.

46. Bret's Journal, 24 Dec 1836, Girard, *Lettres reçues d'Océanie*, doc. 1, 25.

47. Girard, *Lettres reçues d'Océanie*, 2 Jan. 1837, doc. 1, 33. When they reached the Canaries they discovered that two of the four bolts holding the rudder to the stern-post had been lost and a third was hanging loose. To have a new one made they had to remain in the Canaries from 8 January to 27 February 1837. It was probably there that Claude Bret caught the illness that brought about his death on 20 March. I am grateful to Charles Girard for drawing my attention to the matter.

Epilogue

'This venerable founder … had laboured for more than twenty years in the face of contradiction, contempt, discouragement and inadequate means, to make this work of heaven succeed …' Maîtrepierre on Colin.

'He walked not with measured step but with giant strides which, granted, tended to splash mud on the next man, but while the nit-pickers … were still at the beginning of the road … he had already covered an immense distance.' Mayet on Colin.

It took the missionaries over a year before they arrived, in January 1838, at their journey's end at the mouth of the Hokianga River in New Zealand. During that time Colin was busy organising the newly-approved society. With the Brief of Approbation, *Omnium Gentium,* he had achieved what he had worked for over the previous twenty years. The cost to himself was the unwanted responsibility of becoming, perhaps for life, the superior general of the twenty Marist priests who chose him to guide them into what was for all of them uncharted seas. For all Marists he was the major figure. For the brothers, if Champagnat was their beloved father and immediate superior, Colin was still the central superior and Champagnat looked to him to obtain Roman approval for them. Jeanne-Marie Chavoin saw in him the charismatic founder who would write the rule and who would finally obtain approval for the sisters. For Bishop Devie, who was losing him from his diocese, Colin was one of his ablest priests, a canon and vicar general, the superior of the college at Belley to which he had brought order and discipline. The pope and the Curia looked to him to maintain the most far-flung mission in the Church. The missioners looked to him as to a spiritual father. What was Colin like?

Colin was now forty-six years old and at the height of his powers. He was a metre and sixty-four centimetres or five feet four inches tall and somewhat plump.[1] His hair, according to himself, had gone white during the difficult year of 1830-1 while his passports describe him as grey-haired at sixty. He had an aquiline nose, soft blue eyes and a smile that charmed all who met him. Many years later, Mother Marie-Thérèse Dubouché could still say of him: 'Even his face took on the imprint of his virtues, his soft blue eyes and his open and candid smile make you forget his white hair. He reminds you of a child with the

1. Coste, *Lectures,* pp 127-8.

energy and intelligence of a sage.'[2] 'At first sight,' Mayet recalled, 'he appeared to be one of those good, little old country priests, very simple, very timid, not knowing where to put themselves to take up less space, and at the same time, so abounding in kindness.'[3] Earlier he had some difficulty in speaking and at Saint-Irénée, he said, he was unable to read one sentence without hesitation. He cured it by forcing himself to articulate with a dozen pebbles in his mouth but some difficulties remained. If he became excited or angry, however, the words flowed out of him like a torrent. When he was young his sight began to fail, and he followed Father de la Croix d'Azolette's advice to take snuff as a cure. This habit once formed he was not able to break. If later accounts are anything to go by, he was careless in his dress and inattentive to his appearance. He was physically strong but several illnesses and immoderate penances had impaired his health. He often overworked and exhausted himself. A man of boundless activity, he disdained eating and sleeping – 'my great mortifications' he called them.

As for most people, Colin's habitual modes of perception and response had been formed in this early period of his life. The first twenty-five years had been perhaps the most turbulent ever in the history of France and its Church and his parish and family had suffered greatly. Orphaned before he was five, his mother's death had thrown him to depend on his heavenly mother, Mary, at the foot of whose image in the parish church he often took refuge. He had never a thought apparently for a more human love. He had grown up in a world of his own, a quiet shy sensitive boy, given to wandering alone in the woods of Crest where his pious fancy had full play. He went to the seminary to find that aloneness with God which he had previously sought in the woods. Yet even there the great events of the day followed him: the pope's memorable visits to Lyon and the re-consecration of the sanctuary of Our Lady at Fourvière. Later came Napoleon's unending wars, his persecution of the pope, his defeat, his return and his ultimate exile – involving, too, the exile of Cardinal Fesch, Colin's own bishop, who only a few weeks before had ordained him deacon. During the frightening summer of 1815, he could hear the fury of the Bonapartist mob, enraged by news of Waterloo, as they hurled insults and threats over the walls of the seminary at clergy and royalists. Twice he witnessed foreign occupation of the city. Those events had an effect on Colin at this impressionable stage of his life.

Closer to home, his serious illness of 1809, with grasping relatives besieging his death-bed, opened his eyes to the covetousness of human nature. Ever afterwards he resolved to guard himself and his fellow-workers from its crippling

2. Ibid., p. 128. Venerable Mother Marie-Thérèse Dubouché (1809-63), foundress of the congregation of Adoration Réparatrice. She had many contacts with Colin.
3. FA, doc. 232, 8.

cupidity. His experience, apparently, was the cause of a detachment from his family, so great that it astonished some of his contemporaries. A devout, bright and diligent student, he was able to maintain his place among the best in his class, despite frequent illnesses. At the seminary in Lyon, he received the normal, somewhat narrow, training for the priesthood which was aimed at producing a pious obedient priest. The studies, geared towards preaching and confession, taught a strict moral theology. In his final year there, Courveille told him of the call of the Virgin Mary at Le Puy for a society bearing her name, and invited him to take part in the project. 'This suits you,' Colin told himself delightedly. He could now accept the priesthood, whose responsibilities he had dreaded, with joy in his heart. He was one of twelve who were at Fourvière that morning in July 1816 and had made the promise of founding a Society of Mary. Nothing marked him out as exceptional.

Up to about this time – until he was twenty-five, he tells us – he suffered excruciating scruples and torment of soul. Irresolute, he had jibbed at every step that appeared to commit him to the priesthood. That year, 1816, the year of ordination, of the Fourvière promise, of his appointment as assistant priest to his brother at Cerdon, saw the beginning of a change. The joy he experienced at the hope of a society dedicated to Mary suffused the beginnings of his ministry and at Cerdon he experienced those six years of consolation. The timid young priest developed into an excellent pastor. It was probably during this period, when he was at a very formative stage, dealing with more people and reading more widely, that his keen young mind began to understand the needs of his age. Realising that his generation had come through a Revolution where privilege had been abolished and equality underscored, he came to believe that the response of the Church lay in an approach that would be modest and avoid prestige-seeking. A keen sensitivity had resulted from the sufferings and loss which the Revolution had inflicted on him as a child; he transformed it into an appreciation for the feelings of others. Sensitivity in the approach to people became for him a key spiritual principle summed up in his plea that in their work Marists remain 'hidden and unknown in this world'. This unassuming way fitted well not just with his inclination but with his understanding of the modest but essential role of Mary in the Church, first during apostolic times, later during its troubled history, and again in this 'last age'.

From the special graces he received during those years, he set to work to write a rule for a society devoted to Mary, incorporating into it that central intuition. His vision of the future society was idealistic and utopian. The decision to undertake the responsibility of writing this rule, as surprising as it was significant, was inspired, he believed, from on high. The irresistible impulsion to write a rule convinced him that the project of the society would succeed. He linked his whole future with it by solemnly vowing to work at it until it could be laid before the pope. The unwavering support of his brother, Pierre, and of Jeanne-Marie Chavoin, both strong personalities in their own right, helped confirm him in his role. This conviction was powerfully reinforced by his extra-ordinary personal experience at La Coria. Colin showed himself a man of action. He was the moving spirit behind the contacts with bishops and the pope. The letter to Bishop Bigex in October 1819 was almost certainly his init-iative. When, in 1822, he, Pierre and Courveille wrote to Rome, the rule, whose supernatural origins they proposed to explain to the pope, was Colin's. In November of that year it was Colin who travelled to Paris to see the nuncio and other important ecclesiastics. This journey called for considerable courage on the part of the shy young country curate who always experienced a deep repugnance to taking such initiatives. Once he had begun those negotiations he kept at them. In February 1823 it was he who wrote to the nuncio seeking the speedy approval of the society before the division of the dioceses, and fol-lowed up this initiative by going to Paris to see him again.

There was an ascetic, if not heroic, side to his commitment. When Devie invited the group to give missions, despite his fears Colin agreed, accepting that that was how he must start the work of Mary. The years of consolation were over and resolutely, if reluctantly, he set to work. Badly lodged and fed at Belley College, and subject to constant petty persecution, Colin accepted all with cheerfulness. Although he was totally inexperienced, he proved an excellent missioner in the Bugey mountains during the difficult winter months from 1825 to 1829. His unassuming approach – summed up in his oft-repeated for-mula that the missioners were but 'instruments of mercy' – encouraged and won over people. He steered clear of the excesses of some contemporary missions, avoiding political comment, avoiding severe denunciations from the pulpit, and avoiding expense. To catechise the people rather than to stage the grand-style mission frequently held in the towns and cities was what he tried to do. Here he met the hard-working simple country people, listened to their prob-lems and saw their needs. This experience, together with the exhortations of Pope Leo XII and Bishop Devie, combined to make him abandon the narrow theology he had learned in the seminary, for the more compassionate one of St Alphonsus Liguori. Perhaps more than any other, this mission work left its mark on him and his outlook. It deepened his conviction that, in the modern world, jealously conscious of its independence and suspicious of clerical power, a modest unobtrusive approach was the only way to people's hearts. This may well be what Cardinal Castracane had in mind when he commented that Colin understood the times better than any of them. The hardship he and his companions willingly endured during this ministry and the simplicity of their lifestyle, made him look back in nostalgia to this period as to the heroic time of the Marists.

When Devie, impressed by Colin's ability, forced him to take over the running of the college at Belley, Colin rose to a new challenge for which again he had no preparation. He invented no new pedagogy but his spiritual vision, practical commonsense and hard work achieved a transformation in the college. He showed a rare wisdom in framing a body of directives, a flexible skill in governing, combined with a benevolent kindness. Yet he tolerated no insubordination and showed an unshakeable firmness in combating wrongdoing. When the Liberal Catholics, in opposition to the bishops, fired the younger clergy with a dream of a Church free from its compromising connection with the state, the clamour they made repelled him. Although he was almost alone in the college to oppose them, he held firm. When the time was ripe, he took decisive action and restored order.

All the while he sought to further the Marist project, 'the work of Mary' as he, Jeanne-Marie Chavoin and Marcellin Champagnat preferred to call it. From the time, in 1830, he became central superior of the groups in Belley and Lyon, he strove to give them clear direction, reluctant to tolerate any straying from the lines he was convinced were the right ones. Delays and opposition did not deter him. It was in June of that year that he had to endure the persistent pressure of Bishop Devie who, devoted to the renewal of his neglected diocese, hoped to persuade Colin and his group to remain as diocesan missioners. Bringing all the pressure he could to bear on the Marists, dividing them in order to persuade them individually, and attempting to browbeat Colin in stand-up arguments, Devie threw all his skill and the weight of his position into the struggle. Colin held firm. When Devie refused to give him the house he had promised him, Colin, while not hesitating to tell the bishop how angry he was with him, turned fervently to the Blessed Virgin. Under siege from Colin and fearing the contrast that Colin might draw between his stalling tactics and Archbishop de Pins' generosity in Lyon, Devie finally handed over the Capucinière, the first Marist house: as Colin laughingly admitted, he used concessions from one bishop as a lever to extract more from the other.

Knowing that Rome held the key to recognition, he insisted that he be allowed to go to the Holy See. Despite refusals, his perseverance, his determination to call the nuncio to his aid and his appeal to his vow finally paid off and he was allowed to go. What is remarkable in this long crisis was his unwavering faith in the project of the Society of Mary. It gave hope to the little group. In Rome the situation was not as simple as he had expected and little progress was made. Here, too, he showed negotiating skills and perseverance. The 'active courage' of which Maîtrepierre speaks is evident here, for despite reverses and contradictions, he kept at the task. Although he came back from Rome empty-handed, Colin was content, for he had a quiet faith in what he had accomplished there. When, with the quest for missionaries for Oceania, the possibility of a break-through emerged, he acted decisively, committing his tiny group to a mission encompassing an enormous swathe of the globe. Archbishop de Pins, who in 1824 had brushed aside Colin's efforts to link the Marists in Lyon with those in Belley, by now had come to regard Colin highly and recommended the Marists to Rome for the Oceania mission. With the mission came approbation.

A fine intelligence and a resolute will combined in Colin to make him a powerful personality. Normally, he could both go deeply into a problem and see far ahead. His letters in the 1830s show a man who grasped the problems that arose and was able to tackle them. Later on, when an important question came up for discussion, he listened first to everyone else, but when he examined the matter himself, he dug so deeply into it that he brought to light aspects that had never occurred to them. 'They were thunderstruck,' Mayet reported.[4] His approach was neither narrow nor doctrinaire but flexible and broad. Around the year 1838, he expressed liberal views as regards General Carrier, whom many regarded as a public sinner. One confrère suggested to Colin that he was not following the Church's decrees. Times change, he replied. The Church in her wisdom, he added, accommodates herself to the misfortunes of each age, and by acting sensitively accomplishes more.[5]

Throughout his many negotiations, curia, bishops and fellow-Marists commented on Colin's modesty. Firmness was also evident. He knew what he wanted and was determined to get it. What comes through perhaps most of all about Colin over all this period is that he was a passionate man, or more exactly a man of an enduring passion. His one absorbing passion was for the 'work of Mary', for her 'society'. Convinced that the Blessed Virgin wanted this work, he was equally convinced that his task was to bring it to realisation and then step down. He believed, too, that it was his role to give it its rule. Such conviction alone explains not merely his perseverance with the authorities but his success in overcoming his very real personal reluctance. Obstacles made no difference to him. The opposition of the vicars general in Lyon or the more formidable opposition of Devie in Belley, who alternately commanded him as bishop and enticed him by making him vicar general and a canon, did not put him off course. He just trusted in the Blessed Virgin and came back again and again. Courveille's departure and Terraillon's withdrawal may have upset him but does not appear to have discouraged him, as it may have discouraged Champagnat. As Mayet said of him on one occasion when trying to sum up his character, 'Nothing gave him so much energy and strength as obstacles.' When Maîtrepierre jokingly told him that he needed the spur of serious matters, he did not deny it.

If this absorbing passion, this zeal for the 'work of Mary', explains his per-

4. FA, doc. 360, 17.
5. FA, doc. 14, 15.

severance, it also sheds light on his attitude to others. He was not insensitive, but where the great work had to be done, he did not care about his own feelings or those of anyone else. One moment he was in floods of tears at his unexpected election and the fearful responsibilities he knew it would involve; the next moment he jumped to his feet and hurried across to Pierre when it seemed that his brother would be elected assistant, and, with no great attention to Pierre's feelings, he there and then had him withdraw. His justification was the good of the society. Where that was concerned, he was unwilling to brook any opposition. He acted similarly a few years later towards Cholleton despite his affection for him and the many debts he owed him. He rejected his offer to teach moral theology and in Cholleton's presence he publicly supported Father Épalle. 'Father Colin,' Mayet commented on that occasion, 'when it was a question of the good of the society, has eyes only for the society.' For him the respect due to Cholleton was 'of no account' weighed against that good.[6] A certain steeliness is evident in his character.

Although this uncompromising single-mindedness emerges clearly later, in his dealings with Pierre Colin, Jeanne-Marie Chavoin and Terraillon, it surfaced already in his correspondence shortly after he became central superior. His querulous letter of 19 January 1836 complaining of dissension among the priests in Lyon is revealing. While disavowing any wish to be in charge, he insisted that as long as he was superior he should control all negotiations with the diocesan authorities. To assert that control, he was ready to withdraw all the priests from Lyon to Belley. About this time, too, he took a strong line with Devie who forbade the sisters to teach when they moved to Meximieux. Devie, who was canonically the sisters' superior, was seeking to avoid competition between the Marist sisters and other sisters already established in the town. When Devie complained that 'M. Colin did not understand me,' he commented sharply: 'Oh, yes. I understood him quite well, and it is because I understood him that I acted as I did.' Colin, who saw himself as the sisters' superior on the grounds that he was superior of the priests' branch, added: 'He thinks of his diocese, I concern myself with the Society of Mary.'

This forceful, if not authoritarian, attitude emerged, too, in his dealings with the faithful Champagnat, who had done so much to make a reality of the Marist dream. His two letters to him in 1837 and 1839 are proof of his determination to drive the Society along the lines he believed were right, whatever the cost to others. The goal for him was all. If anything could account for forceful actions on his part that caused others to suffer, it was his utter conviction of the importance of the 'work of Mary'. No wonder Devie, who knew him from many a tough encounter, appealed to him to go easier on his men. No wonder that, faced with this clear-headed, determined, single-minded man,

6. FA, doc. 254.

Maîtrepierre, remarking ruefully that 'it is not easy to grow up in the shadow of a genius', commented: 'Founders who are full of their work, who have set up everything, often amid great difficulties, understandably have difficulty in finding satisfactory what others engaged in the same work do.'[7] His great admirer, Mayet, knew how trying he could be for others and noted that he moved with giant strides, but in the process others got splashed with mud.[8] While an authoritarian trait was part of Colin's character, his manner of acting was in line with traditional spirituality that taught that the virtue of humility came through humiliations and that the superior's decision represented the will of God. In lesser matters too, Colin could be angry and show it in impulsive behaviour. In Cerdon he pushed a man into line during a procession with the result that the man stayed away from confession for two years. Colin was mortified when the man told him later, but was then humble enough to admit his ill-considered behaviour. In the college at Belley, he cuffed a boy who lied, and, most remarkable of all, one day during confession he cuffed an apathetic penitent.[9] This action was one he straightaway repented and, again, he was honest enough to admit his fault.

Over the two decades from 1816 to 1836, insensibly and unwillingly Colin came centre-stage. Courveille's inadequacies were the reason. Colin shrank from Courveille's ostentatious ways and feared, too, that, by wanting to push ahead despite the bishops, Courveille was embarking the society on the wrong course. Concern for the project decided him to take the vow to stick by it until it could be submitted to the pope. This took far longer than he expected and when it finally took place, Colin had become, in the eyes of the Roman cardinals, the bishops and his own confrères, the indisputable head of the group. His hope of relinquishing that role to Cholleton at the election of the first superior general, was illusory.

Since Colin did effectively take over the leading role from Courveille, was he, then, an ambitious person? Early on, possibly before Courveille left the scene, some contemporaries hinted at ambition on his part: 'There were those who saw us as ambitious,' Colin said, 'Alas! Ambitious ... Ah! They did not know what violence one did to oneself, how much one suffered to put oneself forward, how many efforts it took just to advance one step.'[10] He often repeated those sentiments of repugnance. David, who knew him well, wrote: 'But when he had to put himself forward in order to prepare the way for the establishment of the society, nothing can express the repugnance against which he had to struggle. 'My mouth said, "Yes." My heart said "No." I fought with God.'[11]

7. FA, doc. 233, 6.
8. FA, doc. 360, 36.
9. OM, doc. 706; FA, docs 234, 4; 235,13.
10. OM, doc. 519, 3.
11. OM, doc. 848, 6.

Jeanne-Marie also bore witness to this repugnance. Indeed, the reason why Colin had so enthusiastically accepted the idea of a society dedicated to Mary, was because he saw in it the possibility of being a priest and still remaining 'hidden and unknown'. It is difficult not to accept his claim that repugnance, not ambition, was uppermost in his mind when he found that he had to come forward and take an active role. A leadership role can grow on one but of that there is no clear evidence in Colin. A born leader, with clear vision, tough mind and powerful energy, ambition should have been natural to him. His timidity and shyness and, especially, that modesty on which Maîtrepierre, Mayet and others remarked, kept him from putting himself forward or seeking the limelight, and allowed him to subordinate his talents to one great spiritual ideal. Even then he worried lest he put too much of himself in the project. All the evidence points to his never wanting to be superior general. He undoubtedly wanted Cholleton, an understandable choice because Cholleton, the revered seminary professor and spiritual director, had played a major role in Colin's own life and in the life of the society from the seminary days, right through the negotiations with de Pins and up to the approbation.

Should Colin be seen as the founder? Colin rejected the title of founder as Maîtrepierre recounted: 'The title of founder really makes him indignant: "Ah! Yes, founders, ah! Wonderful founders! God leads us, sometimes we obey, often we resist, we put up obstacles, and that is all".'[12] For him the initiative to found the Society came solely from the Blessed Virgin. Commendable though those sentiments are, they still leave open the question of founder. Should that title be left to Courveille, who had the original revelation at Le Puy, gave the Society its name and launched it at Fourvière in 1816? Though Courveille's contribution and initial importance cannot be forgotten, yet he faded from the scene without having accomplished much. Colin, moreover, always claimed that he had the idea of the society before Courveille mentioned it, although it is difficult to say precisely what this claim means. Those two great Marist founders, Marcellin Champagnat and Jeanne-Marie Chavoin, saw in Colin the man who made the Society possible. It was he whom Marists honoured as Father Founder even in his lifetime. It was he who gave the Marist priests and sisters a rule of life, both idealistic and practical, in which he bequeathed to them key intuitions that have inspired them since. It was he who, after the long years of negotiations, setbacks and hard toil, finally succeeded in obtaining for the Society of Mary papal approbation, which sealed its status as a religious society capable of helping people to follow Christ in the practice of the evangelical virtues. He it was, too, who began the organisation that originated and successfully sustained a new and significant missionary endeavour in Oceania. Those are remarkable achievements. While in the story of the Society many

12. Keel ed., *Texts,* doc. 164.

people contributed, especially Courveille, Champagnat, Pierre Colin, Jeanne-Marie Chavoin, and Cholleton, it was Colin's ideas and leadership that made it all possible. All those are strong reasons for seeing him as founder.

Since little has been said in this volume about Colin's spiritual life, it could give the impression that he was an organisation man, devoted only to his project. His inner spiritual life has been presented more through his activities than in itself. Yet in a religious founder the spiritual life is the heart of things. It is difficult, if not impossible, however, to enter into the mind and heart of another, to assess his relationship with God, especially when the person is long since dead. In Colin's case, the task is more difficult because of his attachment to a life 'unknown and hidden', which pushed him even to destroy his personal papers. It would be unjust, however, to portray him as just an organiser and negotiator, for all who met him testify there was much more to him than that. How those close to him assessed him spiritually, can be sensed from an account which Maîtrepierre, an observer of some ability, gave on the day of profession: '[W]e all felt the spirit of God hidden in him, and we admired in him an active courage, a solid firmness, a spirit that was subtle and far-seeing, a rare wisdom and, especially, a delightful modesty.'[13] Those who knew him at this time saw him as a man of God. Mayet, who contacted him by letter in 1837 and met him soon after, reported: 'As soon as I had spoken to him for the first time, I had this strong feeling in my heart: That is the man you are looking for.' Convinced that he was in the presence of a saint, Mayet mused: 'Saints have something of God in them that cannot be defined, which stimulates and attracts.'[14] The Curé of Ars also admired him: 'Oh! What a holy priest he is,' he said on one occasion, 'and how he loves the Blessed Virgin!'[15] Colin was undoubtedly a prayerful person who never took a major decision without praying long and hard over it. His instinct when faced with a major task, his reaction to difficulties, his preparation for mission work in the Bugey, all show a man whose first reflex was to turn to God in prayer. 'Without prayer, without the spirit of prayer, we shall achieve nothing,' he told his confrères, and added, 'I'm telling you this because the spirit of God prompts me to.'[16] With the years, as he strove to pass on a spiritual heritage to his confrères, more of the inner core of his own life would emerge.

We have come to no more than midway in Colin's career. During the second half of his life his strengths would become more obvious when, as superior general, he assumed the responsibilities of that role and when, after his retirement, he painfully readjusted to a less prominent position. More varied

---

13. OM, doc. 752, 43.
14. FA, doc. 232, 8.
15. Acta SM, vol. 5, pp. 383-7.
16. FS, doc. 105, 2.

and more stressful situations would occur that would test his character to the limit. Issues would arise, at home and in the missions, which would cast doubt on his judgment of others, challenge his claim to write the rule and even dispute his role as founder.

At this point in his story, to attempt more than an outline of some aspects of the character and temperament of this dedicated and extraordinarily forceful man, would be presumptuous. The sources are inadequate. Colin's methodical burning of his papers over a period of four days in June 1841 eliminated precious personal material that could cast light on the motives for his actions, his relations with others and perhaps his inner doubts and struggles.[17] Although other sources are available, the loss of his own papers limits our understanding of that part of his life. For the period after 1836 the loss is less important, for by then he had become a public person whose official papers were conserved as a matter of course. In addition, ample material is available from other sources. More people would observe, comment and record their often contrasting impressions and views of him. It would be tempting to use the abundant documentation for the second part of Colin's life, to interpret the earlier part. That would be unhistorical, however, for with Colin, as with most people, new facets of temperament emerged in response to new challenges.

Although that monumental set of documents, the *Origines Maristes,* does not extend to that period, a biographer is fortunate to possess a variety of material from different archives, many of which have not yet yielded all their treasures. He has, too, the invaluable pages of the 'Mémoires' of Mayet, the chronicler, which are contemporary for much of the period. All this will be for a future work.

---

17. Among the papers that perished in the bonfire was the precious correspondence with Trinchant, the priest who acted as his agent in Rome and did so much to further Colin's attempt to obtain Roman approbation. Correspondence with Courveille, that might have shed light on later problems, probably perished in it too.

Names and Places occurring frequently

Nicolas-Augustin de La Croix d'Azolette (1779-1861), superior at Alix, Argentière, professor at Saint-Irénée; vicar general to Devie; bishop of Gap; archbishop of Auch.

François-Marie Bigex (1751-1827), professor of theology and philosophy; bishop of Pinerolo; archbishop of Chambéry; helped the early Marists with his advice.

Claude-Marie Bochard (1759-1834), vicar general of the diocese of Lyon; founder of diocesan congregation of the Fathers of the Cross.

Le Bugey, mountainous region 80 km north-east of Lyon, where Marists preached missions.

Benoît-Marie Cabuchet (1758-1813), curé of Saint-Bonnet-le-Troncy; baptised Colin.

Castruccio Castracane degli Antelminelli (1779-1852), secretary of Propaganda, 1828; cardinal, 1833; prefect of Congregation of Indulgences, 1834; cardinal-bishop of Palestrina.

Saint Marcellin Champagnat (1789-1840), b. Marlhes; made Fourvière promise 1816: professed 1836; Marist priest; founded Marist Teaching brothers (FMS) La Valla, 1817; canonised in 1999.

Jeanne-Marie Chavoin [Mother Saint Joseph] (1786-1858), b. Coutouvre; joined the Colins at the presbytery in Cerdon; foundress of the Marist sisters.

Jean Cholleton (1788-1852), professor of moral theology and spiritual director at Saint-Irénée, 1811; vicar general of Lyon, 1824-40; became Marist, 1841.

Pierre Colin (1786-1856), Marist priest, older brother of Jean-Claude; assistant priest at Coutouvre where he met Jeanne-Marie Chavoin; curé of Cerdon 1816-25.

Sébastien Colin (1756-1831), Colin's uncle; same name as Colin's brother Sébastien (1782-1841).

Joseph Courbon (1748-1824), vicar general of the diocese of Lyon.

Jean-Claude Courveille (1787-1866), received the revelation at Le Puy 1812; made Fourvière promise 1816; Marist aspirant to 1826; joined the Benedictines in 1836.

Étienne Déclas (1783-1868), Marist priest; one of the first four to make profession.

Jean-Paul-Gaston de Pins (1766-1850), bishop of Limoges, 1822; apostolic administrator of Lyon, 1823-40.

Alexandre-Raymond Devie (1767-1852), vicar general of Valence, 1813-23; bishop of Belley, 1823-52.

Jacques-André Émery (1732-1811), refounder and superior general of the Sulpicians.

Saint Peter-Julian Eymard (1811-1868), Marist priest; assistant to Colin; later founder of the Fathers of the Blessed Sacrament (SSS), 1856.

Julien Favre (1812-1885), professor of theology, first as diocesan priest and then as Marist at the Marist scholasticate in Belley; second superior general in 1854.

Joseph Fesch (1763-1839), Napoleon's uncle; took the oath to the civil constitution; archbishop of Lyon, 1802; cardinal, 1803; died in exile in Rome.

Giacomo Fransoni (1775-1856), cardinal, 1826; prefect of Propaganda Fide, 1834-56.

Philibert Gardette (1765-1848), superior Saint-Jodard 1802-11 and Saint-Irénée 1812-41.

L'Hermitage, 50 km south-west of Lyon, mother house of the Marist Brothers (FMS).

Jean-Marie Humbert (1795-1873), Marist priest; missionary and bursar of Belley College.

Antoine Jallon (1782-1854), Marist priest; worked in parishes and missions.

Pauline Jaricot (1799-1862), a prime mover in Association for the Propagation of the Faith, 1818; founded *Living Rosary,* 1826.

Jean Jeantin (1824-1895), Marist priest; b. Savoy; author of the six-volume biography of Colin, *Le très révérend Père Colin* (Lyon, 1895-1898).

Benoît Lagniet (1806-1884), Marist priest, assistant to Colin; provincial of Paris, 1852.

Vincenzo Macchi (1770-1860), nuncio at Paris, later cardinal in Rome.

Denis-Joseph Maîtrepierre (1800-1872), Marist priest; novice master 1844-1864.

Gabriel-Claude Mayet (1809-1894), Marist priest; chronicler of the Society of Mary.

Carlo Odescalchi (1786-1841), cardinal, archbishop of Ferrara, 1823; prefect of Congregation of Bishops and Regulars, 1826; vicar general of Rome, 1834.

Jean-Louis Pastre (1779-1839), missionary on Bourbon Island, 1817-28; apostolic prefect, 1822; returned to France, 1828; canon of Saint-Jean's Cathedral, Lyon, 1829.

Jean-Félix Pichat (1787-1829), superior of Belley College; Marist aspirant.

Jean-Baptiste-François Pompallier (1801-1871), ord. 1829; Marist aspirant; first vicar-apostolic Western Oceania, first bishop of Auckland, New Zealand.

Le Puy, town 130 km south-west of Lyon; place of pilgrimage.

Giuseppe Antonio Sala (1762-1839), cardinal; at the Curia dealing with French affairs.

Étienne Séon (1803-1856), Marist priest; ordained 1827.

Étienne Terraillon (1791-1869), one of the first professed Marists; made Fourvière promise 1816; professed 1836; parish priest at Saint-Chamond; elected assistant to Colin in 1836.

Paul Trinchant (1800-1835), canon of Chartres; helped with Marist application for Roman approval.

La Valla, parish, 55 km south-west of Lyon, first house of the Marist Brothers (FMS).

Saint John Mary Vianney (1786-1859), curé of Ars; later member of the Third Order of the Society of Mary.

Popes
Pius VI (1775-1799)
Pius VII (1800-1823)
Leo XII (1823-1829)
Pius VIII (1829-1830)
Gregory XVI (1831-1846)

Rulers of France
Louis XVI (1774-1793)
Napoleon I (1804-1814)
Louis XVIII (1814-1824)
Charles X (1824-1830)
Louis-Philippe (1830-1848)

Important events in France
1789 Revolution
1790 Oath to Civil Constitution of Clergy imposed on clergy
1792 Massacre of priests in Paris
1793 King Louis XVI guillotined; The Terror; Lyon besieged and taken
1794 Fall of Robespierre and end of Terror
1797 Renewed oppression of the Church
1799 Pius VI dies at Valence, a prisoner of the revolutionaries
1799 Napoleon Bonaparte becomes First Consul
1801 Concordat signed
1804 Pius VII crowns Napoleon Emperor
1809 Pius VII excommunicates Napoleon
1814 Napoleon abdicates; Louis XVIII becomes king
1815 Napoleon returns; defeated at Waterloo
1824 Charles X succeeds as king (1824-1830)
1830 Revolution. Louis-Philippe becomes king (1830-1848)

Select Bibliography

ARCHIVAL MATERIAL

Archive of the Marist Sisters, Rome.
Archive of Congregation for the Evangelization of Peoples ('Propaganda Fide'), Rome.
Archive of the Marist Fathers (abbreviated APM), Rome.
Diocesan Archive, Pinerolo, Italy.

CONTEMPORARY NEWSPAPERS, JOURNALS AND PAMPHLETS

L'ami de la religion et du roi; journal ecclésiastique, politique et littéraire, Paris, 1814ff.
Bochard, C.-M., *Pensée pieuse* (Lyon, c.1814-1815) [= OM, doc. 33].
Circulaire de Mgr l'évêque de Belley à l'occasion du Jubilé (Brou, 1826).

CONTEMPORARY WORKS

Bailly, L., *Theologia dogmatica et moralis ad usum seminariorum,* 8 vols (Lyon -Paris, 1810; new edition 1829).
Baldassari, P., *Histoire de l'enlèvement et de la captivité de Pie VI ... traduite de l'italien ... par M. l'abbé de Lacouture* (Paris, 1839).
Bossi, M., *Statistique générale de la France. Département de l'Ain* (Paris, 1808).
Boudon, H.-M., *Dieu Seul, ou association pour l'intérêt de Dieu seul* (Paris-Lyon, 1662).
Chausse, J.M., *Vie de M. l'abbé Jean-Louis Duplay. Notes, souvenirs et monographies sur le diocèse de Lyon (1788-1887),* 2 vols (Lyon-Paris, 1887).
Cognat, J., *Vie de Mgr Alexandre-Raymond Devie, évêque de Belley,* 2 vols (Lyon-Paris, 1865).
Correspondance authentique de la cour de Rome avec la France depuis l'invasion de l'État Romain jusqu'à l'enlèvement du Souverain Pontife (Lyon, 1809).
Fleury, Ch., *Histoire de l'Église,* 20 vols, (Paris, 1691-1720).
Franchi, G. I., *Traité de l'amour du mépris de soi-même* (Lyon, 1803 = *Sull'amore al proprio disprezzo,* Lucca, 1774).
Gosselin, J., *Vie de M. Émery, neuvième supérieur du séminaire et de la compagnie de Saint-Sulpice,* 2 vols (Paris, 1861-1862).
Jeantin, J., *Le très révérend père Colin,* 6 vols (Lyon, 1895-1898).
Jouvancy, Jean-Baptiste, *Christianis Litterarum Magistris de ratione discendi et docendi* (Paris, 1692; completely revised edition 1703).
Abbé Lyonnet, *Le cardinal Fesch, archevêque de Lyon. Fragments biographiques, politiques et religieux pour servir à l'Histoire ecclésiastique contemporaine,* 2 vols (Lyon-Paris, 1841).

Martyrs, confesseurs et serviteurs de la foi (Bourg, 1892).

Rétablissement du culte divin dans l'Église de Notre-Dame de Fourvière, et détails intéressans sur le passage de N. S. Père le Pape Pie VII, à Lyon, le 29 [sic] Novembre, 1804; ainsi que sur son séjour, dans la même Ville, les 17, 18 et 19 Avril 1805, à son retour de Paris (Lyon, 1805).

Rodríguez, A., *Ejercicio de perfección y virtudes cristianas* (Seville, 1609; = *La perfection chrétienne,* Lyon, 1824).

Rohrbacher, R., *Histoire universelle de l'Église catholique,* 13 vols (Paris-Brussels, new edition, 1878-1883).

Rollin, C., *De la Manière d'enseigner et d'étudier les Belles Lettres par rapport à l'esprit et au coeur,* 4 vols (Paris, 1741).

Steyert, A., *Nouvelle Histoire de Lyon et des provinces de Lyonnais – Forez – Beaujolais, Franc-Lyonnais et Dombes,* 4 vols (Lyon, 1899-1939).

Tronson, L., *Examens particuliers sur divers sujets, propres aux ecclésiastiques et à toutes les personnes qui veulent s'avancer dans la perfection,* 2 vols (Lyon, 1690; revised edtion 1740).

PRINTED SOURCES

Coste, J., Fagan, S., Lessard, G. eds, *Antiquiores textus constitutionum Societatis Mariae* (FHSM, 1), 7 fascicles (Rome, 1955).

Coste, J., Lessard, G. eds, *Origines maristes (1786-1836)* (FHSM, 3), 4 vols (Rome, 1960-67), with the collaboration of S. Fagan for volume 2.

Coste, J., Lessard, G. eds, *Autour de la règle,* Vol. 1: *Règlements et pratiques maristes du vivant de Jean-Claude Colin* (FHSM, 8) (Rome, 1991).

Girard, Ch. ed., *Lettres reçues d'Océanie par l'administration générale des pères maristes pendant le généralat de Jean-Claude Colin,* 4 vols (Rome, 1999).

Historical Committees of the Marist Fathers and Marist Sisters eds, *Correspondence of Mother Saint Joseph, Foundress of the Marist Sisters (1786-1858)* (FHSM, 4) (Rome-Anzio, 1966).

Historical Committees of the Marist Fathers and Marist Sisters eds, *Recollections: Mother Saint Joseph, Foundress of the Marist Sisters (1786-1858)* (Rome, 1971).

Historical Committees of the Marist Fathers and Marist Sisters eds, *Index Mother Saint Joseph. Foundress of the Marist Sisters (1786-1858)* (Rome, 1977).

Keel, E. ed., *A Book of Texts for the Study of Marist Spirituality* (Rome, 1993).

Rozier, C. ed., *Écrits de Pierre Chanel* (FHSM, 2) (Rome, 1960).

Ward, A. ed., *... Ever your poor brother. Peter Chanel: Surviving Letters and Futuna Journal* (Rome, 1991).

SECONDARY SOURCES

UNPUBLISHED WORKS

Alonso, L., 'La formación intelectual de Juan Claudio Colin en el Seminario de S. Ireneo de Lyon, 1 nov 1813-22 julio 1816' (Pontifical Gregorian University, thesis, Rome, 1964).

Aubague, Alphonse-Marie, 'Histoire et esprit de la Congrégation de Marie; première et deuxième parties, 1786-1853', (Belley, 1964-5).

Bouchard, G.-M., 'La Prédication morale de Jean-Claude Colin; période 1816-1829', (Pontifical Lateran University, doctoral thesis, Rome, 1973).

Coste, B., 'Mes souvenirs de soixante ans' (copy APM, Rome).

Coste, J., 'L'apparition de la Sainte Vierge au Père Colin sur le chemin de Mérignat' (APM, Fonds Coste, 1956).

Filippucci, M., 'La ripresa dell'attività missionaria nel primo ottocento: la Società di Maria e l'Oceania' (Tesi di Laurea, Università degli Studi di Bari, 1984-1985).

Forissier, A., 'Les deux premiers mois du Supérieur Général' (APM, Rome).

Grange, D.-J., 'Le recrutement du clergé au séminaire Saint-Irénée de Lyon de 1801 à 1815' (Diplôme d'études supérieures, Université de Lyon, Lyon, 1963).

Jacolin, P., 'Apports sur les premières missions maristes dans le Bugey' (APM, 1996-1997).

Lessard, G., 'Une crise d'adolescence: Première communion de J.-C. Colin' (Université Saint-Paul, Ottawa, 1976).

Lessard, G., 'Claudine of Lyon: the French Connection' (Hyattsville, 1981).

Lessard, G. ed., 'Projet d'édition des lettres écrites par Jean-Claude Colin pendant son généralat (1836-1854)', 9 fascicles (Hull-Rome, 1986-1990).

Lessard, G., 'L'ultima fatica di Coste: "Une vision mariale de l'Église: Jean-Claude Colin"', (APM, 1998).

Mayet, G.-Cl., 'Mémoires', 11 Vols, APM.

Rozier, C., 'L'ancêtre dans le placard' (APM).

PUBLISHED WORKS

Allard, P., Saint Marcellin Champagnat, 1789-1840. Père mariste et fondateur des petits frères de Marie (Québec, 1999).

Audinet, J., 'L'enseignement "De Ecclesia" à St Sulpice sous le Premier Empire et les débuts du gallicanisme moderne', L'Ecclésiologie au XIXe siècle. Revue des Sciences Religieuses 34 (1960), 115-139.

Boutry, P., Prêtres et paroisses au pays du Curé d'Ars (Paris, 1986).

Chadwick, O., A History of the Popes 1830-1914 (Oxford, 1998).

Coste, J., 'Les deux plus anciens fragments des Constitutions – The Two Oldest Fragments of the Constitutions', Acta S.M. 3 (1954-55), 468-479.

Coste, J., 'Commentaires historiques sur les Constitutions de la S.M.: Marie dans l'Église naissante et à la fin des temps – Historical Commentary on the Constitutions of the S. M.: The Role of Mary at the Birth of the Church and at the End of Time', *Acta S.M.* 5 (1958-59), 262-281; 418-451; 6 (1960-62), 52-87; 178-197.

Coste, J., *Lectures on Society of Mary History (Marist Fathers). Part I, The Beginnings, 1786-1836; Part II, Father Colin's Generalate, 1836-1854* (Rome, 1965).

Coste, J., 'Commentaires historiques sur les Constitutions de la Société de Marie: De Societatis Spiritu - Historical Commentary on the Constitutions of the Marist Fathers, The Spirit of the Society, nrs. 49-50', *Acta S.M.* 6 (1960-62), 444-533; 581-677.

Coste, J. ed., *A Founder Speaks. Spiritual Talks of Jean-Claude Colin*, English translation by A. Ward (Rome, 1975).

Coste, J. ed., *A Founder Acts. Reminiscences of Jean-Claude Colin by Gabriel-Claude Mayet,* English translation by W. J. Stuart and A. Ward (Rome, 1983).

Coste, J., 'Le mandat donné par ses compagnons à Marcellin Champagnat en 1816. Essai d'histoire de la tradition', *The Study of Marist Spirituality* (Rome, 1984), pp 7-17.

Coste, J., *Studies on the Early Ideas of Jean-Claude Colin - I* (Maristica, 2) (Rome, 1989).

Coste, J., *Une certaine idée de la Société de Marie. Jean-Claude Colin - A Certain Idea of the Society of Mary. Jean-Claude Colin* (Rome, 1990).

Coste, J., 'The Brief "Omnium Gentium"; Two readings of a basic text', *Forum Novum* 2 (1992) 29-49.

Coste, J., *Une vision mariale de l'Église: Jean-Claude Colin – A Marian Vision of the Church: Jean-Claude Colin,* Edited by Gaston Lessard (Maristica, 8) (Rome, 1998).

Costigan, R. F., *Rohrbacher and the Ecclesiology of Ultramontanism* (Rome, 1980).

Cousin, B., Cubells, M., Moulinas, R., *La pique et la croix. Histoire religieuse de la Révolution française* (Paris, 1989).

De Montalembert, C., *Journal intime inédit,* 2 vols, Edited by L. Le Guillou and N. Roger-Taillade (Paris, 1990).

De Montclos, X., 'Benoît Coste', X. de Montclos ed., *Dictionnaire du monde religieux dans la France contemporaine,* vol. 6. *Lyon, Le Lyonnais, Le Beaujolais* (Paris, 1994), pp 125-128.

De Viguerie, J., 'Examen de quelques hypothèses au sujet de la révolution française et de la déchristianisation', *Christianisation et déchristianisation; actes de la neuvième rencontre d'histoire religieuse tenue à Fontevraud les 3, 4, et 5 octobre 1985* (Angers, 1986), pp 177-185.

Drouilly, F., *Les avis de Jean-Claude Colin au personnel du petit séminaire de Belley – Jean-Claude Colin's Instructions to the Staff of the Minor Seminary of Belley* (Maristica, 3) (Rome, 1990).

Dumoulin, C., *Un séminaire français au 19ème siècle: le recrutement, la formation, la vie des clercs à Bourges* (Paris, 1978).

Dudon, R.P., 'Le cardinal Fesch et les séminaires lyonnais', *Études* 96 (1903), 499-526.

Farrell, S., *Achievement from the Depths* (Drummoyne, New South Wales, 1984).

Faure, C., *Cahiers de doléances du Beaujolais pour les États généraux de 1789* (Lyon, 1939).

Forissier, A., *For a Marian Church. Marist Founders and Foundresses,* (Middlegreen, St Paul's Publications, 1992).

Furet, F., 'Constitution civile du clergé', F. Furet and M. Ozouf eds, *Dictionnaire critique de la Révolution française: institutions et créations* (Paris, 1992), pp 207-220.

Furet, J.-B., *Life of Joseph Benedict Marcellin Champagnat 1789-1840. Marist Priest. Founder of the Congregation of the Little Brothers of Mary* (Rome, 1989; Bicentenary edition).

Gadille, J., Fédou, R., Hours, H., Vrégille, B., *Le Diocèse de Lyon* (Paris, 1983).

Garden, M., Bronnert, C., Chappé, B. eds, *Paroisses et communes de France: dictionnaire d'histoire administrative et démographique. Rhône* (Paris, 1978).

Gioannetti, F., *A Spirituality for our Time. Jean-Claude Colin* (Rome, 1989).

Girard, C., 'On the Sources of Colin's Teaching on Humility', *Forum Novum* 4 (1998), 257-293.

Gonnet, P., 'Les Cent Jours à Lyon', *Revue d'histoire de Lyon* 7 (Lyon, 1908), 57-67. 111-123. 186-210. 286-303.

Greiler, A., *Marcellin Champagnat, a Marist Saint: Marist Priest and Founder of the Marist Brothers* (Rome, 1999).

Guillet, C., *La rumeur de Dieu. Apparitions, prophéties et miracles sous la Restauration* (Paris, 1994).

Hosie, S. W., *Anonymous Apostle. The Life of Jean-Claude Colin, Marist,* (New York, 1967).

Hours, H., *Les Papes à Lyon: Pie VII, 1794-1805* (Lyon, 1986).

Hufton, O., 'The Reconstruction of a Church 1796-1801', G. Lewis and C. Lucas eds, *Beyond the Terror. Essays on French Regional and Social History, 1794-1815* (Cambridge, 1983) pp 21-52.

Hufton, O., 'The French Church', W. J. Callahan and D. Higgs eds, *Church and Society in Catholic Europe of the Eighteenth Century* (London, 1979), pp 14-15.

Humbert, G., 'Jalons chronologiques pour une histoire de la pénétration en pays francophones de la pensée et des oeuvres d'Alphonse de Liguori', J. Delumeau ed., *Alphonse de Liguori, pasteur et docteur* (Paris, 1987), pp 369-401.

Jacolin, P., *Jésus appelle les pécheurs. Retraite Pèlerinage en Bugey, Juillet 1999* (Document SM, 52) (Paris, 1999).

Jomand, J., *Le Cardinal Fesch par lui-même* (Lyon, 1970).

Jore, L., *L'Océan Pacifique au temps de la Restauration et de la Monarchie de Juillet (1815-1848),* Vol 1 (Paris, 1969).

Lanfrey, A., 'The Society of Mary as Secret Congregation', *Marist Notebooks* Nr. 9 (1996), 5-14.

Lanfrey, A., 'La Société de Marie comme Congrégation secrète', *Marist Notebooks* Nr. 9 (1996), 15-92.

Lanfrey, A., 'The Legend of the Jesuit of Le Puy', *Marist Notebooks* Nr. 10 (1997), 1-16.

Lanfrey, A., 'Commentaire critique de la lettre du 9 octobre 1819', *Forum Novum* 4 (1997), 95-123.

Lanfrey, A., *Marcellin Champagnat et les Frères Maristes: instituteurs congréganistes au XIXe siècle* (Paris, 1999).

Lathoud, D., *Marie-Pauline Jaricot,* 2 vols (Paris, 1937).

Latreille, A., *L'Église catholique et la révolution française,* 2 vols (Paris, 1946, 1950).

Ledré, C., *Le culte caché sous la révolution: les missions de l'abbé Linsolas* (Paris, 1949).

Leflon, J., *Monsieur Émery, L'Église concordataire et impériale* (Paris, 1946).

Leflon, J., *Eugène de Mazenod, évêque de Marseille, fondateur des missionnaires oblats de Marie immaculée, 1782-1861,* 3 vols (Paris, 1957, 1960, 1965).

Leonhard, Jessica, *Triumph of Failure. Jeanne-Marie Chavoin, Foundress of the Marist Sisters* (Middlegreen, St Paul's Publications, 1998).

Lessard, G., 'Jean-Claude Colin fait voeu d'aller à Rome – Jean-Claude Colin Makes a Vow to Go to Rome', *Forum Novum* 2 (1992), 262-288.

Lessard, G., 'Un trésor pour ces derniers temps', *Forum Novum* 3 (1995-1996), 457-472.

Lessard, G., 'Une lettre inédite de Pierre Colin – An Unpublished Letter of Pierre Colin', *Forum Novum* 4 (1997) 79-94.

Lestra, A., *Histoire secrète de la Congrégation de Lyon. De la clandestinité à la fondation de la Propagation de la Foi* (Paris, 1967).

Linsolas, J., *L'Église clandestine de Lyon pendant la Révolution,* 2 vols (Lyon, 1985, 1987).

Mathieu, Y., 'L'usage colinien de la 'Cité mystique de Dieu' de Marie d'Agreda', *Forum Novum* 3 (1996) 439-456.

McMahon, F., *Travellers in Hope. The Story of Marcellin Champagnat and his Fellow Founders of the Society of Mary* (Rome, 1994).

Plongeron, B., Lerou, P., Darteville, R. eds, *Pratiques religieuses, mentalités et spiritualités dans l'Europe révolutionnaire (1770-1820): Actes du colloque Chantilly 27-29 novembre 1986* (Paris-Turnhout, 1988).

Schmidlin, J., *Histoire des papes de l'époque contemporaine,* Vol. 1, *La papauté et les papes de la restauration (1800-1846)* (Lyon-Paris, 1938, 1940).

Sevrin, E., *Les missions religieuses en France sous la restauration,* vol. 1, *Le missionnaire et la mission* (Saint-Mandé, 1948), vol. 2, *Les missions (1815-1820)* (Paris, 1959).

Sorrel, C., 'Marin Ducrey – Prêtre séculier, enseignant', *La Savoie. Dictionnaire du monde religieux dans la France contemporaine,* vol. 8. (Paris, 1996), 172-173.

Struminski, R., 'Father Colin and the love of self-contempt – Padre Colin e l'amore del disprezzo di se', *Forum Novum* 2 (1993), 196-223.

Tackett, T., *Religion, Revolution and Regional Culture in Eighteenth-Century France. The Ecclesiastical Oath of 1791* (Princeton, 1986).

Trénard, L., *La Révolution française dans la région Rhône-Alpes* (Paris, 1992).

Trochu, F., *The Curé d'Ars: Saint Jean-Marie-Baptiste Vianney* (London, 1927).

Vovelle, M., 'C'est la faute à la Révolution', J. le Goff and R. Rémond eds, *Histoire de la France religieuse,* vol. 3, *XVIIIe-XIXe siècle* (Paris, 1991), 261-271.

Whelan, Ch., *The Marist Story, (3) The Bugey Experience* (Sidcup, 1996).

Wiltgen, R. M., *The Founding of the Roman Catholic Church in Oceania, 1825-1850* (Canberra, 1979).

Zind, P., *Les nouvelles congrégations de Frères enseignants en France de 1800 à 1830* (Saint-Genis-Laval, 1969).

Index

Numbers refer to pages of the present work. General references to Jean-Claude Colin (= JCC) are not given. General references to 'France', 'Rome' and so forth are omitted. Titles of books and journals are in italics. 'St' = Saint, and 'Bl' = Blessed. Words assimilated into English are given their English spelling.

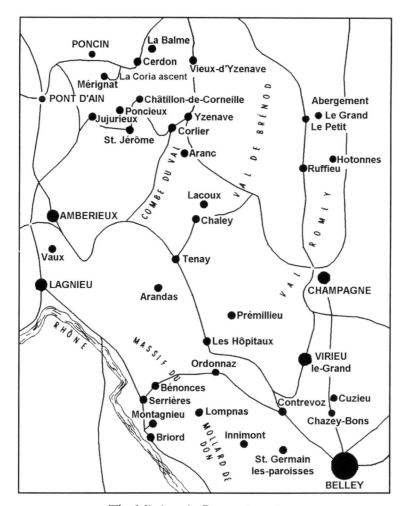

The Missions in Bugey 1824-1829

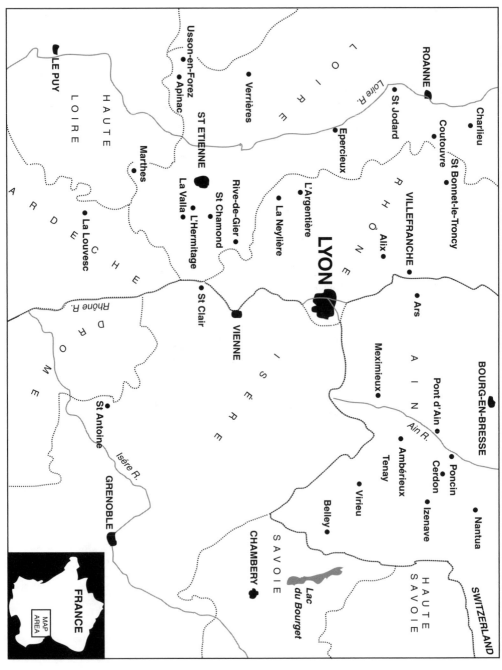

Places of Marist Origins

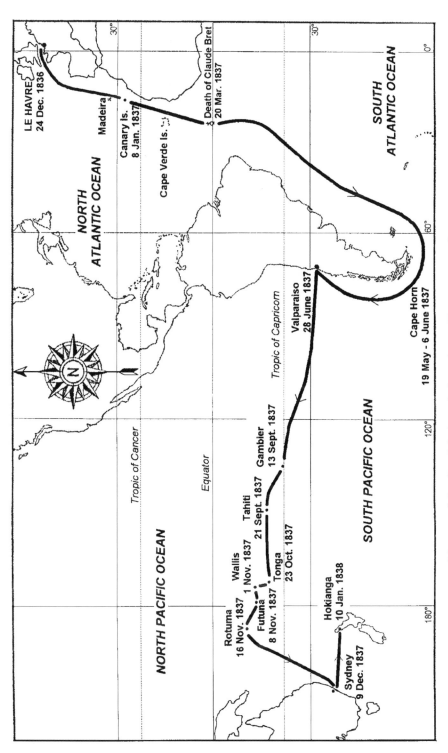

Voyage of the first Marist missionaries 24 Dec 1836 - 10 Jan 1838